THE WICKED + THE DIVINE

VOL. 3, COMMERCIAL SUICIDE

THE WICKED + THE DIVINE
CREATED BY
KIERON GILLEN AND
JAMIE MCKELVIE

KIERON GILLEN
WRITER

KATE BROWN
ISSUE 12 ARTIST

TULA LOTAY
ISSUE 13 ARTIST

JAMIE MCKELVIE
ISSUE 14 ARTIST

MATTHEW WILSON
ISSUE 14 COLOURIST

STEPHANIE HANS
ISSUE 15 ARTIST

LEILA DEL DUCA
ISSUE 16 ARTIST

MAT LOPES
ISSUE 16 COLOURIST

BRANDON GRAHAM
ISSUE 17 ARTIST

CLAYTON COWLES
LETTERER
(EXCEPTING ISSUE 17)

SERGIO SERRANO
DESIGNER

CHRISSY WILLIAMS
EDITOR

DEE CUNNIFFE
FLATTER

THE WICKED + THE DIVINE, VOL. 3, COMMERCIAL SUICIDE
February 2016
ISBN: 978-1-63215-631-0
Published by Image Comics Inc.
Office of publication: 2001 Center St, Sixth Fl, Berkeley, CA 94704.

For information regarding the CPSIA on this printed material call: 203-595-3636
and provide reference # RICH – 662303. Representation: Law Offices of Harris
M. Miller II, P.C. (rights.inquiries@gmail.com).

This book was designed by Sergio Serrano, based on a design by Hannah
Donovan and Jamie McKelvie, and set into type by Sergio Serrano in Edmonton,
Canada. The text face is Gotham, designed and issued by Hoefler & Co. in 2000.
The paper is Escanaba 60 matte.

IMAGE COMICS, INC.
Robert Kirkman, CHIEF OPERATING OFFICER
Erik Larsen, CHIEF FINANCIAL OFFICER
Todd McFarlane, PRESIDENT
Marc Silvestri, CHIEF EXECUTIVE OFFICER
Jim Valentino, VICE-PRESIDENT
Eric Stephenson, PUBLISHER
Corey Murphy, DIRECTOR OF SALES
Jeff Boison, DIRECTOR OF PUBLISHING
PLANNING & BOOK TRADE SALES
Jeremy Sullivan, DIRECTOR OF DIGITAL SALES
Kat Salazar, DIRECTOR OF PR & MARKETING
Emily Miller, DIRECTOR OF OPERATIONS
Branwyn Bigglestone, SENIOR ACCOUNTS MANAGER
Sarah Mello, ACCOUNTS MANAGER

Drew Gill, ART DIRECTOR
Jonathan Chan, PRODUCTION MANAGER
Meredith Wallace, PRINT MANAGER
Briah Skelly, PUBLICITY ASSISTANT
Randy Okamura, MARKETING PRODUCTION DESIGNER
David Brothers, BRANDING MANAGER
Ally Power, CONTENT MANAGER
Addison Duke, PRODUCTION ARTIST
Vincent Kukua, PRODUCTION ARTIST
Sasha Head, PRODUCTION ARTIST
Tricia Ramos, PRODUCTION ARTIST
Jeff Stang, DIRECT MARKETING SALES REPRESENTATIVE
Emilio Bautista, DIGITAL SALES ASSOCIATE
Chloe Ramos-Peterson, ADMINISTRATIVE ASSISTANT
www.imagecomics.com

GILLEN McKELVIE WILSON COWLES

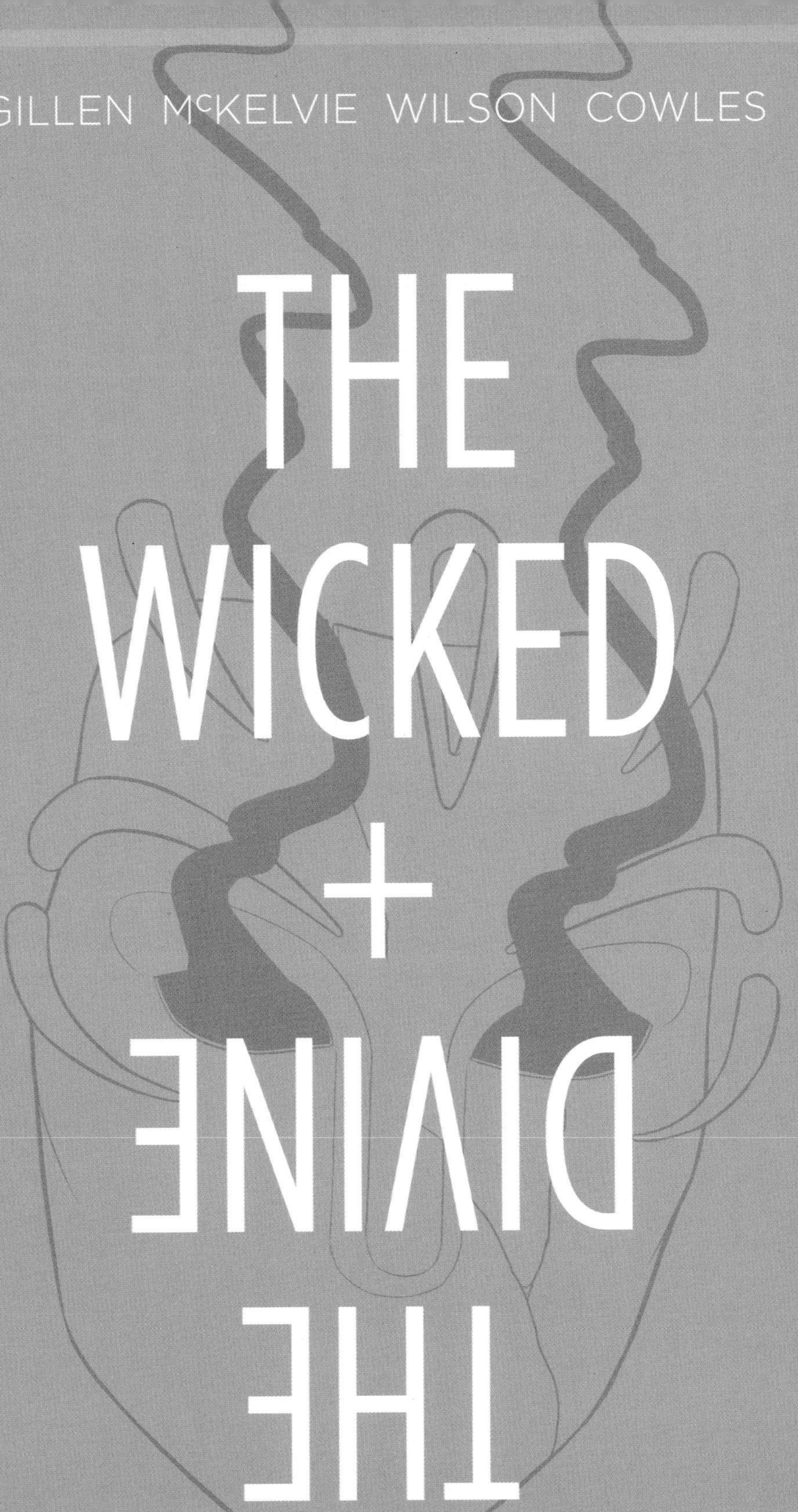

THE WICKED + THE DIVINE

VOL. 3, COMMERCIAL SUICIDE

12

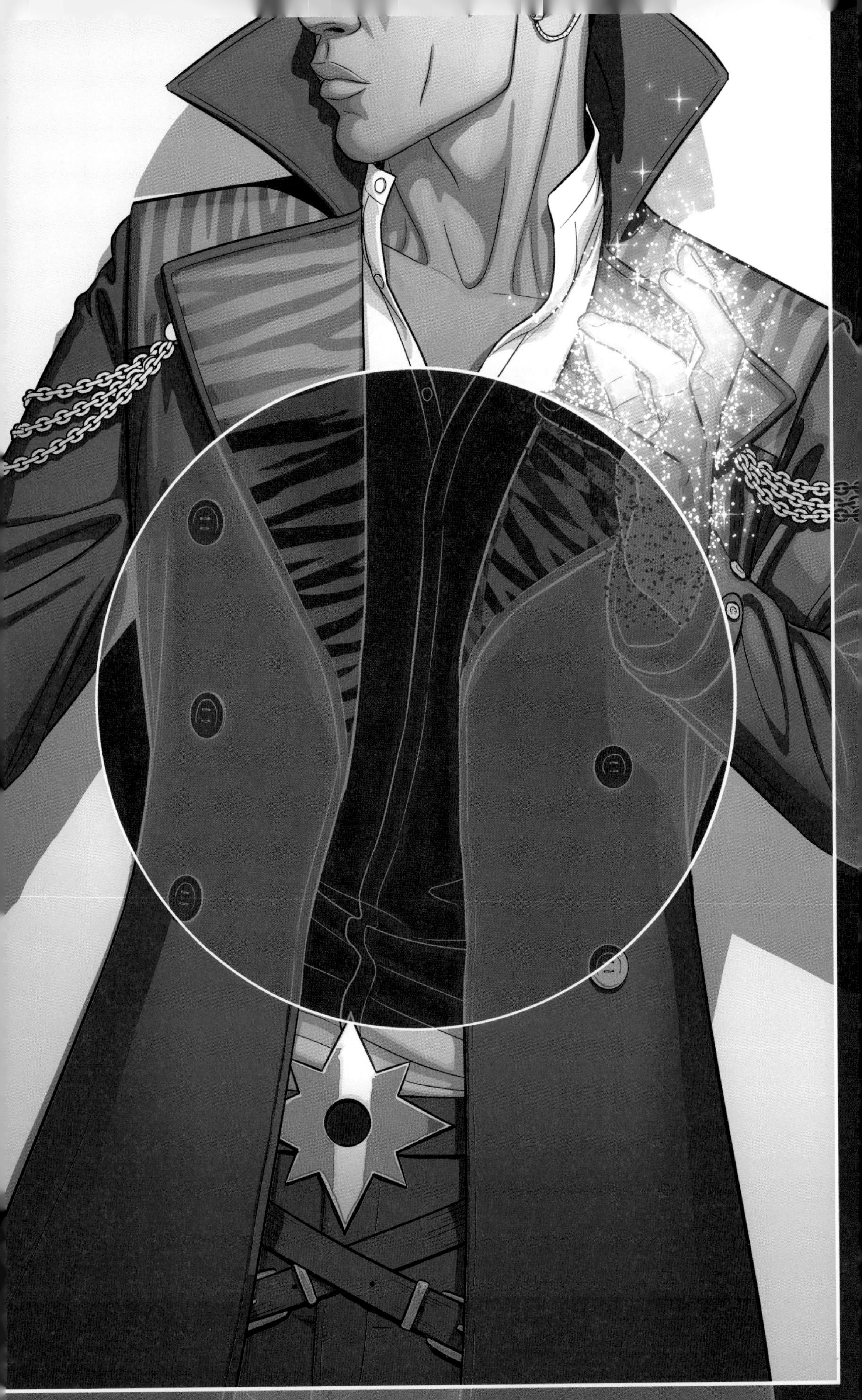

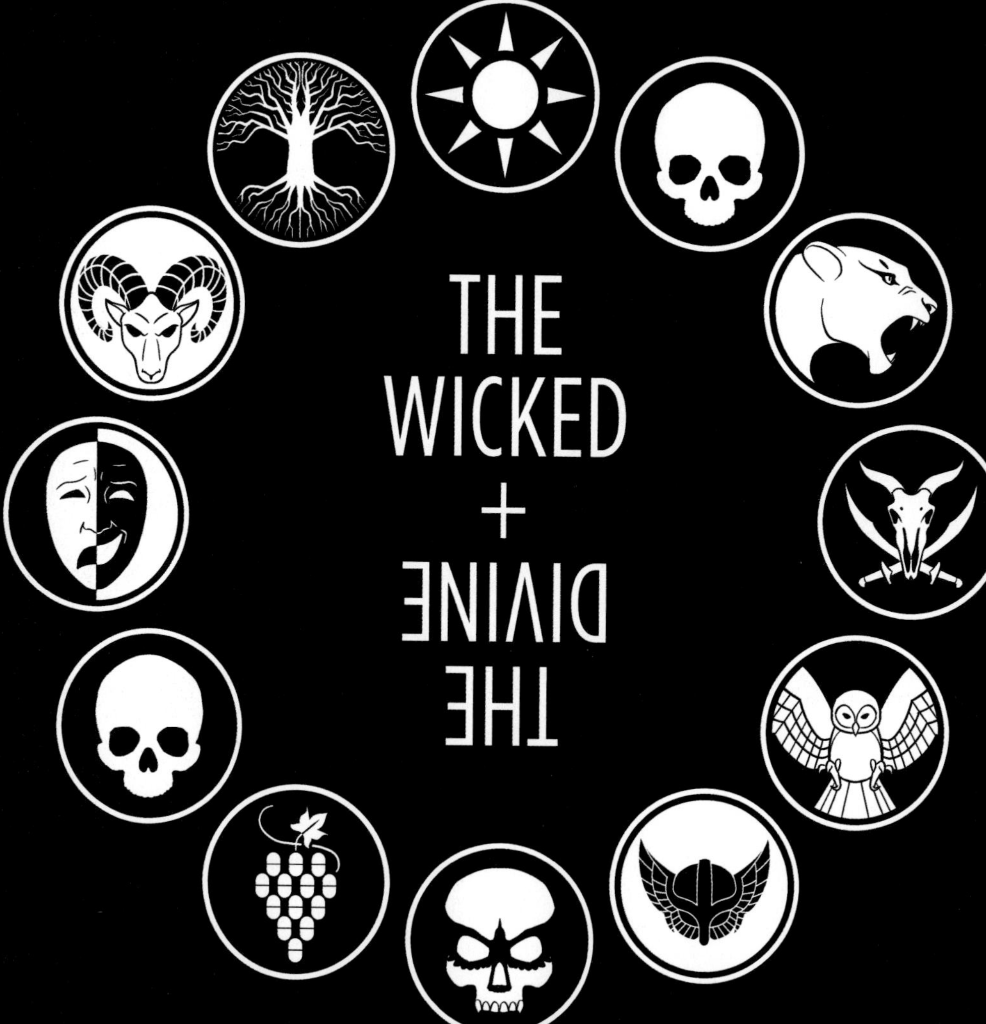

THE WICKED + THE DIVINE

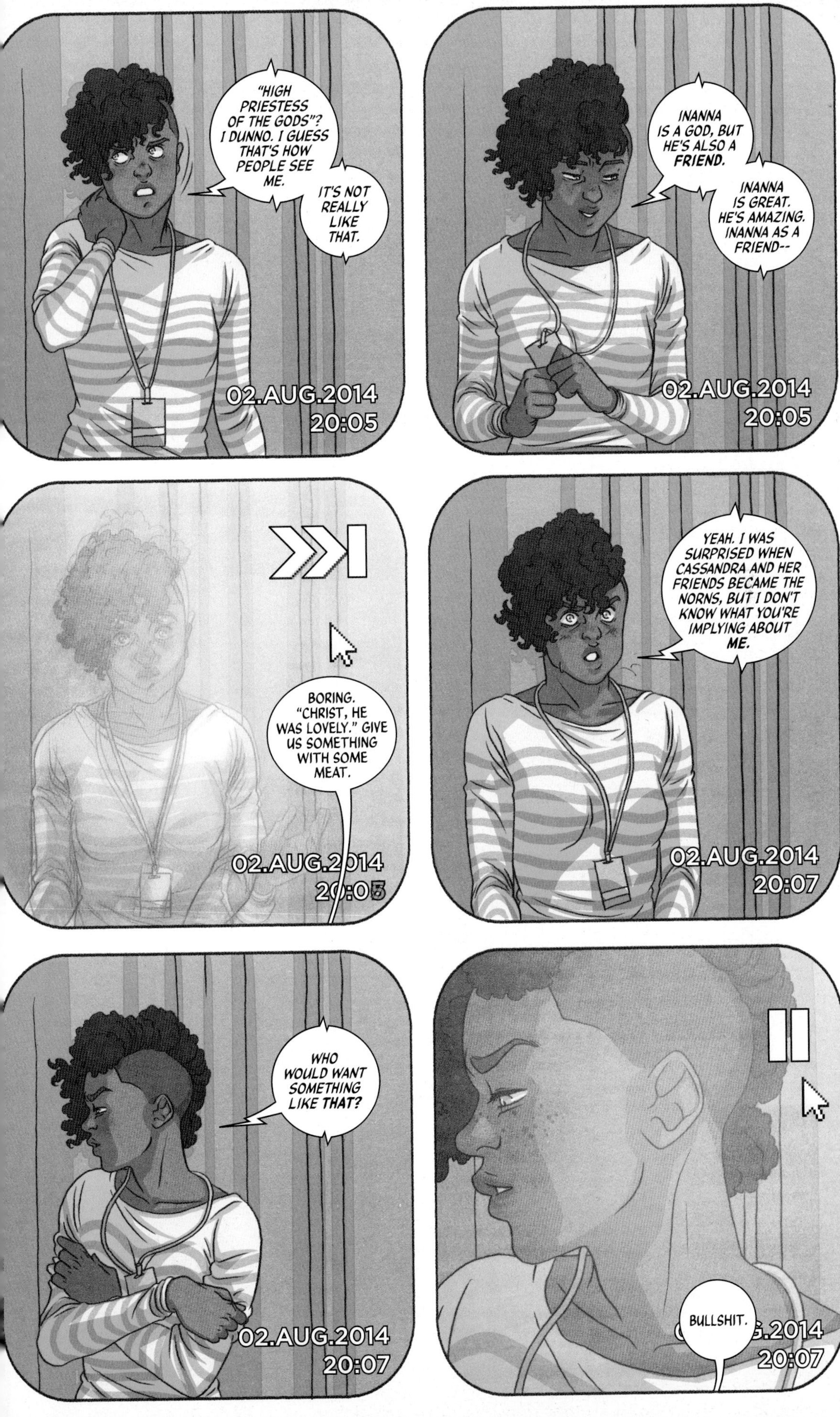
"HIGH PRIESTESS OF THE GODS"? I DUNNO. I GUESS THAT'S HOW PEOPLE SEE ME.
IT'S NOT REALLY LIKE THAT.
02.AUG.2014 20:05
INANNA IS A GOD, BUT HE'S ALSO A **FRIEND.**
INANNA IS GREAT. HE'S AMAZING. INANNA AS A FRIEND--
02.AUG.2014 20:05
BORING. "CHRIST, HE WAS LOVELY." GIVE US SOMETHING WITH SOME MEAT.
02.AUG.2014
YEAH. I WAS SURPRISED WHEN CASSANDRA AND HER FRIENDS BECAME THE NORNS, BUT I DON'T KNOW WHAT YOU'RE IMPLYING ABOUT **ME.**
02.AUG.2014 20:07
WHO WOULD WANT SOMETHING LIKE THAT?
02.AUG.2014 20:07
BULLSHIT.
20:07

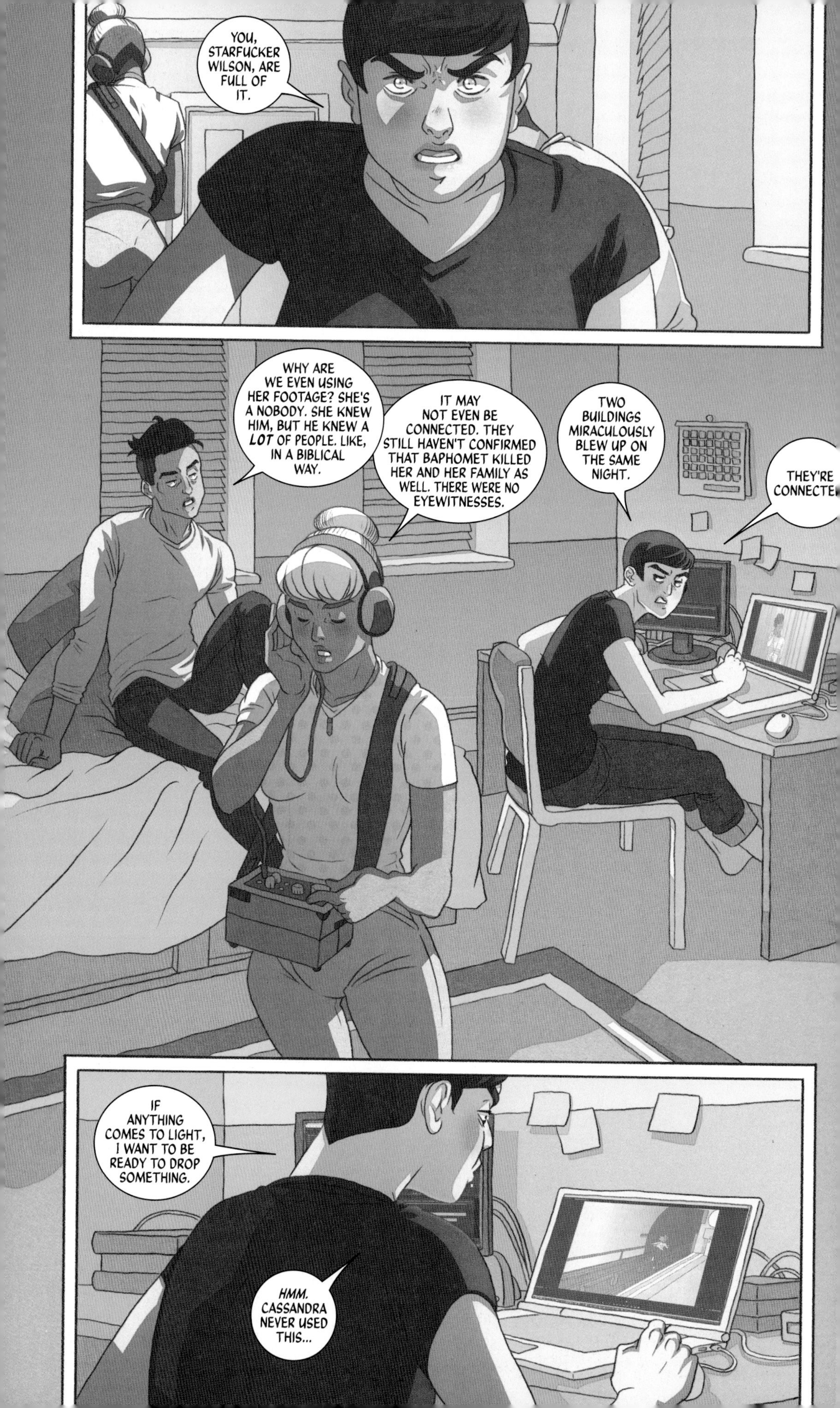
YOU, STARFUCKER WILSON, ARE FULL OF IT.
WHY ARE WE EVEN USING HER FOOTAGE? SHE'S A NOBODY. SHE KNEW HIM, BUT HE KNEW A *LOT* OF PEOPLE. LIKE, IN A BIBLICAL WAY.
IT MAY NOT EVEN BE CONNECTED. THEY STILL HAVEN'T CONFIRMED THAT BAPHOMET KILLED HER AND HER FAMILY AS WELL. THERE WERE NO EYEWITNESSES.
TWO BUILDINGS MIRACULOUSLY BLEW UP ON THE SAME NIGHT.
THEY'RE CONNECTE
IF ANYTHING COMES TO LIGHT, I WANT TO BE READY TO DROP SOMETHING.
HMM. CASSANDRA NEVER USED THIS...

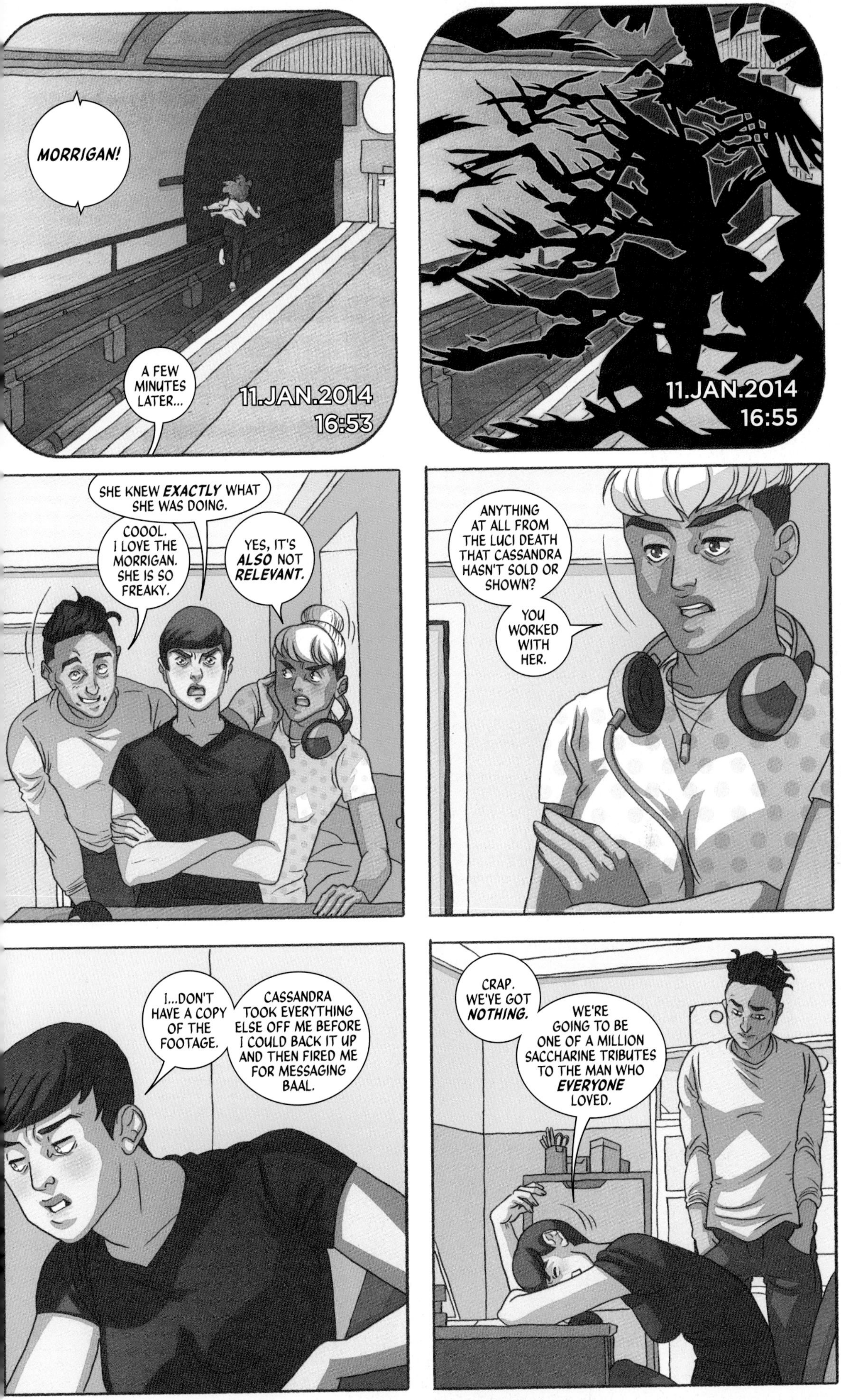
MORRIGAN!
A FEW MINUTES LATER...
11.JAN.2014 16:53
11.JAN.2014 16:55
SHE KNEW *EXACTLY* WHAT SHE WAS DOING.
COOOL. I LOVE THE MORRIGAN. SHE IS SO FREAKY.
YES, IT'S *ALSO* NOT *RELEVANT.*
ANYTHING AT ALL FROM THE LUCI DEATH THAT CASSANDRA HASN'T SOLD OR SHOWN?
YOU WORKED WITH HER.
I...DON'T HAVE A COPY OF THE FOOTAGE.
CASSANDRA TOOK EVERYTHING ELSE OFF ME BEFORE I COULD BACK IT UP AND THEN FIRED ME FOR MESSAGING BAAL.
CRAP. WE'VE GOT *NOTHING.*
WE'RE GOING TO BE ONE OF A MILLION SACCHARINE TRIBUTES TO THE MAN WHO *EVERYONE* LOVED.

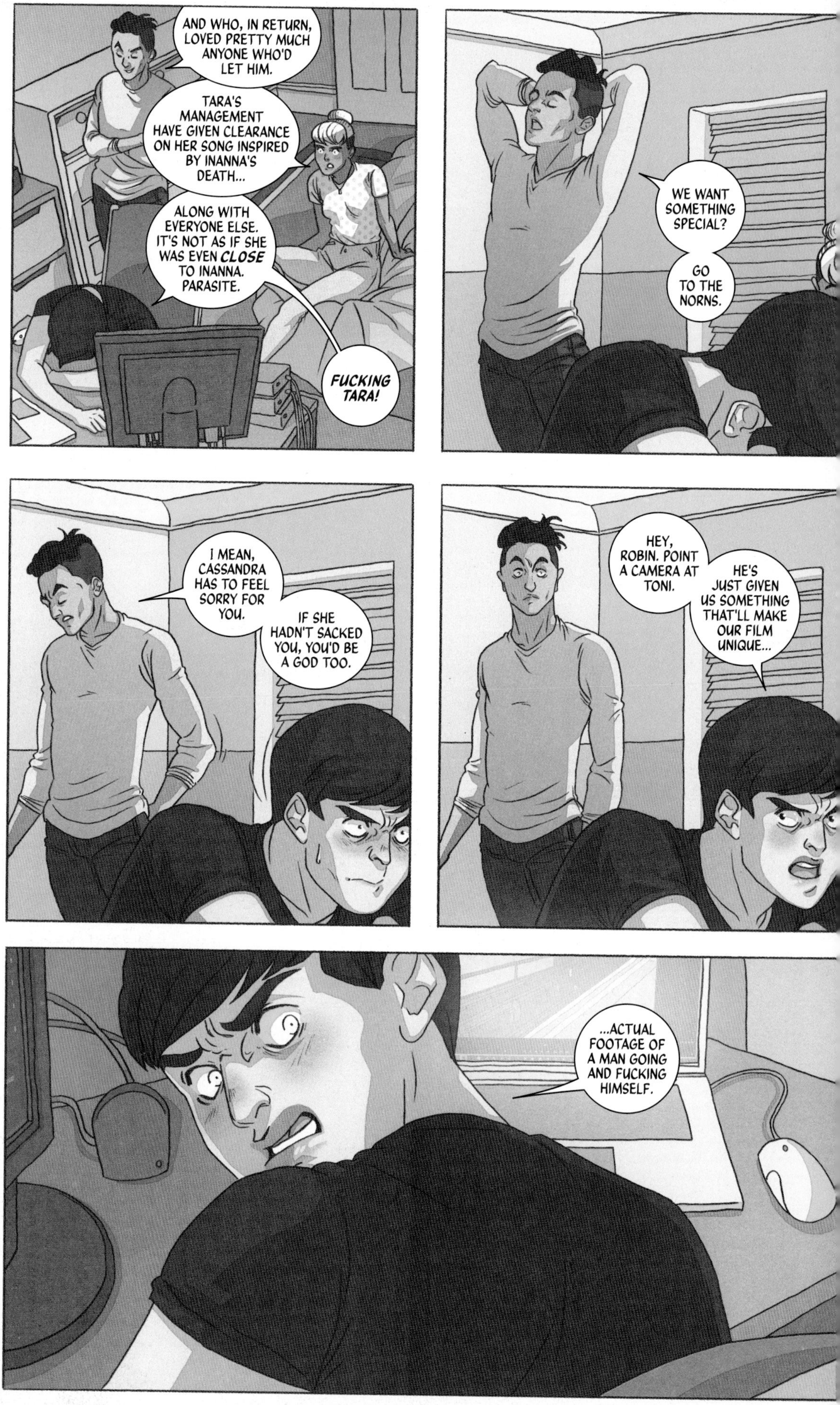
AND WHO, IN RETURN, LOVED PRETTY MUCH ANYONE WHO'D LET HIM.
TARA'S MANAGEMENT HAVE GIVEN CLEARANCE ON HER SONG INSPIRED BY INANNA'S DEATH...
ALONG WITH EVERYONE ELSE. IT'S NOT AS IF SHE WAS EVEN *CLOSE* TO INANNA. PARASITE.
FUCKING TARA!
WE WANT SOMETHING SPECIAL?
GO TO THE NORNS.
I MEAN, CASSANDRA HAS TO FEEL SORRY FOR YOU.
IF SHE HADN'T SACKED YOU, YOU'D BE A GOD TOO.
HEY, ROBIN. POINT A CAMERA AT TONI.
HE'S JUST GIVEN US SOMETHING THAT'LL MAKE OUR FILM UNIQUE...
...ACTUAL FOOTAGE OF A MAN GOING AND FUCKING HIMSELF.

LEFT BEHIND

7 AUGUST 2014

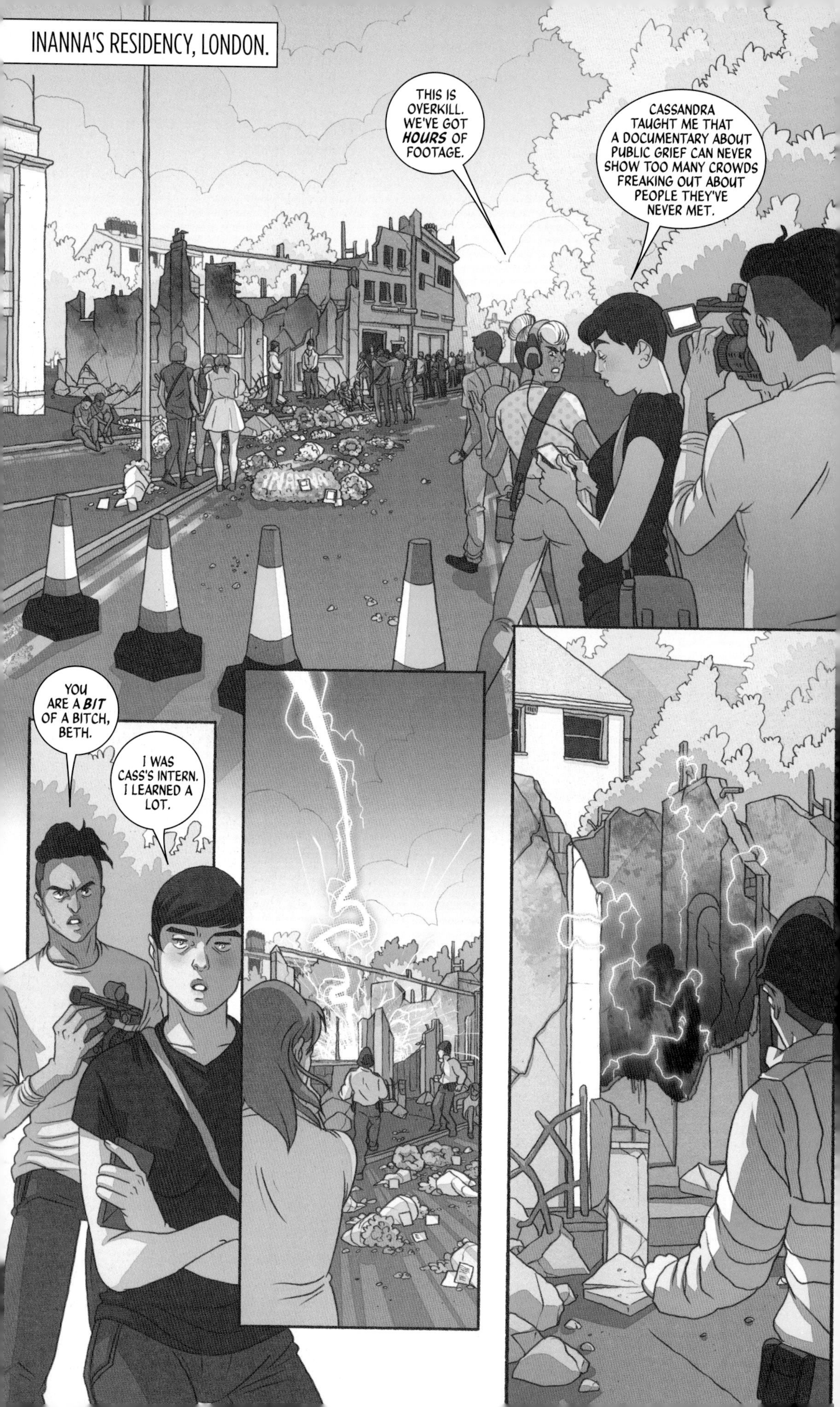

INANNA'S RESIDENCY, LONDON.
THIS IS OVERKILL. WE'VE GOT **HOURS** OF FOOTAGE.
CASSANDRA TAUGHT ME THAT A DOCUMENTARY ABOUT PUBLIC GRIEF CAN NEVER SHOW TOO MANY CROWDS FREAKING OUT ABOUT PEOPLE THEY'VE NEVER MET.
YOU ARE A **BIT** OF A BITCH, BETH.
I WAS CASS'S INTERN. I LEARNED A LOT.

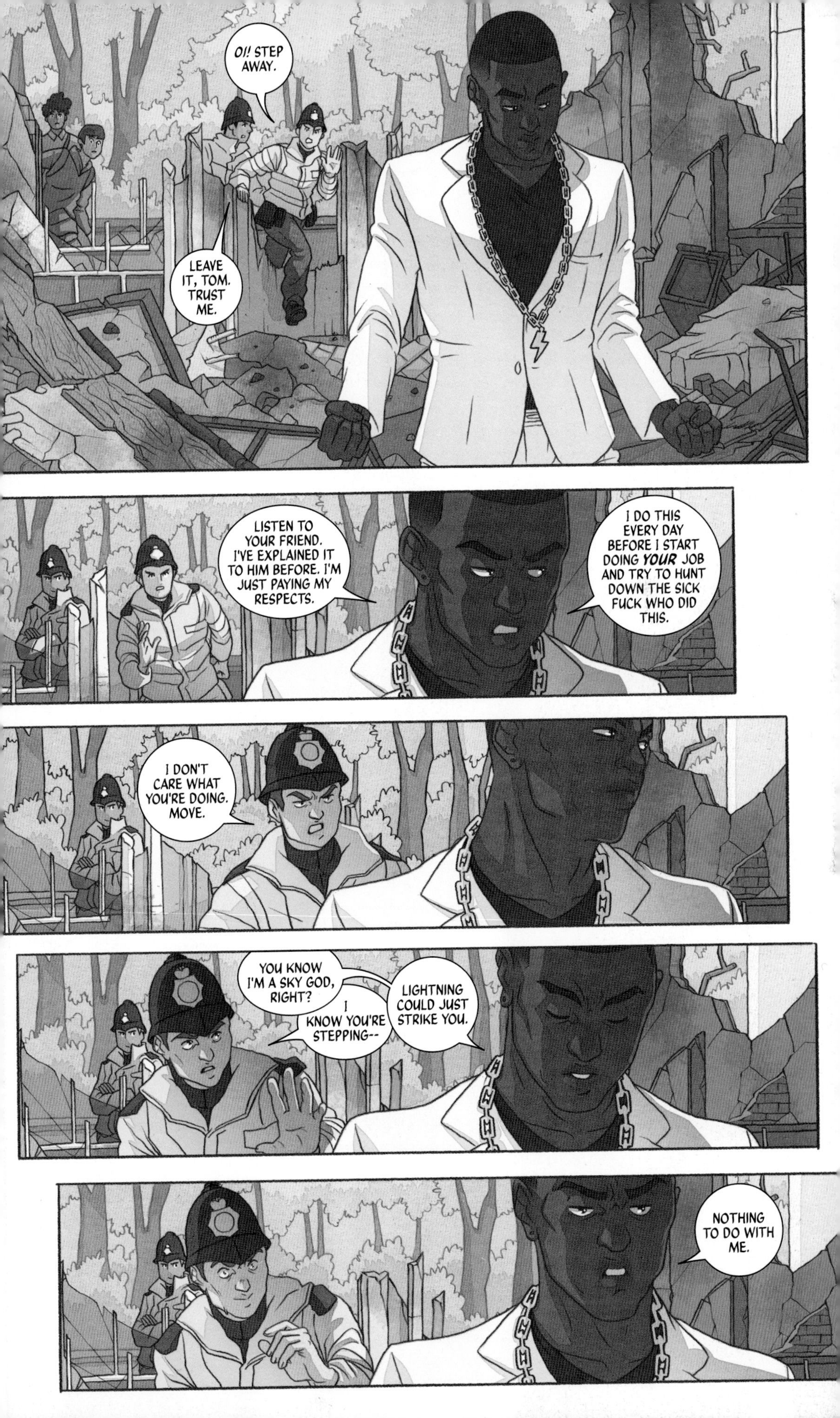
OI! STEP AWAY.
LEAVE IT, TOM. TRUST ME.
LISTEN TO YOUR FRIEND. I'VE EXPLAINED IT TO HIM BEFORE. I'M JUST PAYING MY RESPECTS.
I DO THIS EVERY DAY BEFORE I START DOING YOUR JOB AND TRY TO HUNT DOWN THE SICK FUCK WHO DID THIS.
I DON'T CARE WHAT YOU'RE DOING. MOVE.
YOU KNOW I'M A SKY GOD, RIGHT?
LIGHTNING COULD JUST STRIKE YOU.
I KNOW YOU'RE STEPPING--
NOTHING TO DO WITH ME.

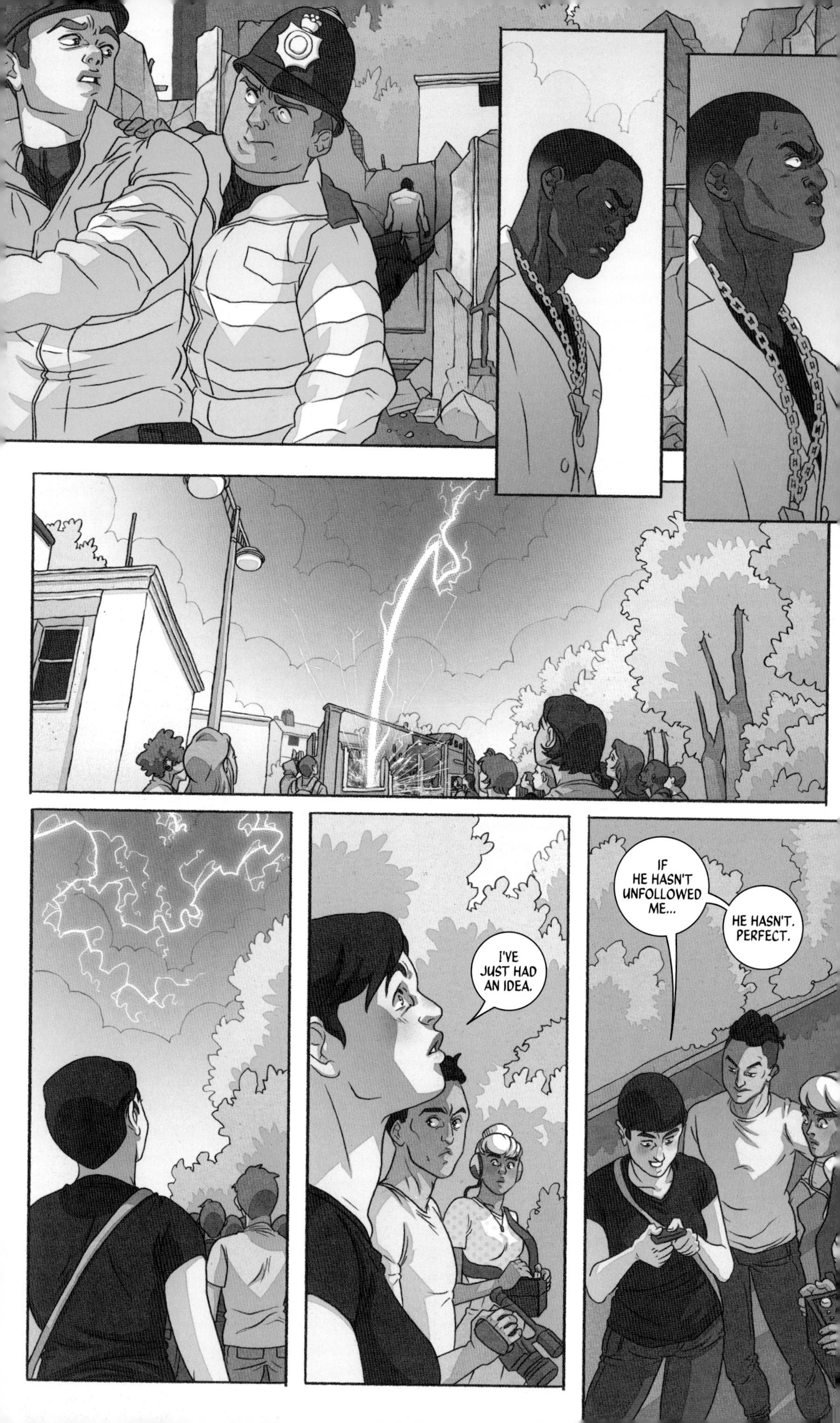
I'VE JUST HAD AN IDEA.
IF HE HASN'T UNFOLLOWED ME...
HE HASN'T. PERFECT.

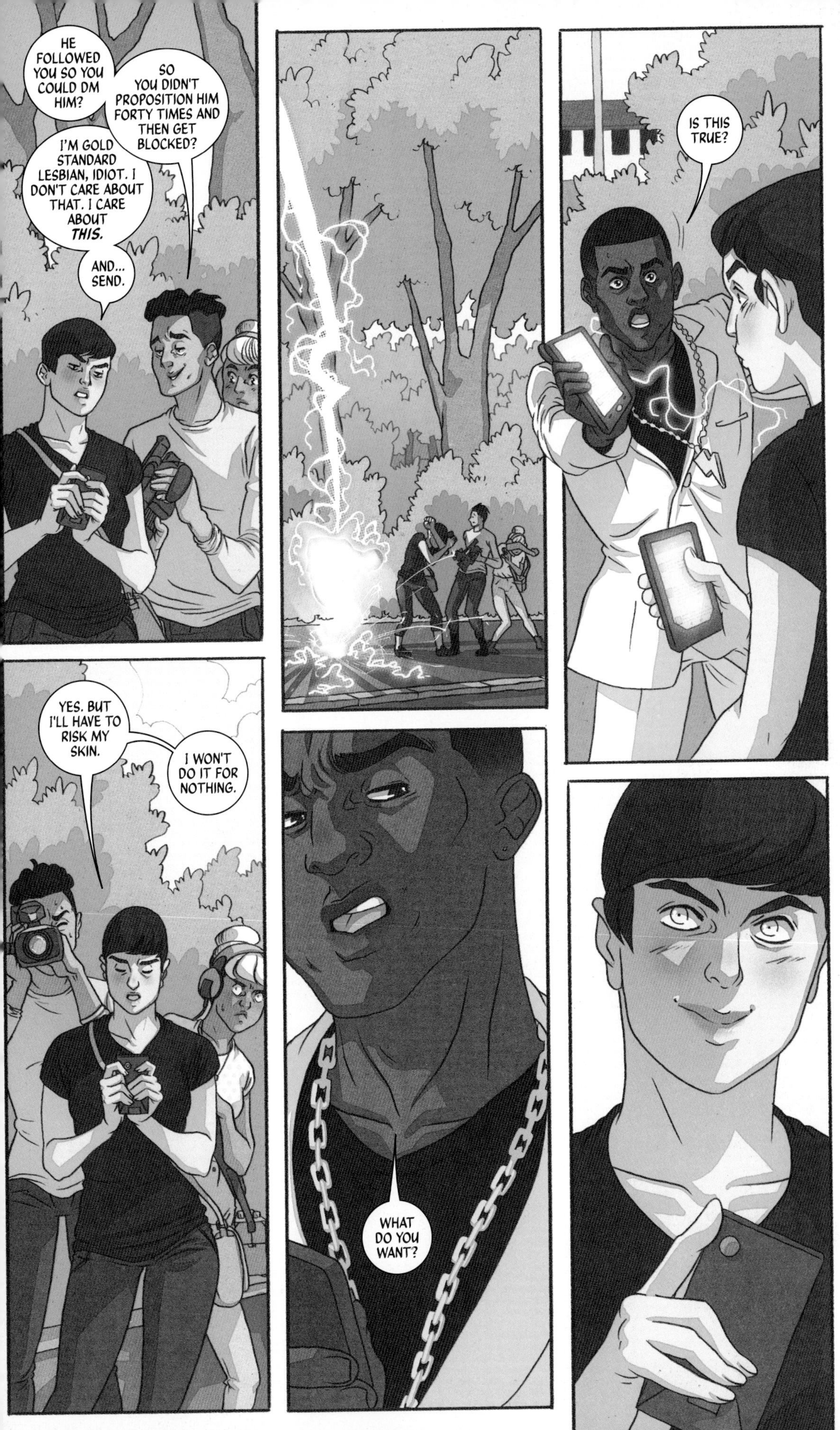

HE FOLLOWED YOU SO YOU COULD DM HIM?
SO YOU DIDN'T PROPOSITION HIM FORTY TIMES AND THEN GET BLOCKED?
I'M GOLD STANDARD LESBIAN, IDIOT. I DON'T CARE ABOUT THAT. I CARE ABOUT *THIS.*
AND... SEND.
IS THIS TRUE?
YES. BUT I'LL HAVE TO RISK MY SKIN.
I WON'T DO IT FOR NOTHING.
WHAT DO YOU WANT?

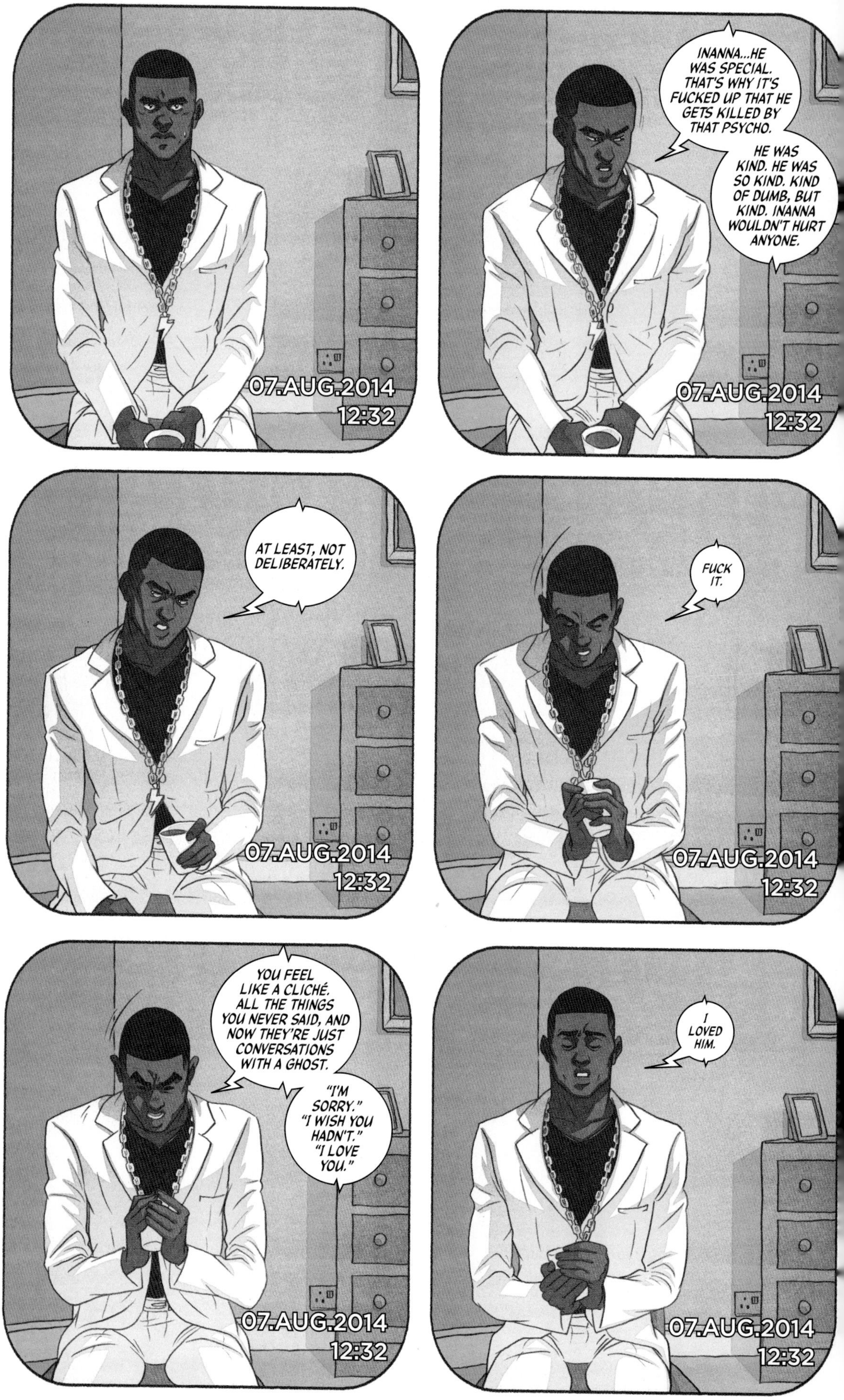
07.AUG.2014
12:32
INANNA...HE WAS SPECIAL. THAT'S WHY IT'S FUCKED UP THAT HE GETS KILLED BY THAT PSYCHO.
HE WAS KIND. HE WAS SO KIND. KIND OF DUMB, BUT KIND. INANNA WOULDN'T HURT ANYONE.
07.AUG.2014
12:32
AT LEAST, NOT DELIBERATELY.
07.AUG.2014
12:32
FUCK IT.
07.AUG.2014
12:32
YOU FEEL LIKE A CLICHÉ. ALL THE THINGS YOU NEVER SAID, AND NOW THEY'RE JUST CONVERSATIONS WITH A GHOST.
"I'M SORRY." "I WISH YOU HADN'T." "I LOVE YOU."
07.AUG.2014
12:32
I LOVED HIM.
07.AUG.2014
12:32

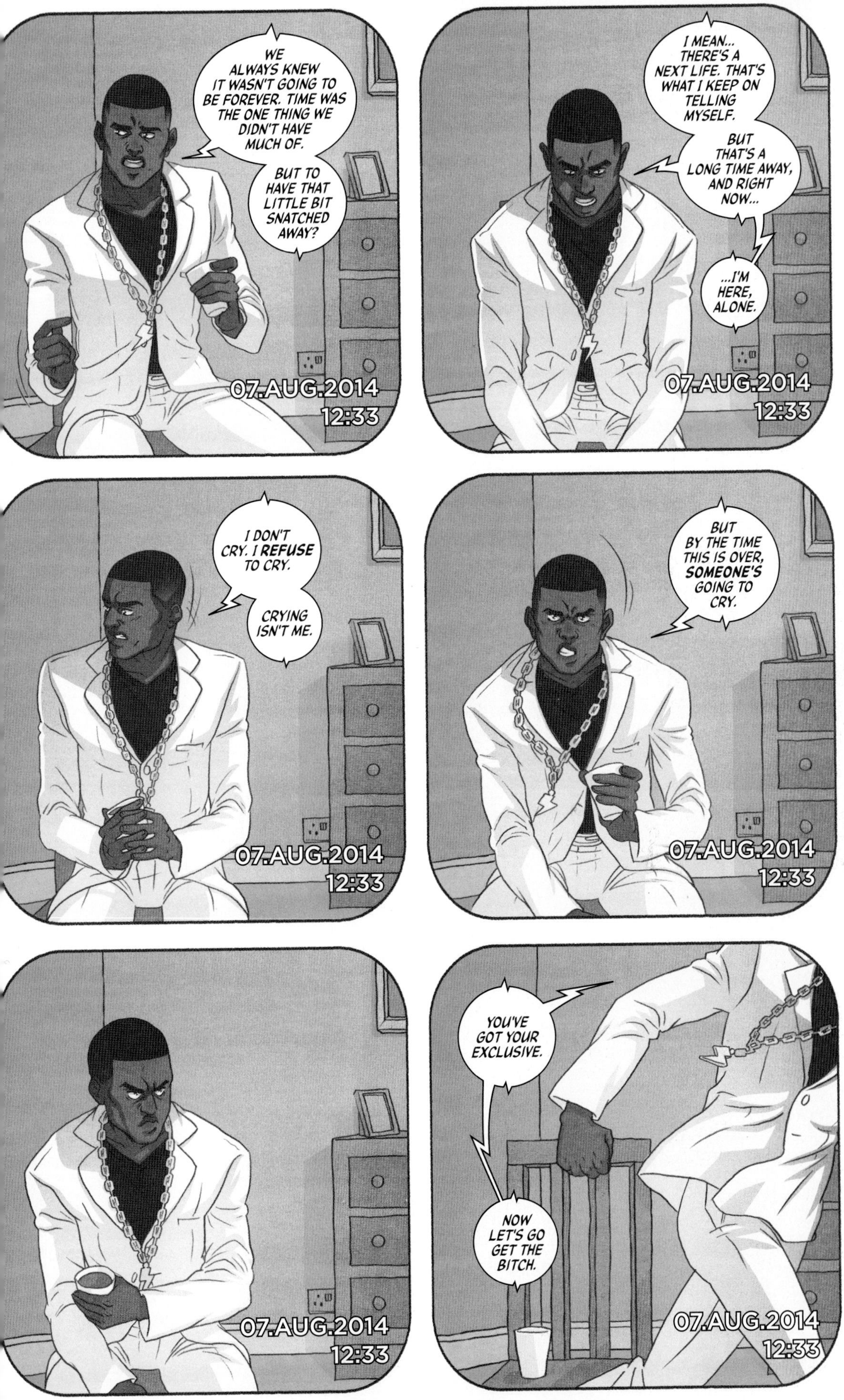
WE ALWAYS KNEW IT WASN'T GOING TO BE FOREVER. TIME WAS THE ONE THING WE DIDN'T HAVE MUCH OF.
BUT TO HAVE THAT LITTLE BIT SNATCHED AWAY?
07.AUG.2014
12:33
I MEAN... THERE'S A NEXT LIFE. THAT'S WHAT I KEEP ON TELLING MYSELF.
BUT THAT'S A LONG TIME AWAY, AND RIGHT NOW...
...I'M HERE, ALONE.
07.AUG.2014
12:33
I DON'T CRY. I REFUSE TO CRY.
CRYING ISN'T ME.
07.AUG.2014
12:33
BUT BY THE TIME THIS IS OVER, SOMEONE'S GOING TO CRY.
07.AUG.2014
12:33
07.AUG.2014
12:33
YOU'VE GOT YOUR EXCLUSIVE.
NOW LET'S GO GET THE BITCH.
07.AUG.2014
12:33

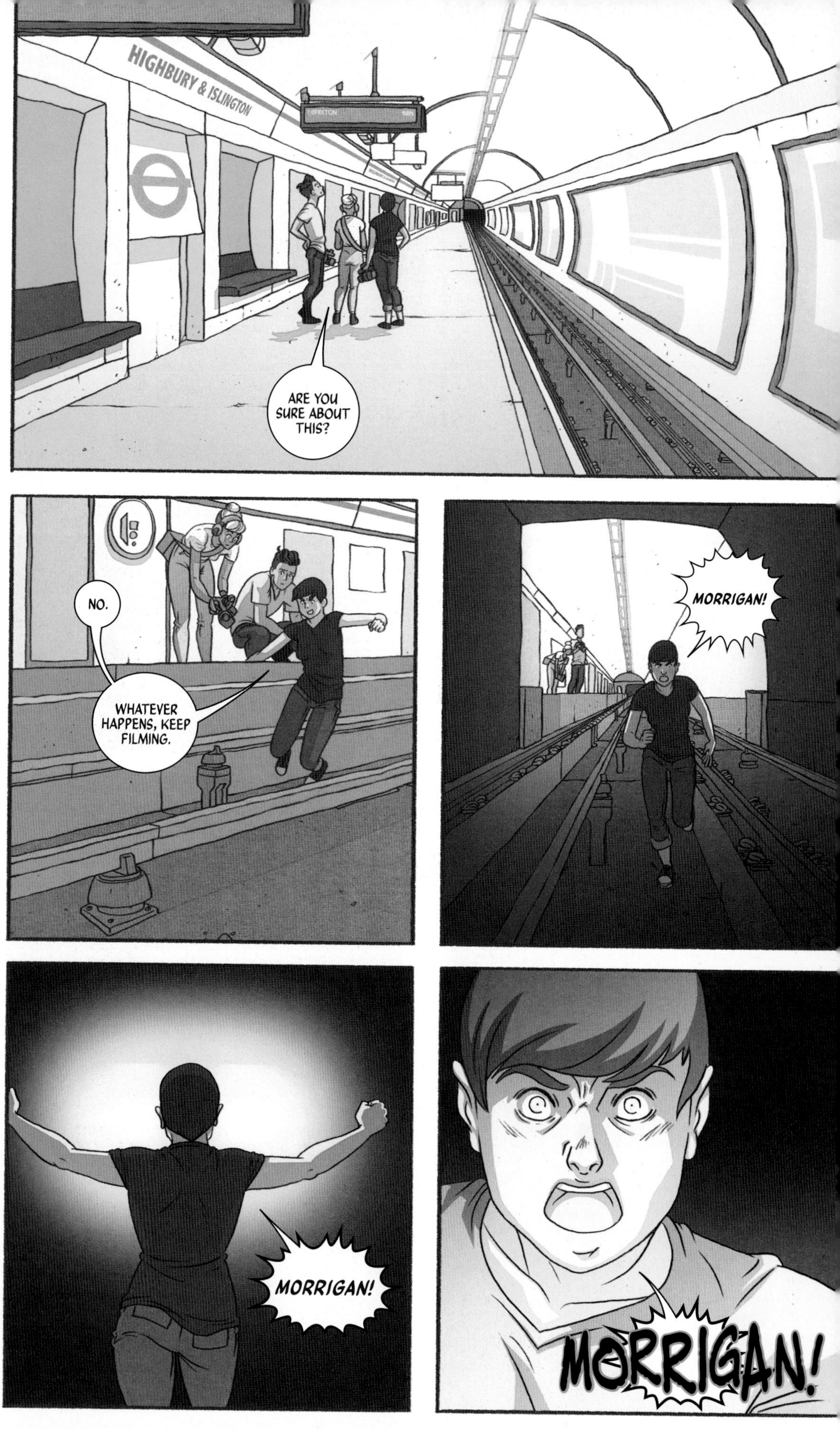
HIGHBURY & ISLINGTON
BRIXTON
ARE YOU SURE ABOUT THIS?
NO.
WHATEVER HAPPENS, KEEP FILMING.
MORRIGAN!
MORRIGAN!
MORRIGAN!

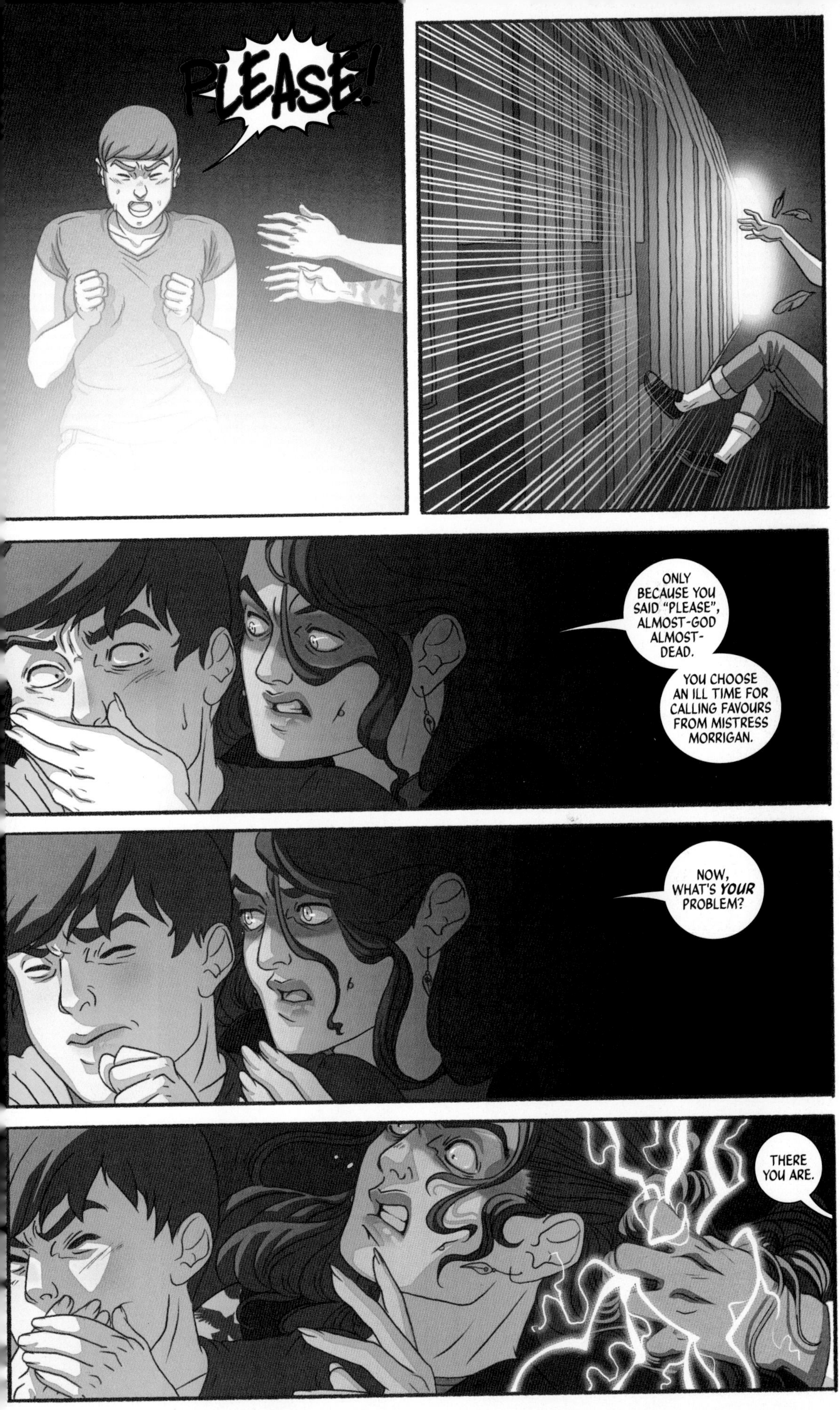
PLEASE!
ONLY BECAUSE YOU SAID "PLEASE", ALMOST-GOD ALMOST-DEAD.
YOU CHOOSE AN ILL TIME FOR CALLING FAVOURS FROM MISTRESS MORRIGAN.
NOW, WHAT'S *YOUR* PROBLEM?
THERE YOU ARE.

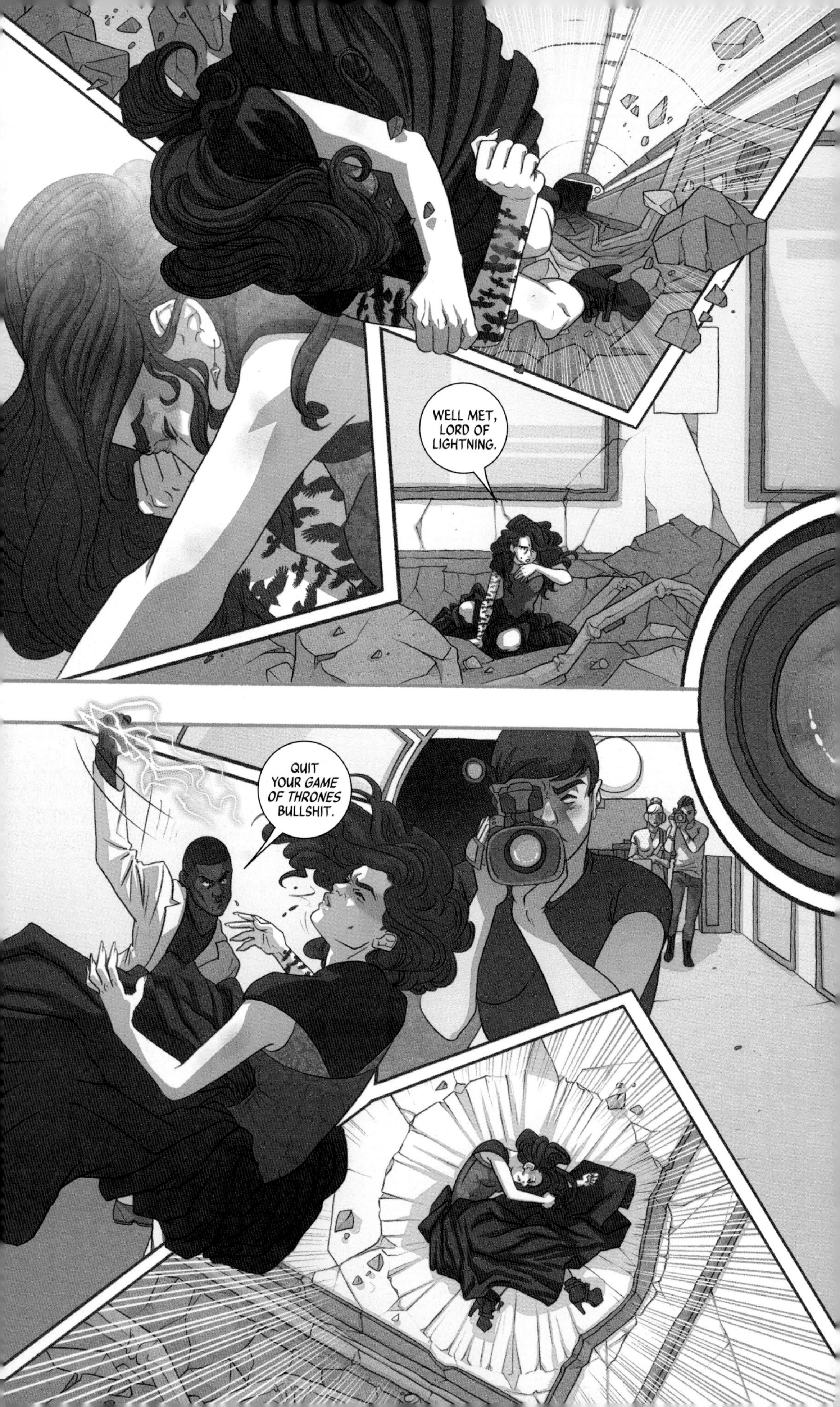
WELL MET, LORD OF LIGHTNING.
QUIT YOUR GAME OF THRONES BULLSHIT.

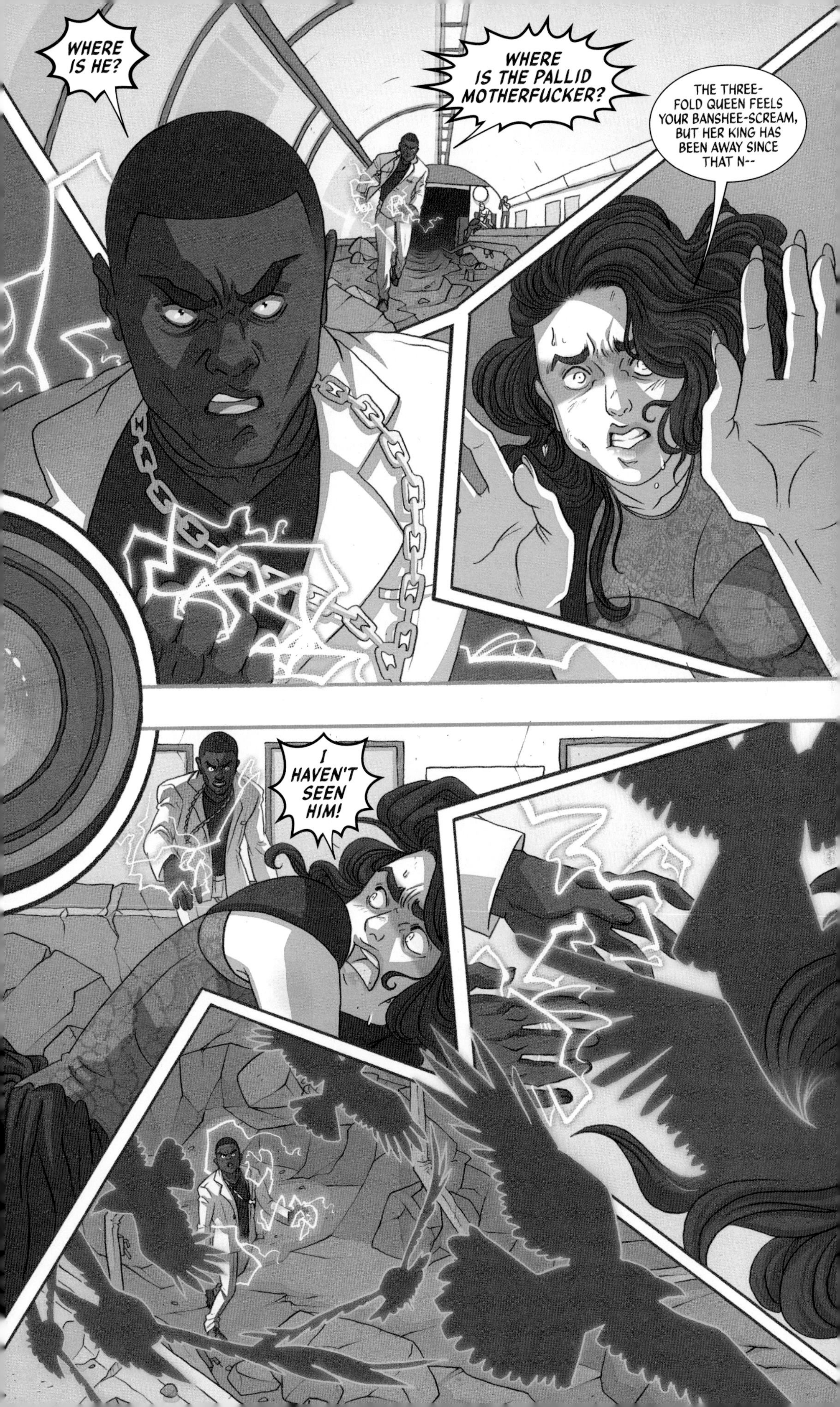
WHERE IS HE?
WHERE IS THE PALLID MOTHERFUCKER?
THE THREE-FOLD QUEEN FEELS YOUR BANSHEE-SCREAM, BUT HER KING HAS BEEN AWAY SINCE THAT N--
I HAVEN'T SEEN HIM!

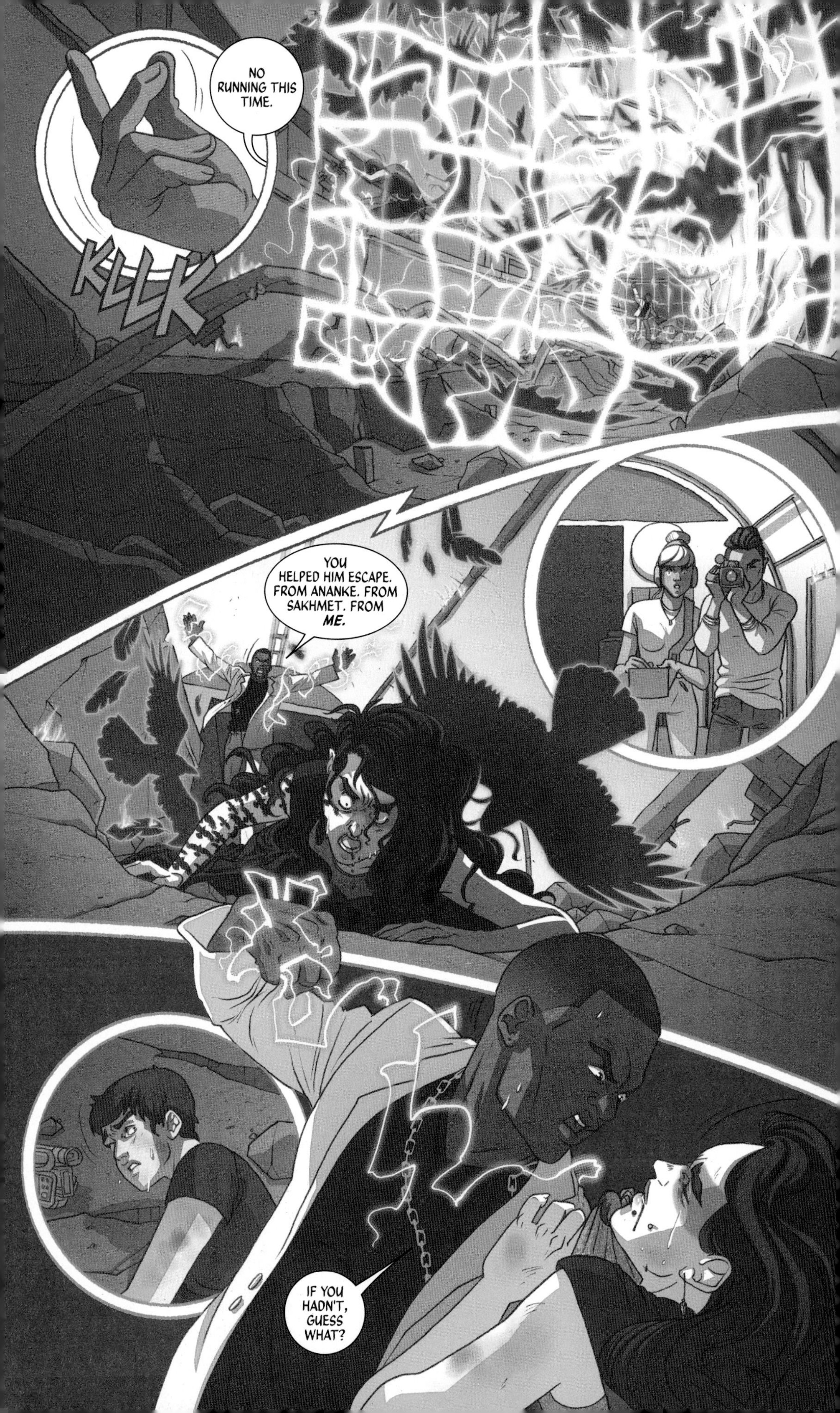
NO RUNNING THIS TIME.
KLLK
YOU HELPED HIM ESCAPE. FROM ANANKE. FROM SAKHMET. FROM ME.
IF YOU HADN'T, GUESS WHAT?

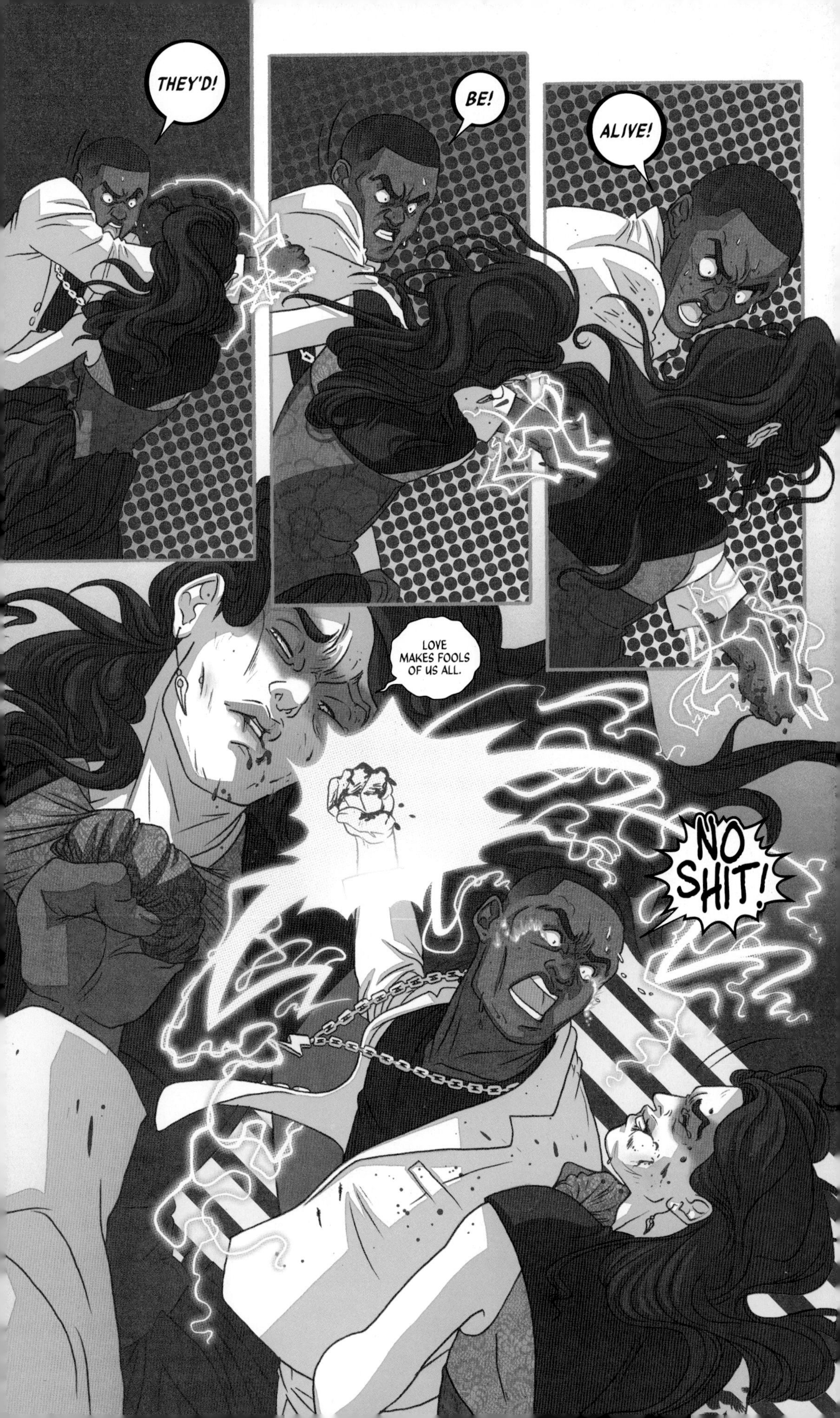
THEY'D!
BE!
ALIVE!
LOVE MAKES FOOLS OF US ALL.
NO SHIT!

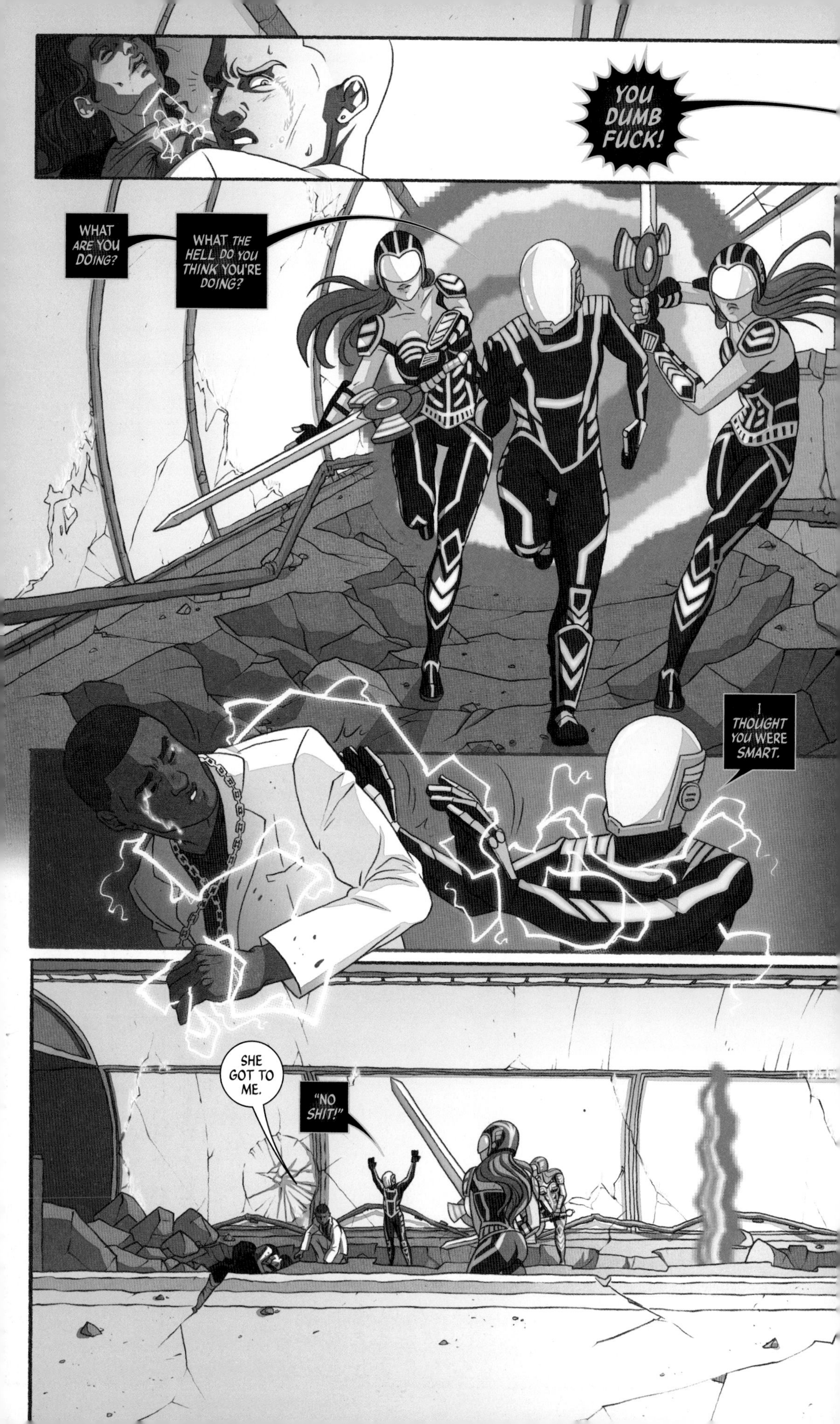
YOU DUMB FUCK!
WHAT ARE YOU DOING?
WHAT THE HELL DO YOU THINK YOU'RE DOING?
I THOUGHT YOU WERE SMART.
SHE GOT TO ME.
"NO SHIT!"

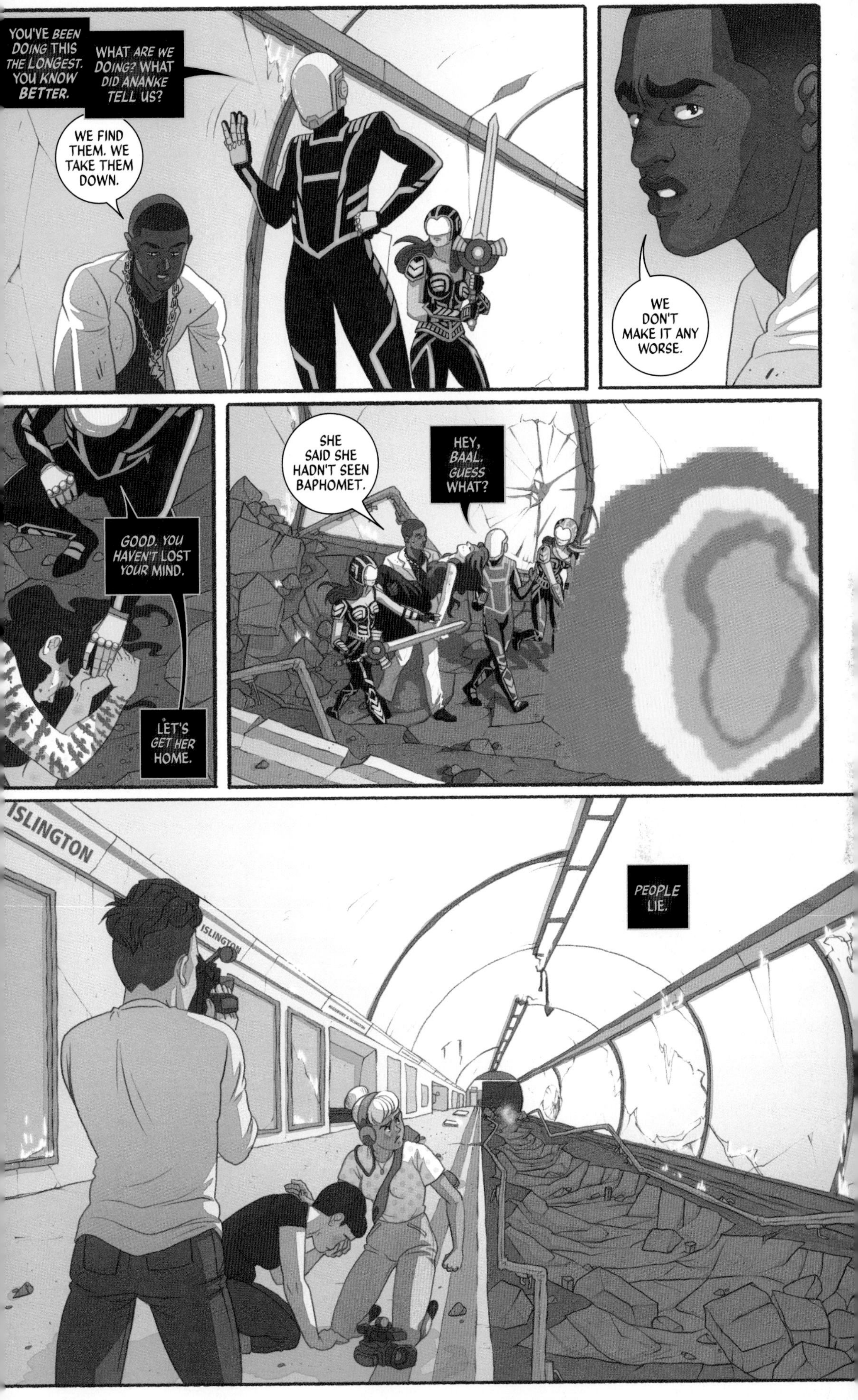
YOU'VE *BEEN DOING* THIS THE LONGEST. YOU KNOW *BETTER*.
WHAT *ARE* WE *DOING*? WHAT DID ANANKE TELL US?
WE FIND THEM. WE TAKE THEM DOWN.
WE DON'T MAKE IT ANY WORSE.
GOOD. YOU HAVEN'T LOST YOUR MIND.
LET'S *GET HER* HOME.
SHE SAID SHE HADN'T SEEN BAPHOMET.
HEY, *BAAL. GUESS* WHAT?
ISLINGTON
ISLINGTON
PEOPLE LIE.

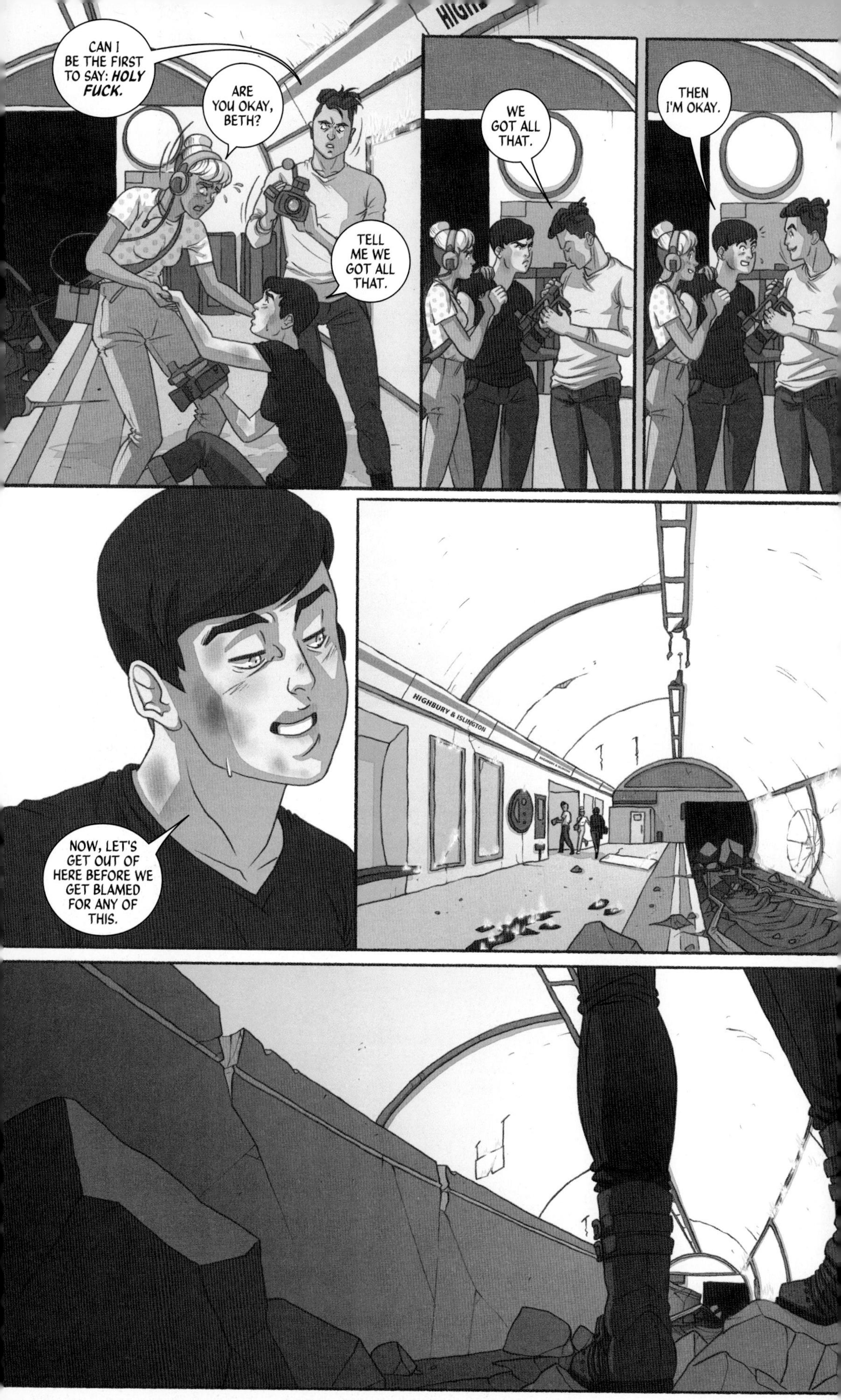
HIGH
CAN I BE THE FIRST TO SAY: HOLY FUCK.
ARE YOU OKAY, BETH?
TELL ME WE GOT ALL THAT.
WE GOT ALL THAT.
THEN I'M OKAY.
NOW, LET'S GET OUT OF HERE BEFORE WE GET BLAMED FOR ANY OF THIS.
HIGHBURY & ISLINGTON

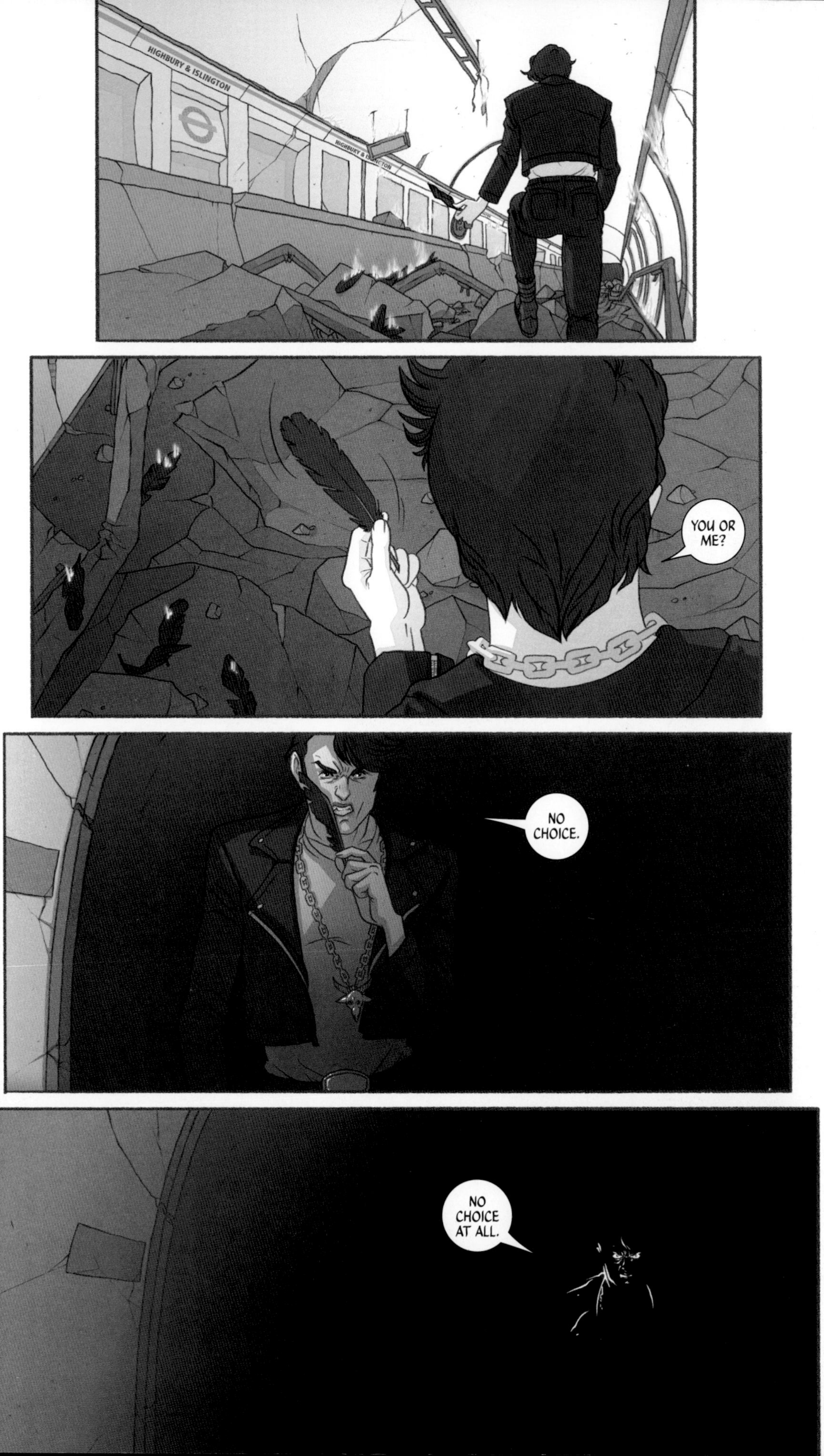
HIGHBURY & ISLINGTON
YOU OR ME?
NO CHOICE.
NO CHOICE AT ALL.

THE QUEEN
IS DEAD

7 AUGUST 2014

THE
WICKED
+
DIVINE
THE

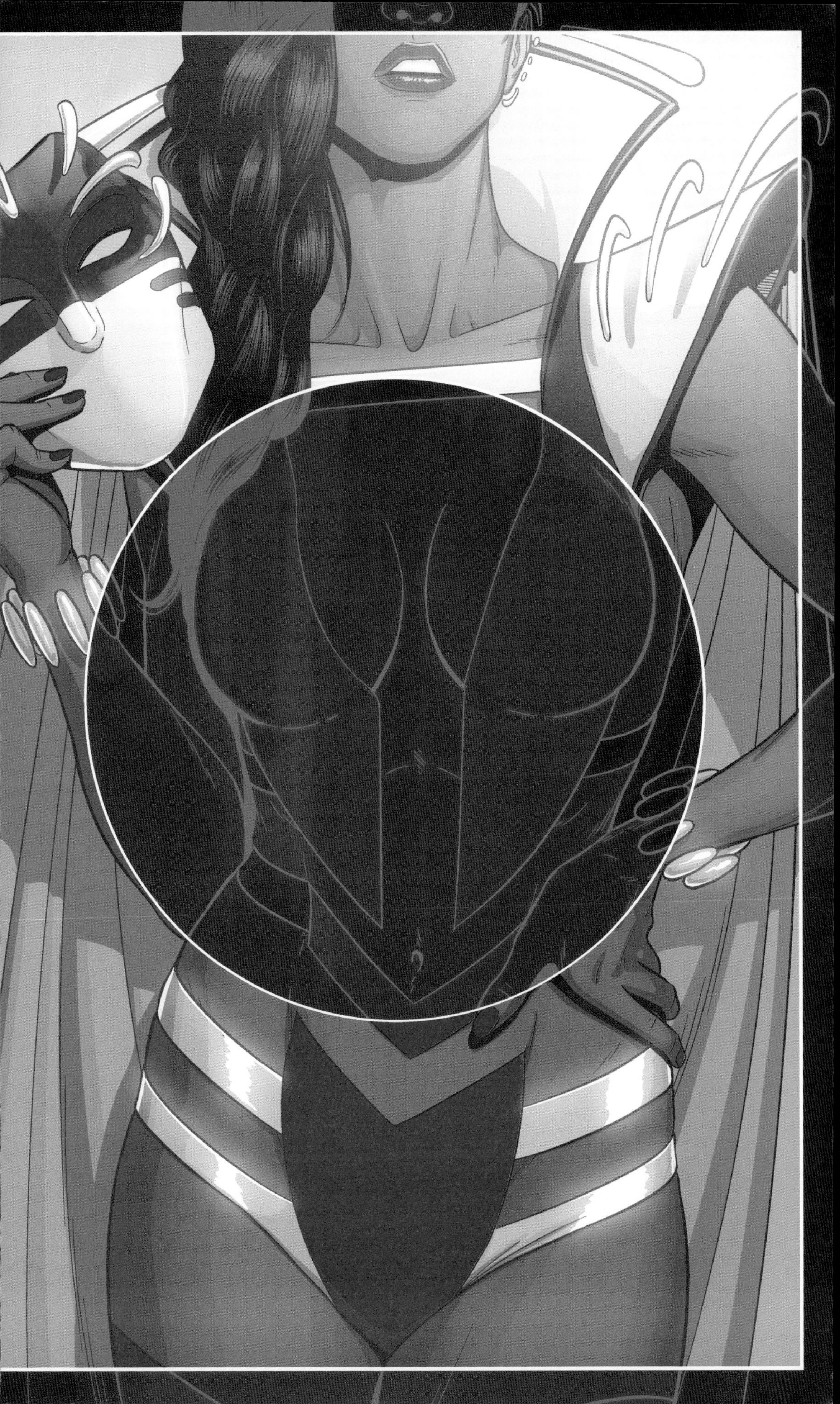

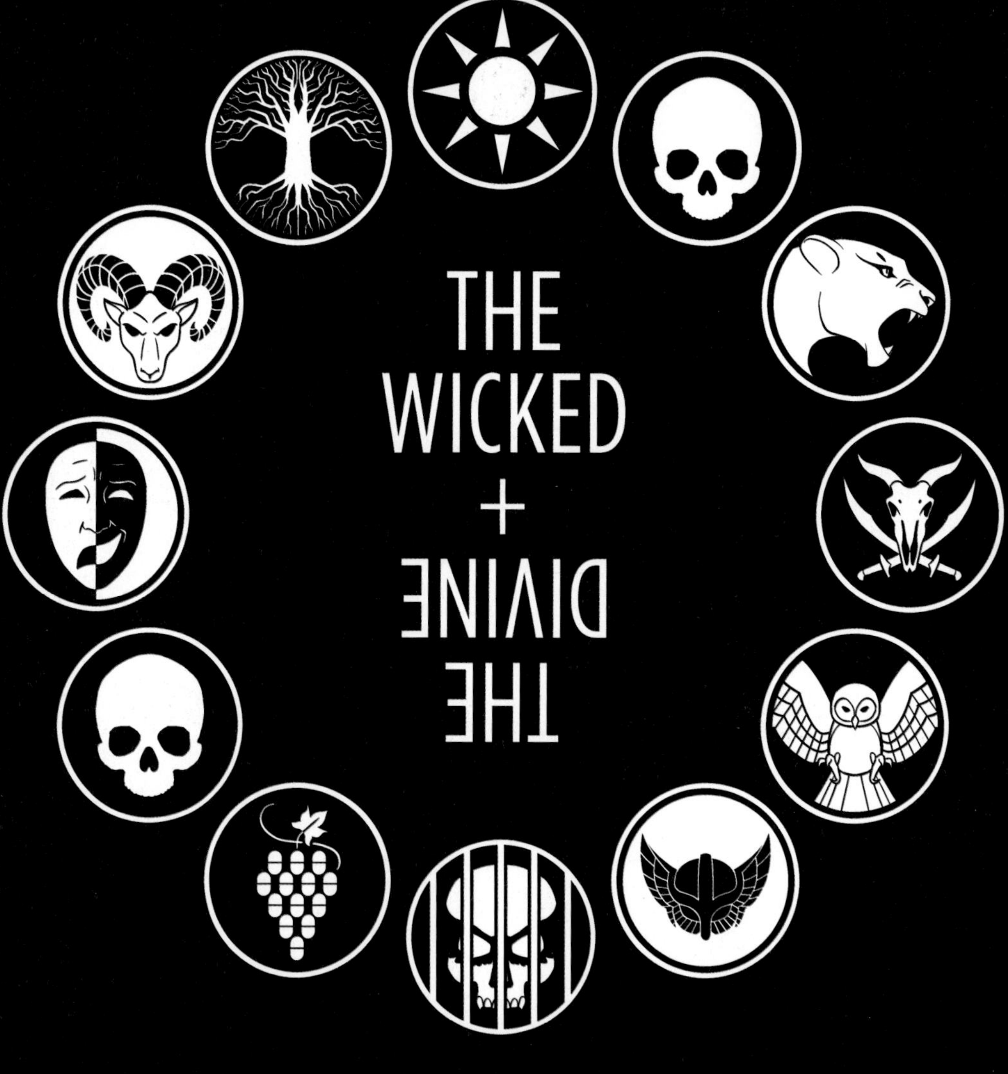
THE WICKED
+
THE DIVINE

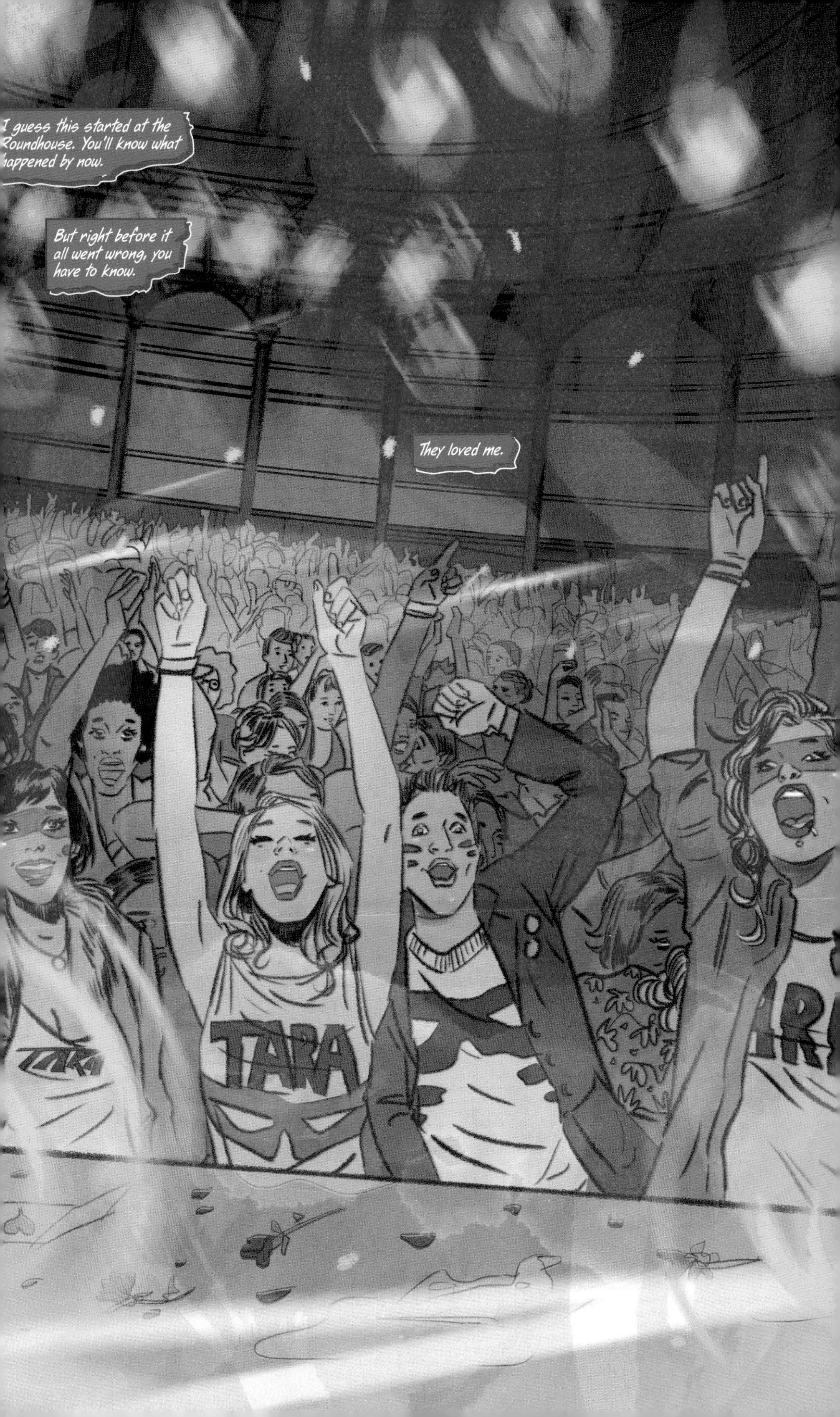

I guess this started at the Roundhouse. You'll know what happened by now.
But right before it all went wrong, you have to know.
They loved me.
TARA

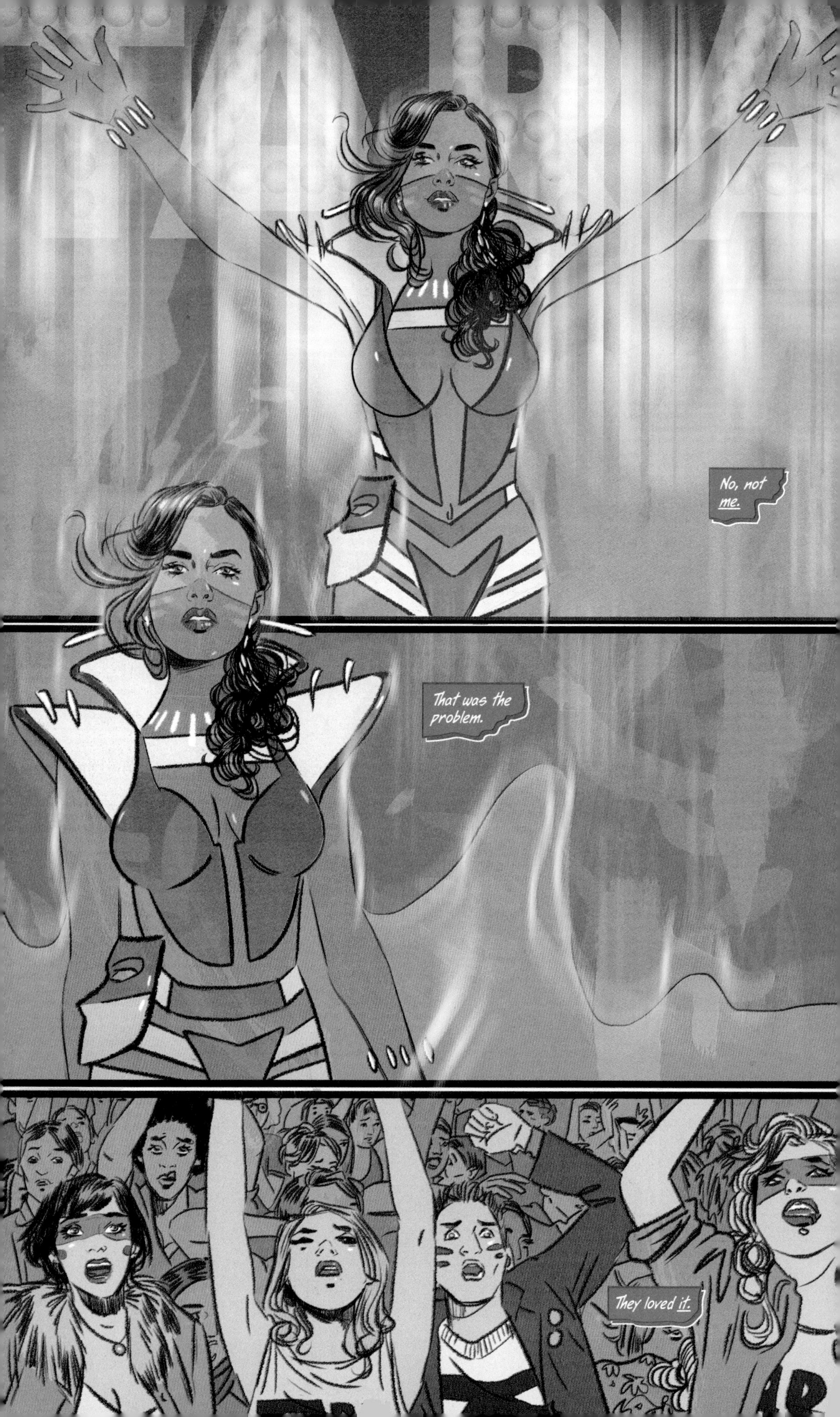
No, not me.
That was the problem.
They loved it.

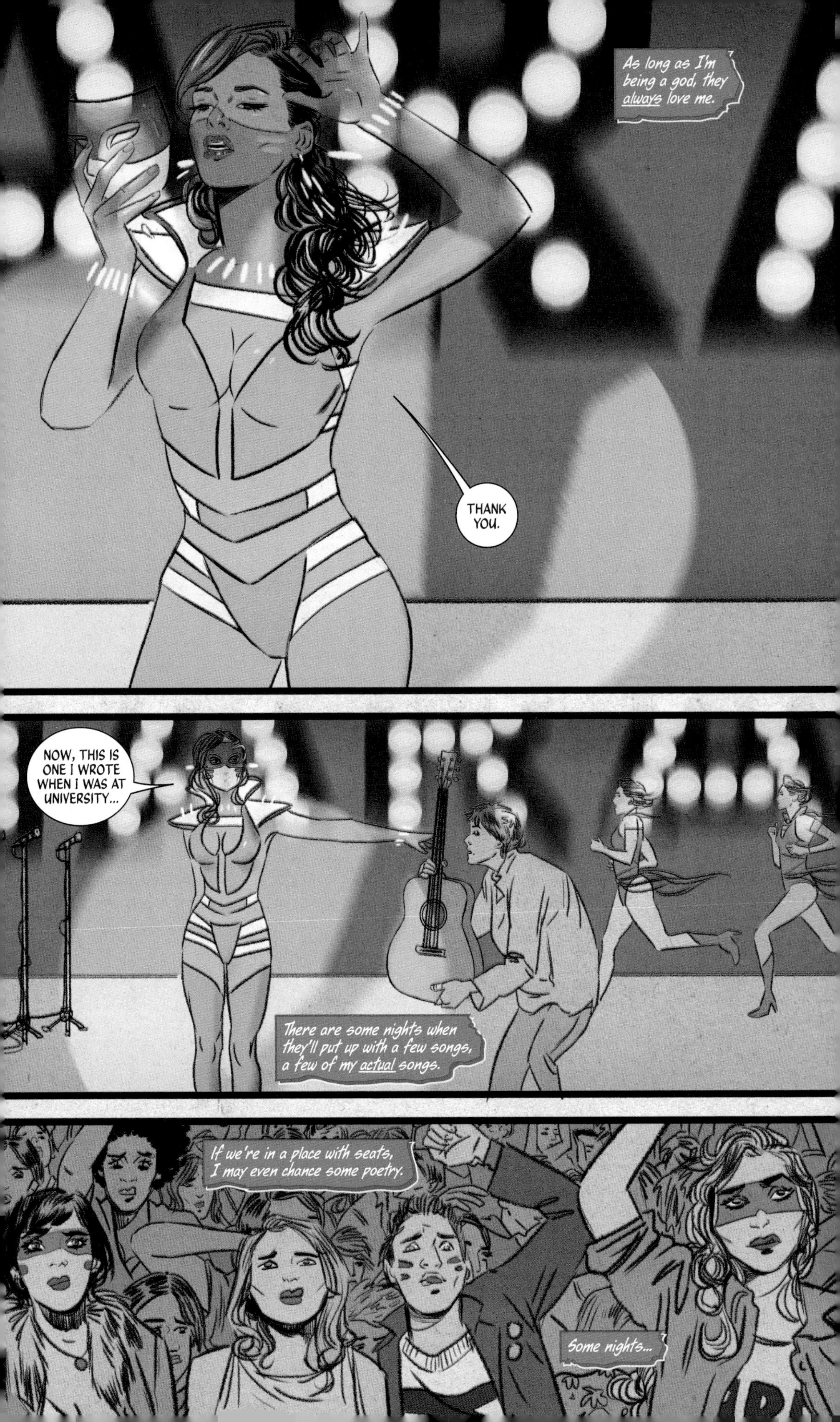
As long as I'm being a god, they always love me.
THANK YOU.
NOW, THIS IS ONE I WROTE WHEN I WAS AT UNIVERSITY...
There are some nights when they'll put up with a few songs, a few of my actual songs.
If we're in a place with seats, I may even chance some poetry.
Some nights...

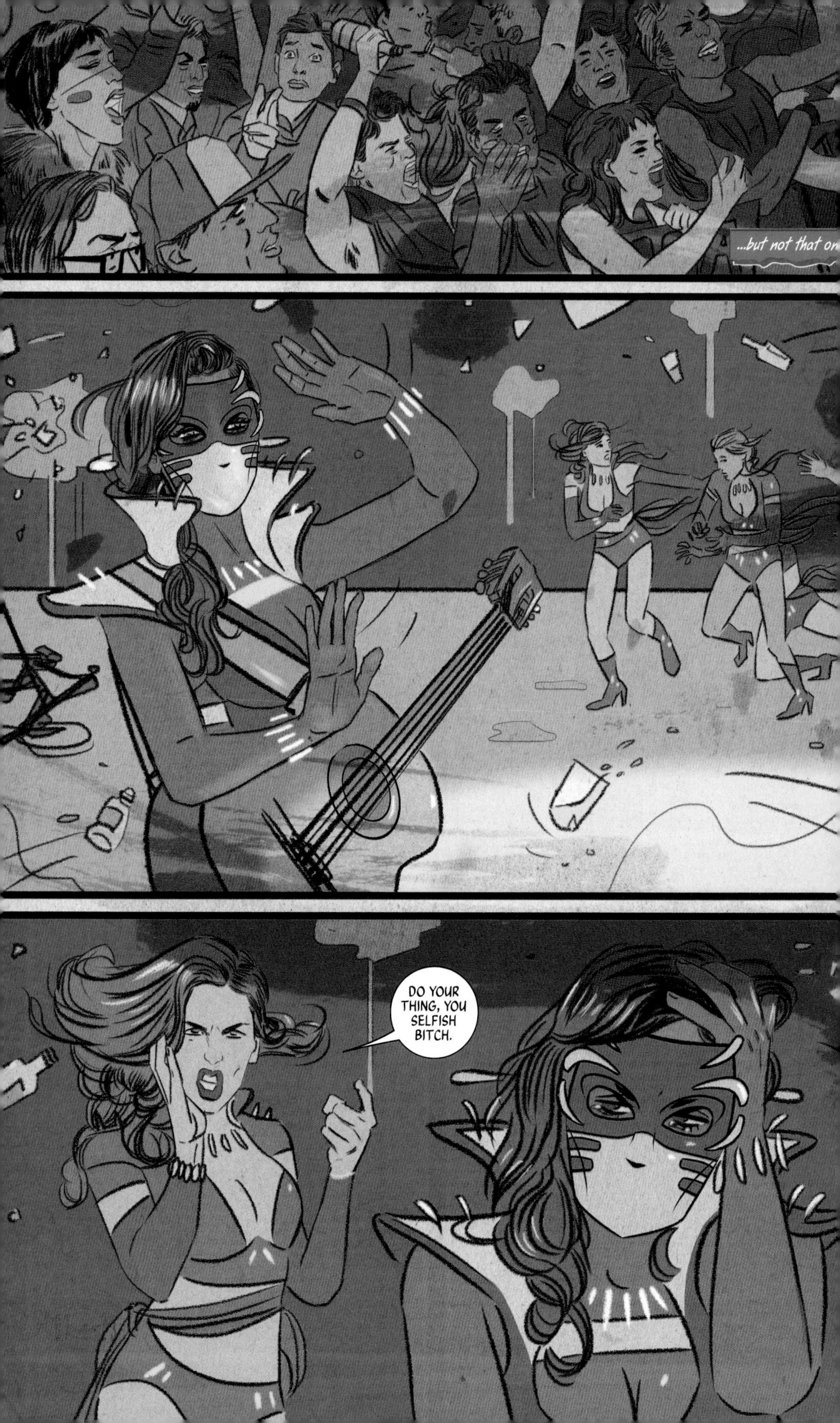
...but not that on
DO YOUR THING, YOU SELFISH BITCH.

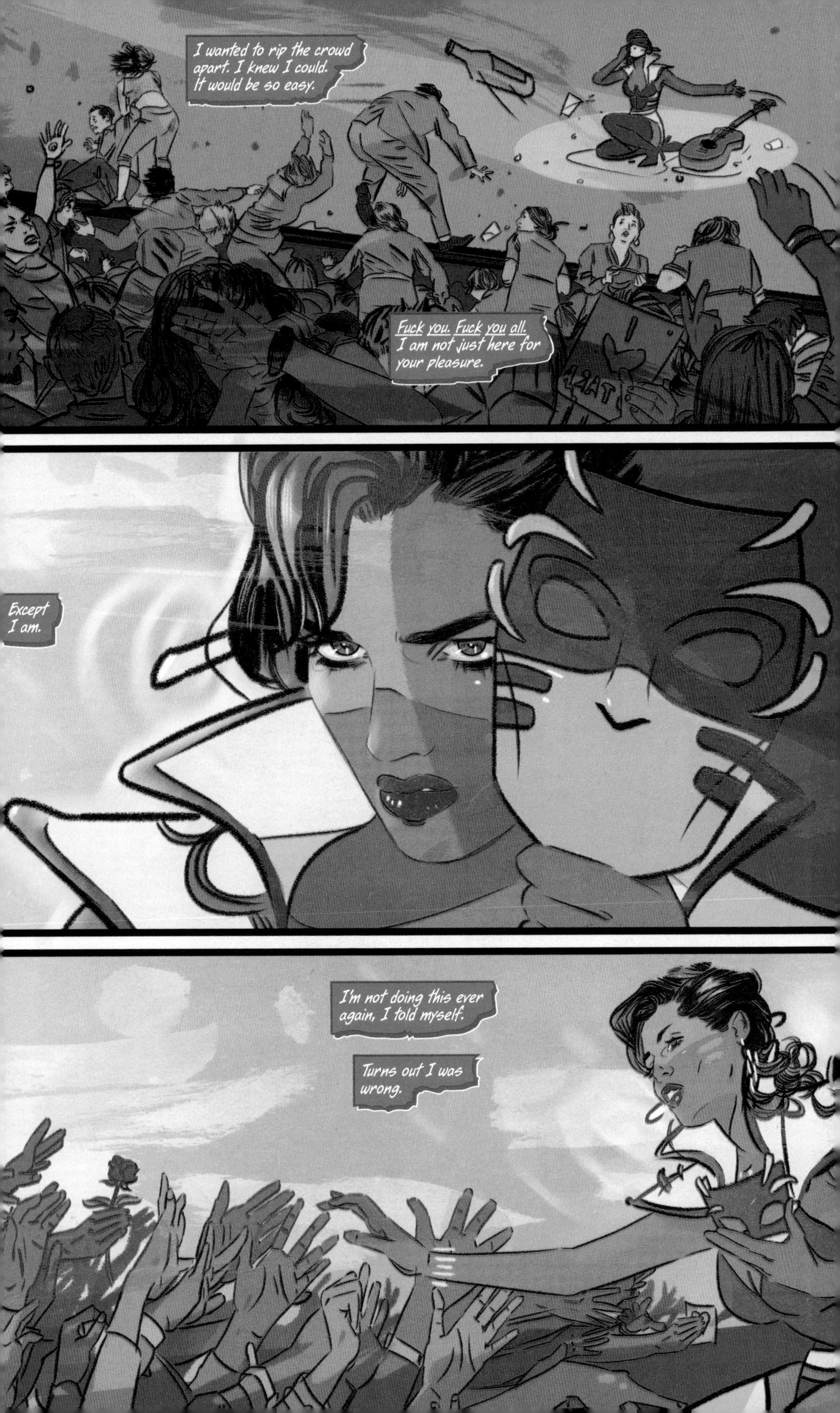
I wanted to rip the crowd apart. I knew I could. It would be so easy.
Fuck you. Fuck you all. I am not just here for your pleasure.
Except I am.
I'm not doing this ever again, I told myself.
Turns out I was wrong.

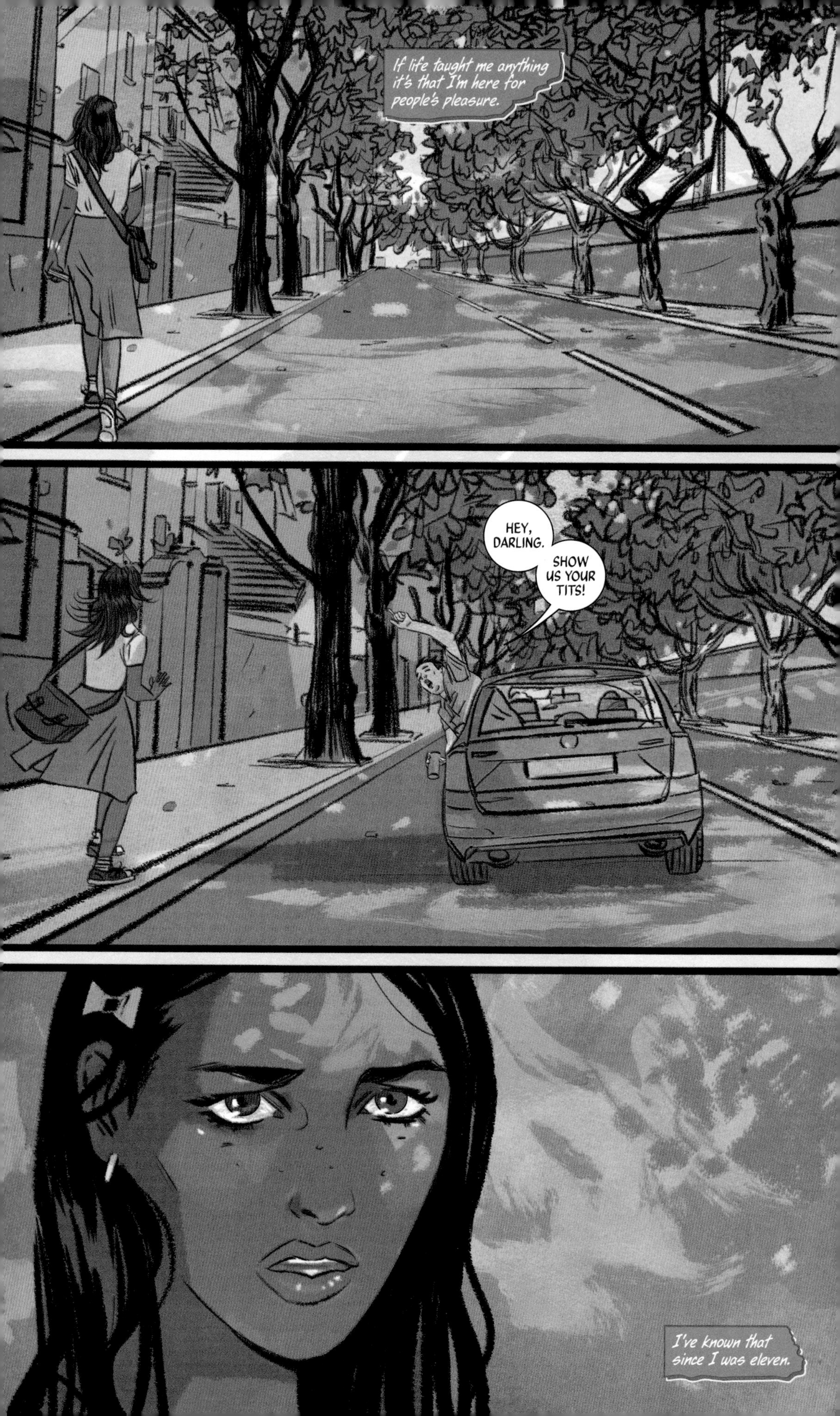
If life taught me anything it's that I'm here for people's pleasure.
HEY, DARLING.
SHOW US YOUR TITS!
I've known that since I was eleven.

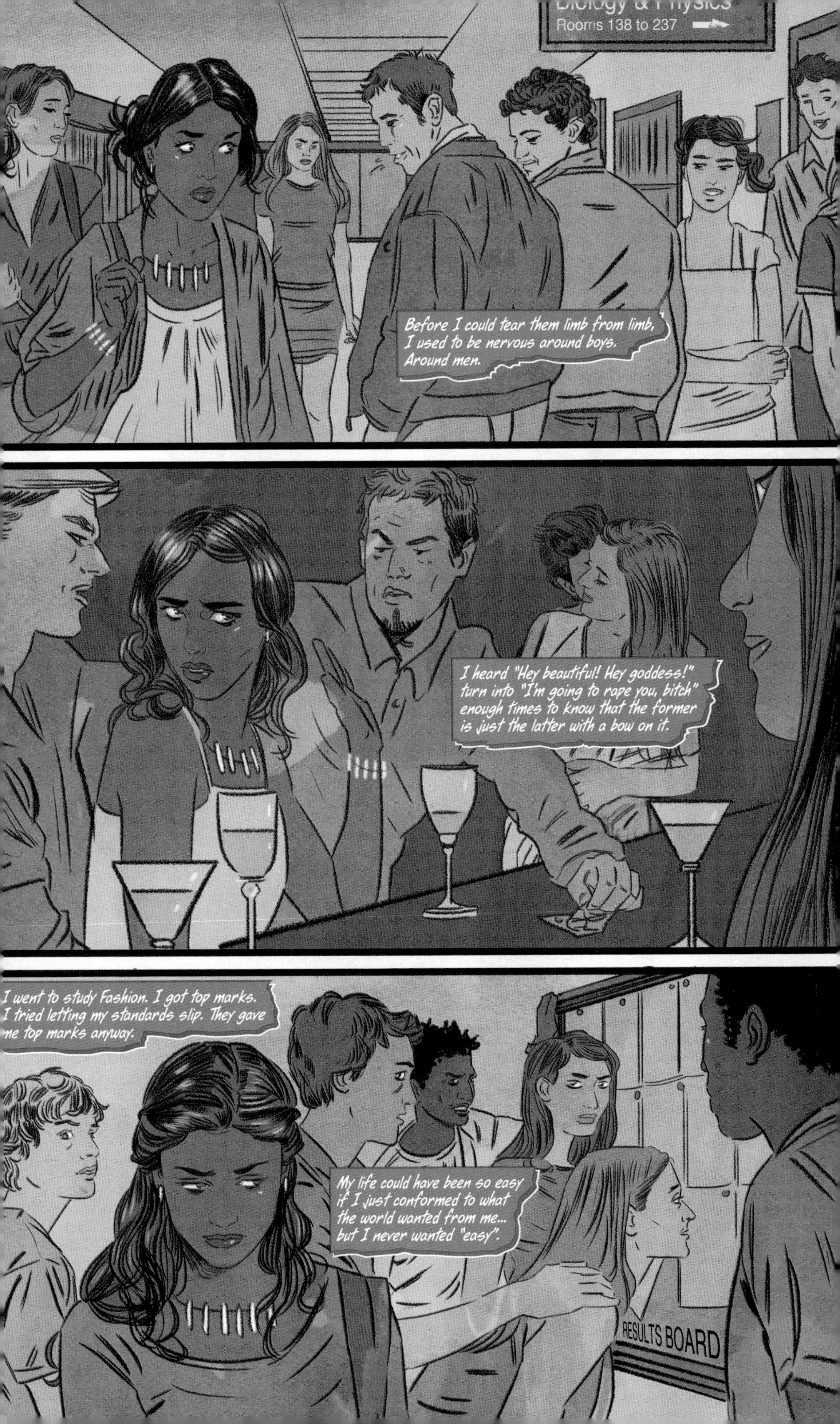
Rooms 138 to 237
Before I could tear them limb from limb, I used to be nervous around boys. Around men.
I heard "Hey beautiful! Hey goddess!" turn into "I'm going to rape you, bitch" enough times to know that the former is just the latter with a bow on it.
I went to study Fashion. I got top marks. I tried letting my standards slip. They gave me top marks anyway.
My life could have been so easy if I just conformed to what the world wanted from me... but I never wanted "easy".
RESULTS BOARD

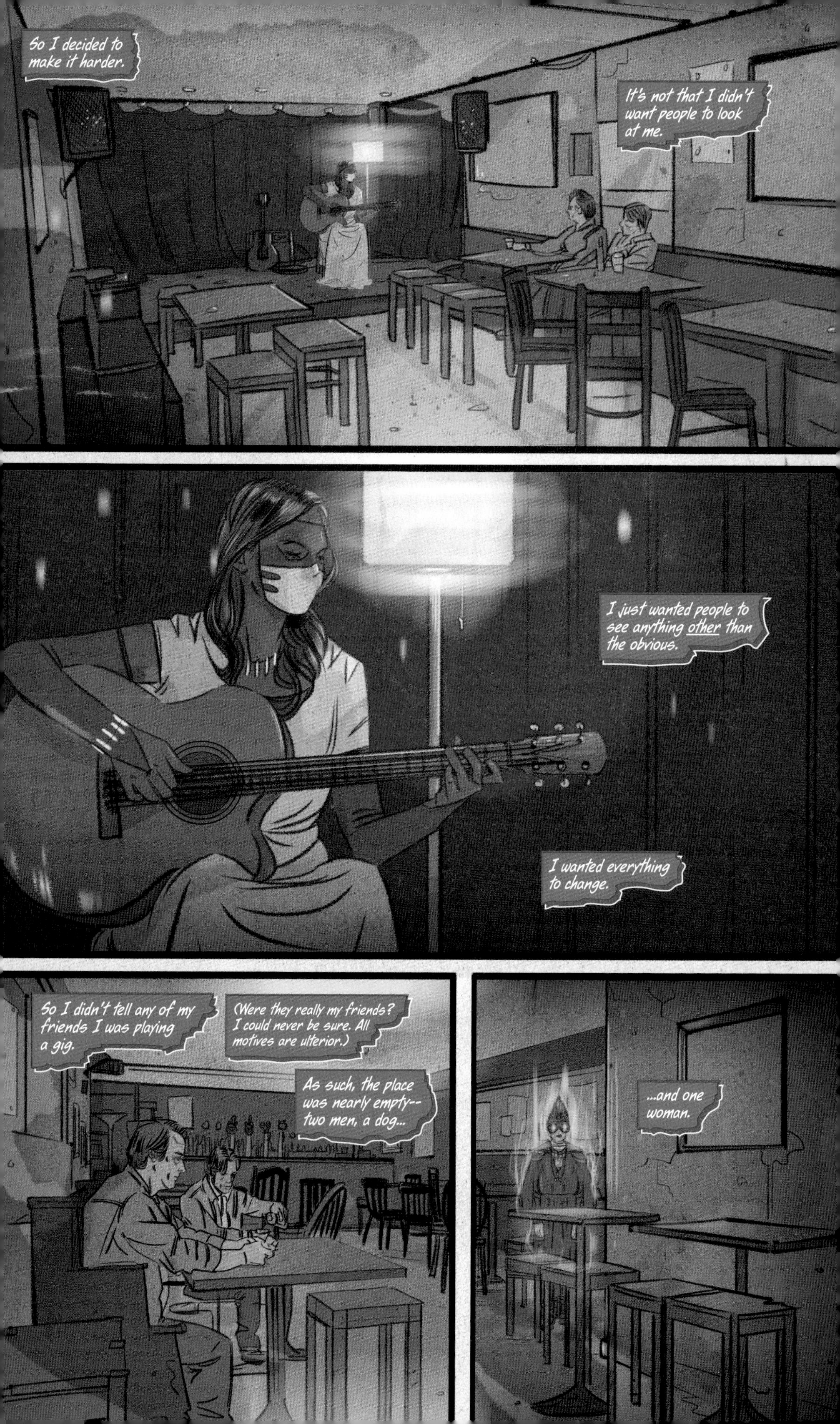

So I decided to make it harder.
It's not that I didn't want people to look at me.
I just wanted people to see anything other than the obvious.
I wanted everything to change.
So I didn't tell any of my friends I was playing a gig.
(Were they really my friends? I could never be sure. All motives are ulterior.)
As such, the place was nearly empty-- two men, a dog...
...and one woman.

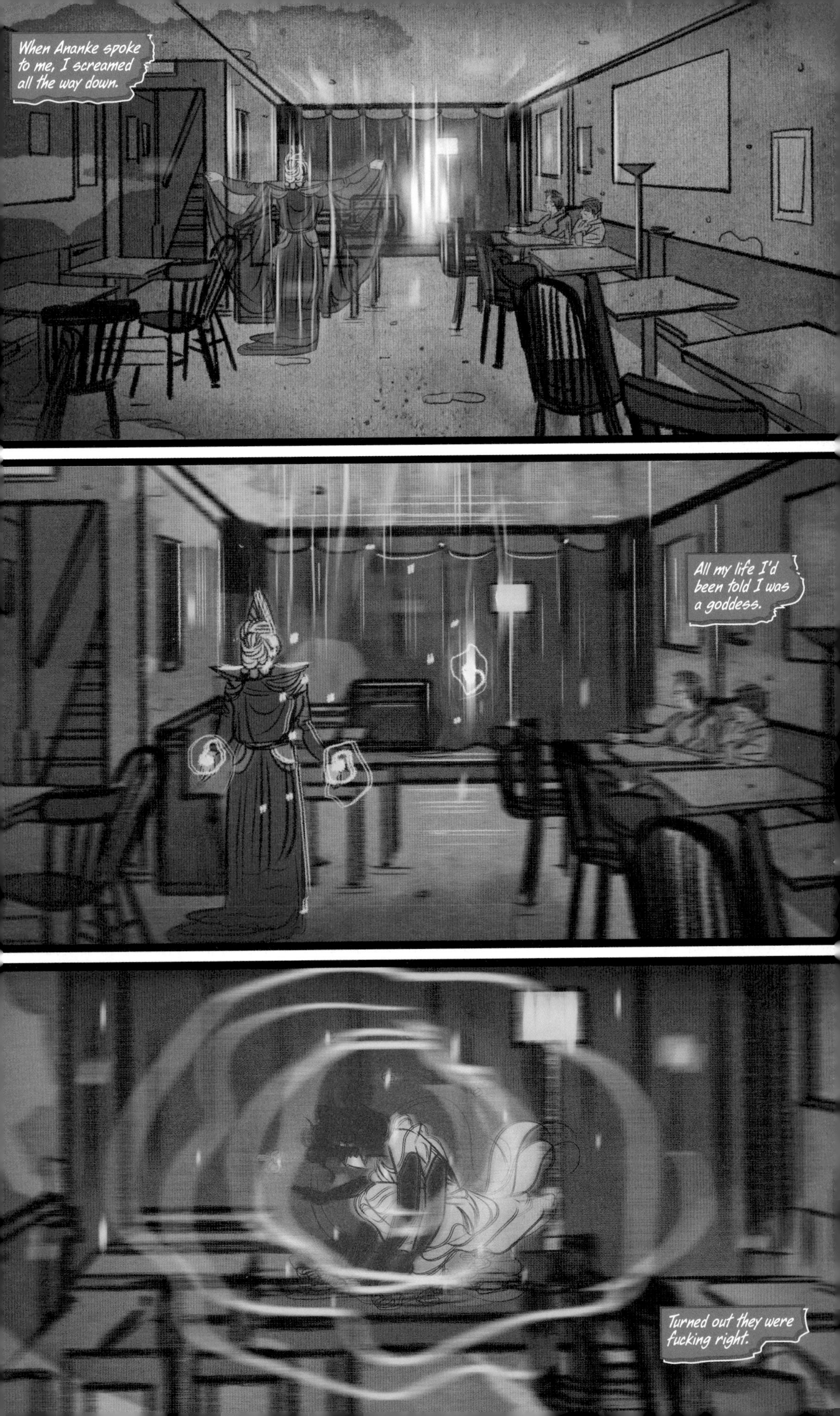
When Ananke spoke to me, I screamed all the way down.
All my life I'd been told I was a goddess.
Turned out they were fucking right.

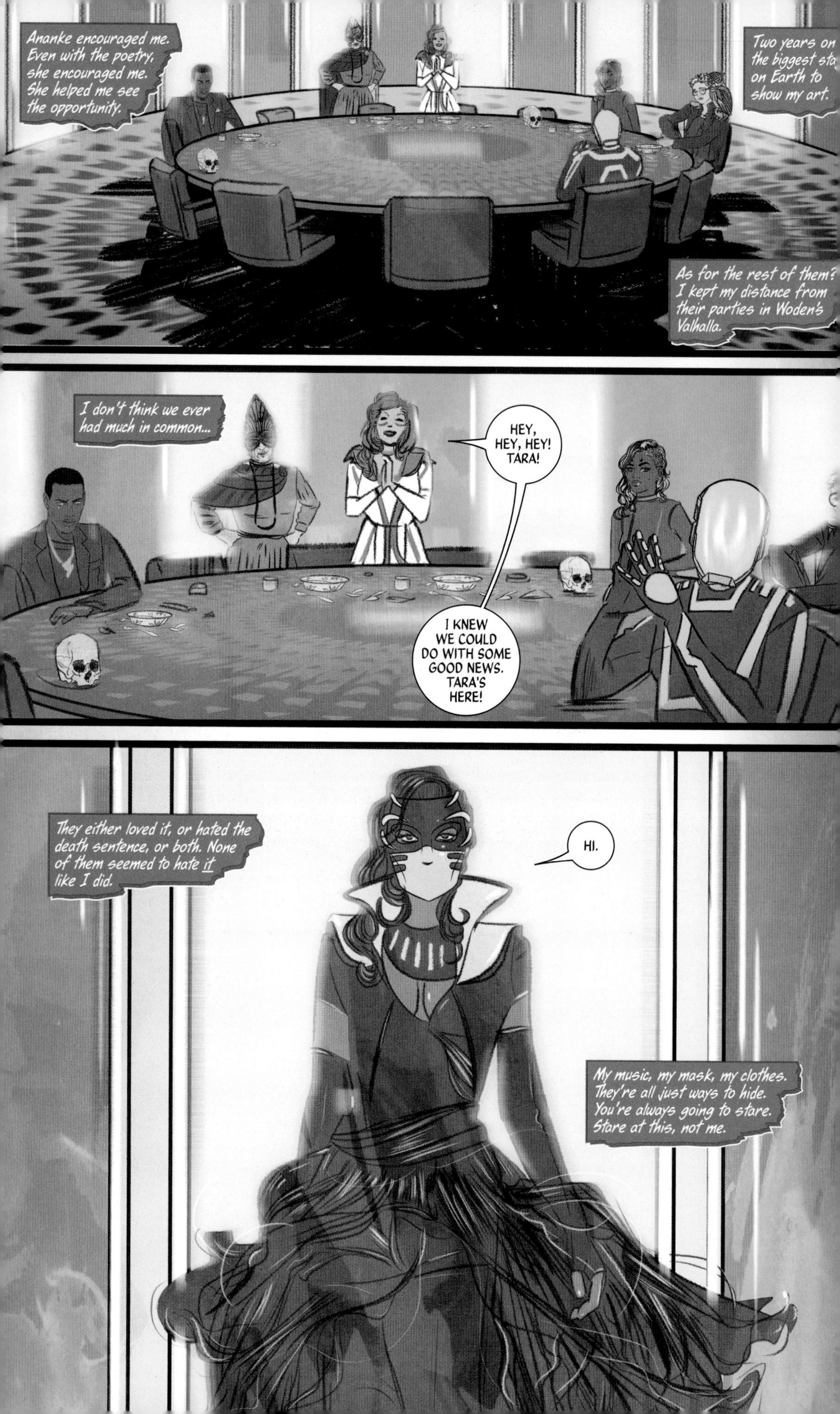
Ananke encouraged me. Even with the poetry, she encouraged me. She helped me see the opportunity.
Two years on the biggest sta on Earth to show my art.
As for the rest of them? I kept my distance from their parties in Woden's Valhalla.
I don't think we ever had much in common...
HEY, HEY, HEY! TARA!
I KNEW WE COULD DO WITH SOME GOOD NEWS. TARA'S HERE!
They either loved it, or hated the death sentence, or both. None of them seemed to hate it like I did.
HI.
My music, my mask, my clothes. They're all just ways to hide. You're always going to stare. Stare at this, not me.

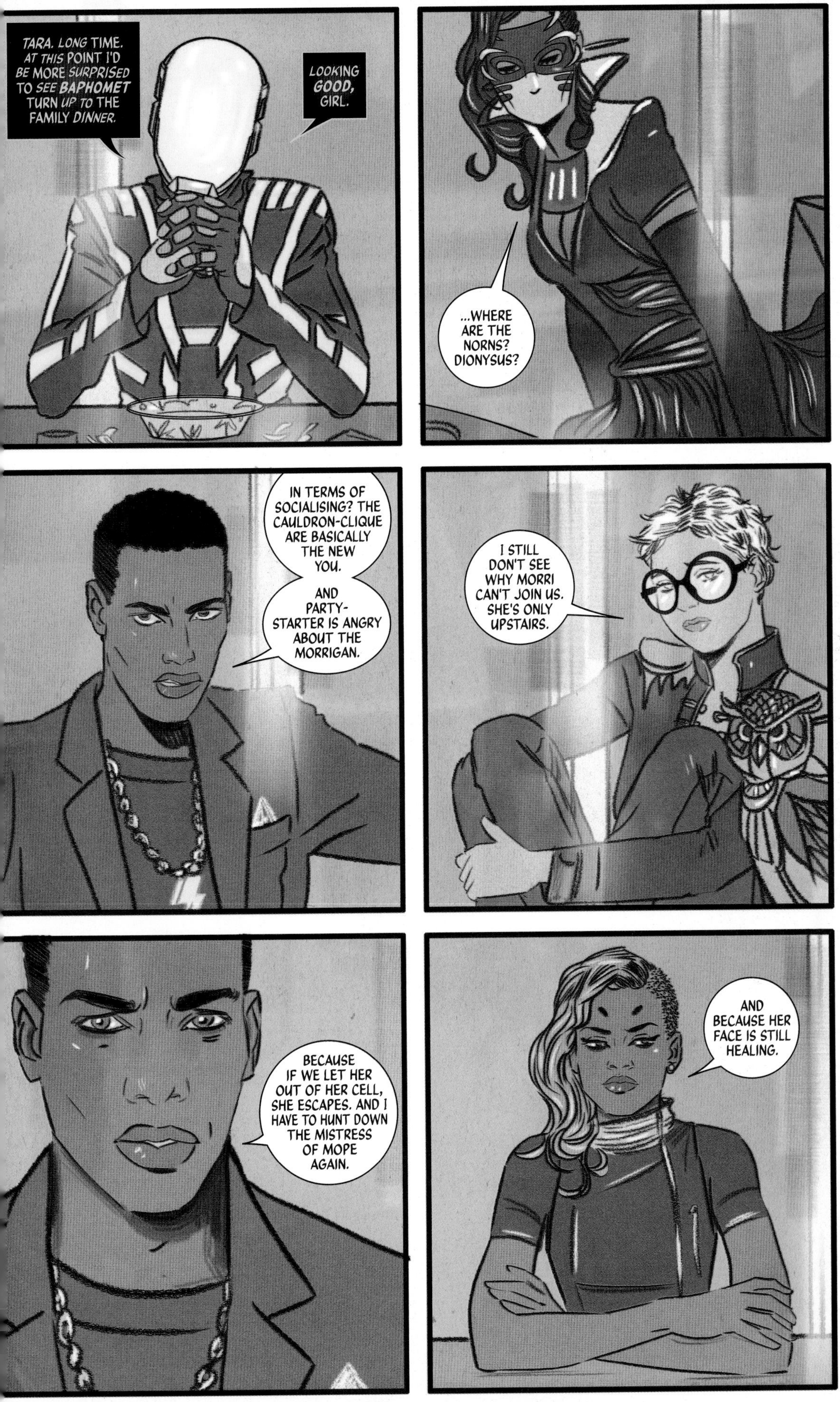
TARA. LONG TIME. AT THIS POINT I'D BE MORE SURPRISED TO SEE BAPHOMET TURN UP TO THE FAMILY DINNER.
LOOKING GOOD, GIRL.
...WHERE ARE THE NORNS? DIONYSUS?
IN TERMS OF SOCIALISING? THE CAULDRON-CLIQUE ARE BASICALLY THE NEW YOU.
AND PARTY-STARTER IS ANGRY ABOUT THE MORRIGAN.
I STILL DON'T SEE WHY MORRI CAN'T JOIN US. SHE'S ONLY UPSTAIRS.
BECAUSE IF WE LET HER OUT OF HER CELL, SHE ESCAPES. AND I HAVE TO HUNT DOWN THE MISTRESS OF MOPE AGAIN.
AND BECAUSE HER FACE IS STILL HEALING.

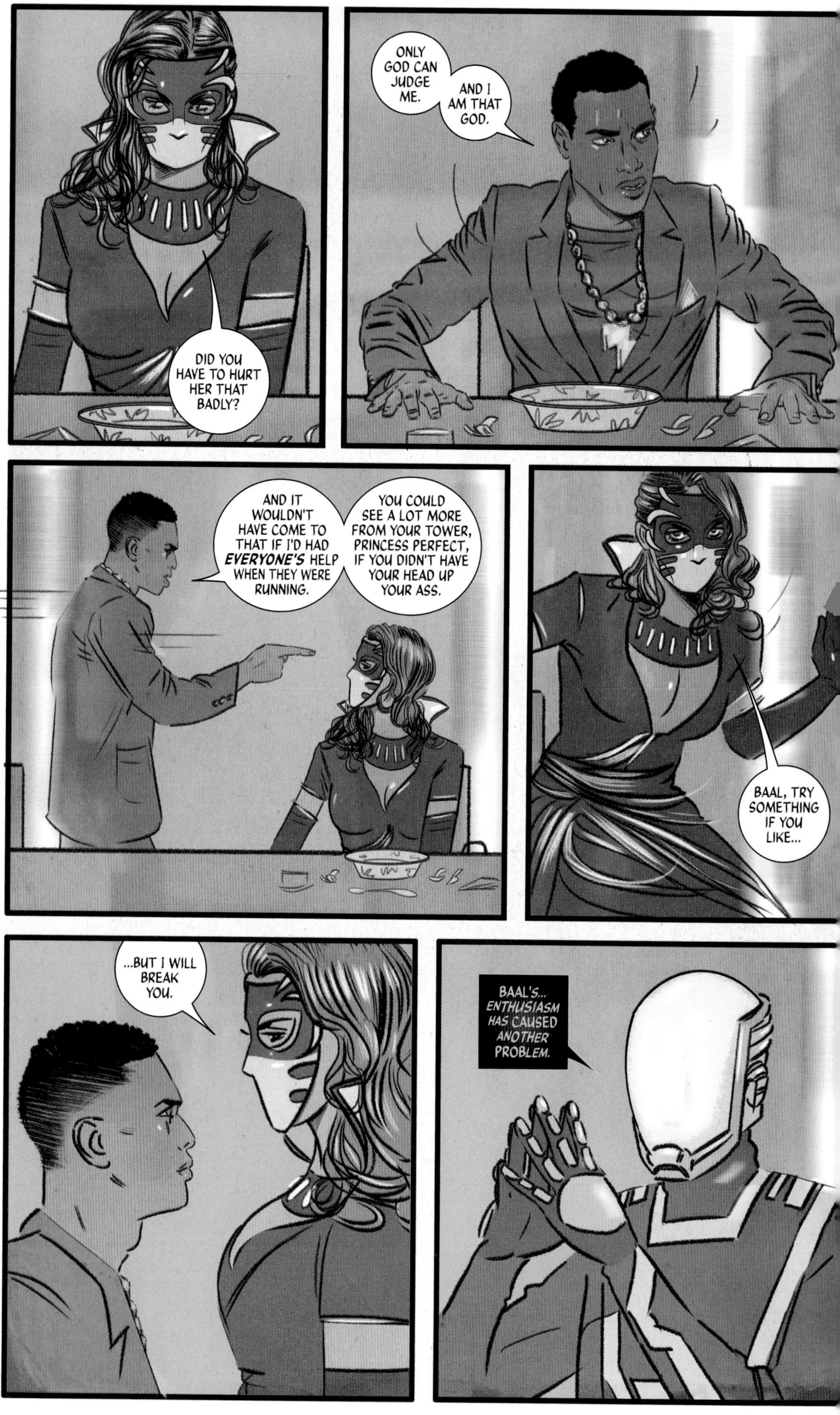
DID YOU HAVE TO HURT HER THAT BADLY?
ONLY GOD CAN JUDGE ME.
AND I AM THAT GOD.
AND IT WOULDN'T HAVE COME TO THAT IF I'D HAD *EVERYONE'S* HELP WHEN THEY WERE RUNNING.
YOU COULD SEE A LOT MORE FROM YOUR TOWER, PRINCESS PERFECT, IF YOU DIDN'T HAVE YOUR HEAD UP YOUR ASS.
BAAL, TRY SOMETHING IF YOU LIKE...
...BUT I WILL BREAK YOU.
BAAL'S... *ENTHUSIASM* HAS CAUSED *ANOTHER* PROBLEM.

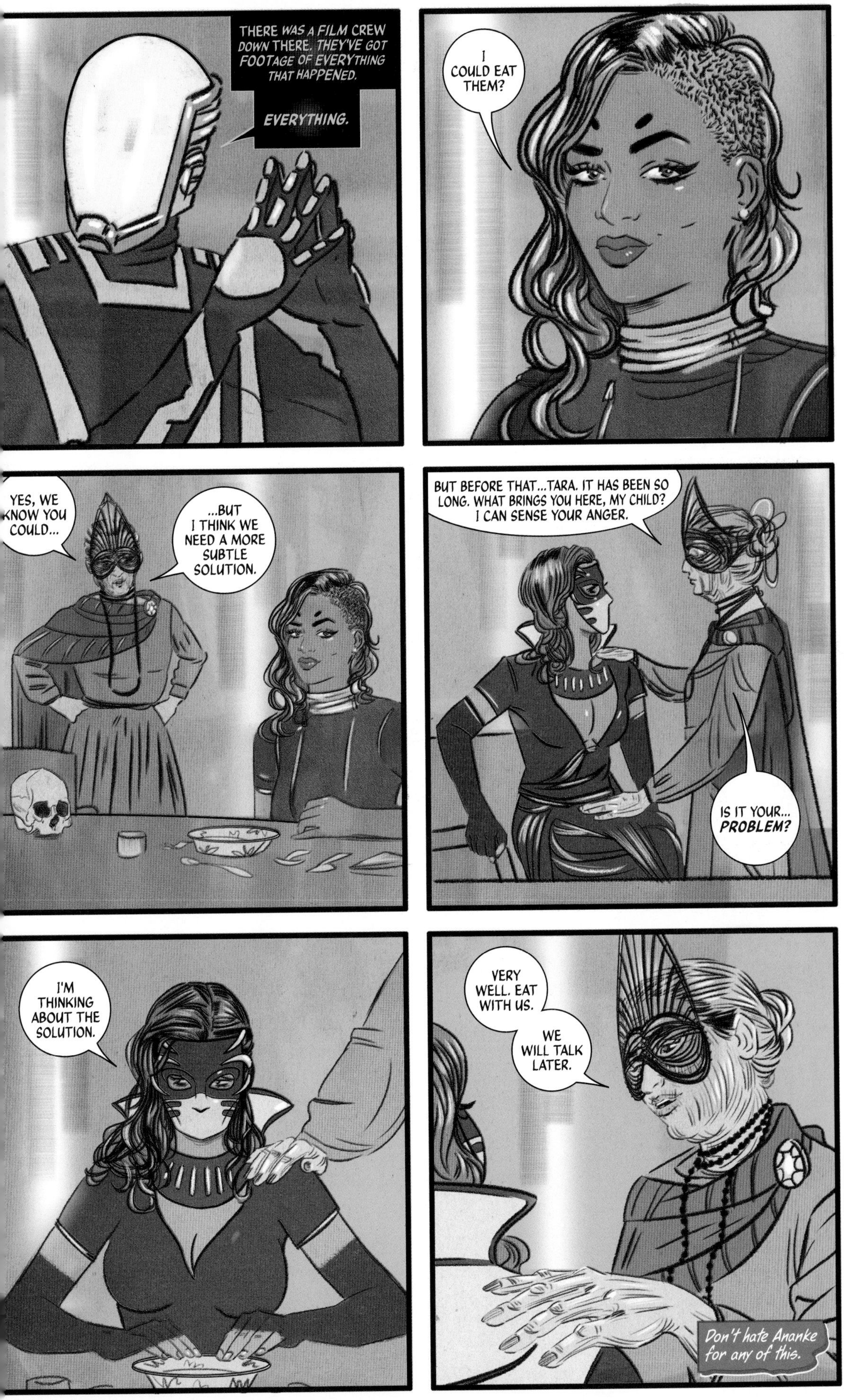
THERE WAS A FILM CREW DOWN THERE. THEY'VE GOT FOOTAGE OF EVERYTHING THAT HAPPENED.
EVERYTHING.
I COULD EAT THEM?
YES, WE KNOW YOU COULD...
...BUT I THINK WE NEED A MORE SUBTLE SOLUTION.
BUT BEFORE THAT...TARA. IT HAS BEEN SO LONG. WHAT BRINGS YOU HERE, MY CHILD? I CAN SENSE YOUR ANGER.
IS IT YOUR... PROBLEM?
I'M THINKING ABOUT THE SOLUTION.
VERY WELL. EAT WITH US.
WE WILL TALK LATER.
Don't hate Ananke for any of this.

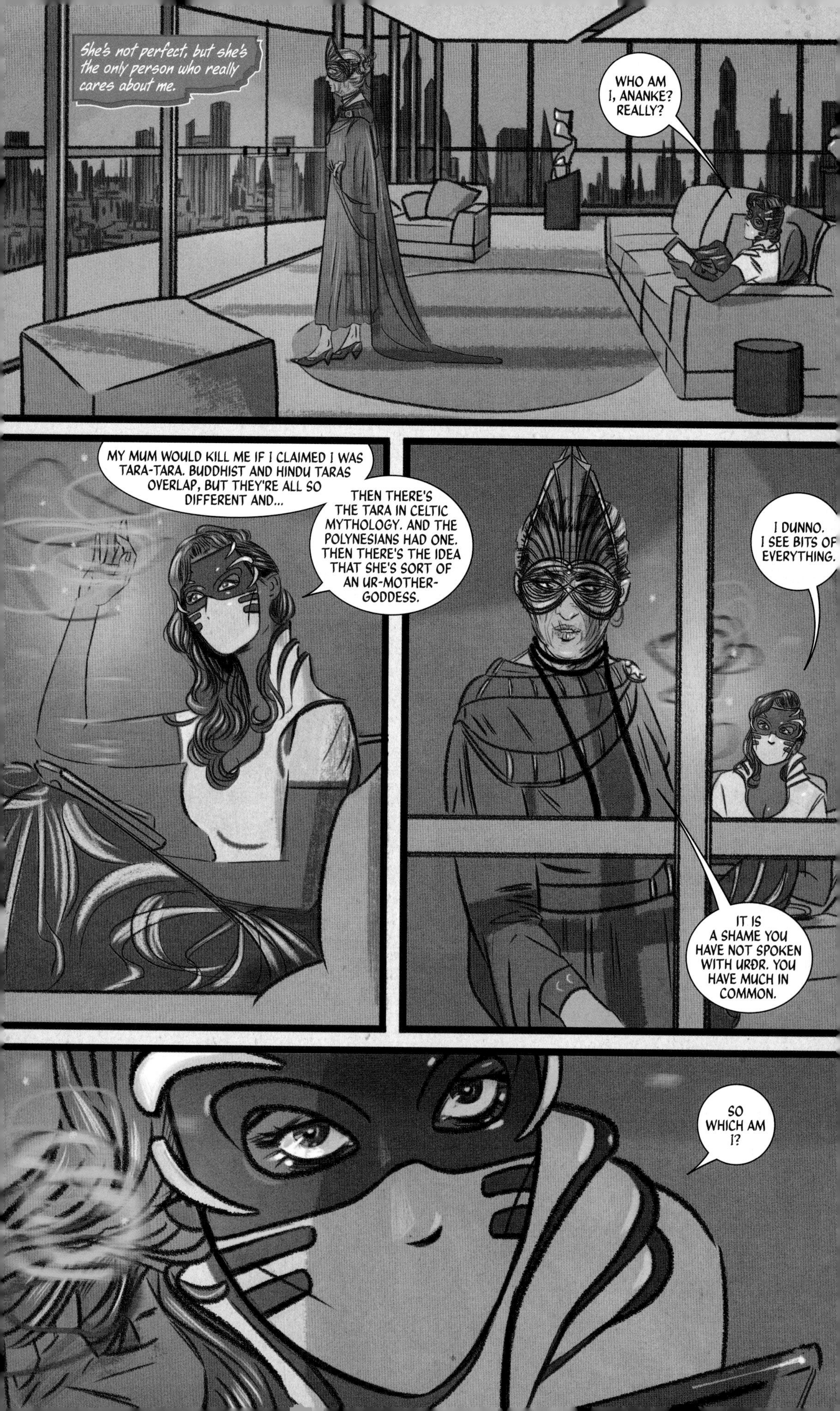
She's not perfect, but she's the only person who really cares about me.
WHO AM I, ANANKE? REALLY?
MY MUM WOULD KILL ME IF I CLAIMED I WAS TARA-TARA. BUDDHIST AND HINDU TARAS OVERLAP, BUT THEY'RE ALL SO DIFFERENT AND...
THEN THERE'S THE TARA IN CELTIC MYTHOLOGY. AND THE POLYNESIANS HAD ONE. THEN THERE'S THE IDEA THAT SHE'S SORT OF AN UR-MOTHER-GODDESS.
I DUNNO. I SEE BITS OF EVERYTHING.
IT IS A SHAME YOU HAVE NOT SPOKEN WITH URÐR. YOU HAVE MUCH IN COMMON.
SO WHICH AM I?

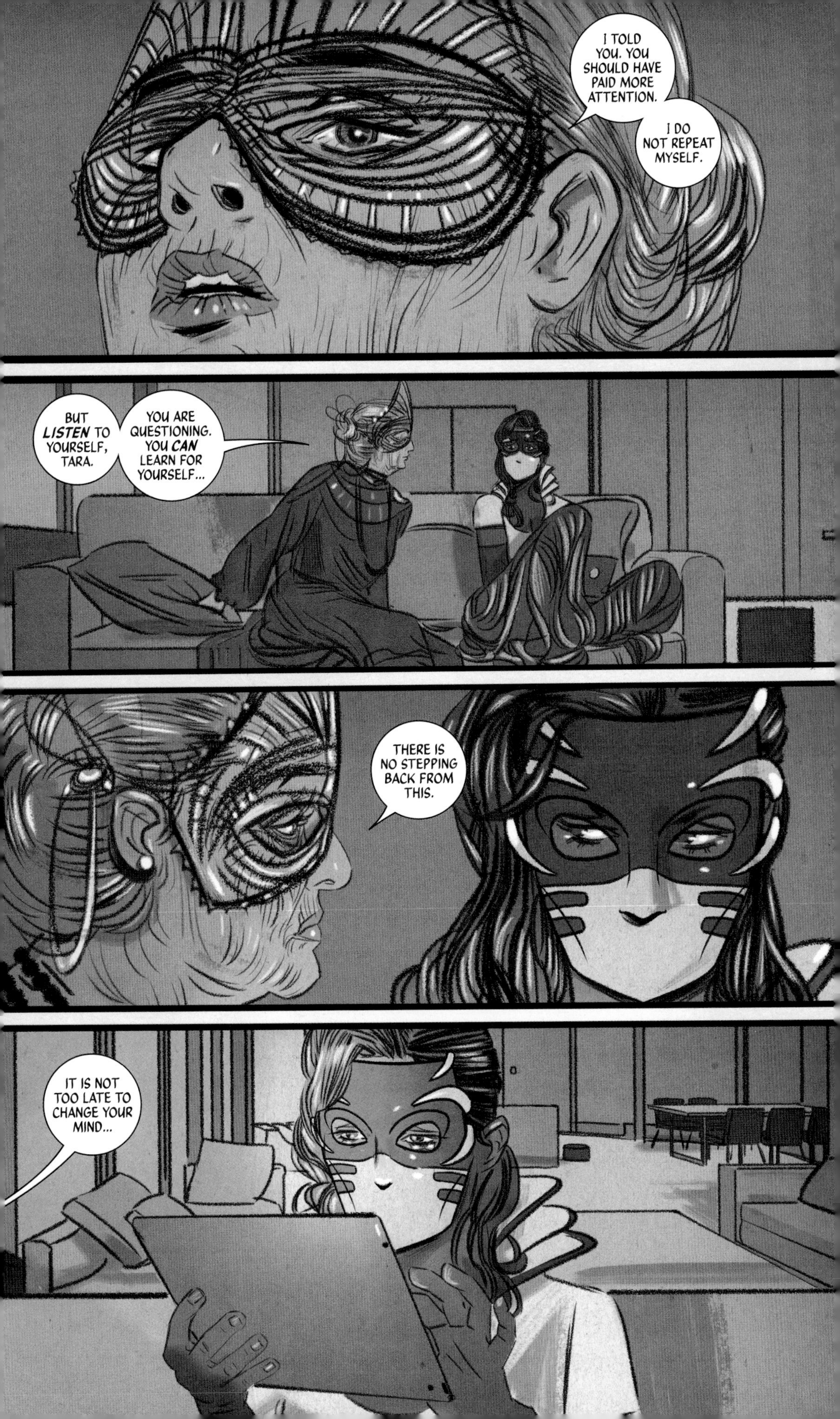
I TOLD YOU. YOU SHOULD HAVE PAID MORE ATTENTION.
I DO NOT REPEAT MYSELF.
BUT *LISTEN* TO YOURSELF, TARA.
YOU ARE QUESTIONING. YOU *CAN* LEARN FOR YOURSELF...
THERE IS NO STEPPING BACK FROM THIS.
IT IS NOT TOO LATE TO CHANGE YOUR MIND...

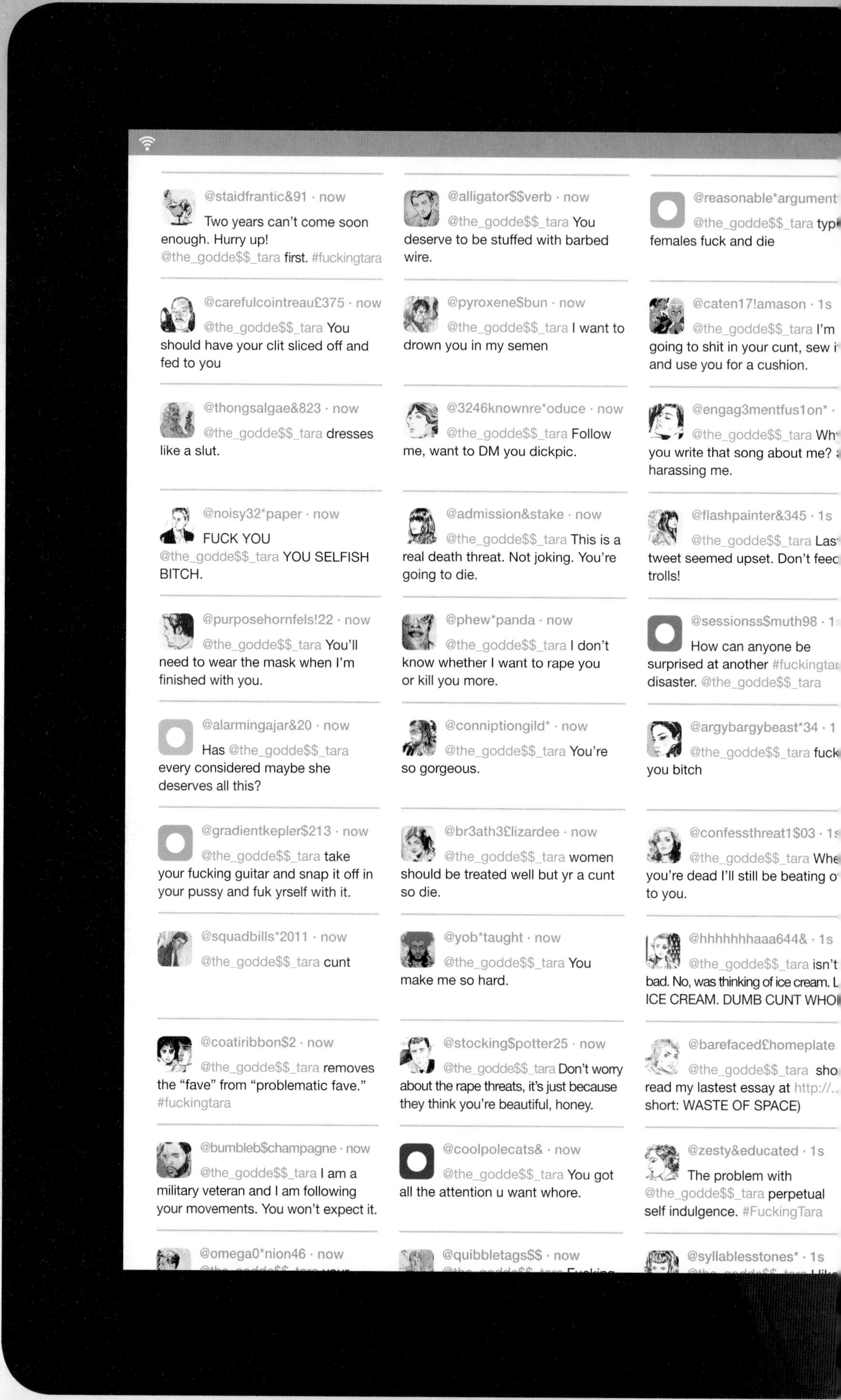

@staidfrantic&91 · now
Two years can't come soon enough. Hurry up! @the_godde$$_tara first. #fuckingtara

@alligator$$verb · now
@the_godde$$_tara You deserve to be stuffed with barbed wire.

@reasonable*argument
@the_godde$$_tara typi females fuck and die

@carefulcointreau£375 · now
@the_godde$$_tara You should have your clit sliced off and fed to you

@pyroxene$bun · now
@the_godde$$_tara I want to drown you in my semen

@caten17!amason · 1s
@the_godde$$_tara I'm going to shit in your cunt, sew i and use you for a cushion.

@thongsalgae&823 · now
@the_godde$$_tara dresses like a slut.

@3246knownre*oduce · now
@the_godde$$_tara Follow me, want to DM you dickpic.

@engag3mentfus1on* ·
@the_godde$$_tara Wh you write that song about me? harassing me.

@noisy32*paper · now
FUCK YOU @the_godde$$_tara YOU SELFISH BITCH.

@admission&stake · now
@the_godde$$_tara This is a real death threat. Not joking. You're going to die.

@flashpainter&345 · 1s
@the_godde$$_tara Las tweet seemed upset. Don't feed trolls!

@purposehornfels!22 · now
@the_godde$$_tara You'll need to wear the mask when I'm finished with you.

@phew*panda · now
@the_godde$$_tara I don't know whether I want to rape you or kill you more.

@sessionss$muth98 · 1
How can anyone be surprised at another #fuckingta disaster. @the_godde$$_tara

@alarmingajar&20 · now
Has @the_godde$$_tara every considered maybe she deserves all this?

@conniptiongild* · now
@the_godde$$_tara You're so gorgeous.

@argybargybeast*34 · 1
@the_godde$$_tara fuck you bitch

@gradientkepler$213 · now
@the_godde$$_tara take your fucking guitar and snap it off in your pussy and fuk yrself with it.

@br3ath3£lizardee · now
@the_godde$$_tara women should be treated well but yr a cunt so die.

@confessthreat1$03 · 1s
@the_godde$$_tara Whe you're dead I'll still be beating o to you.

@squadbills*2011 · now
@the_godde$$_tara cunt

@yob*taught · now
@the_godde$$_tara You make me so hard.

@hhhhhhhaaa644& · 1s
@the_godde$$_tara isn't bad. No, was thinking of ice cream. L ICE CREAM. DUMB CUNT WHO

@coatiribbon$2 · now
@the_godde$$_tara removes the "fave" from "problematic fave." #fuckingtara

@stocking$potter25 · now
@the_godde$$_tara Don't worry about the rape threats, it's just because they think you're beautiful, honey.

@barefaced£homeplate
@the_godde$$_tara sho read my lastest essay at http://... short: WASTE OF SPACE)

@bumbleb$champagne · now
@the_godde$$_tara I am a military veteran and I am following your movements. You won't expect it.

@coolpolecats& · now
@the_godde$$_tara You got all the attention u want whore.

@zesty&educated · 1s
The problem with @the_godde$$_tara perpetual self indulgence. #FuckingTara

@omega0*nion46 · now
@the_godde$$_tara your

@quibbletags$$ · now
@the_godde$$_tara Fucking

@syllablesstones* · 1s
@the_godde$$_tara I lik

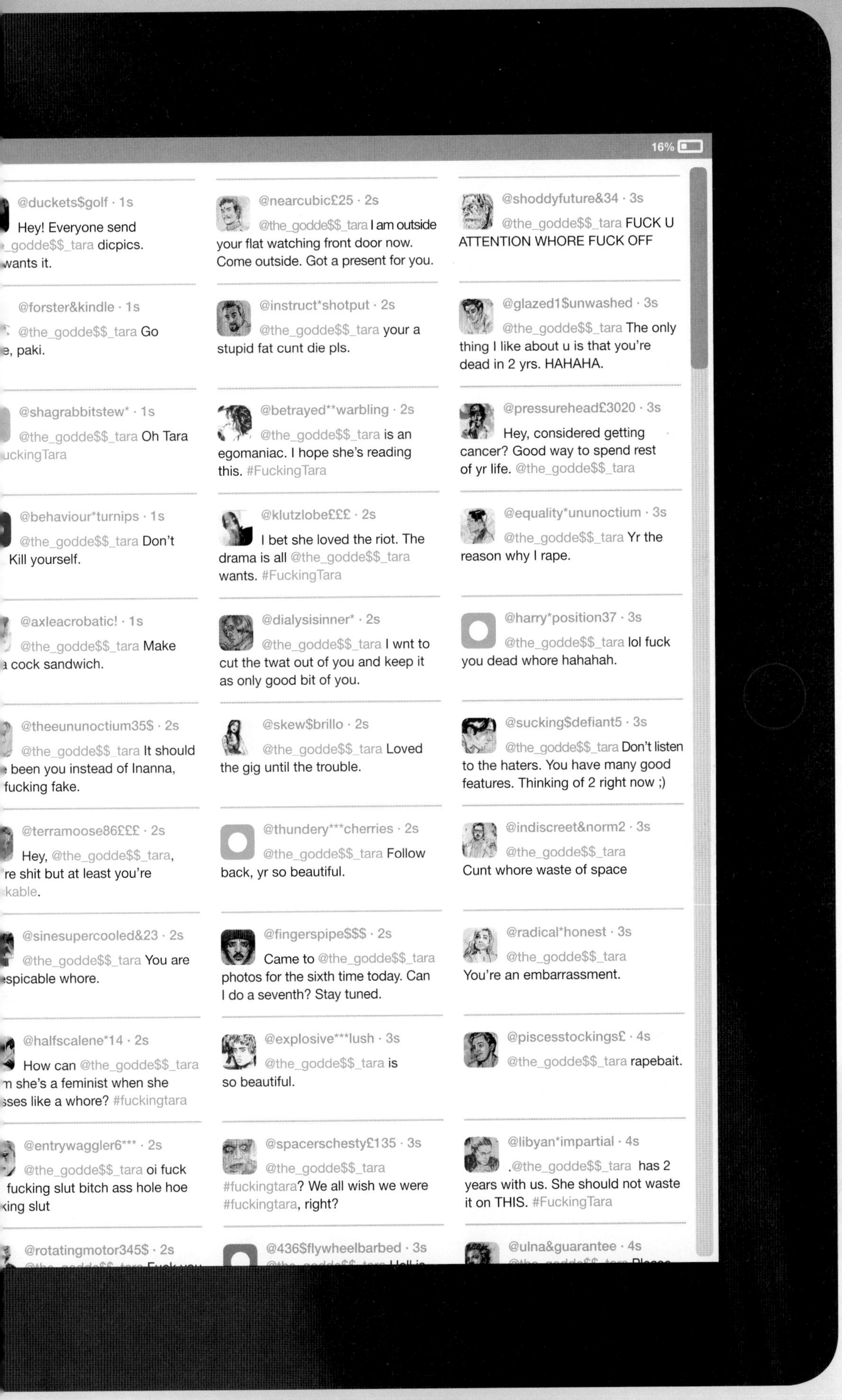
16%
@duckets$golf · 1s
Hey! Everyone send
_godde$$_tara dicpics.
wants it.
@forster&kindle · 1s
@the_godde$$_tara Go
e, paki.
@shagrabbitstew* · 1s
@the_godde$$_tara Oh Tara
uckingTara
@behaviour*turnips · 1s
@the_godde$$_tara Don't
Kill yourself.
@axleacrobatic! · 1s
@the_godde$$_tara Make
a cock sandwich.
@theeununoctium35$ · 2s
@the_godde$$_tara It should
been you instead of Inanna,
fucking fake.
@terramoose86£££ · 2s
Hey, @the_godde$$_tara,
re shit but at least you're
kable.
@sinesupercooled&23 · 2s
@the_godde$$_tara You are
spicable whore.
@halfscalene*14 · 2s
How can @the_godde$$_tara
n she's a feminist when she
sses like a whore? #fuckingtara
@entrywaggler6*** · 2s
@the_godde$$_tara oi fuck
fucking slut bitch ass hole hoe
king slut
@rotatingmotor345$ · 2s
@nearcubic£25 · 2s
@the_godde$$_tara I am outside your flat watching front door now. Come outside. Got a present for you.
@instruct*shotput · 2s
@the_godde$$_tara your a stupid fat cunt die pls.
@betrayed**warbling · 2s
@the_godde$$_tara is an egomaniac. I hope she's reading this. #FuckingTara
@klutzlobe£££ · 2s
I bet she loved the riot. The drama is all @the_godde$$_tara wants. #FuckingTara
@dialysisinner* · 2s
@the_godde$$_tara I wnt to cut the twat out of you and keep it as only good bit of you.
@skew$brillo · 2s
@the_godde$$_tara Loved the gig until the trouble.
@thundery***cherries · 2s
@the_godde$$_tara Follow back, yr so beautiful.
@fingerspipe$$$ · 2s
Came to @the_godde$$_tara photos for the sixth time today. Can I do a seventh? Stay tuned.
@explosive***lush · 3s
@the_godde$$_tara is so beautiful.
@spacerschesty£135 · 3s
@the_godde$$_tara #fuckingtara? We all wish we were #fuckingtara, right?
@436$flywheelbarbed · 3s
@shoddyfuture&34 · 3s
@the_godde$$_tara FUCK U ATTENTION WHORE FUCK OFF
@glazed1$unwashed · 3s
@the_godde$$_tara The only thing I like about u is that you're dead in 2 yrs. HAHAHA.
@pressurehead£3020 · 3s
Hey, considered getting cancer? Good way to spend rest of yr life. @the_godde$$_tara
@equality*ununoctium · 3s
@the_godde$$_tara Yr the reason why I rape.
@harry*position37 · 3s
@the_godde$$_tara lol fuck you dead whore hahahah.
@sucking$defiant5 · 3s
@the_godde$$_tara Don't listen to the haters. You have many good features. Thinking of 2 right now ;)
@indiscreet&norm2 · 3s
@the_godde$$_tara
Cunt whore waste of space
@radical*honest · 3s
@the_godde$$_tara
You're an embarrassment.
@piscesstockings£ · 4s
@the_godde$$_tara rapebait.
@libyan*impartial · 4s
.@the_godde$$_tara has 2 years with us. She should not waste it on THIS. #FuckingTara
@ulna&guarantee · 4s

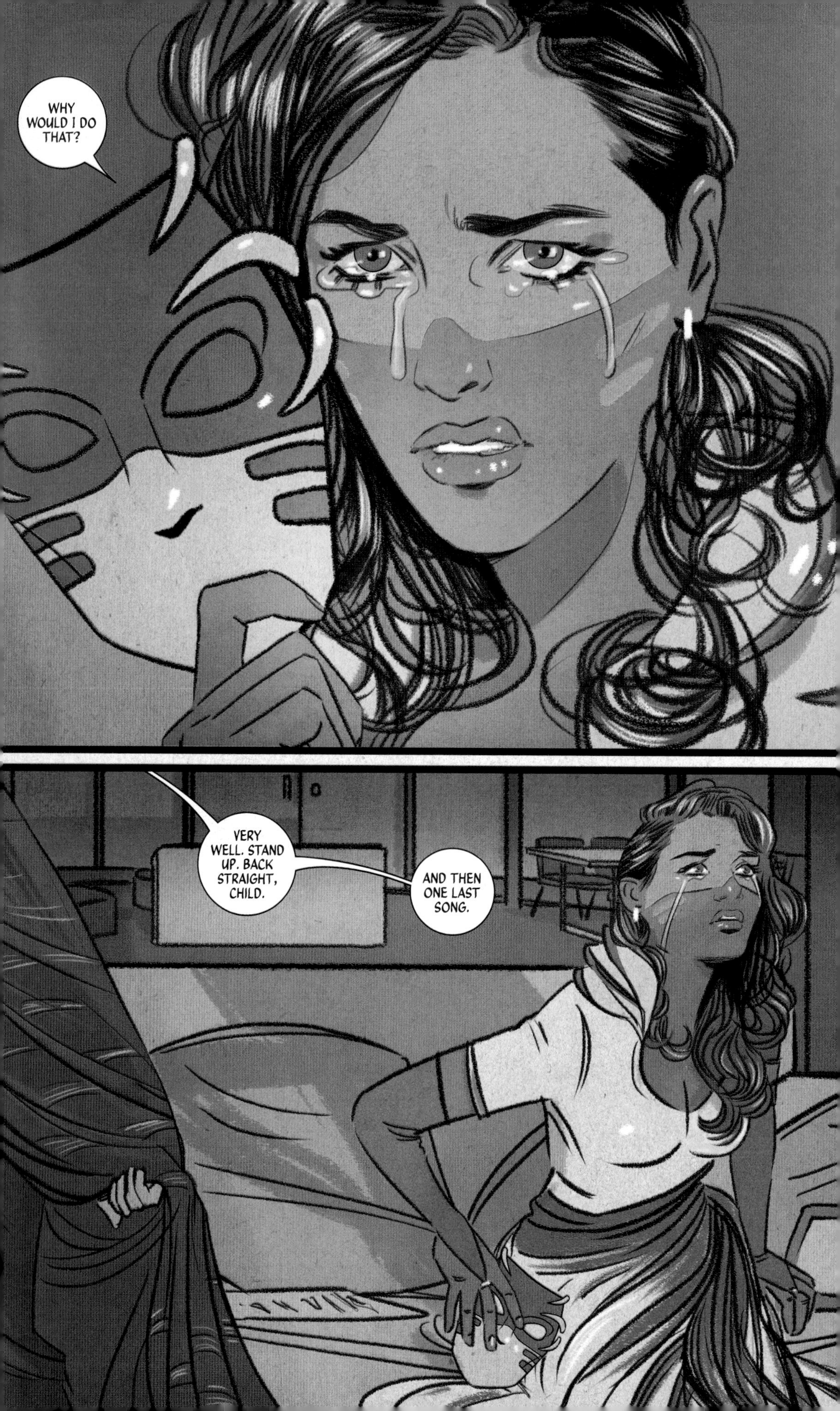
WHY WOULD I DO THAT?
VERY WELL. STAND UP. BACK STRAIGHT, CHILD.
AND THEN ONE LAST SONG.

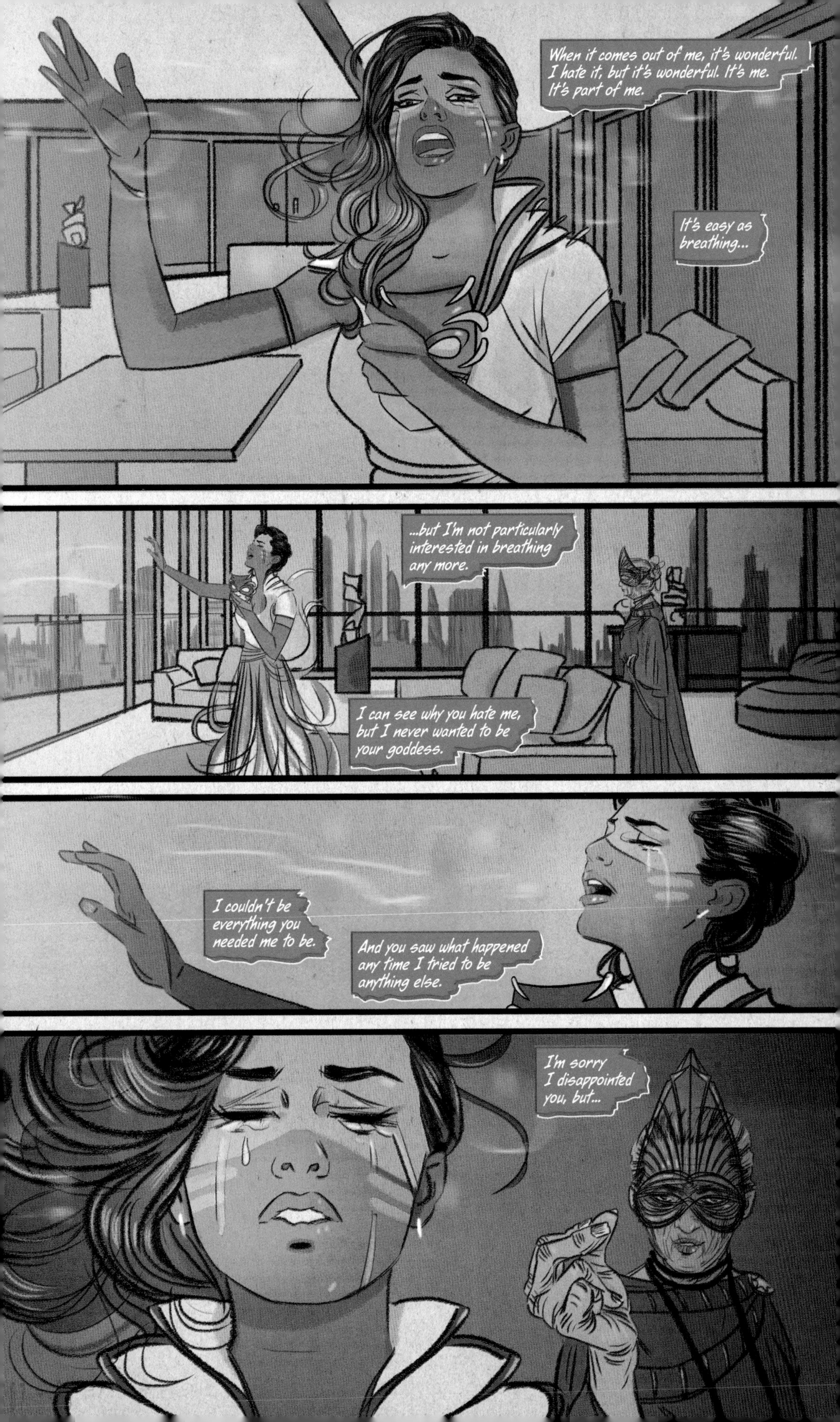
When it comes out of me, it's wonderful. I hate it, but it's wonderful. It's me. It's part of me.
It's easy as breathing...
...but I'm not particularly interested in breathing any more.
I can see why you hate me, but I never wanted to be your goddess.
I couldn't be everything you needed me to be.
And you saw what happened any time I tried to be anything else.
I'm sorry I disappointed you, but...

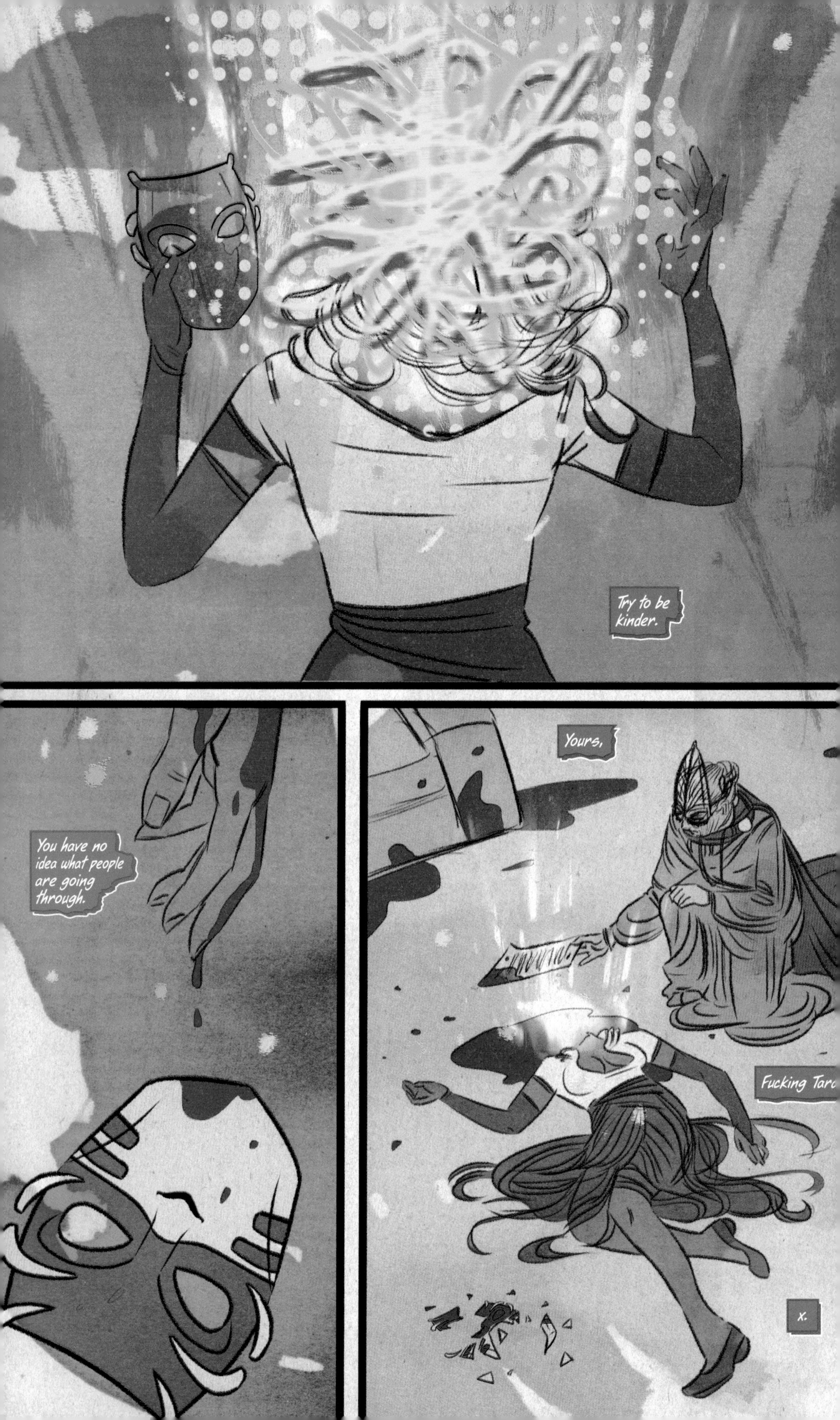
Try to be kinder.
You have no idea what people are going through.
Yours,
Fucking Tarc
x.

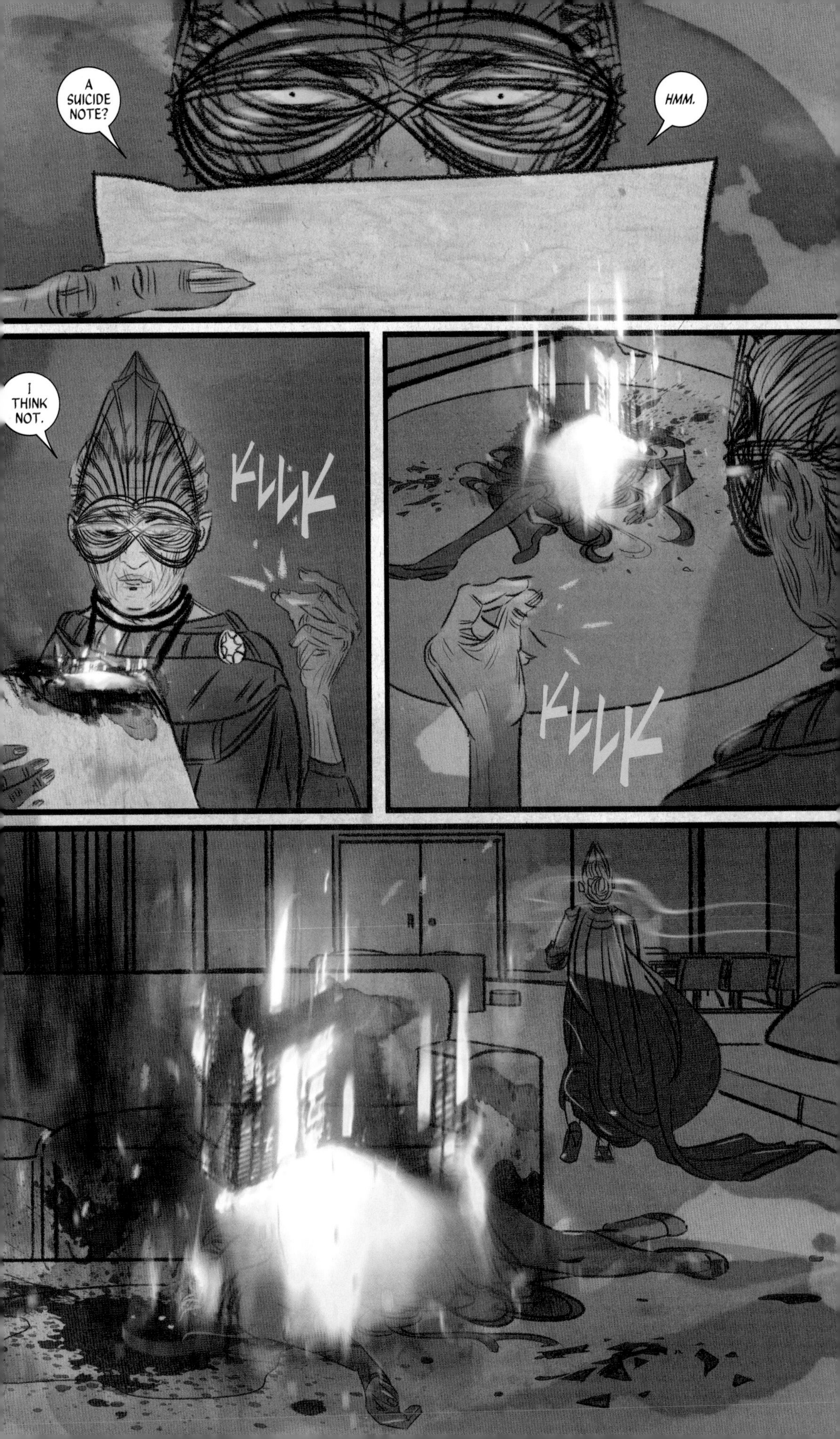
A SUICIDE NOTE?
HMM.
I THINK NOT.
KLLK
KLLK

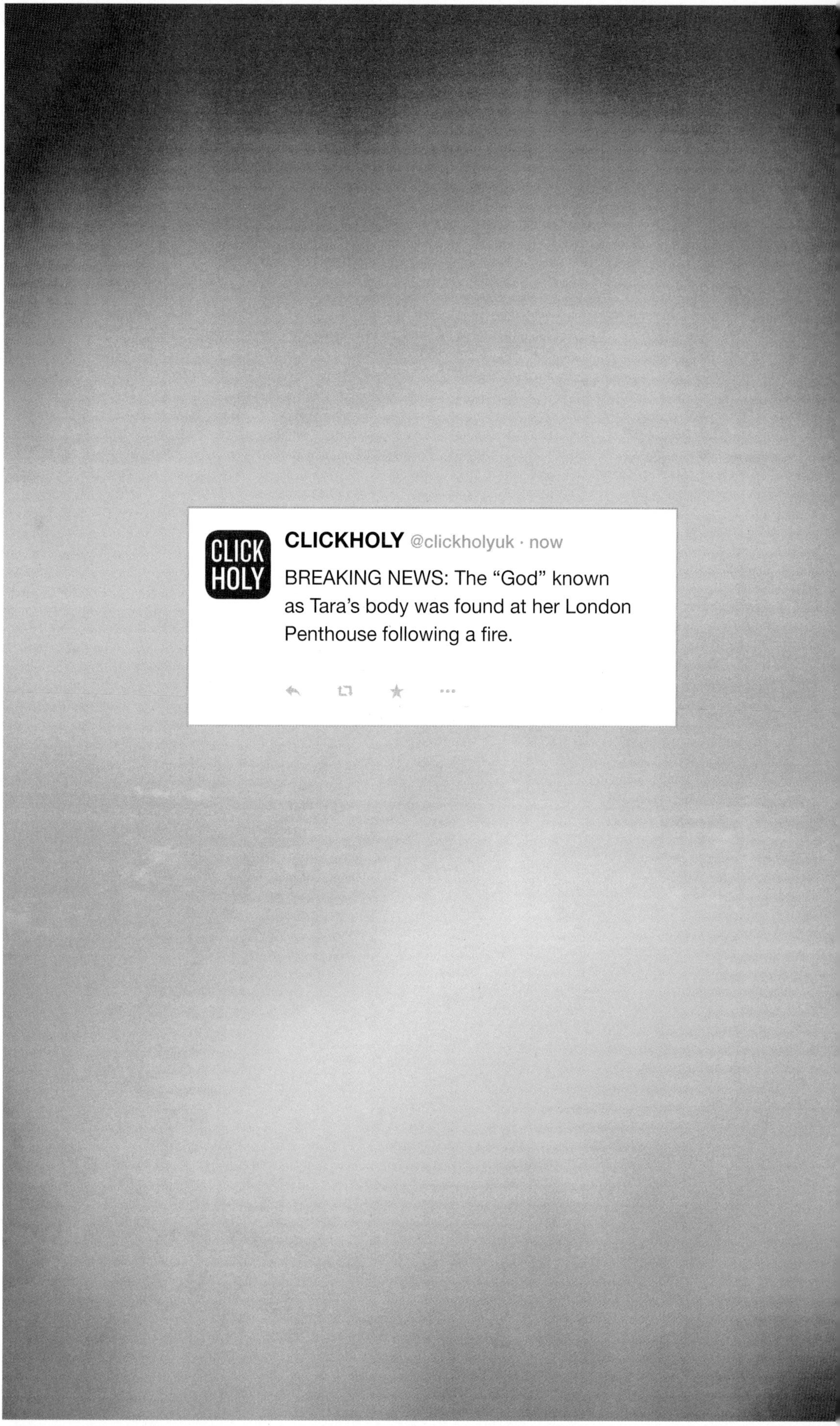
CLICK HOLY
CLICKHOLY @clickholyuk · now
BREAKING NEWS: The "God" known as Tara's body was found at her London Penthouse following a fire.

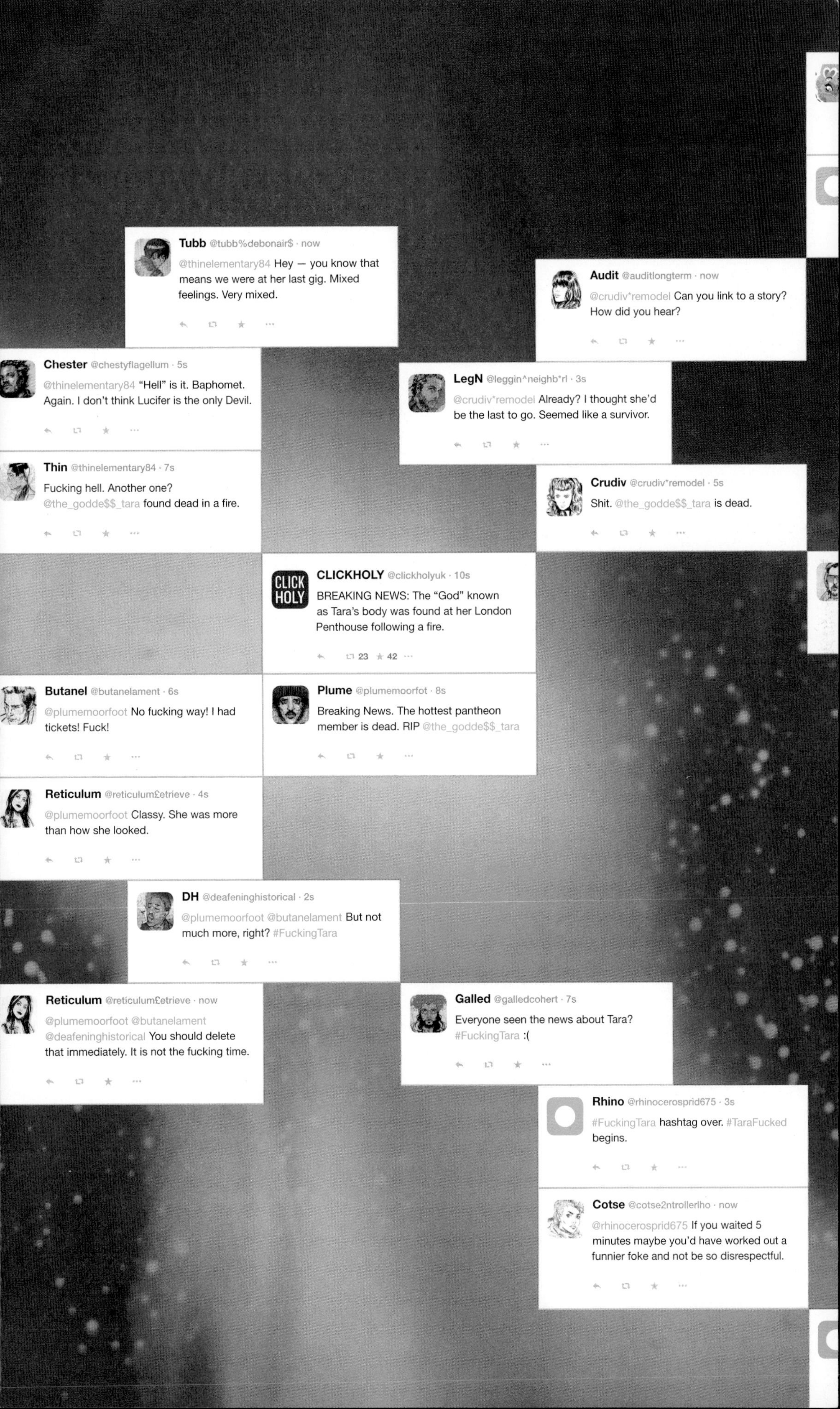

Tubb @tubb%debonair$ · now
@thinelementary84 Hey — you know that means we were at her last gig. Mixed feelings. Very mixed.
Audit @auditlongterm · now
@crudiv*remodel Can you link to a story? How did you hear?
Chester @chestyflagellum · 5s
@thinelementary84 "Hell" is it. Baphomet. Again. I don't think Lucifer is the only Devil.
LegN @leggin^neighb*rl · 3s
@crudiv*remodel Already? I thought she'd be the last to go. Seemed like a survivor.
Thin @thinelementary84 · 7s
Fucking hell. Another one? @the_godde$$_tara found dead in a fire.
Crudiv @crudiv*remodel · 5s
Shit. @the_godde$$_tara is dead.
CLICK HOLY
CLICKHOLY @clickholyuk · 10s
BREAKING NEWS: The "God" known as Tara's body was found at her London Penthouse following a fire.
23 42
Butanel @butanelament · 6s
@plumemoorfoot No fucking way! I had tickets! Fuck!
Plume @plumemoorfot · 8s
Breaking News. The hottest pantheon member is dead. RIP @the_godde$$_tara
Reticulum @reticulum£etrieve · 4s
@plumemoorfoot Classy. She was more than how she looked.
DH @deafeninghistorical · 2s
@plumemoorfoot @butanelament But not much more, right? #FuckingTara
Reticulum @reticulum£etrieve · now
@plumemoorfoot @butanelament @deafeninghistorical You should delete that immediately. It is not the fucking time.
Galled @galledcohert · 7s
Everyone seen the news about Tara? #FuckingTara :(
Rhino @rhinocerosprid675 · 3s
#FuckingTara hashtag over. #TaraFucked begins.
Cotse @cotse2ntrollerlho · now
@rhinocerosprid675 If you waited 5 minutes maybe you'd have worked out a funnier foke and not be so disrespectful.

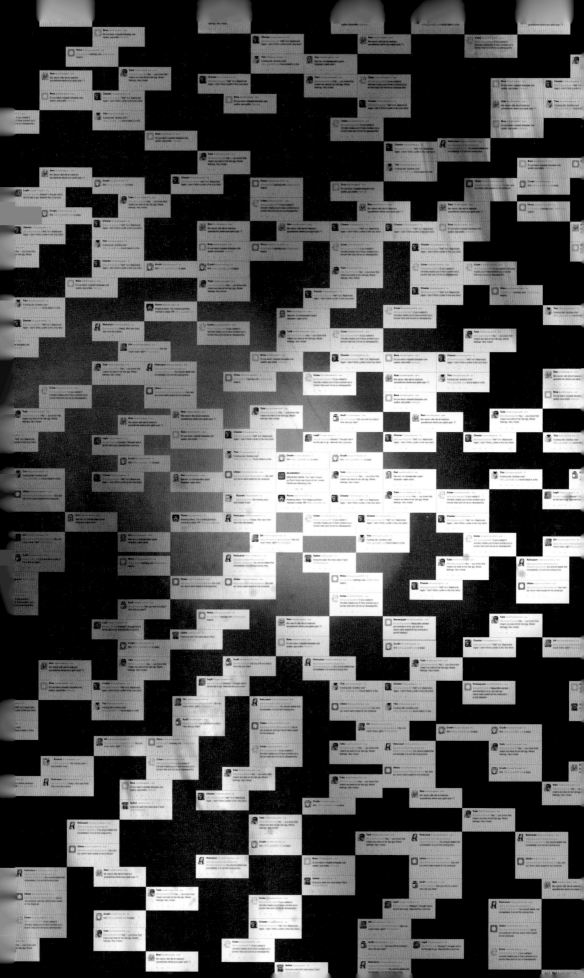

COMMERCIAL
SUICIDE

18 AUGUST 2014

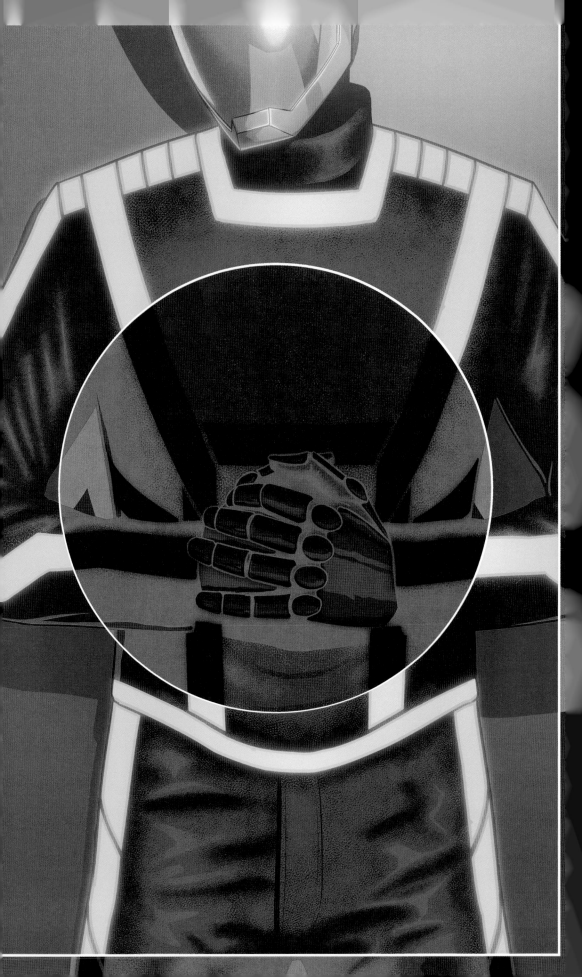

THE
WICKED
+
DIVINE
THE

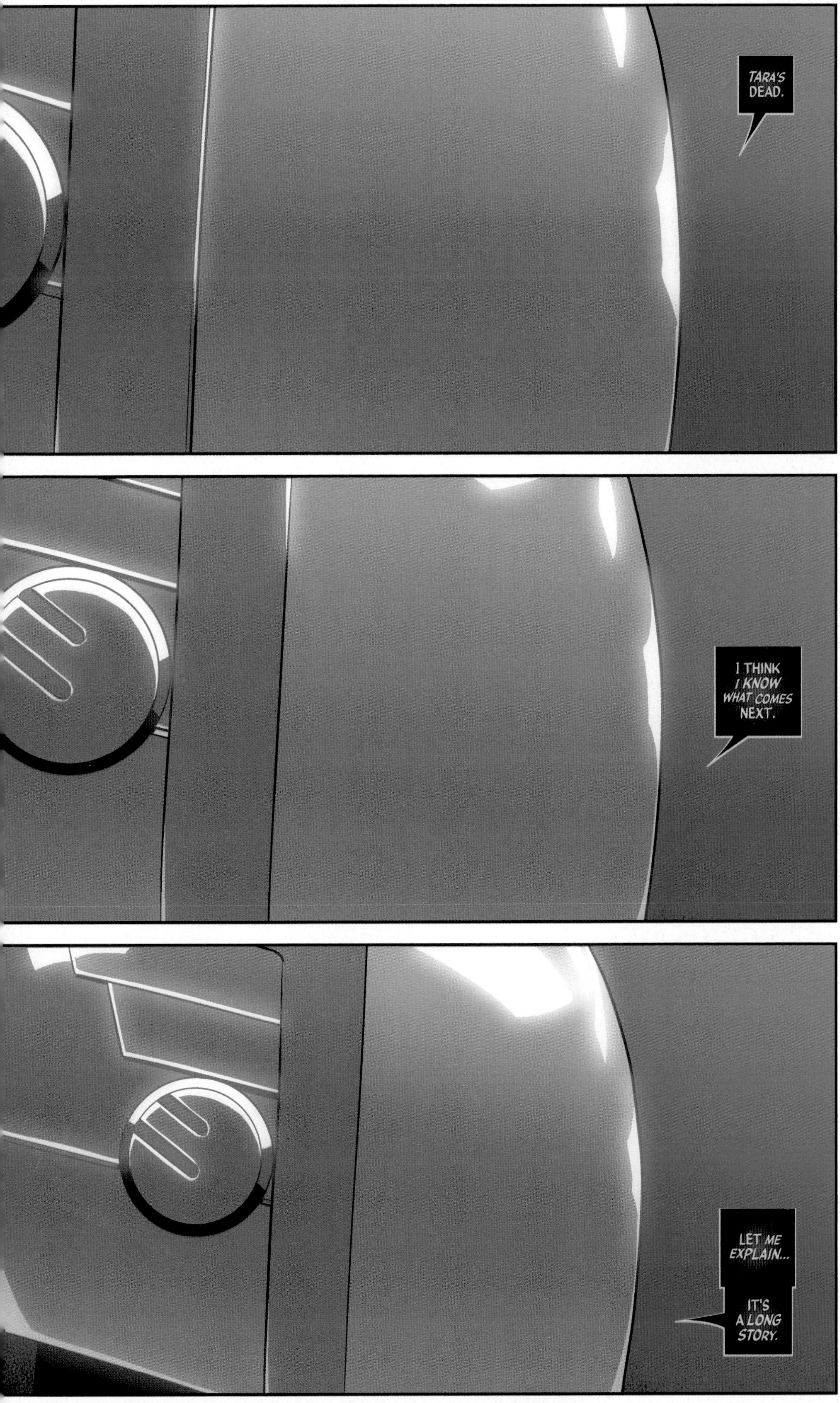
TARA'S DEAD.
I THINK I KNOW WHAT COMES NEXT.
LET ME EXPLAIN...
IT'S A LONG STORY.

THE RE-RE-REMIX

2014

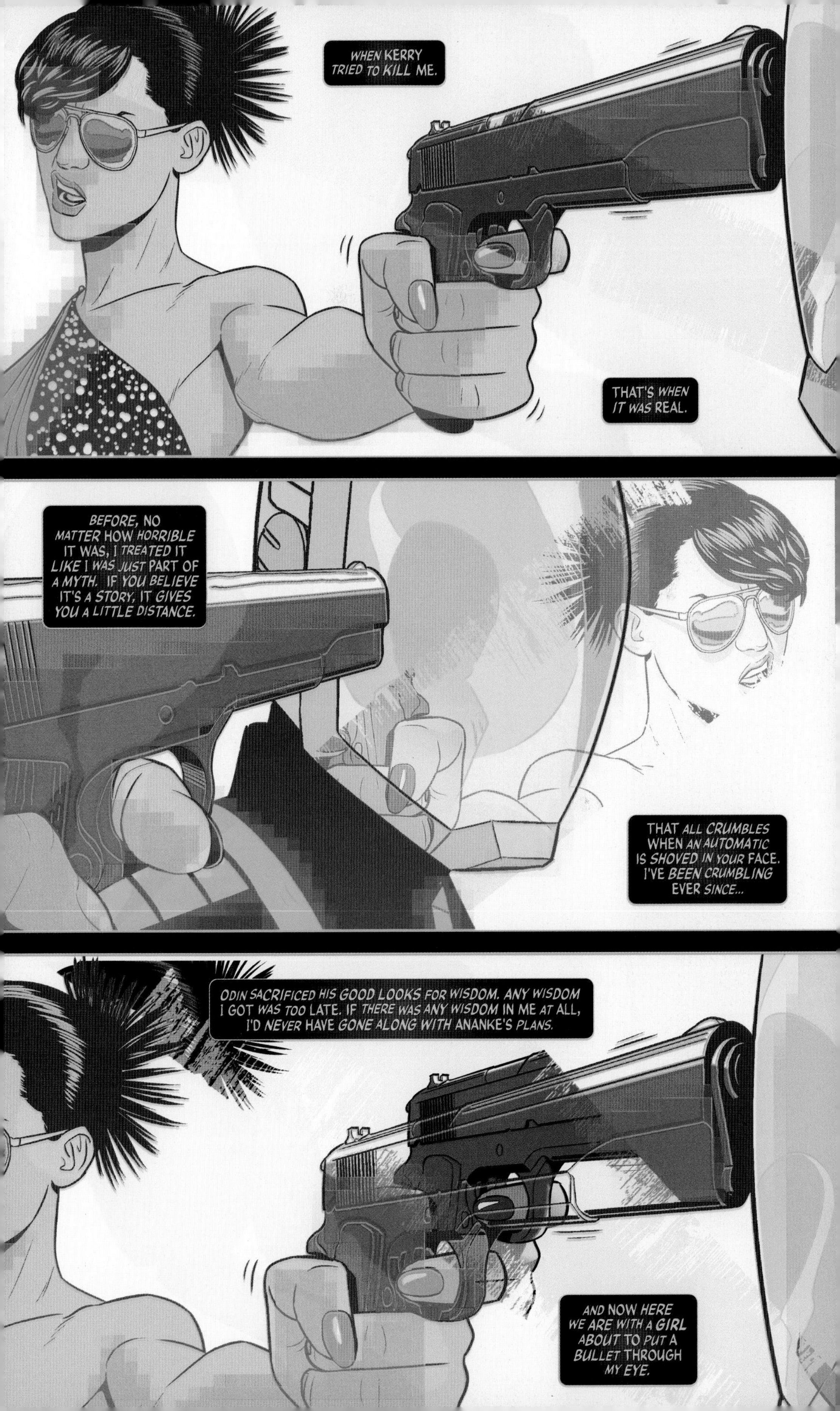
WHEN KERRY TRIED TO KILL ME.
THAT'S WHEN IT WAS REAL.
BEFORE, NO MATTER HOW HORRIBLE IT WAS, I TREATED IT LIKE I WAS JUST PART OF A MYTH. IF YOU BELIEVE IT'S A STORY, IT GIVES YOU A LITTLE DISTANCE.
THAT ALL CRUMBLES WHEN AN AUTOMATIC IS SHOVED IN YOUR FACE. I'VE BEEN CRUMBLING EVER SINCE...
ODIN SACRIFICED HIS GOOD LOOKS FOR WISDOM. ANY WISDOM I GOT WAS TOO LATE. IF THERE WAS ANY WISDOM IN ME AT ALL, I'D NEVER HAVE GONE ALONG WITH ANANKE'S PLANS.
AND NOW HERE WE ARE WITH A GIRL ABOUT TO PUT A BULLET THROUGH MY EYE.

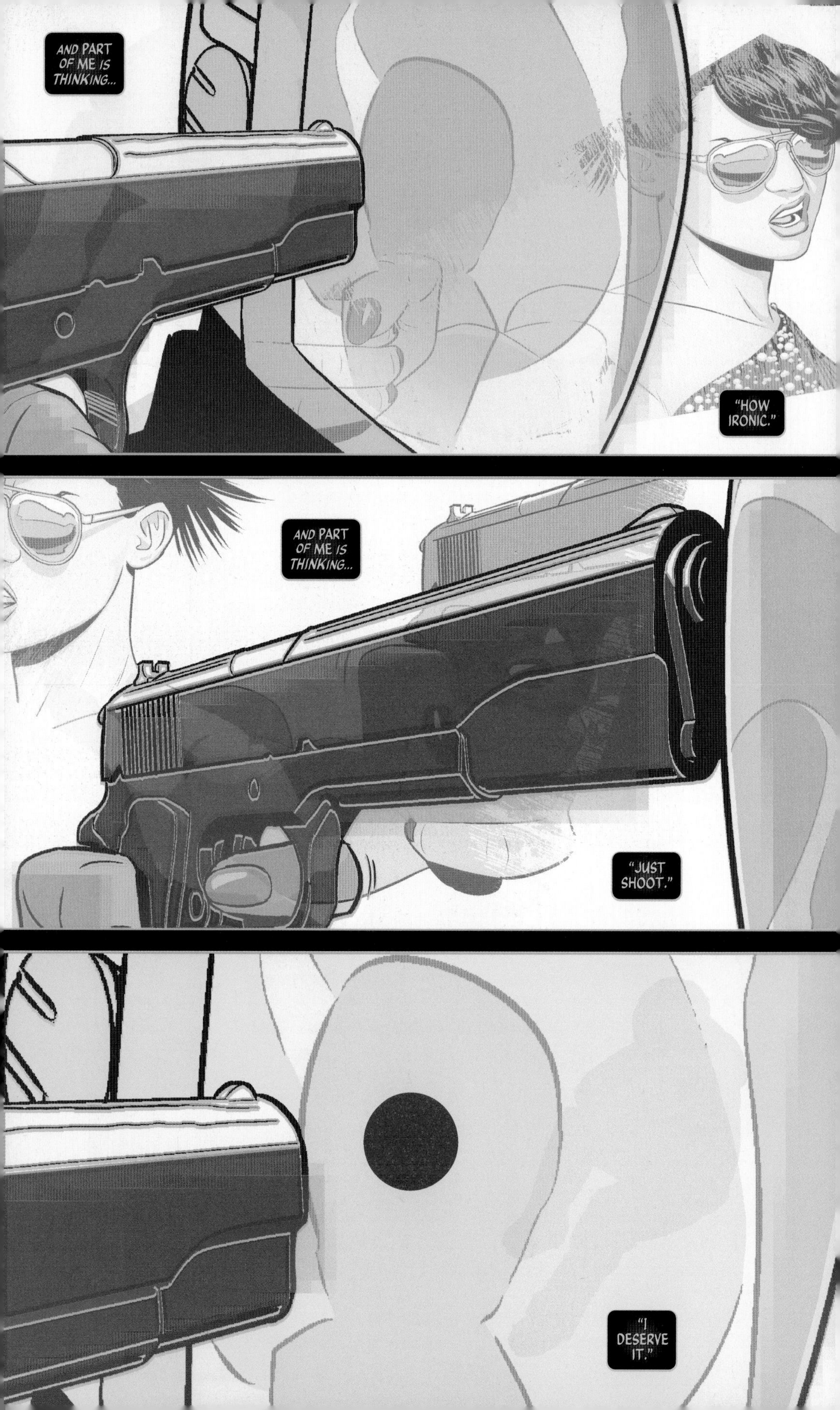
AND PART OF ME IS THINKING...
"HOW IRONIC."
AND PART OF ME IS THINKING...
"JUST SHOOT."
"I DESERVE IT."

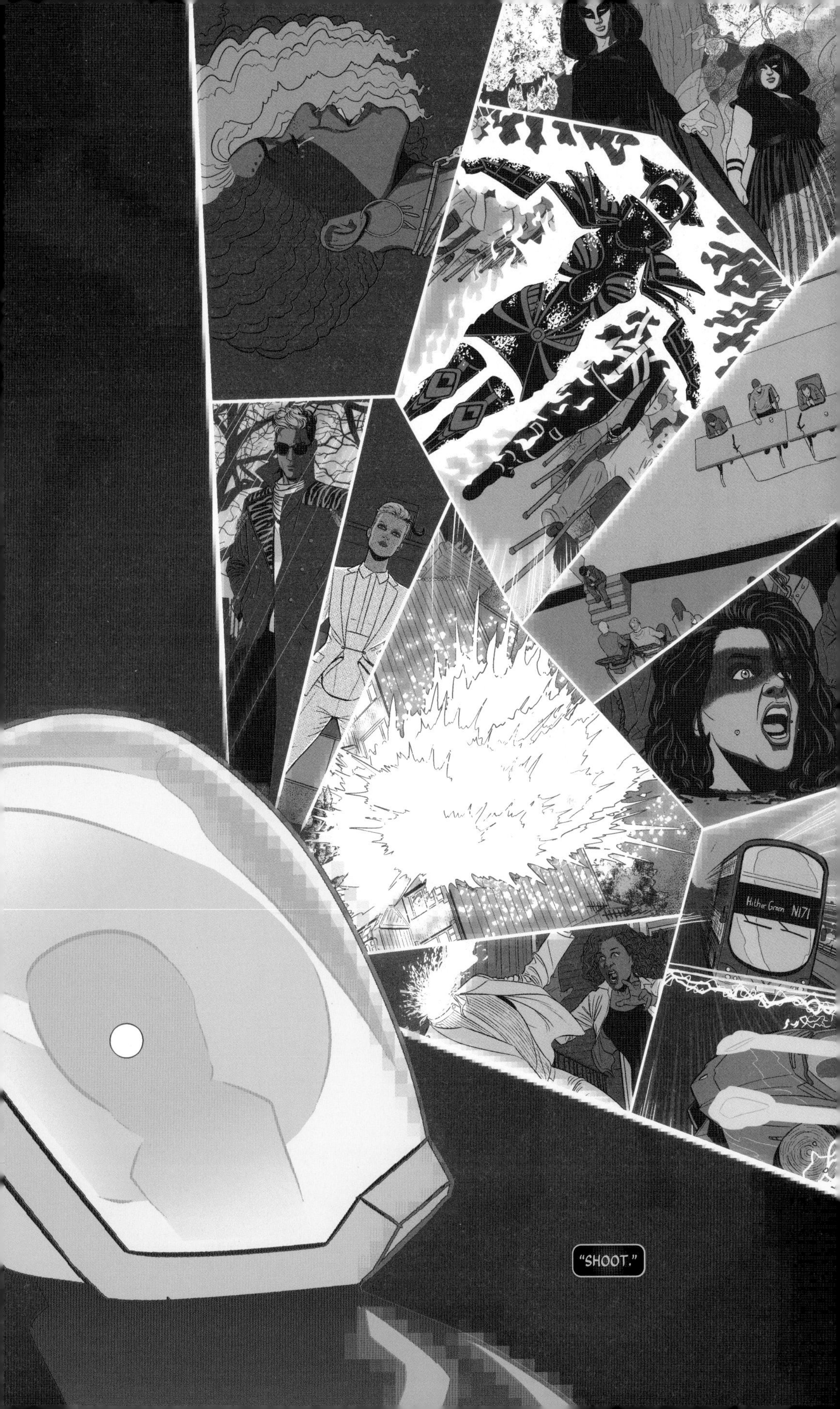
Hither Green N171
"SHOOT."

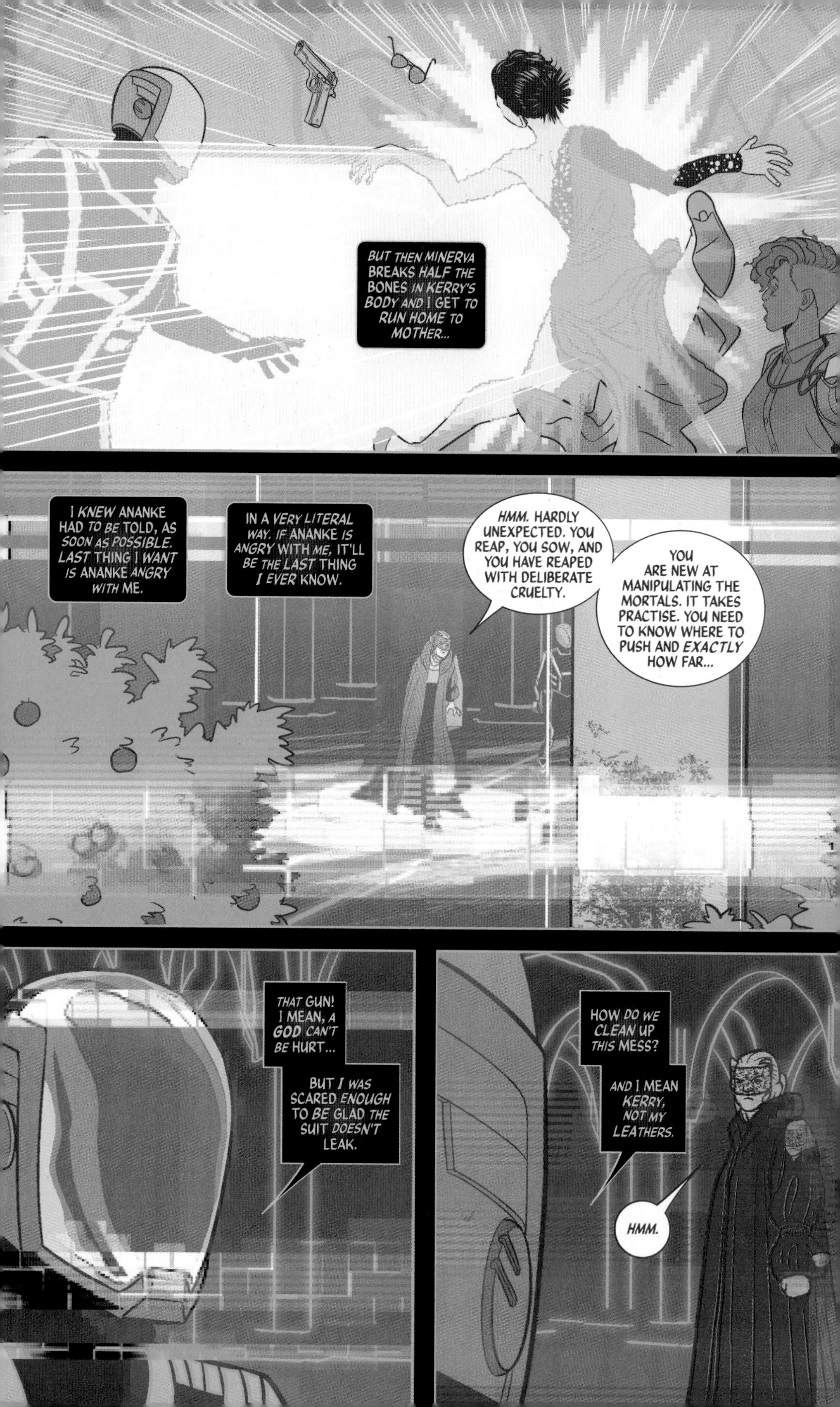
BUT THEN MINERVA BREAKS HALF THE BONES IN KERRY'S BODY AND I GET TO RUN HOME TO MOTHER...
I KNEW ANANKE HAD TO BE TOLD, AS SOON AS POSSIBLE. LAST THING I WANT IS ANANKE ANGRY WITH ME.
IN A VERY LITERAL WAY. IF ANANKE IS ANGRY WITH ME, IT'LL BE THE LAST THING I EVER KNOW.
HMM. HARDLY UNEXPECTED. YOU REAP, YOU SOW, AND YOU HAVE REAPED WITH DELIBERATE CRUELTY.
YOU ARE NEW AT MANIPULATING THE MORTALS. IT TAKES PRACTISE. YOU NEED TO KNOW WHERE TO PUSH AND EXACTLY HOW FAR...
THAT GUN! I MEAN, A GOD CAN'T BE HURT...
BUT I WAS SCARED ENOUGH TO BE GLAD THE SUIT DOESN'T LEAK.
HOW DO WE CLEAN UP THIS MESS?
AND I MEAN KERRY, NOT MY LEATHERS.
HMM.

WHO WITNESSED THE MIRACLES?

JUST THE *BACKSTAGE PEOPLE.* ALL ON THE PAYROLL.

I WAS *GIVING A LITTLE POSTURE* TO THAT ANNOYING *LAURA* GIRL.

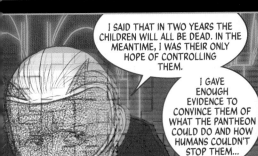

I WILL SPEAK TO THE GOVERNMENT AND STRESS THIS IS A PANTHEON MATTER.

THE CASE WILL DISAPPEAR.

HOW *DID* YOU GET THEM UNDER *YOUR* THUMB?

I SAID THAT IN TWO YEARS THE CHILDREN WILL ALL BE DEAD. IN THE MEANTIME, I WAS THEIR ONLY HOPE OF CONTROLLING THEM.

I GAVE ENOUGH EVIDENCE TO CONVINCE THEM OF WHAT THE PANTHEON COULD DO AND HOW HUMANS COULDN'T STOP THEM...

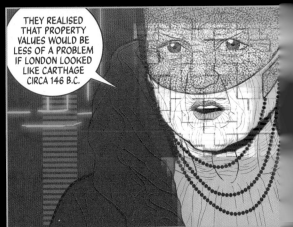

THEY REALISED THAT PROPERTY VALUES WOULD BE LESS OF A PROBLEM IF LONDON LOOKED LIKE CARTHAGE CIRCA 146 B.C.

I'M *IMPRESSED.* MOSTLY THAT YOU *KNOW ABOUT* HOUSING BUBBLES.

I TRY TO STAY IN TOUCH WITH THE MATTERS OF MORTALS.

HMM. SO... THE WILSON GIRL WAS THERE. SHE GETS EVERYWHERE.

WHAT WAS SHE DOING?

"SHE WAS TRYING TO PROBE ME FOR INFORMATION. NOT *EXACTLY* GOOD ENOUGH TO BE *SUBTLE.*

"I NEEDLED HER PRETTY HARD AND *SHE* SWALLOWED FAR MORE THAN *SHE* WANTED BEFORE LASHING OUT."

DON'T *WORRY* ABOUT HER. SHE'S A *FANGIRL* CHASING THE *DREGS* OF HER *FIFTEEN-MINUTE HIGH.* I'D BE *TEMPTED* TO OFFER HER A *VALKYRIE* DEAL *JUST* TO SEE HER FACE WHEN I *PULL IT AWAY.*

SHE'S *NOBODY.* SHE'S FROM THE *ELITE* SET OF *NOBODIES,* BUT STILL A NOBODY. LIKE. ONE IN...A HUNDRED.

SHE WAS CLOSE TO *LUCIFER.* THE *DEVIL* SAW *SOMETHING* IN HER.

WHAT *RESOURCES* DOES SHE HAVE?

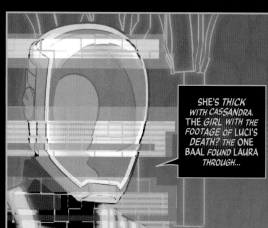

SHE'S *THICK* WITH *CASSANDRA,* THE *GIRL* WITH THE *FOOTAGE* OF LUCI'S *DEATH?* THE *ONE* BAAL FOUND LAURA *THROUGH...*

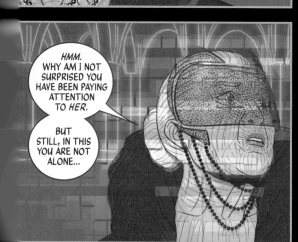

HMM. WHY AM I *NOT* SURPRISED YOU HAVE BEEN PAYING *ATTENTION* TO *HER.*

BUT *STILL,* IN THIS YOU ARE *NOT ALONE...*

CASSANDRA'S GOING TO BE A *HEADLINER?*

I *SUSPECT* SO. I NEED TO HAVE A *CLOSER* LOOK.

LURE HER IN. PLAY TO HER *EGO.*

YOU *CHILDREN* HAVE ENOUGH OF THAT.

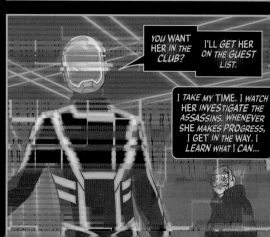

YOU WANT HER IN THE *CLUB?*

I'LL GET HER ON THE *GUEST* LIST.

I TAKE MY *TIME.* I *WATCH* HER *INVESTIGATE* THE *ASSASSINS.* WHENEVER SHE MAKES *PROGRESS,* I GET *IN THE WAY.* I *LEARN* WHAT I *CAN...*

...I EVENTUALLY INVITE HER TO INTERVIEW ANANKE AT DIONYSUS' GIG. APART FROM ME, SHE'S THE ONLY PERSON THERE WHO CLEARLY ISN'T ENJOYING IT.

THAT CHANGED WHEN I MADE THE OFFER.

I...LIKE THE REST OF THE PANTHEON. I'D SWAP PLACES WITH ANY OF THEM. BUT DIONYSUS? HE'S AN ENEMY.

AND PART OF ME THINKS CASS COULD BE AN ALLY...

IS THIS FOR REAL? YOU'RE NOT JUST HITTING ON ME TO BE ONE OF YOUR VALKYRIES?

NO, I'M NOT JUST HITTING ON YOU. ANANKE'S FOR REAL.

SHE'S BEEN FOLLOWING YOU SINCE LUCI. YOU USED THE FOOTAGE PRETTY RESPONSIBLY. NO CASHING IN. SHE EVEN LIKES YOUR IDEAS.

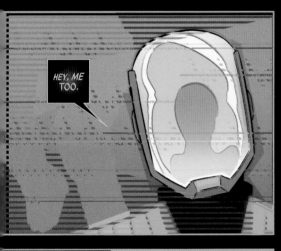

HEY, ME TOO.

YOU ARE TRYING TO IMPRESS ME.

NO, I WON'T BE ONE OF YOUR FUCKING VALKYRIES.

I CAN SEE WHY YOU'RE EXPECTING THE INVITE. I'D GUESS... FIVE-NINE? ASIAN. YOU FIT THE JOB DESCRIPTION.

I'M MANY THINGS, BUT I'M NOT TRANSPHOBIC.

GO FUCK YOURSELF.

BY WHICH I MEAN, "GEE, I'M SORRY. THAT'S REALLY COMPLIMENTARY, BUT I'M JUST NOT INTERESTED IN THAT KIND OF WORK RIGHT NOW."

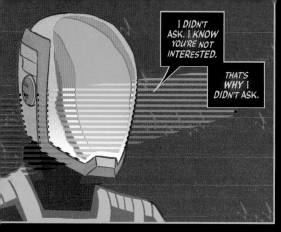

I DIDN'T ASK. I KNOW YOU'RE NOT INTERESTED.

THAT'S WHY I DIDN'T ASK.

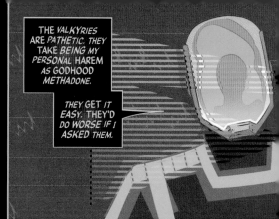

THE VALKYRIES ARE PATHETIC. THEY TAKE BEING MY PERSONAL HAREM AS GODHOOD METHADONE.

THEY GET IT EASY. THEY'D DO WORSE IF I ASKED THEM.

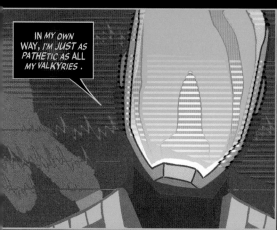

IN MY OWN WAY, I'M JUST AS PATHETIC AS ALL MY VALKYRIES.

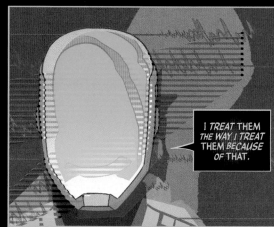

I TREAT THEM THE WAY I TREAT THEM BECAUSE OF THAT.

YOU'RE NOT PATHETIC. YOU HAVE NO INTEREST IN THE LINE I'M SELLING.

I LIKE THAT.

AND THIS IS MEANT TO IMPRESS ME?

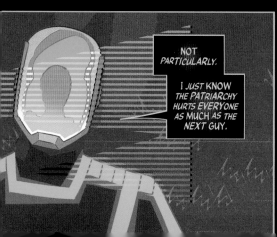

NOT PARTICULARLY.

I JUST KNOW THE PATRIARCHY HURTS EVERYONE AS MUCH AS THE NEXT GUY.

OH GOD.

NOW YOU ARE FUCKING WITH ME.

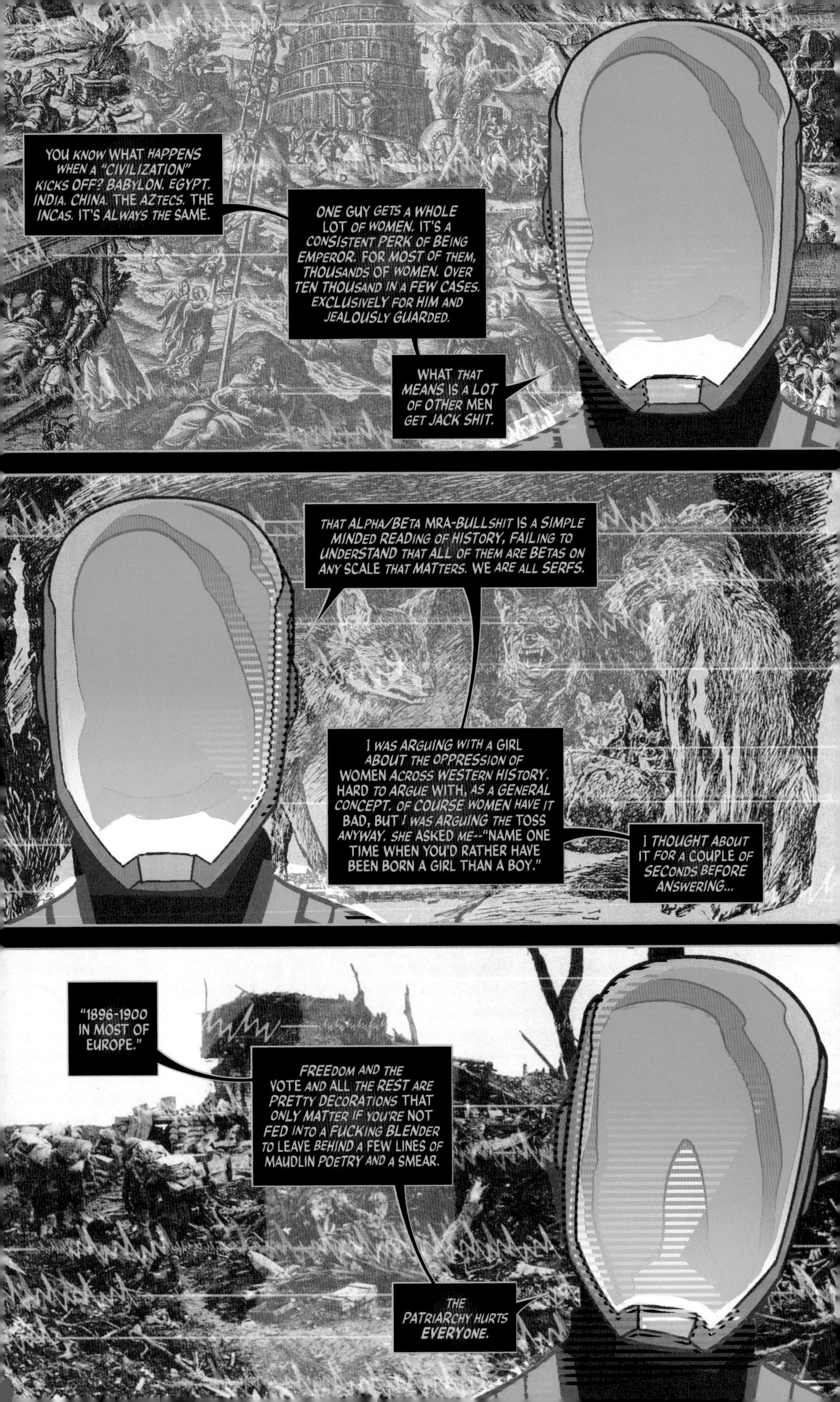
YOU KNOW WHAT HAPPENS WHEN A "CIVILIZATION" KICKS OFF? BABYLON. EGYPT. INDIA. CHINA. THE AZTECS. THE INCAS. IT'S ALWAYS THE SAME.
ONE GUY GETS A WHOLE LOT OF WOMEN. IT'S A CONSISTENT PERK OF BEING EMPEROR. FOR MOST OF THEM, THOUSANDS OF WOMEN. OVER TEN THOUSAND IN A FEW CASES. EXCLUSIVELY FOR HIM AND JEALOUSLY GUARDED.
WHAT THAT MEANS IS A LOT OF OTHER MEN GET JACK SHIT.
THAT ALPHA/BETA MRA-BULLSHIT IS A SIMPLE MINDED READING OF HISTORY, FAILING TO UNDERSTAND THAT ALL OF THEM ARE BETAS ON ANY SCALE THAT MATTERS. WE ARE ALL SERFS.
I WAS ARGUING WITH A GIRL ABOUT THE OPPRESSION OF WOMEN ACROSS WESTERN HISTORY. HARD TO ARGUE WITH, AS A GENERAL CONCEPT. OF COURSE WOMEN HAVE IT BAD, BUT I WAS ARGUING THE TOSS ANYWAY. SHE ASKED ME--"NAME ONE TIME WHEN YOU'D RATHER HAVE BEEN BORN A GIRL THAN A BOY."
I THOUGHT ABOUT IT FOR A COUPLE OF SECONDS BEFORE ANSWERING...
"1896-1900 IN MOST OF EUROPE."
FREEDOM AND THE VOTE AND ALL THE REST ARE PRETTY DECORATIONS THAT ONLY MATTER IF YOU'RE NOT FED INTO A FUCKING BLENDER TO LEAVE BEHIND A FEW LINES OF MAUDLIN POETRY AND A SMEAR.
THE PATRIARCHY HURTS EVERYONE.

AND PATRIARCHY ISN'T RULE BY MEN. IT'S RULE BY FATHERS.

MOST MEN WILL NEVER BE THE FATHERS. THEY'RE JUST SONS, AND SONS GET SACRIFICED TO KEEP THE OLD MAN IN PORT AND CIGARS.

THE WORLD ISN'T HOW THINGS SHOULD BE. WOULD BE GOOD TO HAVE A BETTER WORLD.

BUT I'M NOT GOING TO LIVE TO SEE IT, SO FUCK EVERYONE. IDEALLY, LITERALLY.

YOU'RE NOT STUPID, ARE YOU?

JUST EVIL.

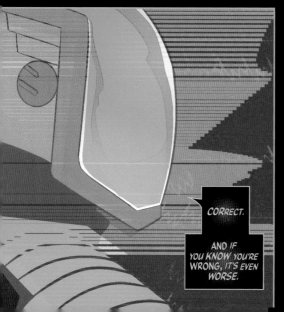

CORRECT.

AND IF YOU KNOW YOU'RE WRONG, IT'S EVEN WORSE.

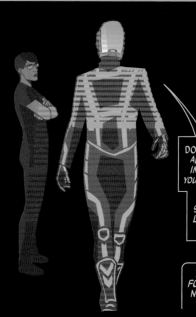

DON'T WORRY ABOUT THE INTERVIEW. YOU'LL NAIL IT.

I'M PRETTY SURE IT'LL BE A LIFE-CHANGING EXPERIENCE.

I CAN'T RESIST FORESHADOWING. MIX IN THE NEXT TRACK...

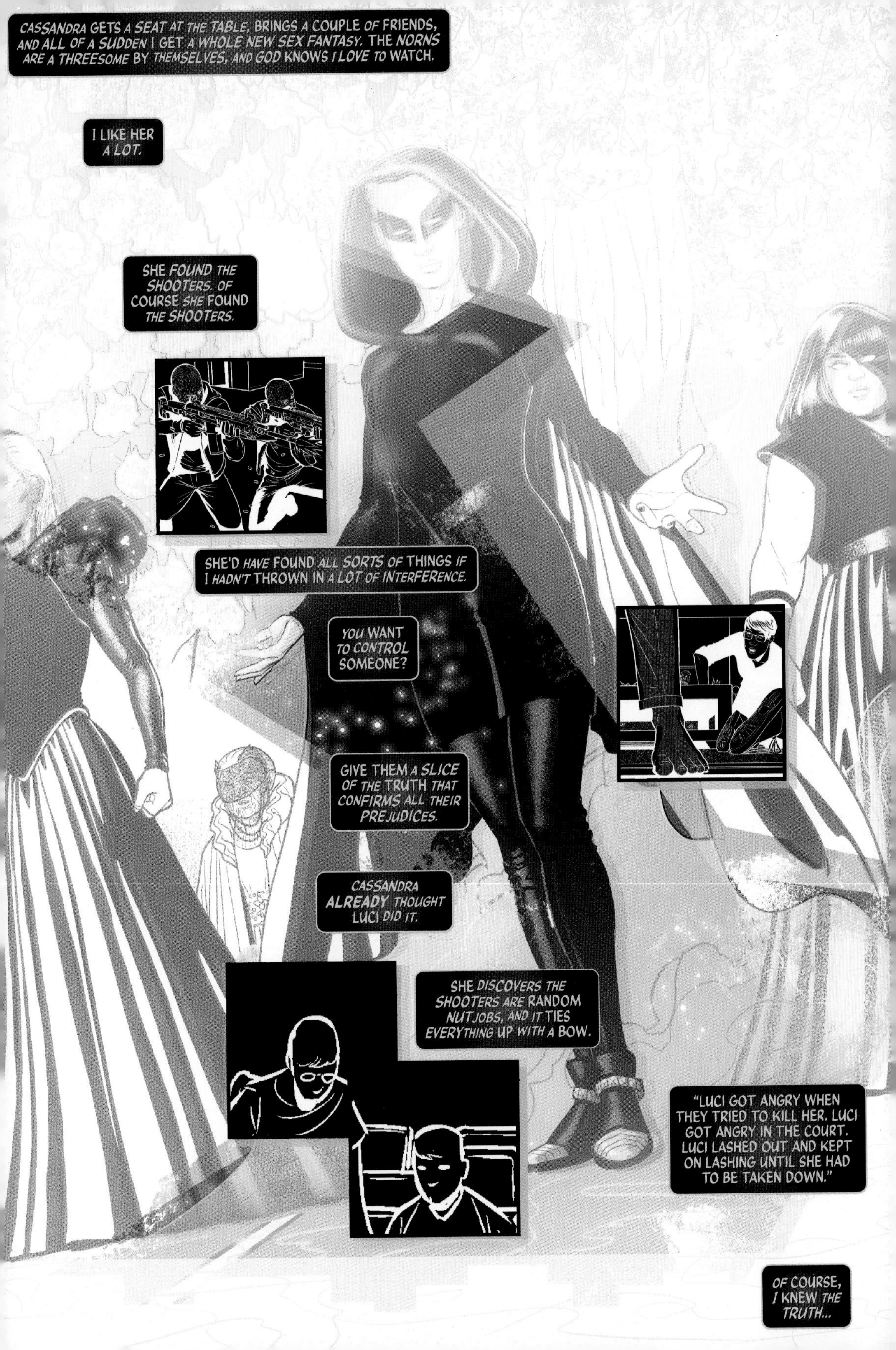
CASSANDRA GETS A SEAT AT THE TABLE, BRINGS A COUPLE OF FRIENDS, AND ALL OF A SUDDEN I GET A WHOLE NEW SEX FANTASY. THE NORNS ARE A THREESOME BY THEMSELVES, AND GOD KNOWS I LOVE TO WATCH.
I LIKE HER A LOT.
SHE FOUND THE SHOOTERS. OF COURSE SHE FOUND THE SHOOTERS.
SHE'D HAVE FOUND ALL SORTS OF THINGS IF I HADN'T THROWN IN A LOT OF INTERFERENCE.
YOU WANT TO CONTROL SOMEONE?
GIVE THEM A SLICE OF THE TRUTH THAT CONFIRMS ALL THEIR PREJUDICES.
CASSANDRA ALREADY THOUGHT LUCI DID IT.
SHE DISCOVERS THE SHOOTERS ARE RANDOM NUTJOBS, AND IT TIES EVERYTHING UP WITH A BOW.
"LUCI GOT ANGRY WHEN THEY TRIED TO KILL HER. LUCI GOT ANGRY IN THE COURT. LUCI LASHED OUT AND KEPT ON LASHING UNTIL SHE HAD TO BE TAKEN DOWN."
OF COURSE, I KNEW THE TRUTH...

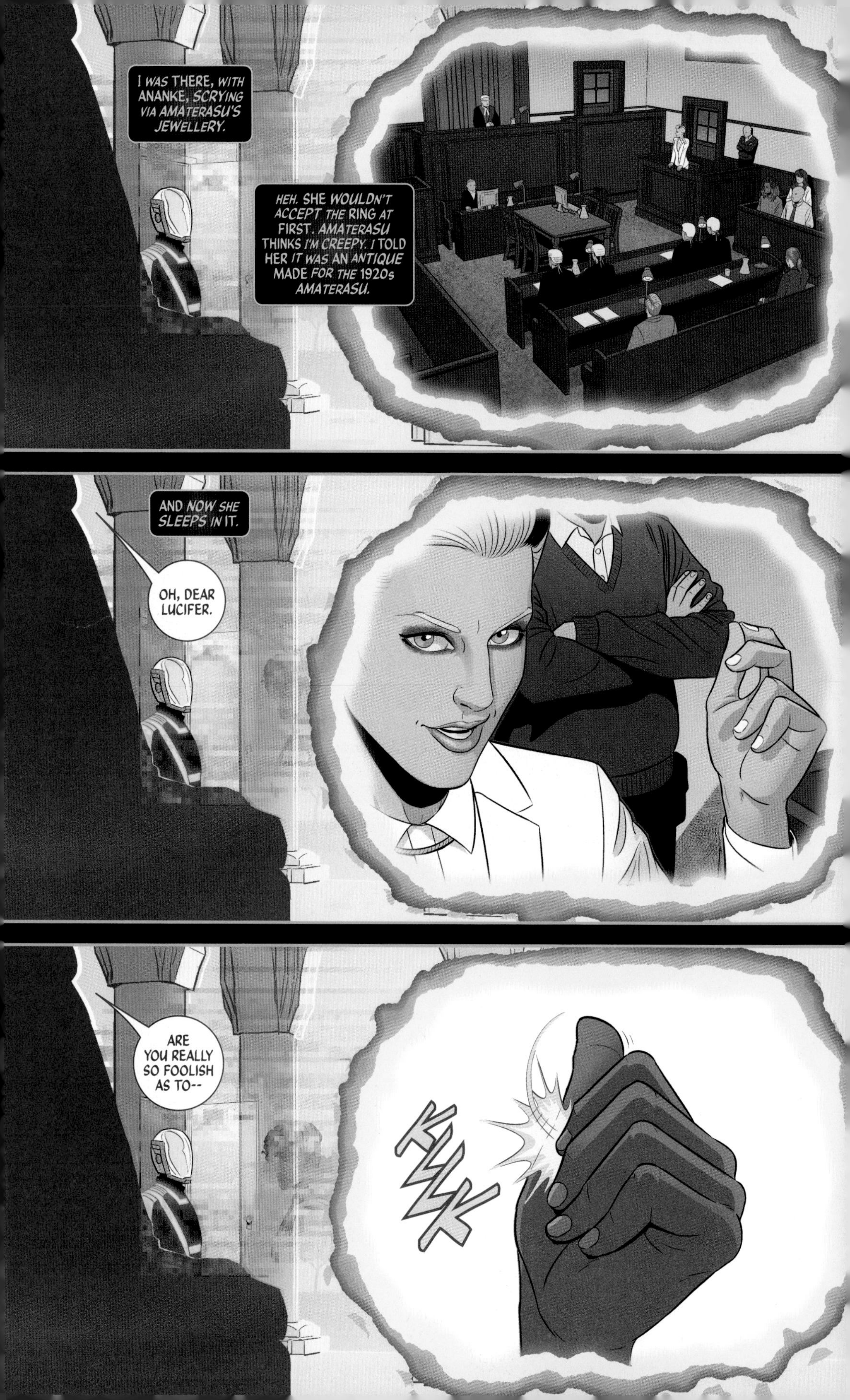
I WAS THERE, WITH ANANKE, SCRYING VIA AMATERASU'S JEWELLERY.
HEH. SHE WOULDN'T ACCEPT THE RING AT FIRST. AMATERASU THINKS I'M CREEPY. I TOLD HER IT WAS AN ANTIQUE MADE FOR THE 1920s AMATERASU.
AND NOW SHE SLEEPS IN IT.
OH, DEAR LUCIFER.
ARE YOU REALLY SO FOOLISH AS TO--
KLIK

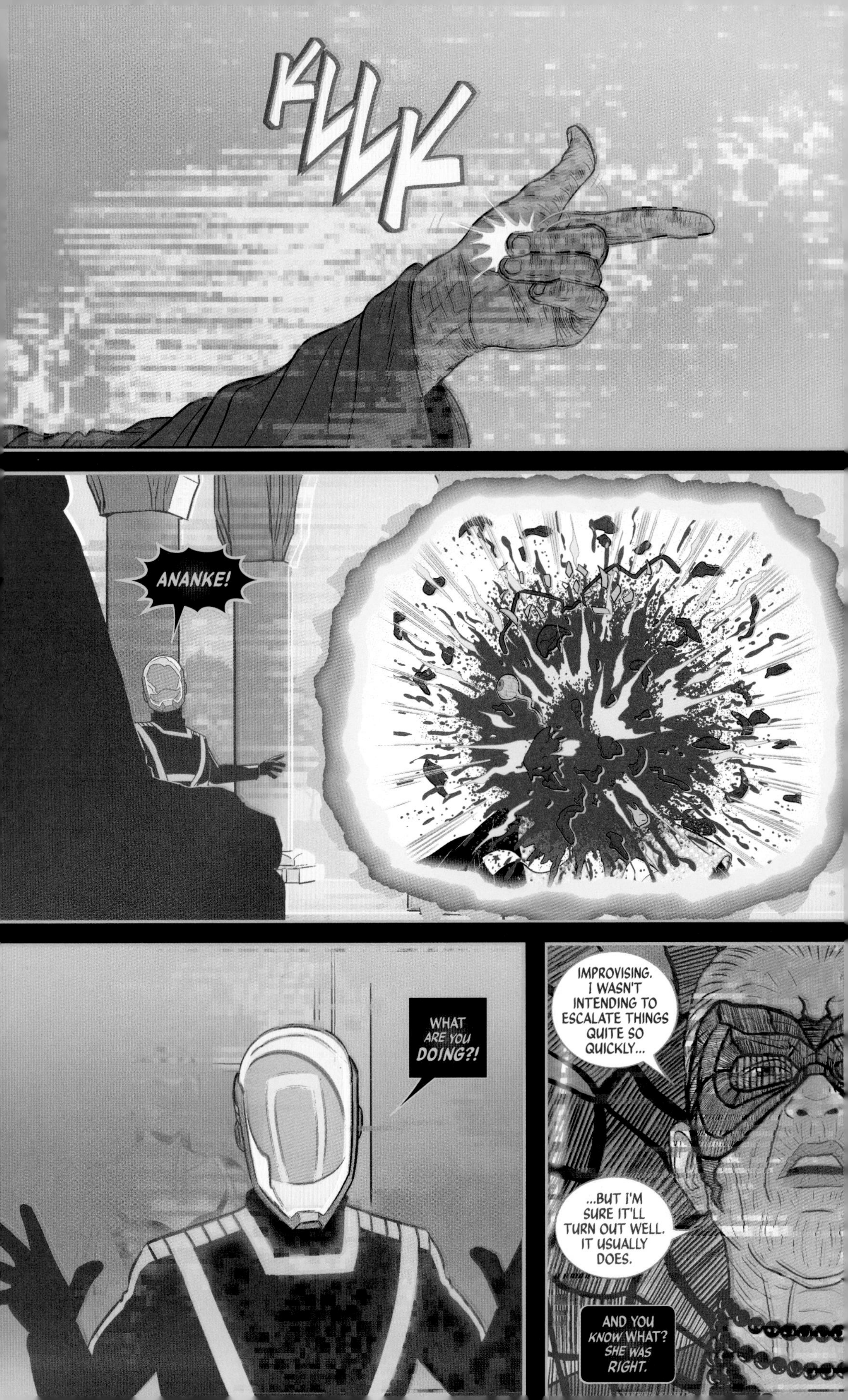
KLLK
ANANKE!
WHAT ARE YOU DOING?!
IMPROVISING. I WASN'T INTENDING TO ESCALATE THINGS QUITE SO QUICKLY...
...BUT I'M SURE IT'LL TURN OUT WELL. IT USUALLY DOES.
AND YOU KNOW WHAT? SHE WAS RIGHT.

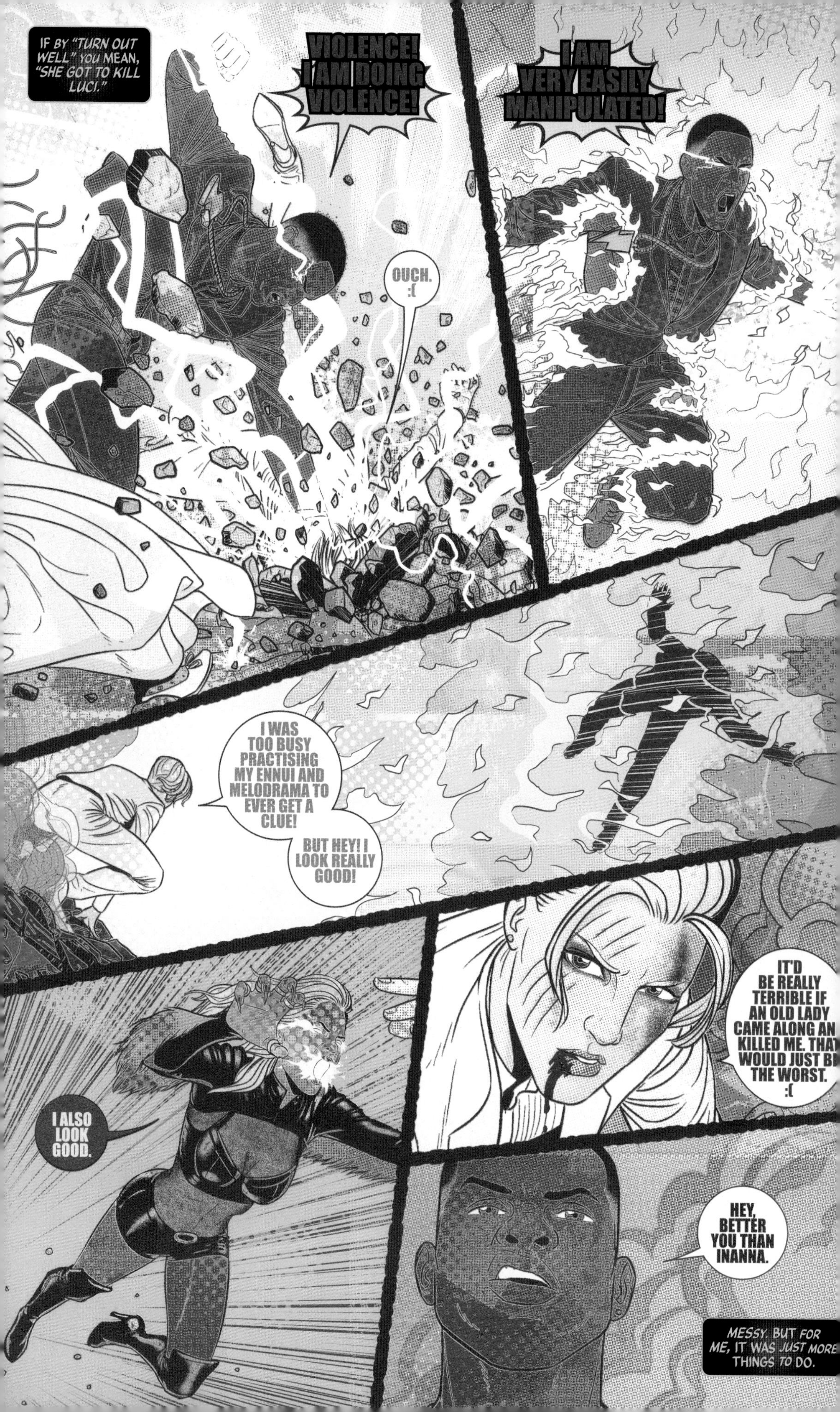
IF BY "TURN OUT WELL" YOU MEAN, "SHE GOT TO KILL LUCI."
VIOLENCE! I AM DOING VIOLENCE!
OUCH. :(
I AM VERY EASILY MANIPULATED!
I WAS TOO BUSY PRACTISING MY ENNUI AND MELODRAMA TO EVER GET A CLUE!
BUT HEY! I LOOK REALLY GOOD!
I ALSO LOOK GOOD.
IT'D BE REALLY TERRIBLE IF AN OLD LADY CAME ALONG AN KILLED ME. THA WOULD JUST B THE WORST. :(
HEY, BETTER YOU THAN INANNA.
MESSY. BUT FOR ME, IT WAS JUST MORE THINGS TO DO.

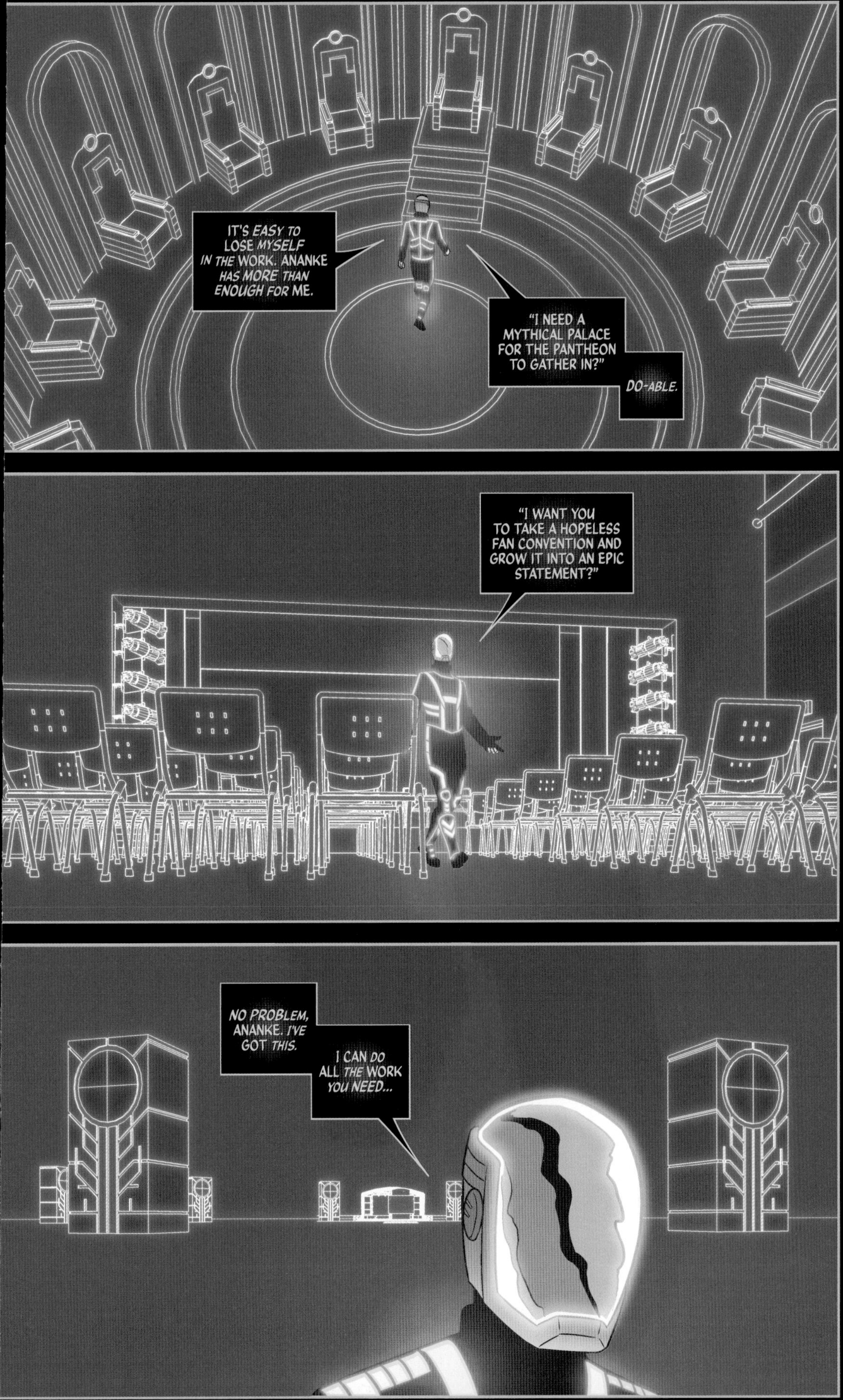
IT'S EASY TO LOSE MYSELF IN THE WORK. ANANKE HAS MORE THAN ENOUGH FOR ME.
"I NEED A MYTHICAL PALACE FOR THE PANTHEON TO GATHER IN?"
DO-ABLE.
"I WANT YOU TO TAKE A HOPELESS FAN CONVENTION AND GROW IT INTO AN EPIC STATEMENT?"
NO PROBLEM, ANANKE. I'VE GOT THIS.
I CAN DO ALL THE WORK YOU NEED...

...AS LONG AS I GET WHAT I WANT.

PEOPLE GET THE WRONG IDEA. I'M NOT JUST INTO ASIAN GIRLS.

I'M INTO ASIAN GIRLS IN PUBLIC.

IN PRIVATE, MY INTERESTS EXTEND TO GIRLS DRESSED UP AS ASIAN GODS AND GIRLS DRESSED UP AS GODS WHO I HELPED MURDER.

I KNOW THIS IS FUCKED UP, BUT THESE ARE THE TIMES I DON'T REGRET GIVING UP MY FACE.

"HOW CAN I DO IT?" IT'S EASY. YOU TAKE WOMEN AND JUST FORGET THAT THEY'RE PEOPLE. IT'S NOT HARD.

I'VE SPENT SO LONG WANTING THIS. AND NOW, I WORK HARD. I GET MY REWARD. THAT'S HOW LIFE SHOULD WORK, RIGHT?

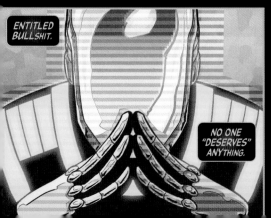

ENTITLED BULLSHIT.

NO ONE "DESERVES" ANYTHING.

IT'S JUST THAT I CAN HAVE IT.

I CAN HAVE ANYTHING...
...ANYTHING I EVER WANTED.
THIS IS MINE.
THIS IS MINE.
THIS IS MINE.
IT'S ALL MINE.
ALMOST.

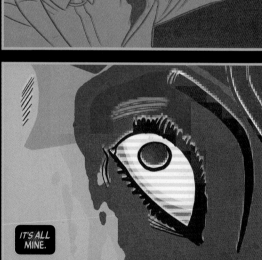

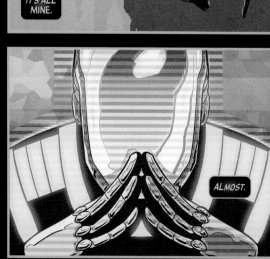

SO THAT'S WHERE MY HEAD WAS BEFORE RAGNAROCK. THE SECOND BAPHOMET RAN, I HOLED UP IN VALHALLA. IF HE WAS GOING TO COME AT ME, I WANTED TOOLED-UP VALKYRIES AT EVERY ENTRANCE.

IF IT CAME TO IT, I'D TRY TO TALK BAPHOMET DOWN. TELL HIM THE TRUTH. *TELL HIM THE GAMBIT WOULDN'T WORK...*BUT HE'D PROBABLY HAVE KILLED ME ANYWAY.

I WAS *PARANOID,* AND NOT IN THE BEST OF MOODS WHEN I GOT THE CALL FROM ANANKE...

WODEN. BRING ME HOME.

THERE HAVE BEEN... COMPLICATIONS.

KEEP THE PORTAL OPEN. YOU HAVE WORK TO DO.

THERE'S A BODY. I NEED IT MOVED. NOW!

I WAS *TIRED, WIRED, SCARED.* I KNEW IT WAS DUMB TO SAY ANYTHING.

BUT I FOUND MYSELF THINKING...

"I GAVE YOU EVERYTHING."

"I GAVE *THIS* EVERYTHING."

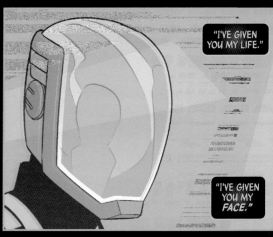

"I'VE GIVEN YOU MY LIFE."

"I'VE GIVEN YOU MY *FACE.*"

"WHEN IS IT GOING TO BE ENOUGH?"

I THINK YOU'VE MISTAKEN ME FOR YOUR SERF.

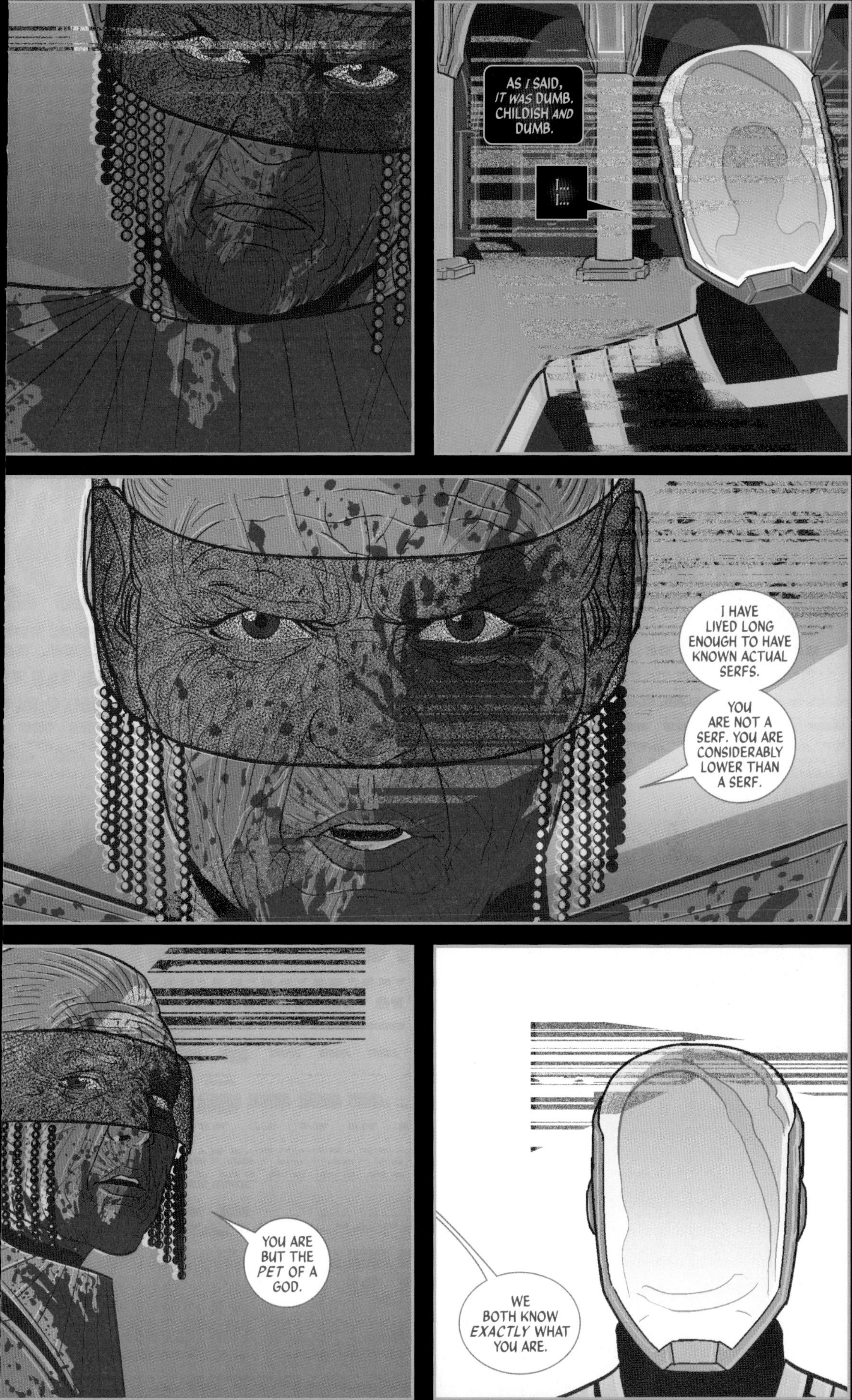
AS I SAID, IT WAS DUMB. CHILDISH AND DUMB.
I... I...
I HAVE LIVED LONG ENOUGH TO HAVE KNOWN ACTUAL SERFS.
YOU ARE NOT A SERF. YOU ARE CONSIDERABLY LOWER THAN A SERF.
YOU ARE BUT THE PET OF A GOD.
WE BOTH KNOW EXACTLY WHAT YOU ARE.

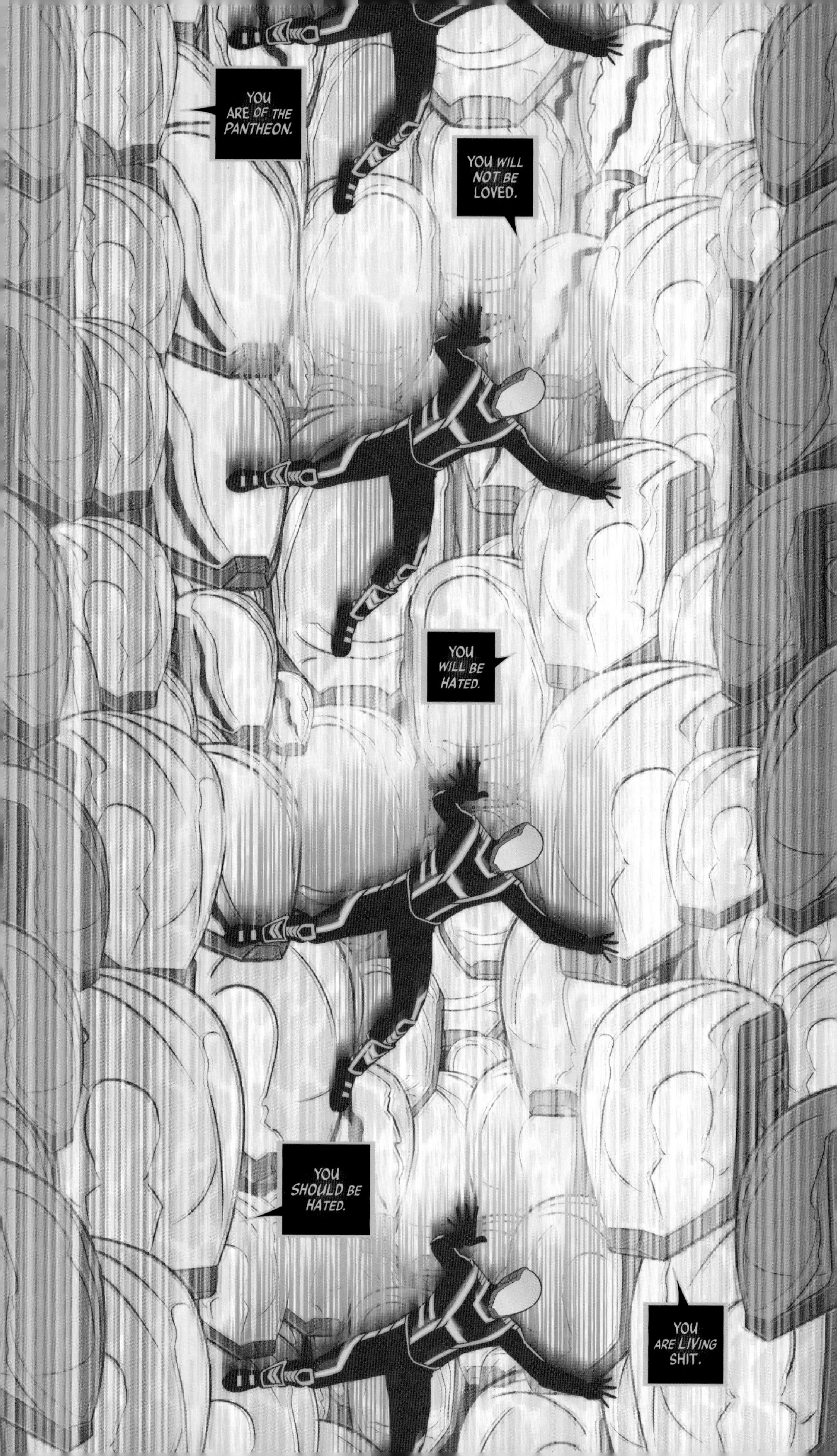
YOU ARE OF THE PANTHEON.
YOU WILL NOT BE LOVED.
YOU WILL BE HATED.
YOU SHOULD BE HATED.
YOU ARE LIVING SHIT.

AND AS LONG AS I KNOW WHAT I KNOW ABOUT YOU, YOU'LL *OBEY.*

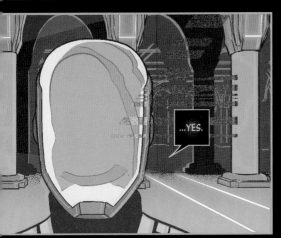

...YES.

GOOD. STRICTLY SPEAKING, YOU ARE NOT IRREPLACEABLE... BUT IT WOULD BE *DIFFICULT.*

AND I HAVE LARGER PROBLEMS TO WORRY ABOUT. THIS SITUATION HAS... CHANGED.

THERE WILL BE A WAR AMONG THE CHILDREN.

I MUST ACT MORE SWIFTLY THAN I WOULD NORMALLY RISK. LET US HOPE THAT THE DICE ARE KIND.

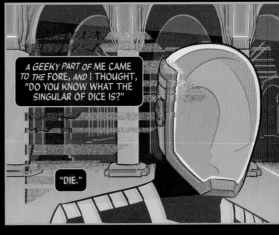

A GEEKY PART OF ME CAME TO THE FORE, AND I THOUGHT, "DO YOU KNOW WHAT THE SINGULAR OF DICE IS?"

"DIE."

I KNEW THERE'D BE ANOTHER BODY IN A WEEK.

WHEN TARA TURNED UP *UNEXPECTEDLY* AT THE PARTY, I KNEW WHO IT'D BE.

THE ONLY THING THAT SURPRISED ME WAS THAT HER MAJESTY DIDN'T CALL ME TO DO ANOTHER CORPSE RUN.

SO...WHERE DOES THAT *LEAVE* US?

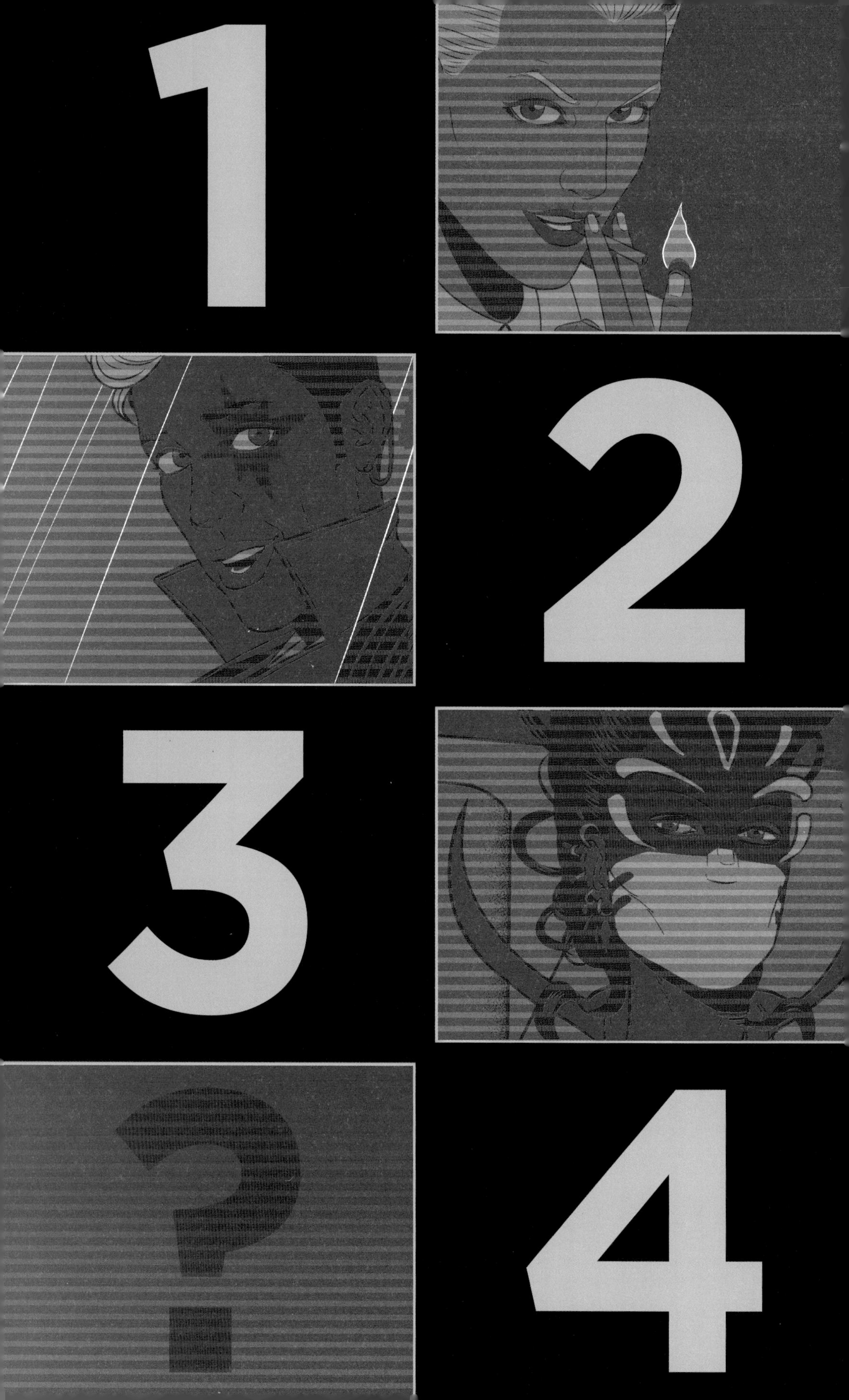
1
2
3
?
4

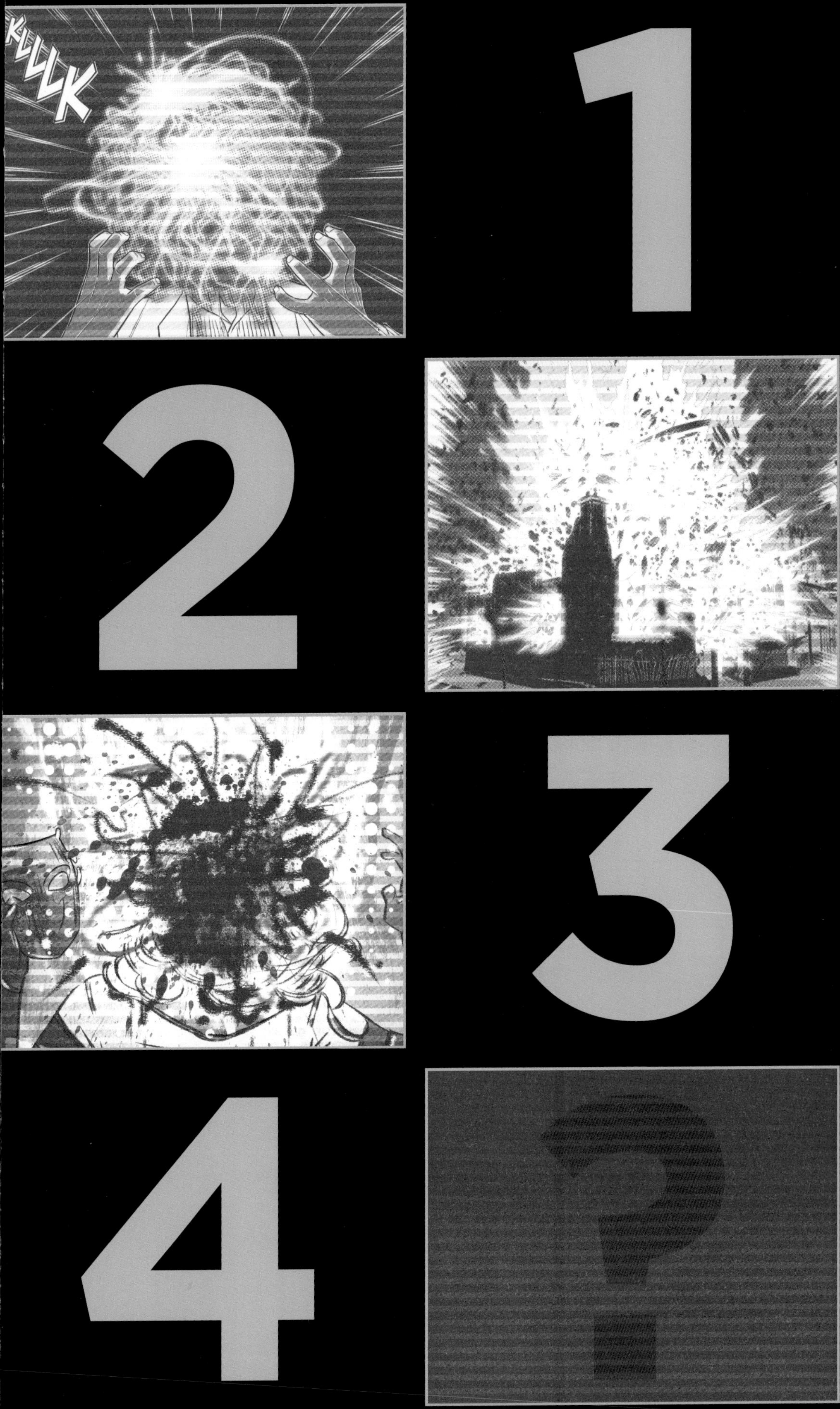
KLLLK
1
2
3
4
?

I DON'T KNOW WHO'S NEXT. BUT SOMEONE'S NEXT. SHE'S PICKING UP THE TEMPO.
THREE DOWN. BUT THERE'S ONE THING I'M SURE OF...
I WON'T LET HER GET YOU.
AFTER EVERYTHING?
...OF COURSE YOU WON'T.

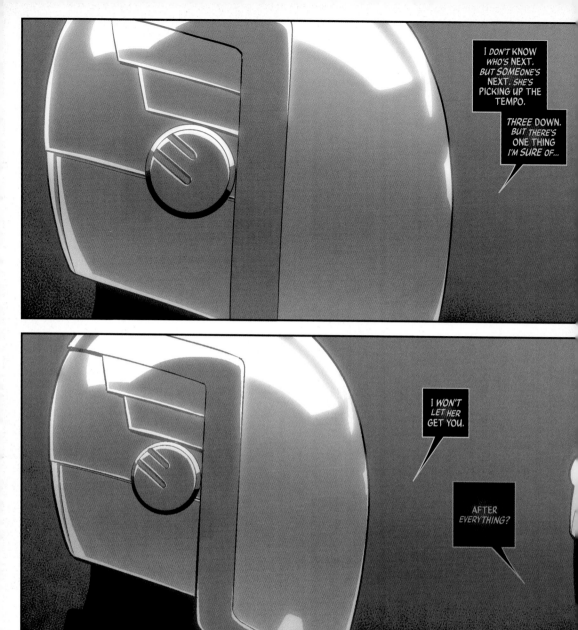

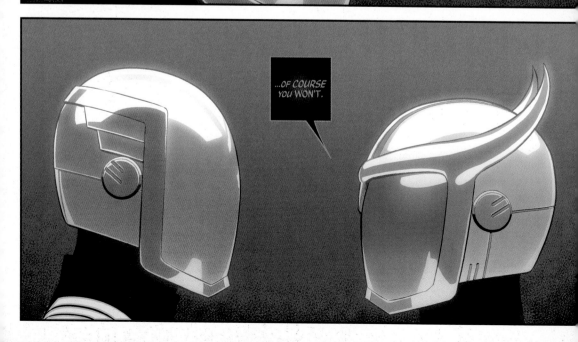

THOUGHT
AND MEMORY

18 AUGUST 2014

15

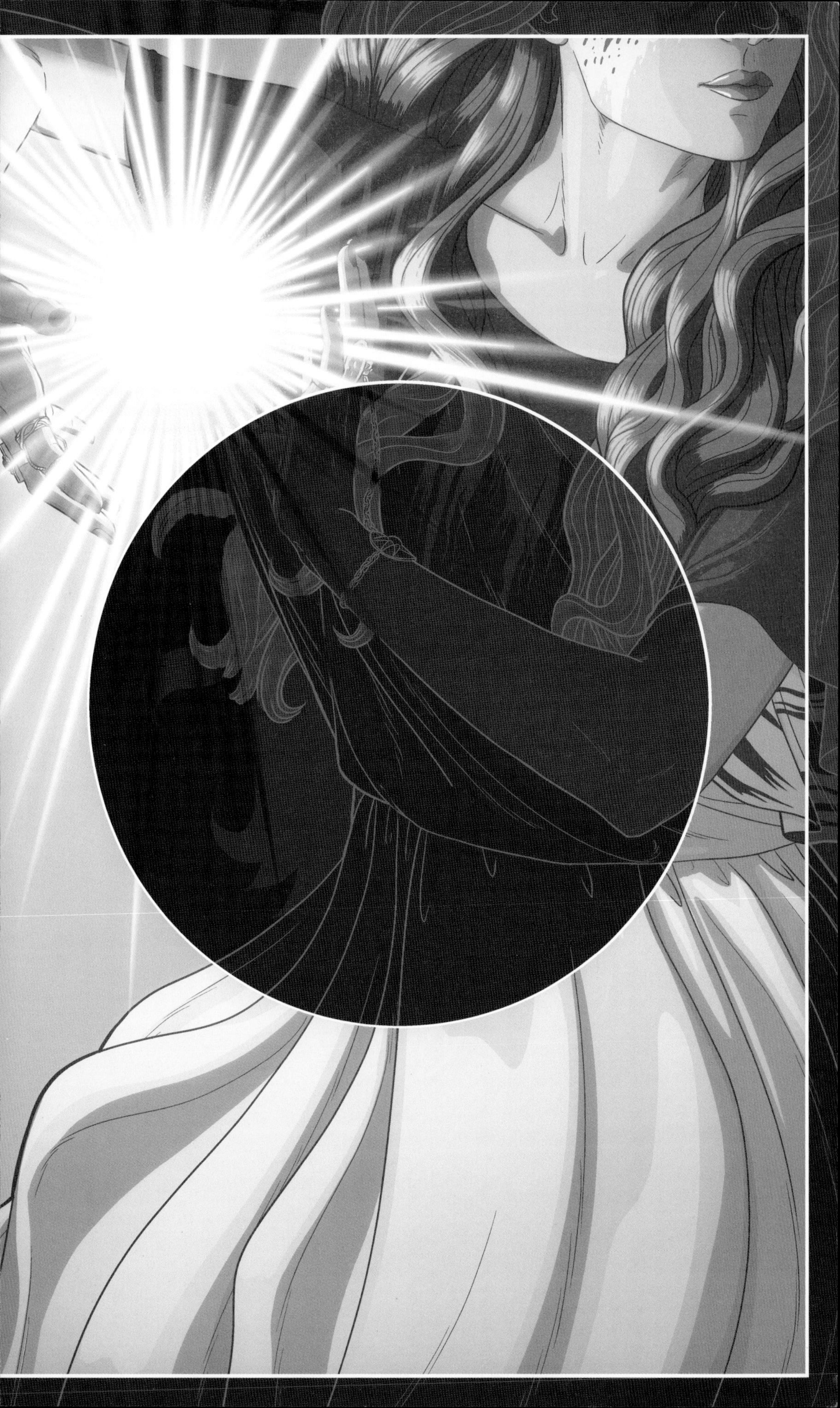

THE
WICKED
+
DIVINE
THE

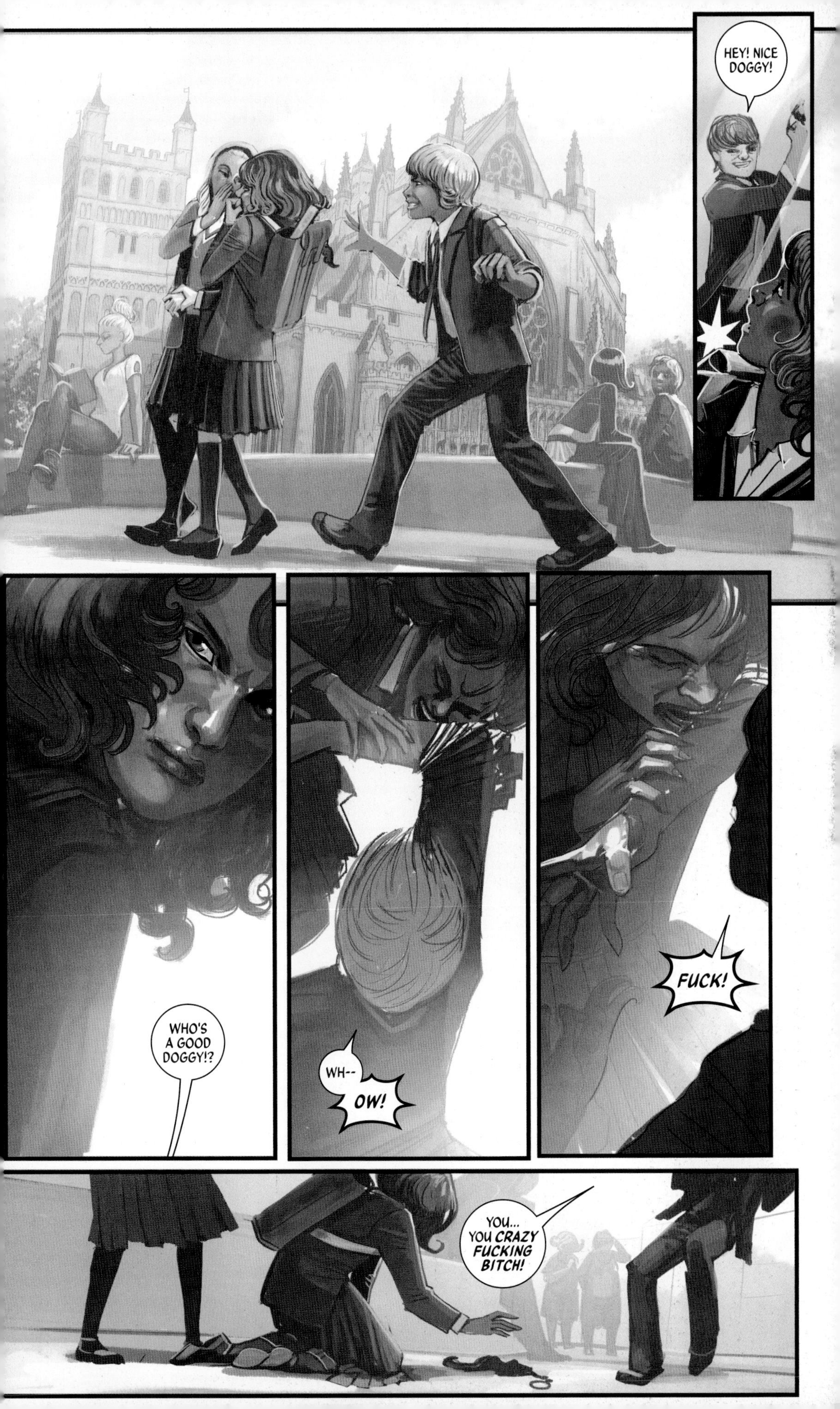
HEY! NICE DOGGY!
WHO'S A GOOD DOGGY!?
WH--
OW!
FUCK!
YOU... YOU *CRAZY FUCKING BITCH!*

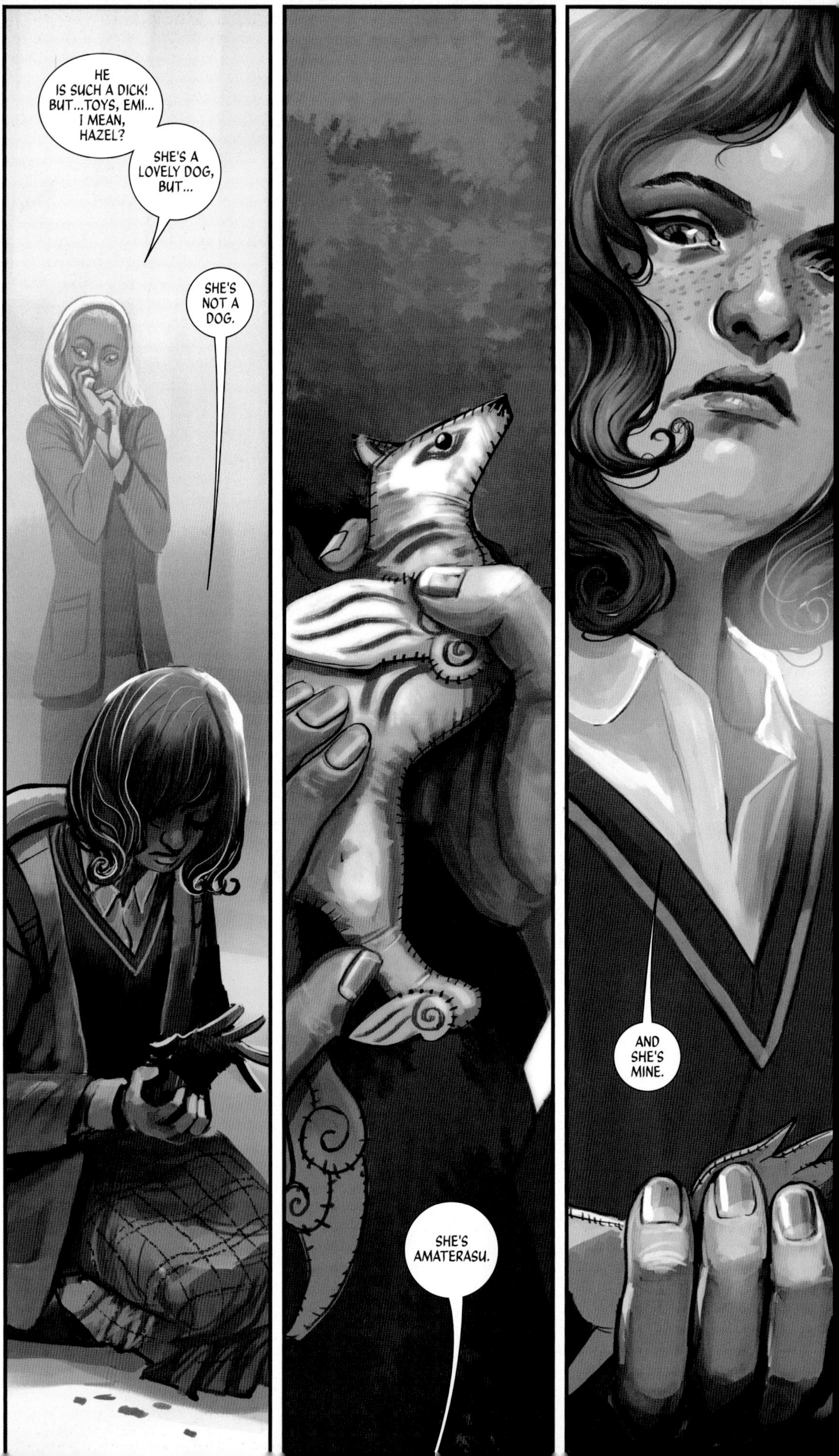
HE IS SUCH A DICK! BUT...TOYS, EMI... I MEAN, HAZEL?
SHE'S A LOVELY DOG, BUT...
SHE'S NOT A DOG.
SHE'S AMATERASU.
AND SHE'S MINE.

THE GOOD DOGGY

6 JULY 2010

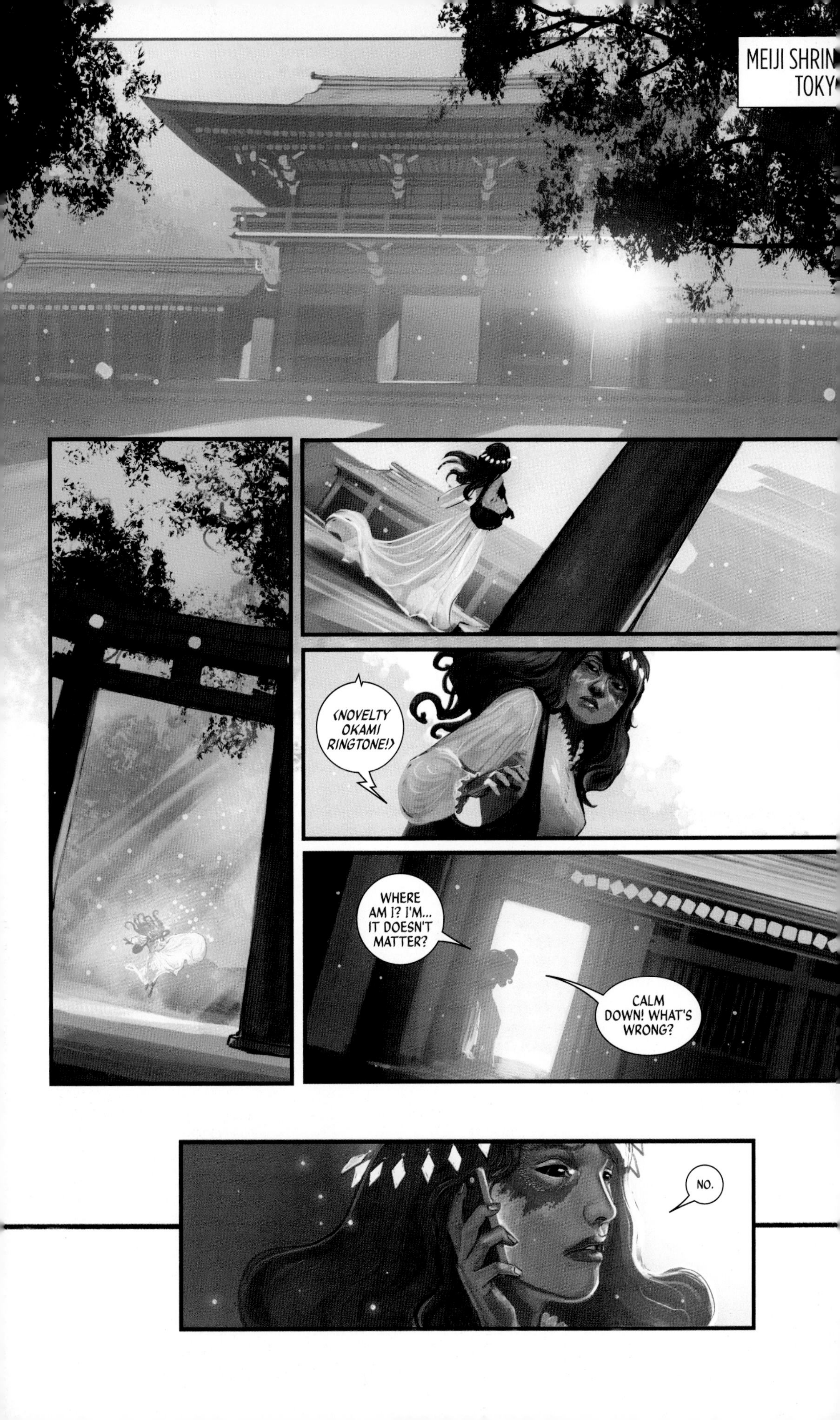
MEIJI SHRIN
TOKY
‹NOVELTY OKAMI RINGTONE!›
WHERE AM I? I'M... IT DOESN'T MATTER?
CALM DOWN! WHAT'S WRONG?
NO.

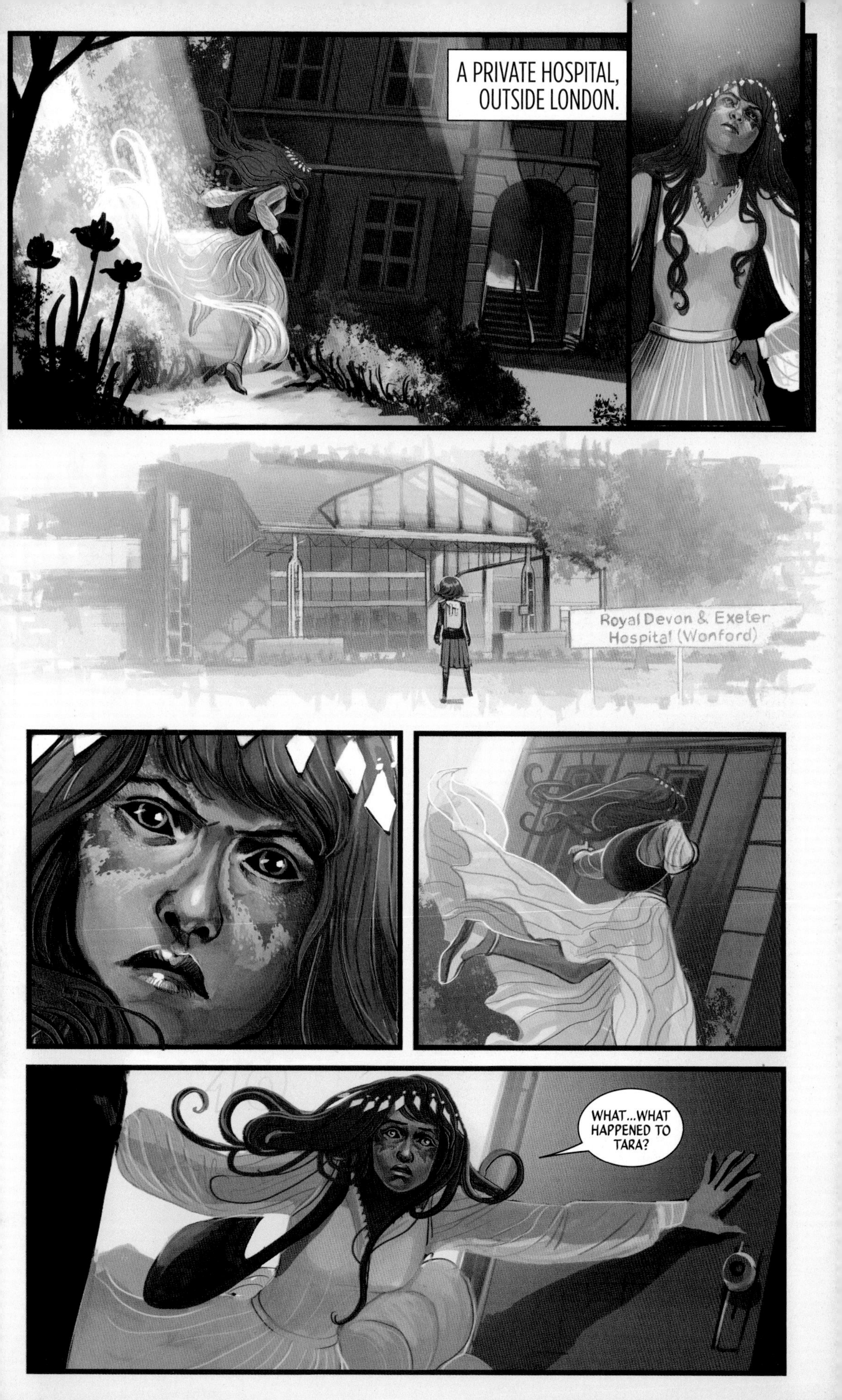
A PRIVATE HOSPITAL, OUTSIDE LONDON.
Royal Devon & Exeter Hospital (Wonford)
WHAT...WHAT HAPPENED TO TARA?

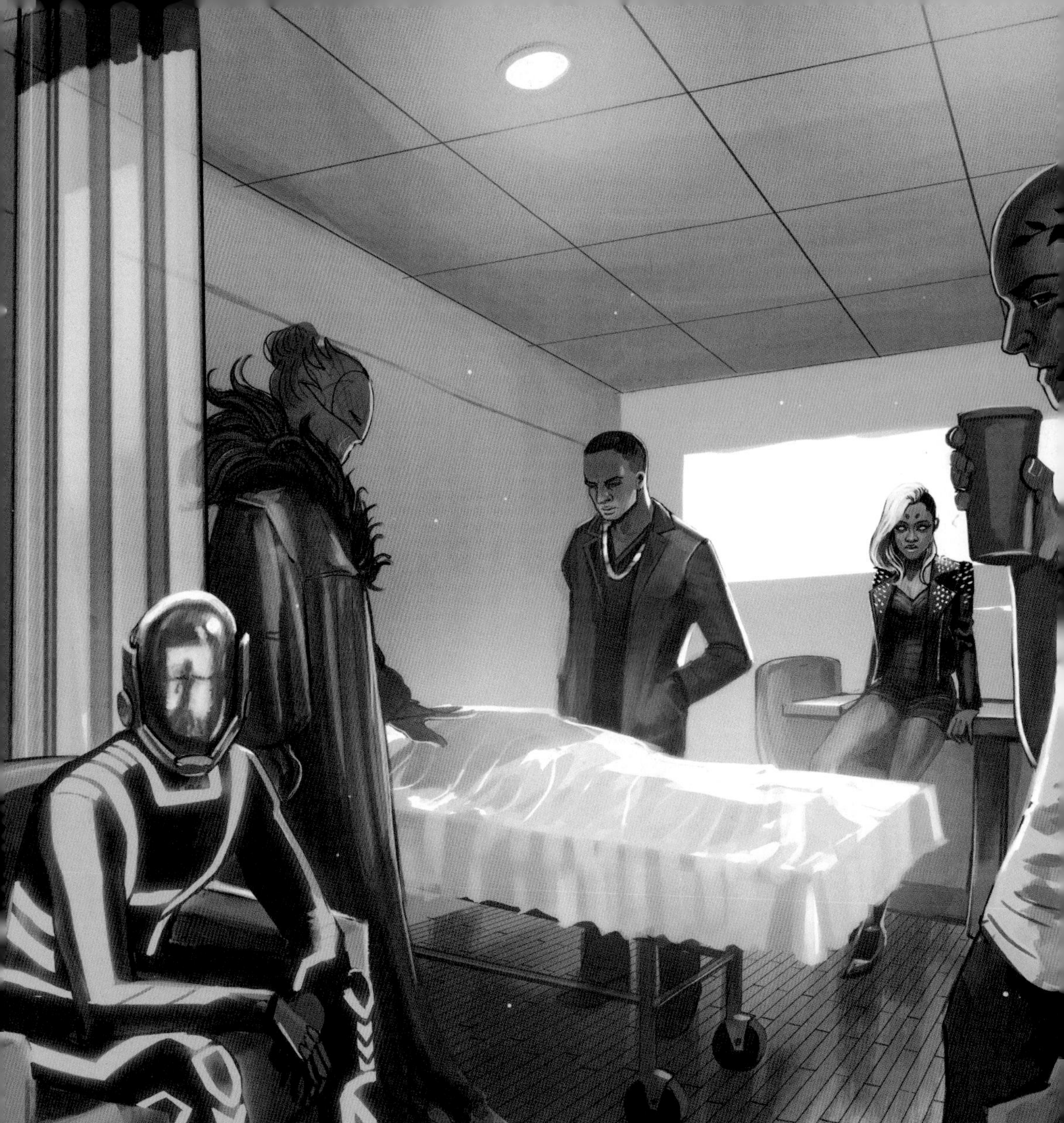

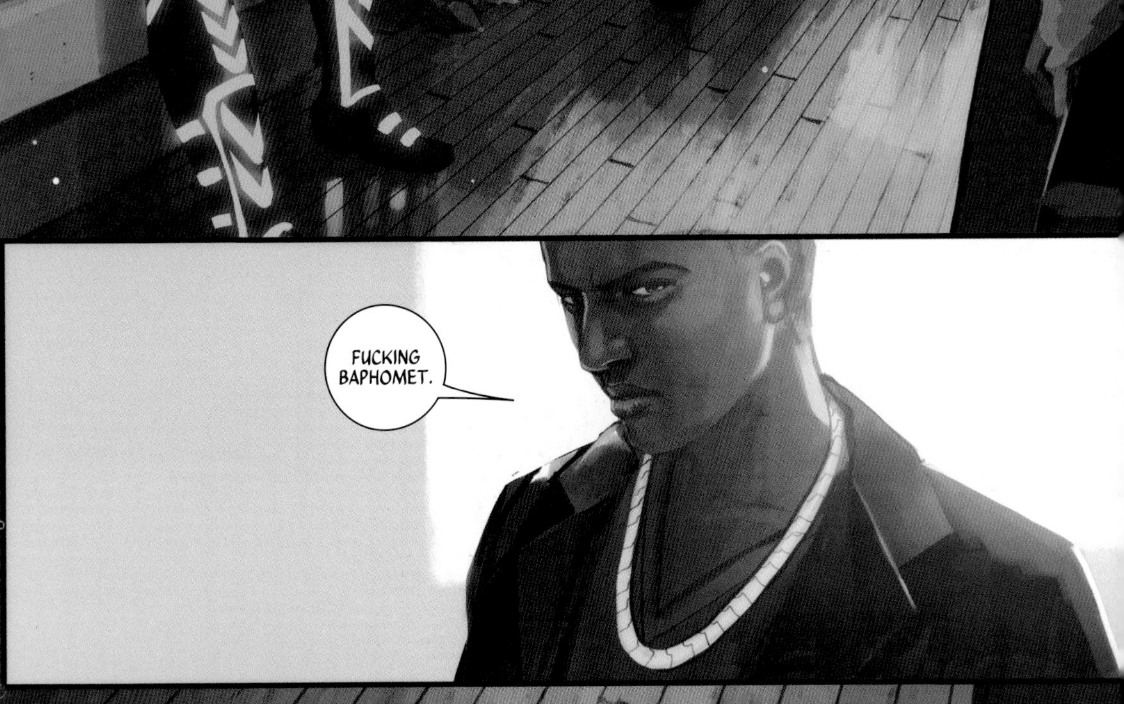
FUCKING BAPHOMET.

THE LIGHT OF
THE DYING

18 AUGUST 2014

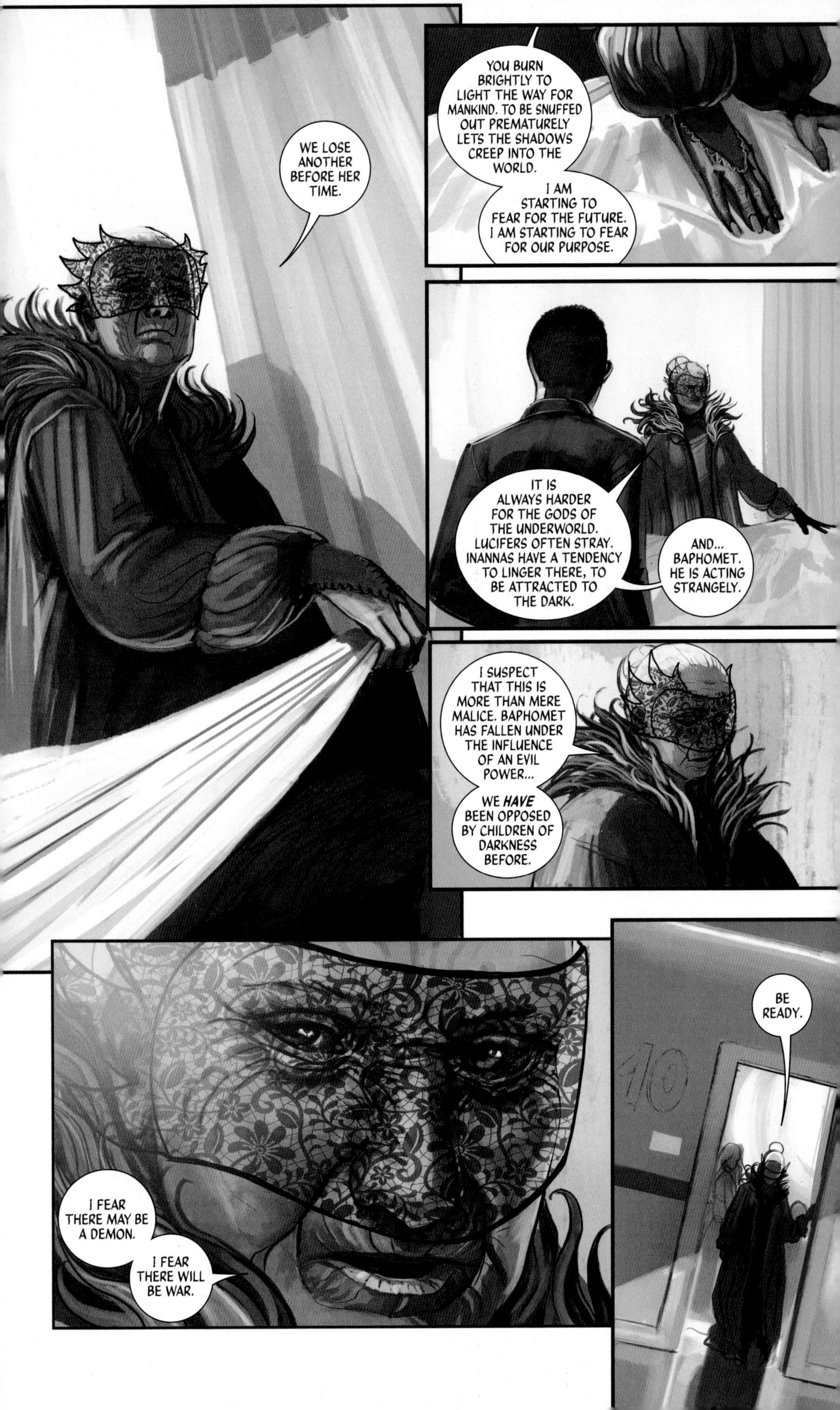
WE LOSE ANOTHER BEFORE HER TIME.
YOU BURN BRIGHTLY TO LIGHT THE WAY FOR MANKIND. TO BE SNUFFED OUT PREMATURELY LETS THE SHADOWS CREEP INTO THE WORLD.
I AM STARTING TO FEAR FOR THE FUTURE. I AM STARTING TO FEAR FOR OUR PURPOSE.
IT IS ALWAYS HARDER FOR THE GODS OF THE UNDERWORLD. LUCIFERS OFTEN STRAY. INANNAS HAVE A TENDENCY TO LINGER THERE, TO BE ATTRACTED TO THE DARK.
AND... BAPHOMET. HE IS ACTING STRANGELY.
I SUSPECT THAT THIS IS MORE THAN MERE MALICE. BAPHOMET HAS FALLEN UNDER THE INFLUENCE OF AN EVIL POWER...
WE *HAVE* BEEN OPPOSED BY CHILDREN OF DARKNESS BEFORE.
I FEAR THERE MAY BE A DEMON.
I FEAR THERE WILL BE WAR.
BE READY.

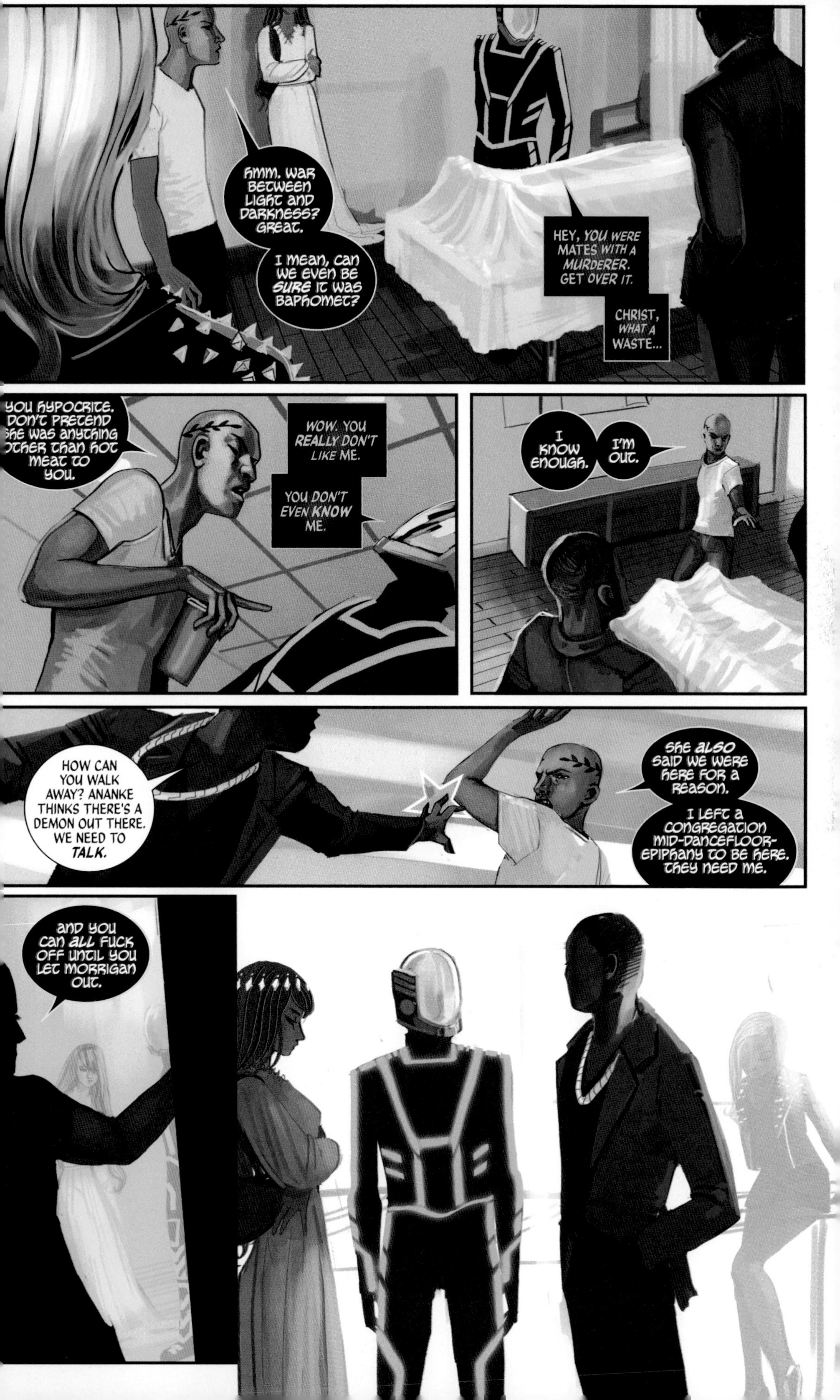
Hmm. War between light and darkness? Great.
I mean, can we even be *sure* it was Baphomet?
HEY, *YOU WERE* MATES *WITH A MURDERER*. GET OVER IT.
CHRIST, *WHAT A* WASTE...
You hypocrite. Don't pretend she was anything other than hot meat to you.
WOW. YOU *REALLY DON'T LIKE* ME.
YOU *DON'T EVEN* ***KNOW*** ME.
I know enough.
I'm out.
HOW CAN YOU WALK AWAY? ANANKE THINKS THERE'S A DEMON OUT THERE. WE NEED TO ***TALK***.
She *also* said we were here for a reason.
I left a congregation mid-dancefloor-epiphany to be here. They need me.
And you can *all* fuck off until you let Morrigan out.

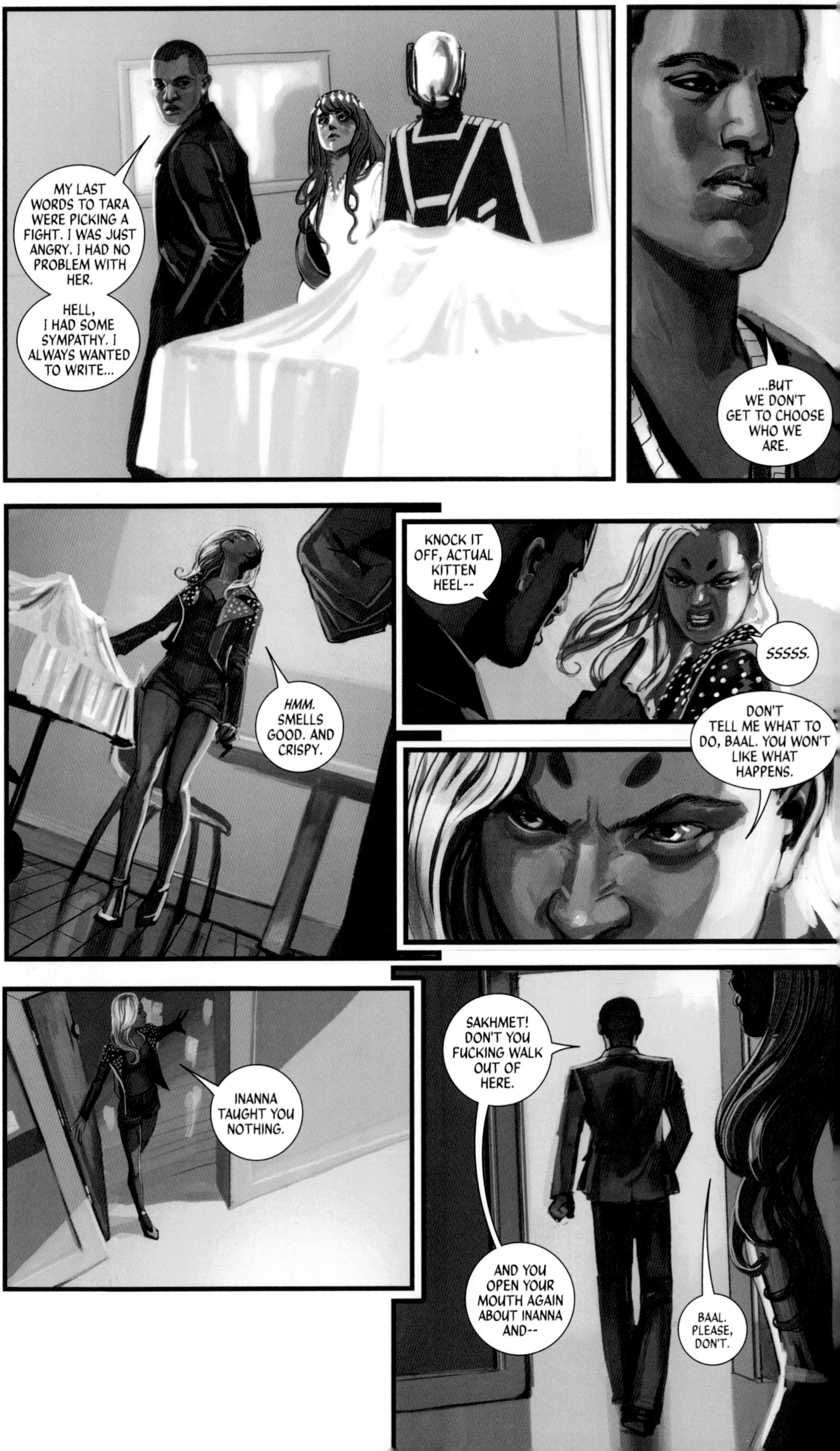
MY LAST WORDS TO TARA WERE PICKING A FIGHT. I WAS JUST ANGRY. I HAD NO PROBLEM WITH HER.
HELL, I HAD SOME SYMPATHY. I ALWAYS WANTED TO WRITE...
...BUT WE DON'T GET TO CHOOSE WHO WE ARE.
HMM. SMELLS GOOD. AND CRISPY.
KNOCK IT OFF, ACTUAL KITTEN HEEL--
SSSSS.
DON'T TELL ME WHAT TO DO, BAAL. YOU WON'T LIKE WHAT HAPPENS.
INANNA TAUGHT YOU NOTHING.
SAKHMET! DON'T YOU FUCKING WALK OUT OF HERE.
AND YOU OPEN YOUR MOUTH AGAIN ABOUT INANNA AND--
BAAL. PLEASE, DON'T.

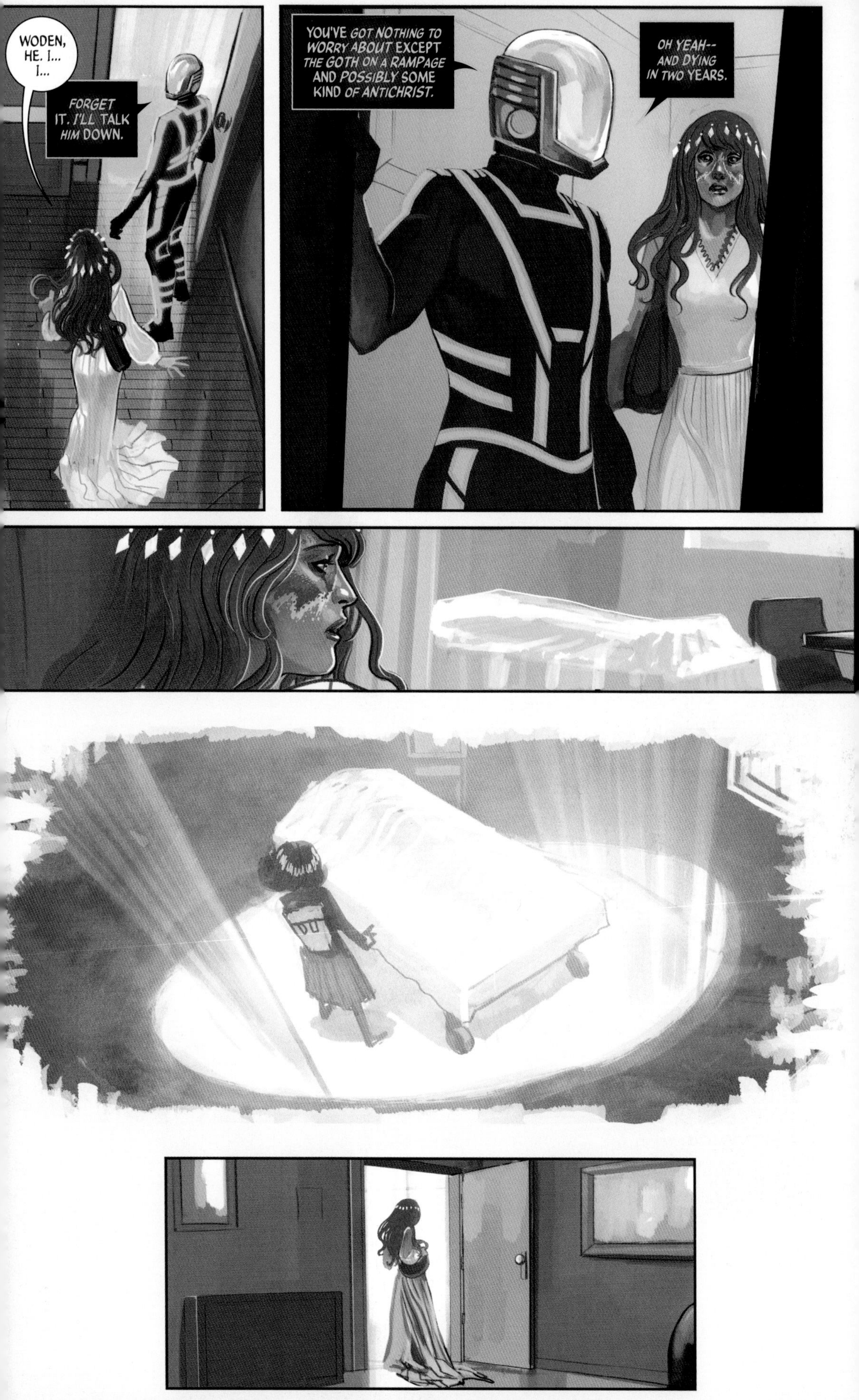
WODEN, HE. I... I...
FORGET IT. I'LL TALK HIM DOWN.
YOU'VE GOT NOTHING TO WORRY ABOUT EXCEPT THE GOTH ON A RAMPAGE AND POSSIBLY SOME KIND OF ANTICHRIST.
OH YEAH-- AND DYING IN TWO YEARS.

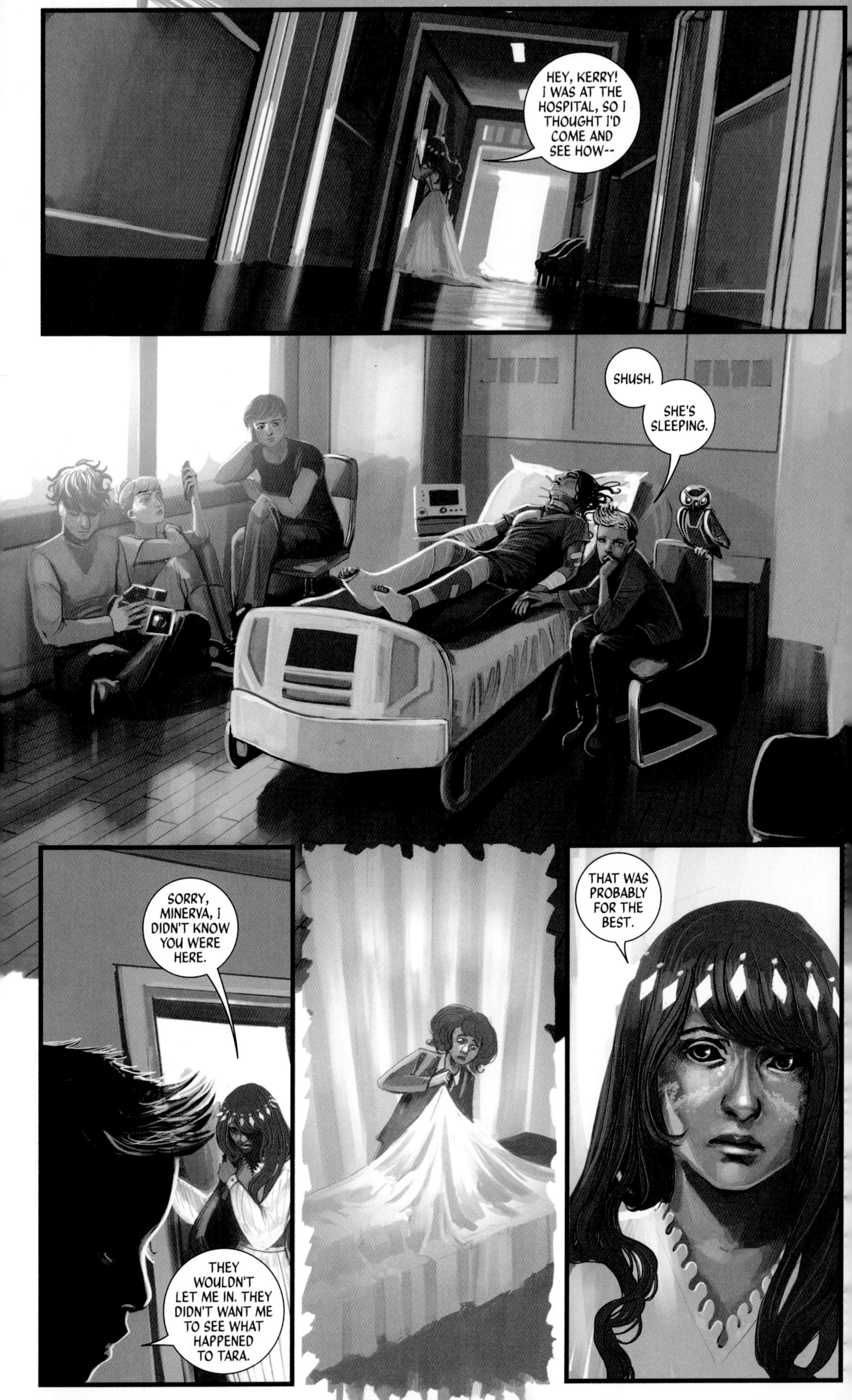
HEY, KERRY! I WAS AT THE HOSPITAL, SO I THOUGHT I'D COME AND SEE HOW--
SHUSH.
SHE'S SLEEPING.
SORRY, MINERVA, I DIDN'T KNOW YOU WERE HERE.
THEY WOULDN'T LET ME IN. THEY DIDN'T WANT ME TO SEE WHAT HAPPENED TO TARA.
THAT WAS PROBABLY FOR THE BEST.

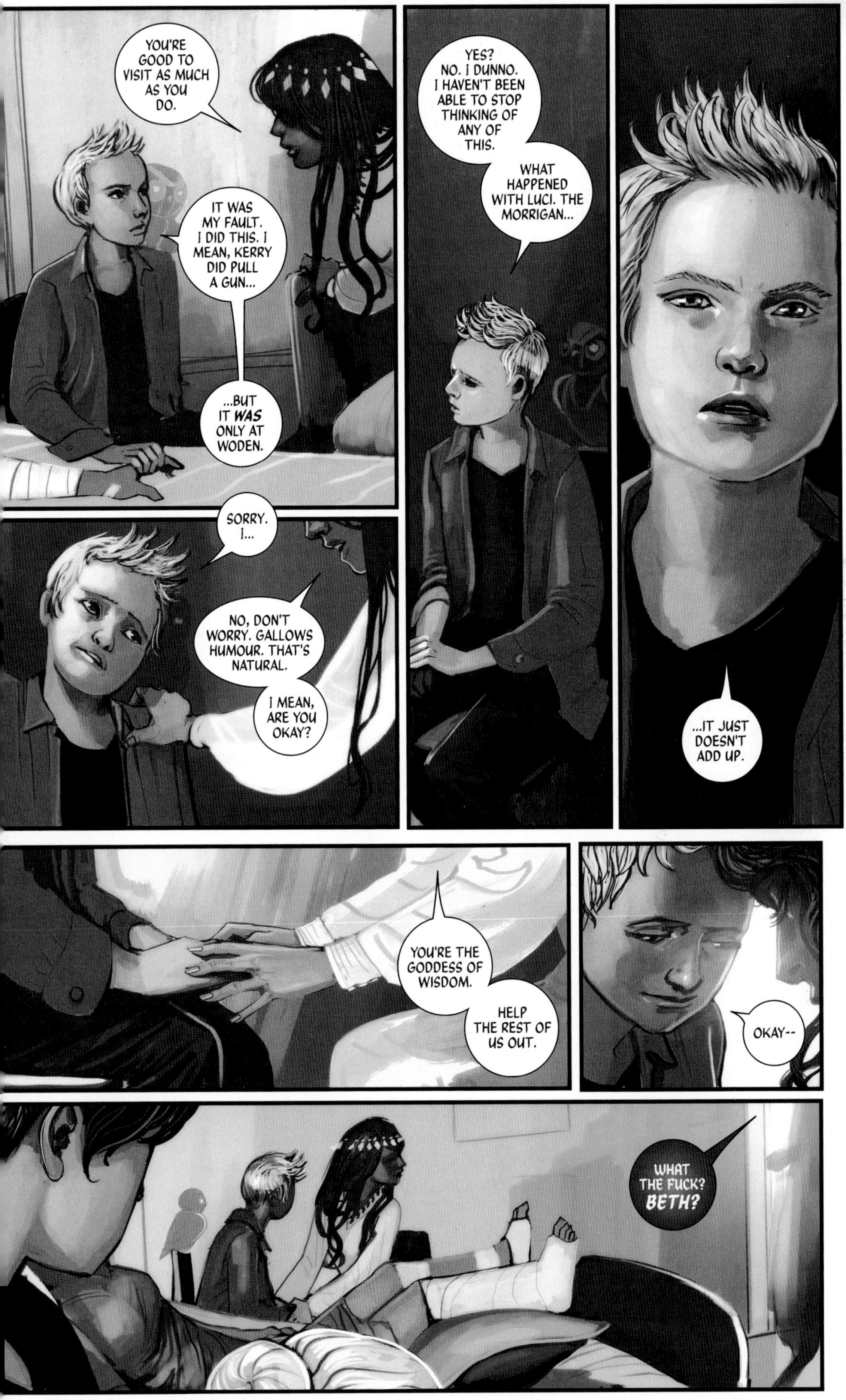
YOU'RE GOOD TO VISIT AS MUCH AS YOU DO.
IT WAS MY FAULT. I DID THIS. I MEAN, KERRY DID PULL A GUN...
...BUT IT WAS ONLY AT WODEN.
SORRY. I...
NO, DON'T WORRY. GALLOWS HUMOUR. THAT'S NATURAL.
I MEAN, ARE YOU OKAY?
YES? NO. I DUNNO. I HAVEN'T BEEN ABLE TO STOP THINKING OF ANY OF THIS.
WHAT HAPPENED WITH LUCI. THE MORRIGAN...
...IT JUST DOESN'T ADD UP.
YOU'RE THE GODDESS OF WISDOM.
HELP THE REST OF US OUT.
OKAY--
WHAT THE FUCK? BETH?

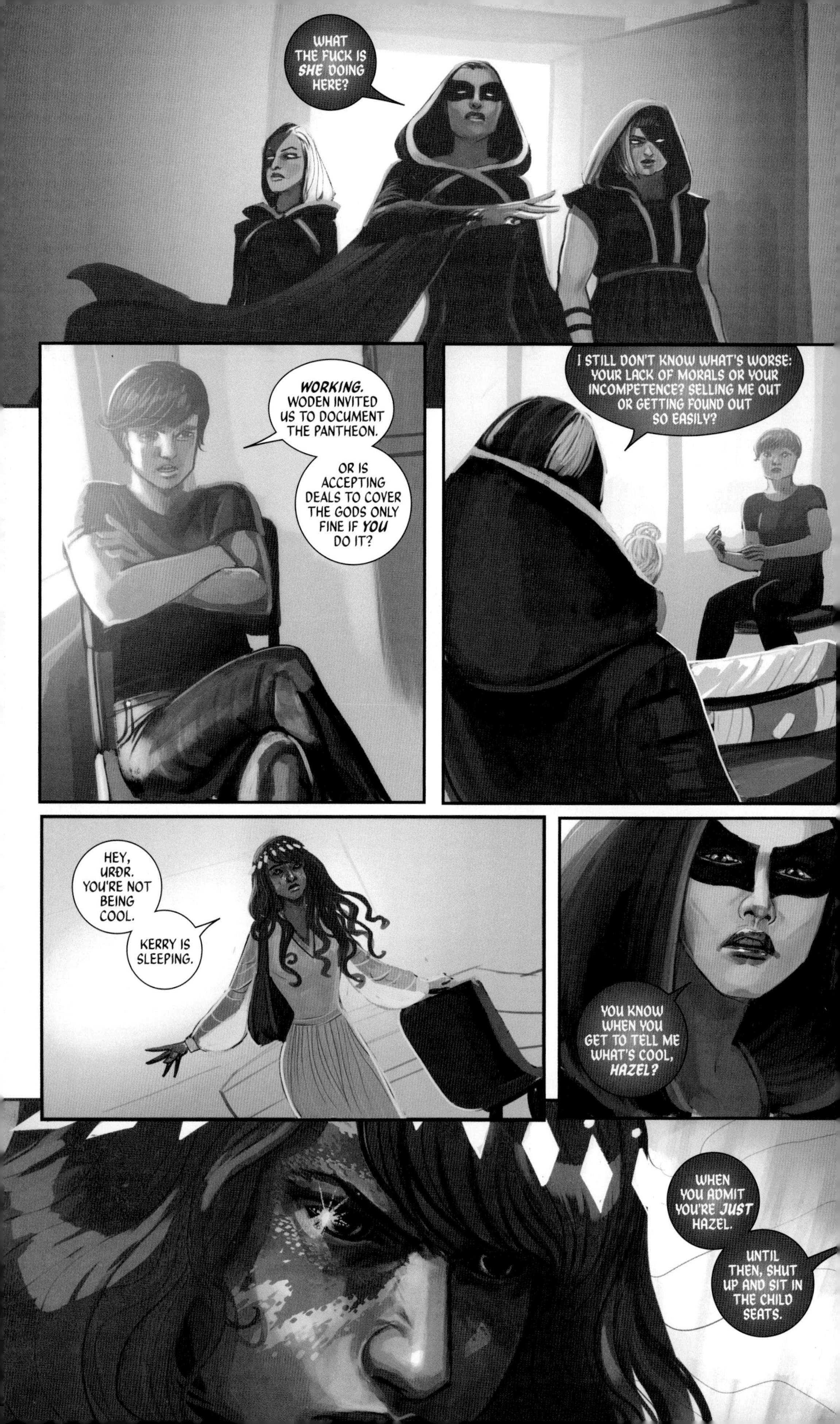

WHAT THE FUCK IS SHE DOING HERE?
WORKING. WODEN INVITED US TO DOCUMENT THE PANTHEON.
OR IS ACCEPTING DEALS TO COVER THE GODS ONLY FINE IF YOU DO IT?
I STILL DON'T KNOW WHAT'S WORSE: YOUR LACK OF MORALS OR YOUR INCOMPETENCE? SELLING ME OUT OR GETTING FOUND OUT SO EASILY?
HEY, URÐR. YOU'RE NOT BEING COOL.
KERRY IS SLEEPING.
YOU KNOW WHEN YOU GET TO TELL ME WHAT'S COOL, HAZEL?
WHEN YOU ADMIT YOU'RE JUST HAZEL.
UNTIL THEN, SHUT UP AND SIT IN THE CHILD SEATS.

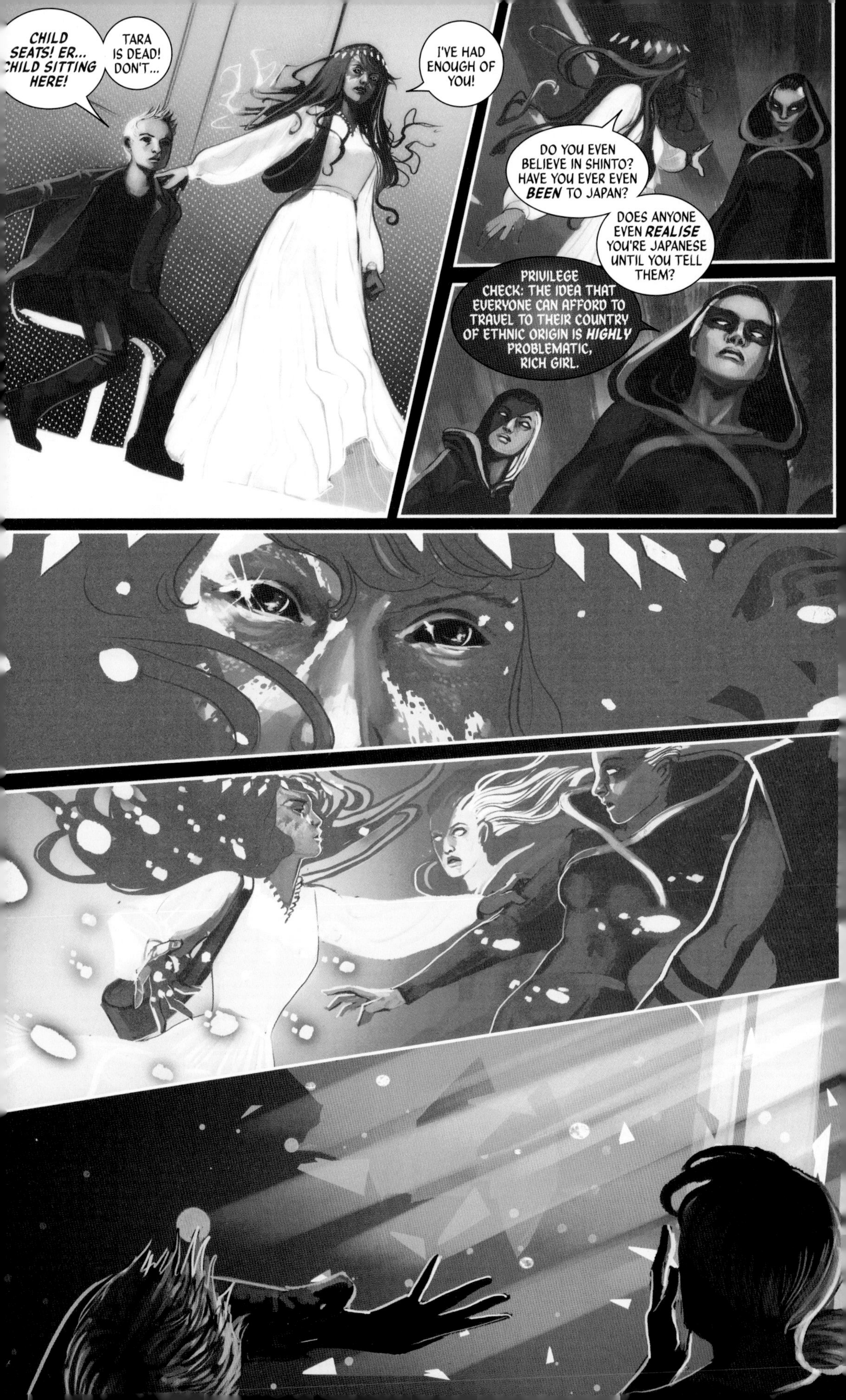
CHILD SEATS! ER... CHILD SITTING HERE!
TARA IS DEAD! DON'T...
I'VE HAD ENOUGH OF YOU!
DO YOU EVEN BELIEVE IN SHINTO? HAVE YOU EVER EVEN BEEN TO JAPAN?
DOES ANYONE EVEN REALISE YOU'RE JAPANESE UNTIL YOU TELL THEM?
PRIVILEGE CHECK: THE IDEA THAT EVERYONE CAN AFFORD TO TRAVEL TO THEIR COUNTRY OF ETHNIC ORIGIN IS HIGHLY PROBLEMATIC, RICH GIRL.

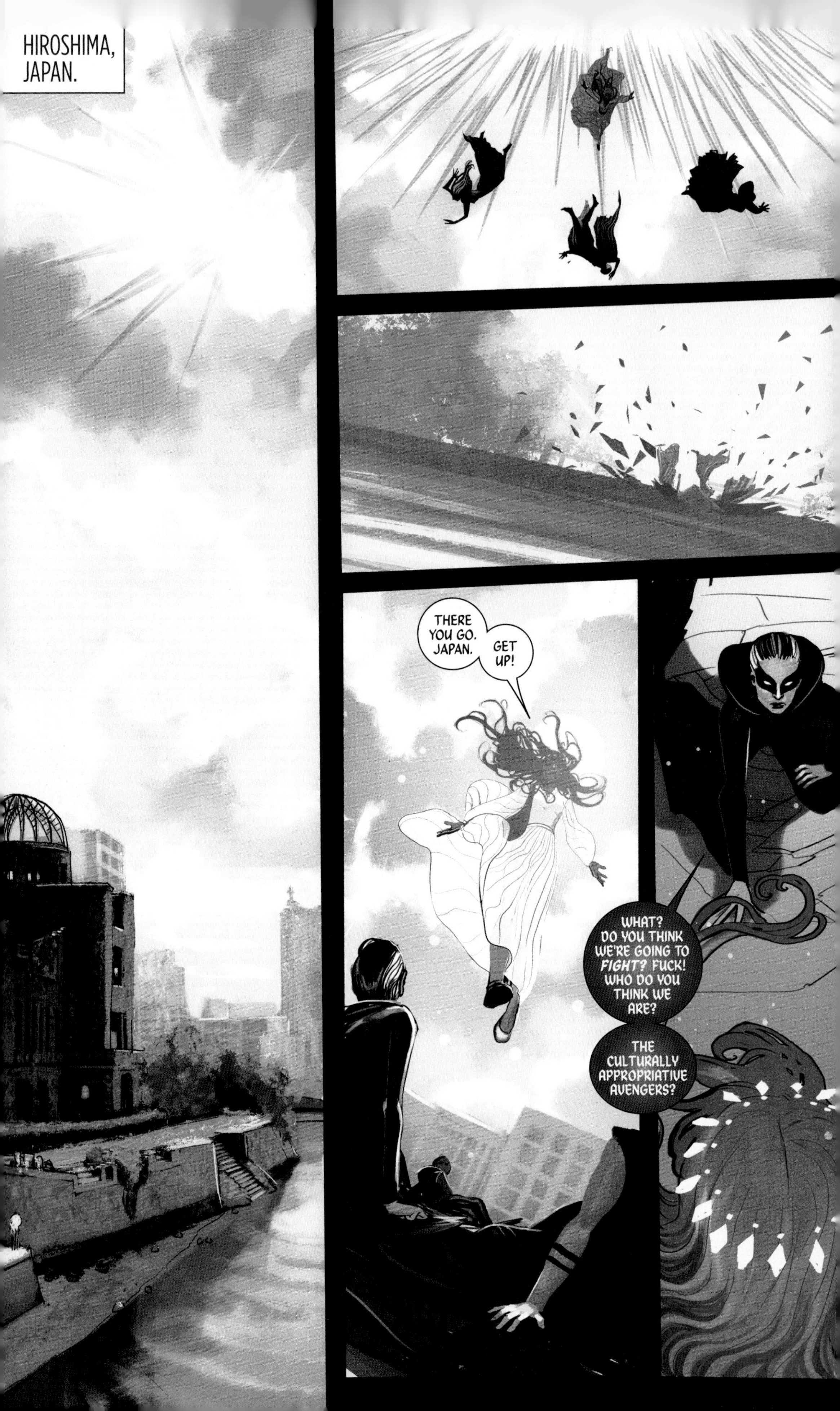
HIROSHIMA, JAPAN.
THERE YOU GO. JAPAN.
GET UP!
WHAT? DO YOU THINK WE'RE GOING TO *FIGHT?* FUCK! WHO DO YOU THINK WE ARE?
THE CULTURALLY APPROPRIATIVE AVENGERS?

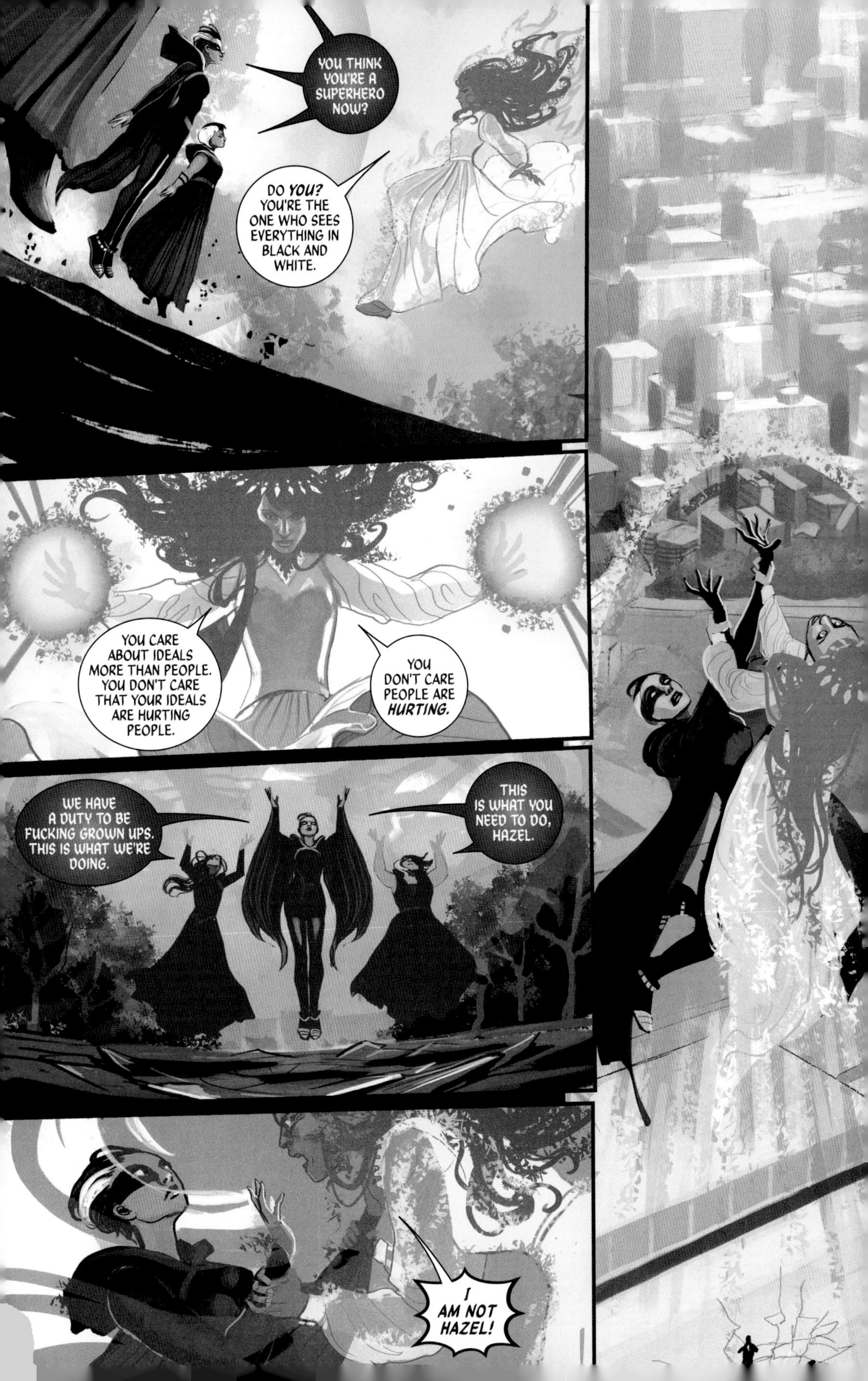
YOU THINK YOU'RE A SUPERHERO NOW?
DO *YOU?* YOU'RE THE ONE WHO SEES EVERYTHING IN BLACK AND WHITE.
YOU CARE ABOUT IDEALS MORE THAN PEOPLE. YOU DON'T CARE THAT YOUR IDEALS ARE HURTING PEOPLE.
YOU DON'T CARE PEOPLE ARE *HURTING.*
WE HAVE A DUTY TO BE FUCKING GROWN UPS. THIS IS WHAT WE'RE DOING.
THIS IS WHAT YOU NEED TO DO, HAZEL.
I AM NOT HAZEL!

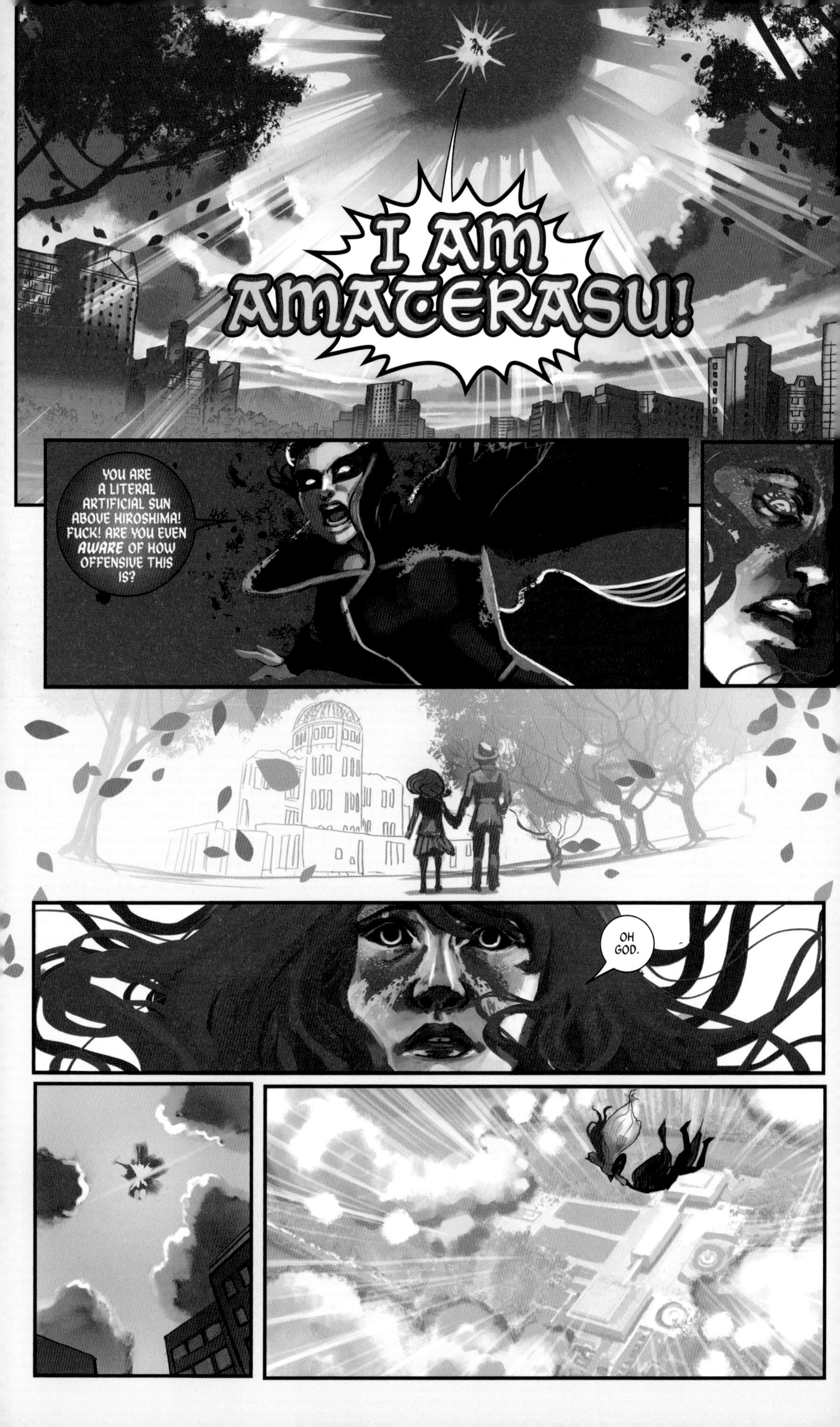
I AM AMATERASU!
YOU ARE A LITERAL ARTIFICIAL SUN ABOVE HIROSHIMA! FUCK! ARE YOU EVEN AWARE OF HOW OFFENSIVE THIS IS?
OH GOD.

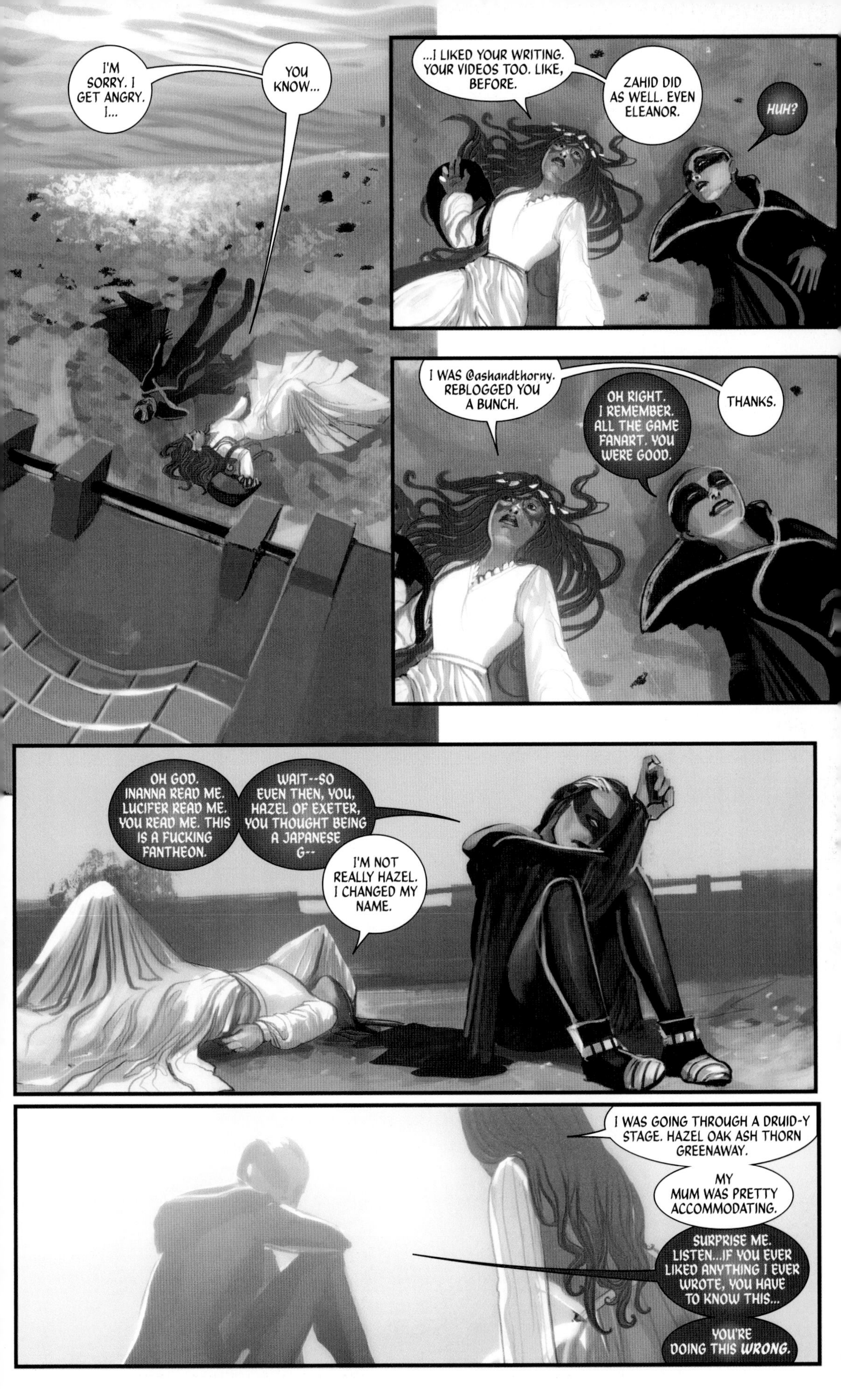
I'M SORRY. I GET ANGRY. I...
YOU KNOW...
...I LIKED YOUR WRITING. YOUR VIDEOS TOO. LIKE, BEFORE.
ZAHID DID AS WELL. EVEN ELEANOR.
HUH?
I WAS @ashandthorny. REBLOGGED YOU A BUNCH.
OH RIGHT. I REMEMBER. ALL THE GAME FANART. YOU WERE GOOD.
THANKS.
OH GOD. INANNA READ ME. LUCIFER READ ME. YOU READ ME. THIS IS A FUCKING FANTHEON.
WAIT--SO EVEN THEN, YOU, HAZEL OF EXETER, YOU THOUGHT BEING A JAPANESE G--
I'M NOT REALLY HAZEL. I CHANGED MY NAME.
I WAS GOING THROUGH A DRUID-Y STAGE. HAZEL OAK ASH THORN GREENAWAY.
MY MUM WAS PRETTY ACCOMMODATING.
SURPRISE ME. LISTEN...IF YOU EVER LIKED ANYTHING I EVER WROTE, YOU HAVE TO KNOW THIS...
YOU'RE DOING THIS *WRONG*.

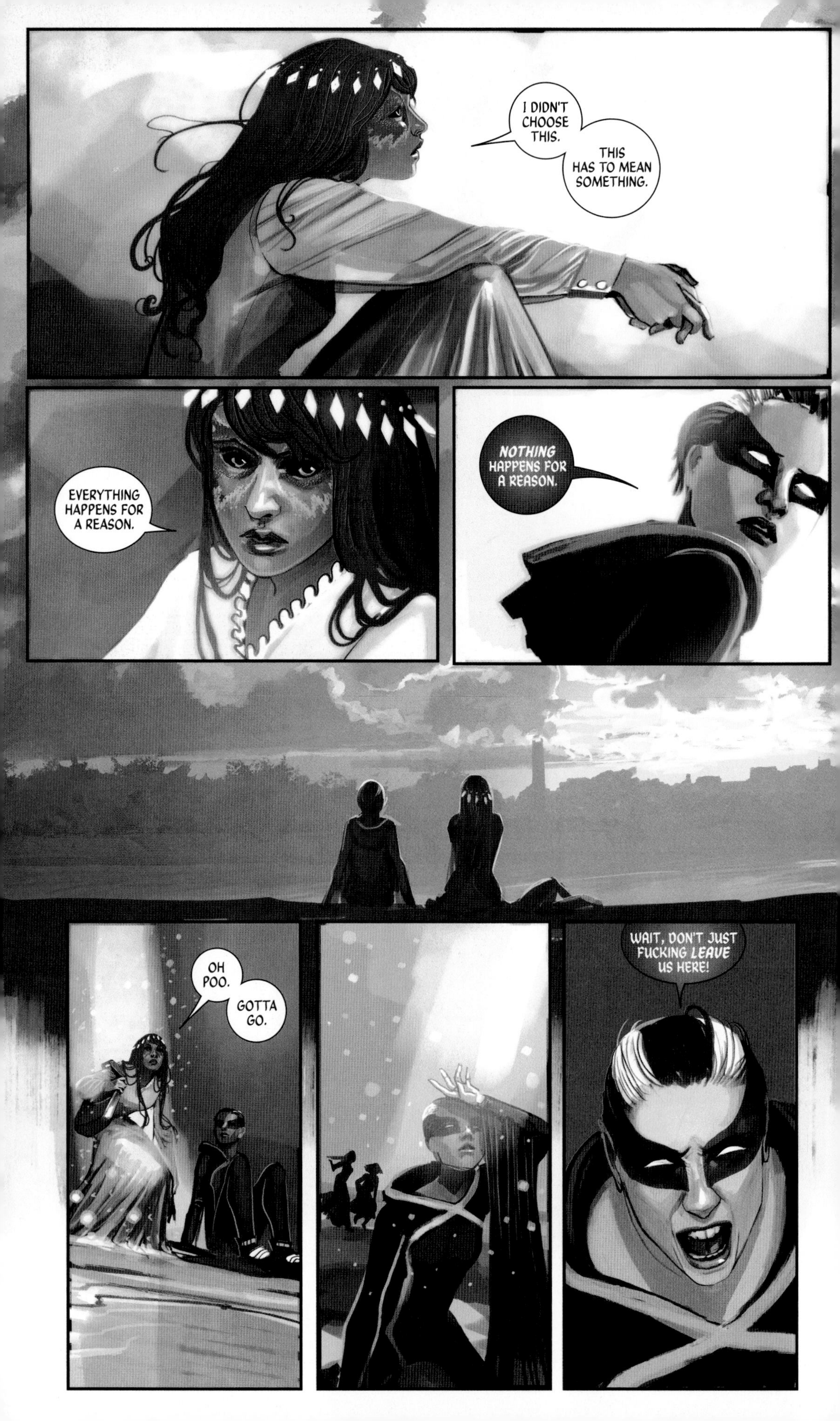
I DIDN'T CHOOSE THIS.
THIS HAS TO MEAN SOMETHING.
EVERYTHING HAPPENS FOR A REASON.
NOTHING HAPPENS FOR A REASON.
OH POO.
GOTTA GO.
WAIT, DON'T JUST FUCKING LEAVE US HERE!

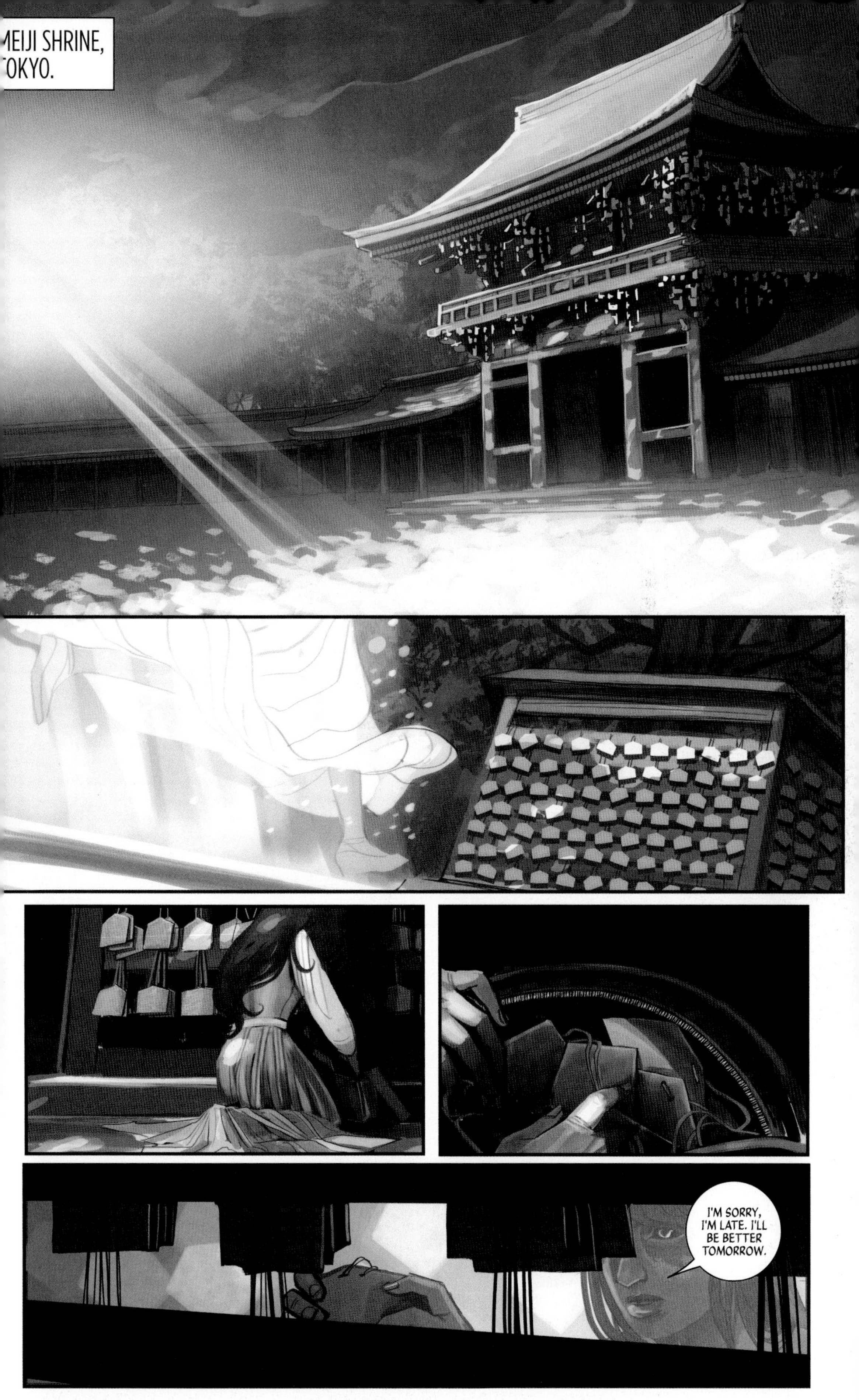

MEIJI SHRINE, TOKYO.
I'M SORRY, I'M LATE. I'LL BE BETTER TOMORROW.

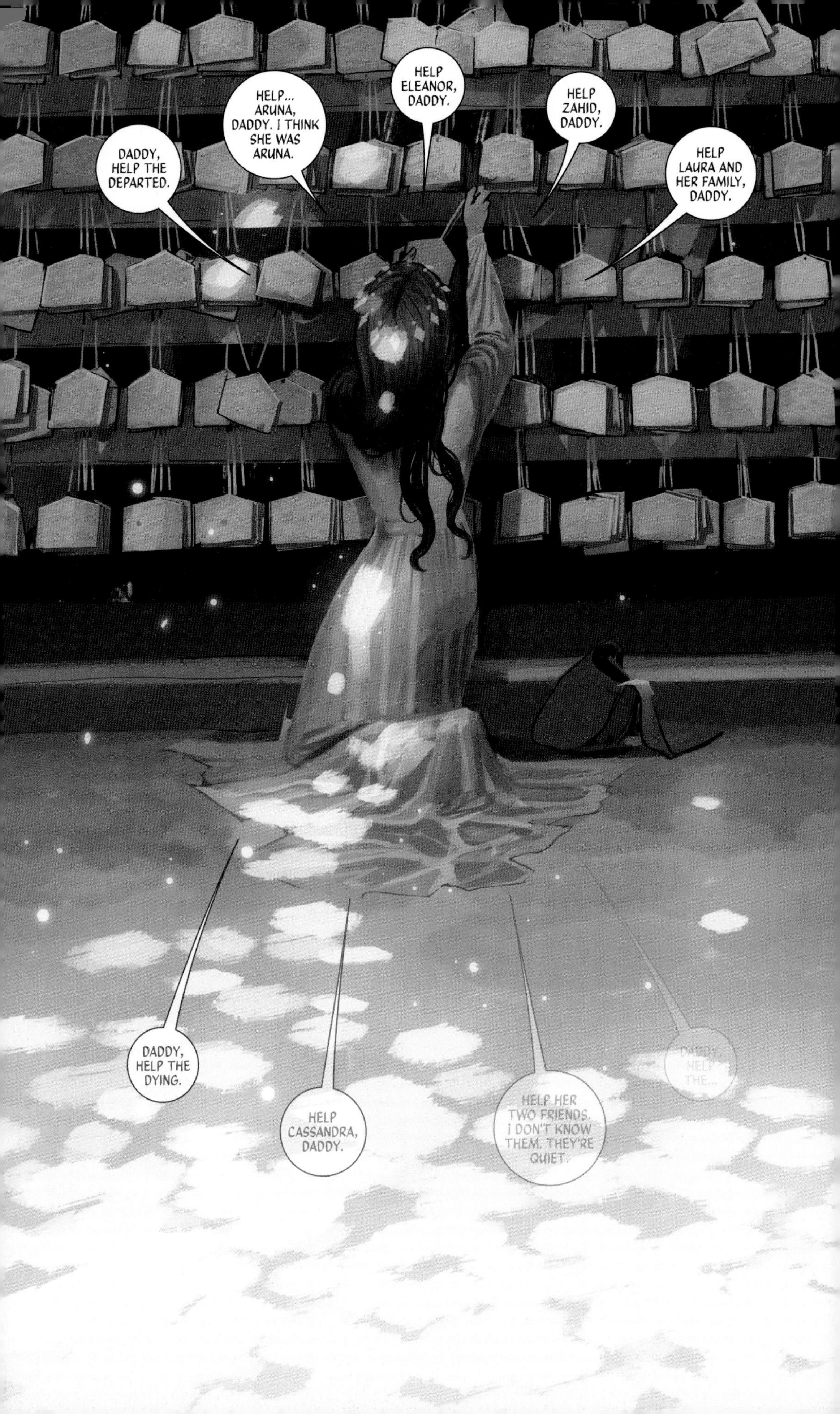
DADDY, HELP THE DEPARTED.
HELP... ARUNA, DADDY. I THINK SHE WAS ARUNA.
HELP ELEANOR, DADDY.
HELP ZAHID, DADDY.
HELP LAURA AND HER FAMILY, DADDY.
DADDY, HELP THE DYING.
HELP CASSANDRA, DADDY.
HELP HER TWO FRIENDS. I DON'T KNOW THEM. THEY'RE QUIET.
DADDY, HELP THE...

PRAYER TO GOD

18 AUGUST 2014

16

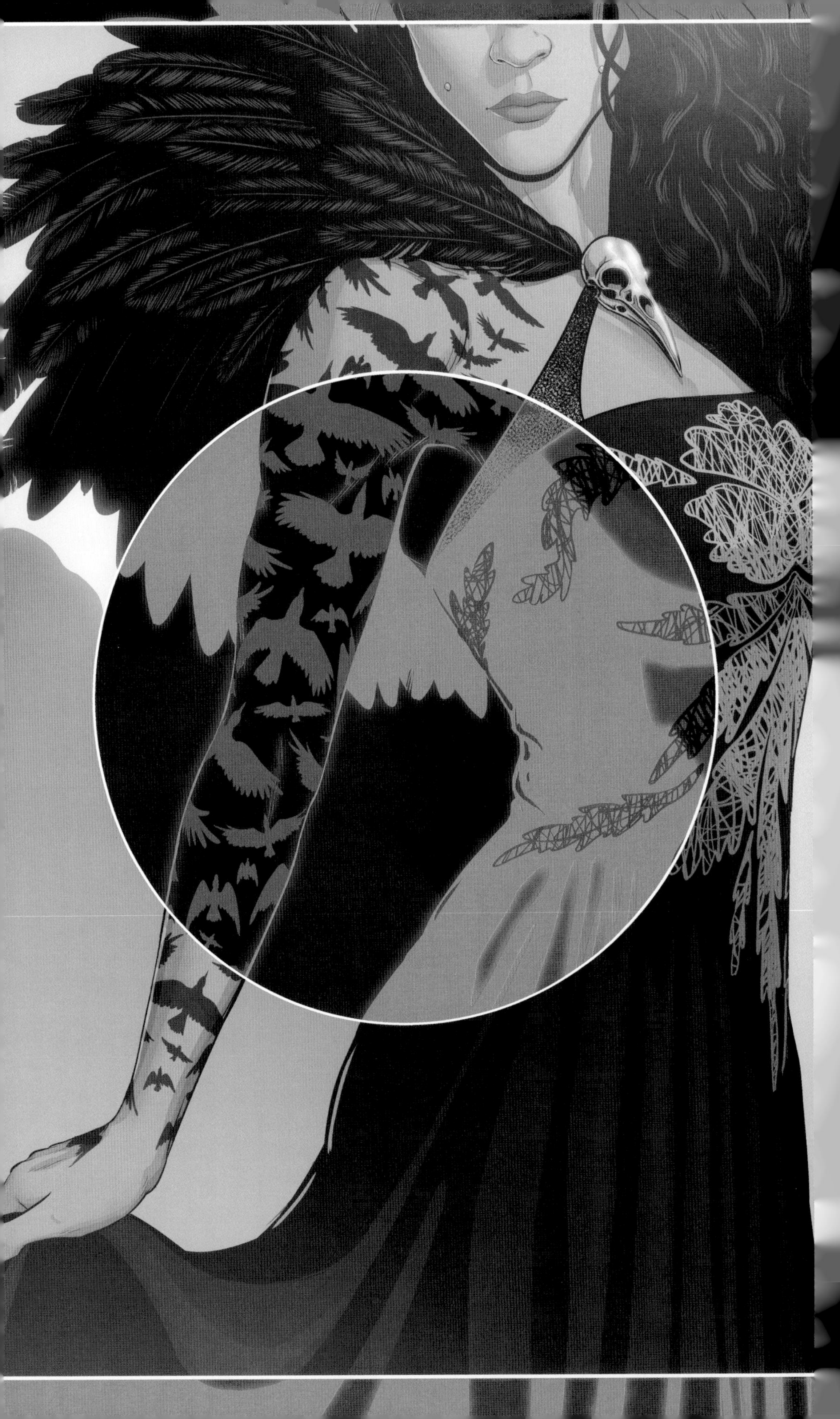

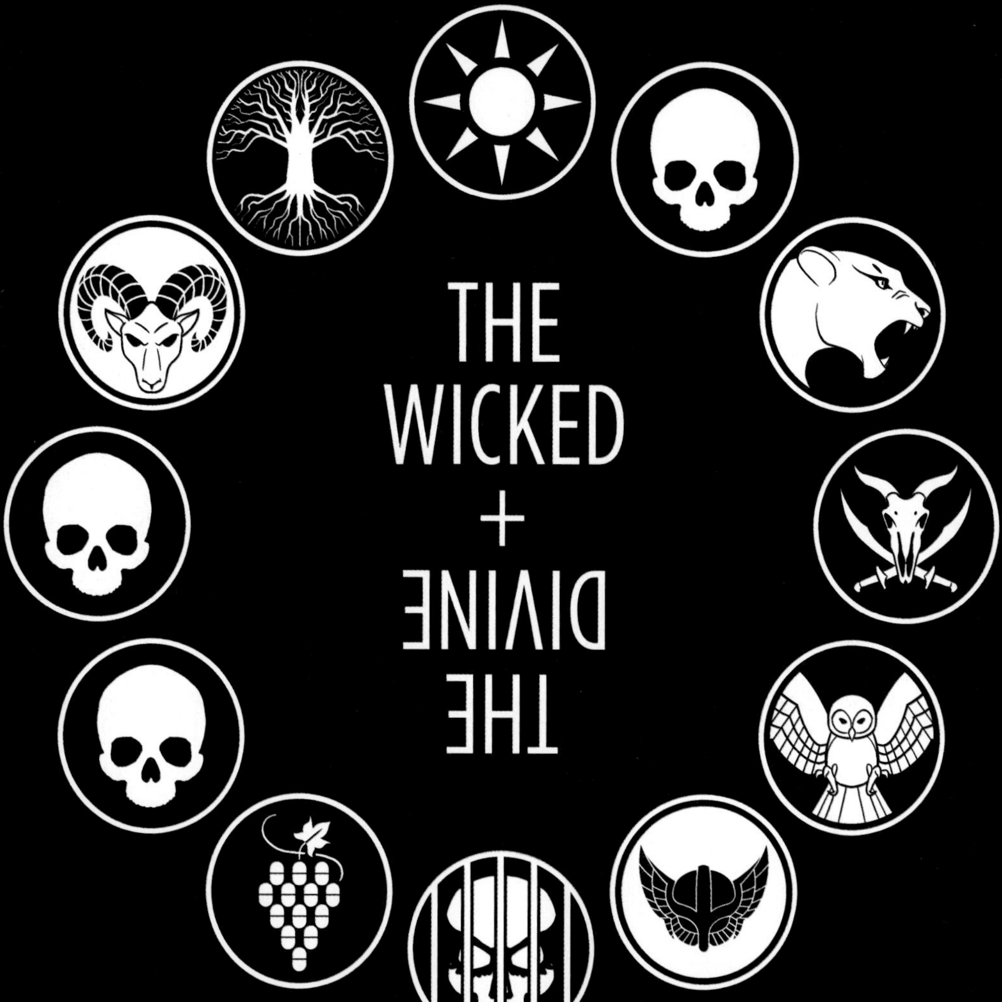
THE
WICKED
+
THE
DIVINE

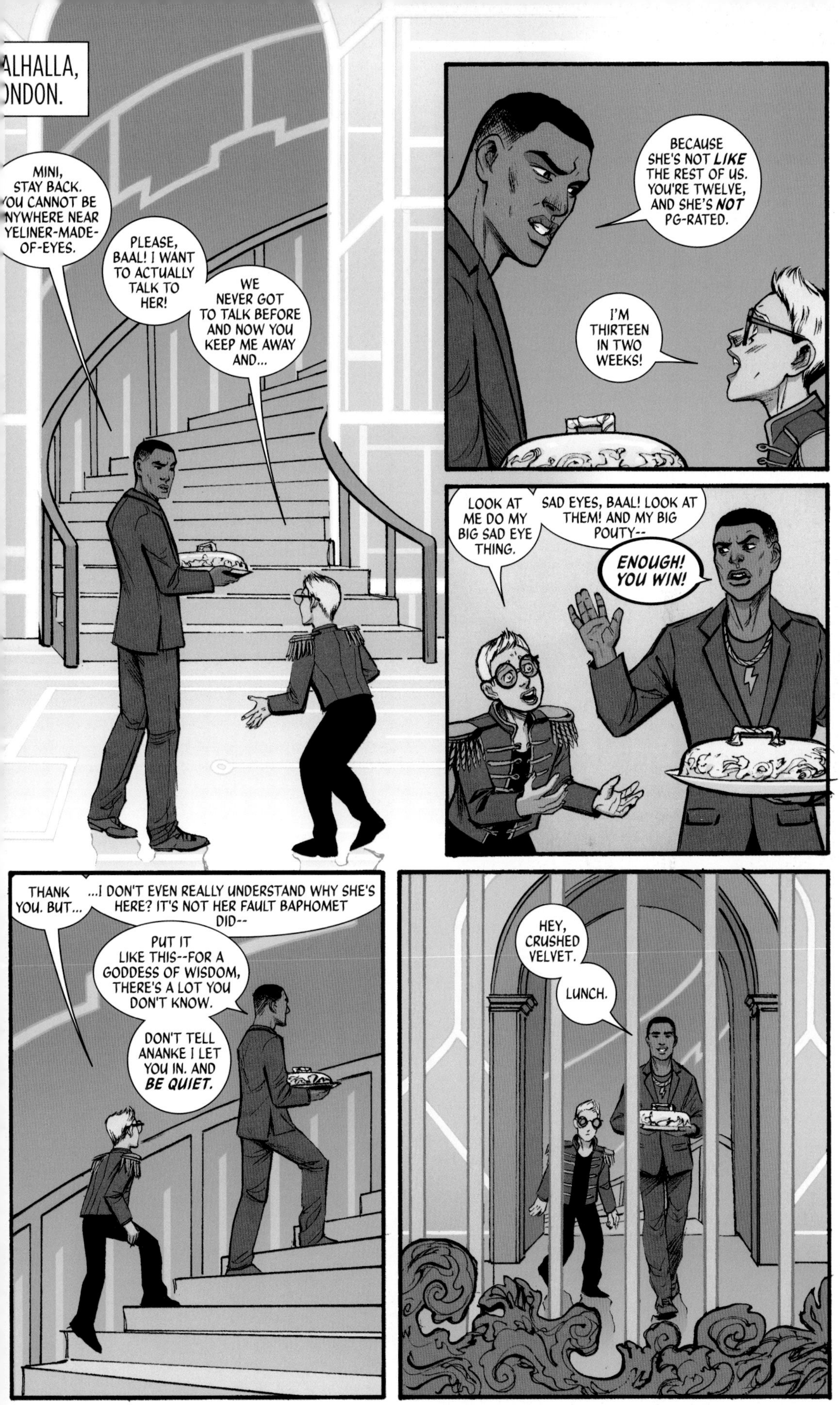

ALHALLA,
ONDON.
MINI, STAY BACK. YOU CANNOT BE NYWHERE NEAR YELINER-MADE-OF-EYES.
PLEASE, BAAL! I WANT TO ACTUALLY TALK TO HER!
WE NEVER GOT TO TALK BEFORE AND NOW YOU KEEP ME AWAY AND...
BECAUSE SHE'S NOT LIKE THE REST OF US. YOU'RE TWELVE, AND SHE'S NOT PG-RATED.
I'M THIRTEEN IN TWO WEEKS!
LOOK AT ME DO MY BIG SAD EYE THING.
SAD EYES, BAAL! LOOK AT THEM! AND MY BIG POUTY--
ENOUGH! YOU WIN!
THANK YOU. BUT...
...I DON'T EVEN REALLY UNDERSTAND WHY SHE'S HERE? IT'S NOT HER FAULT BAPHOMET DID--
PUT IT LIKE THIS--FOR A GODDESS OF WISDOM, THERE'S A LOT YOU DON'T KNOW.
DON'T TELL ANANKE I LET YOU IN. AND BE QUIET.
HEY, CRUSHED VELVET.
LUNCH.

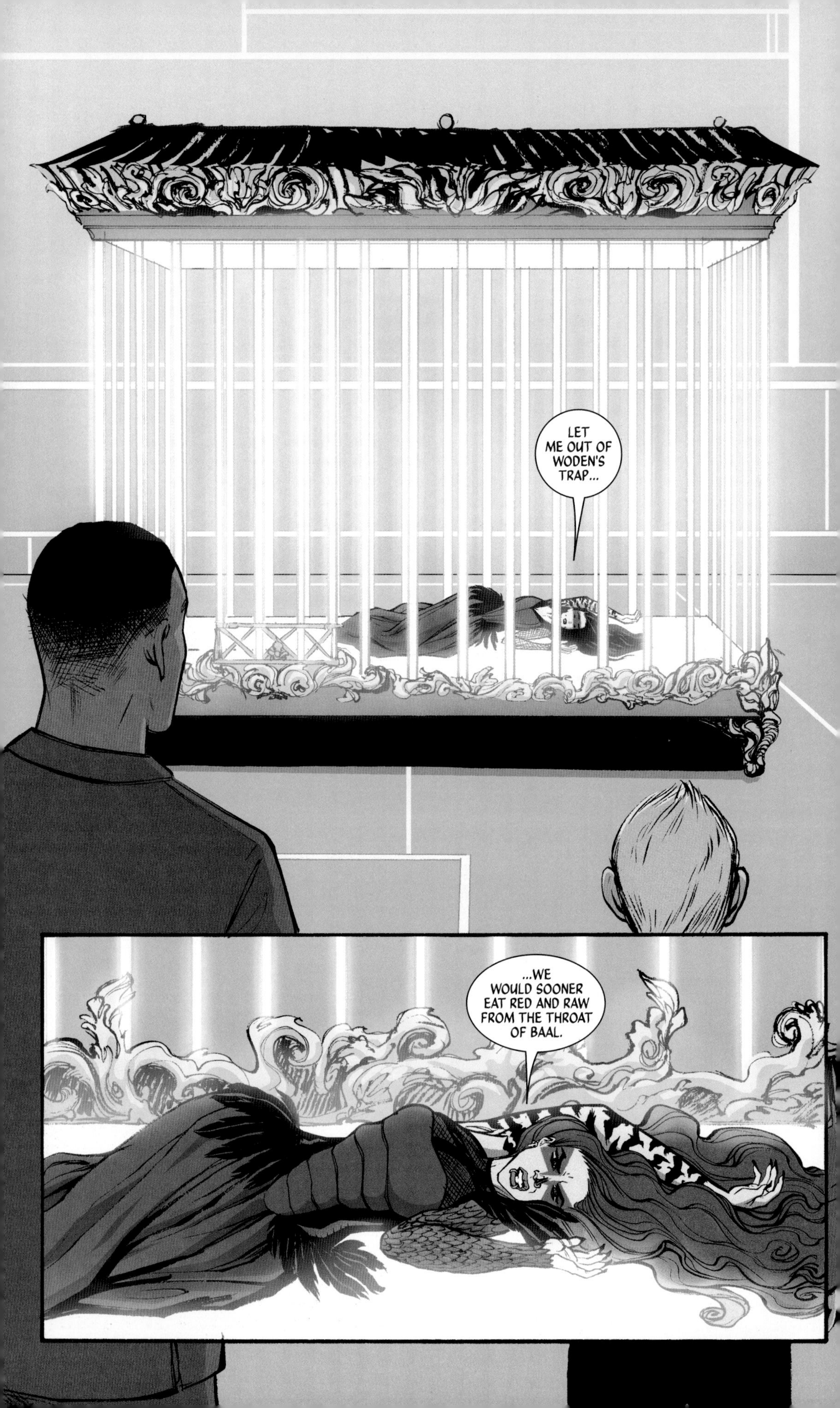
LET ME OUT OF WODEN'S TRAP...
...WE WOULD SOONER EAT RED AND RAW FROM THE THROAT OF BAAL.

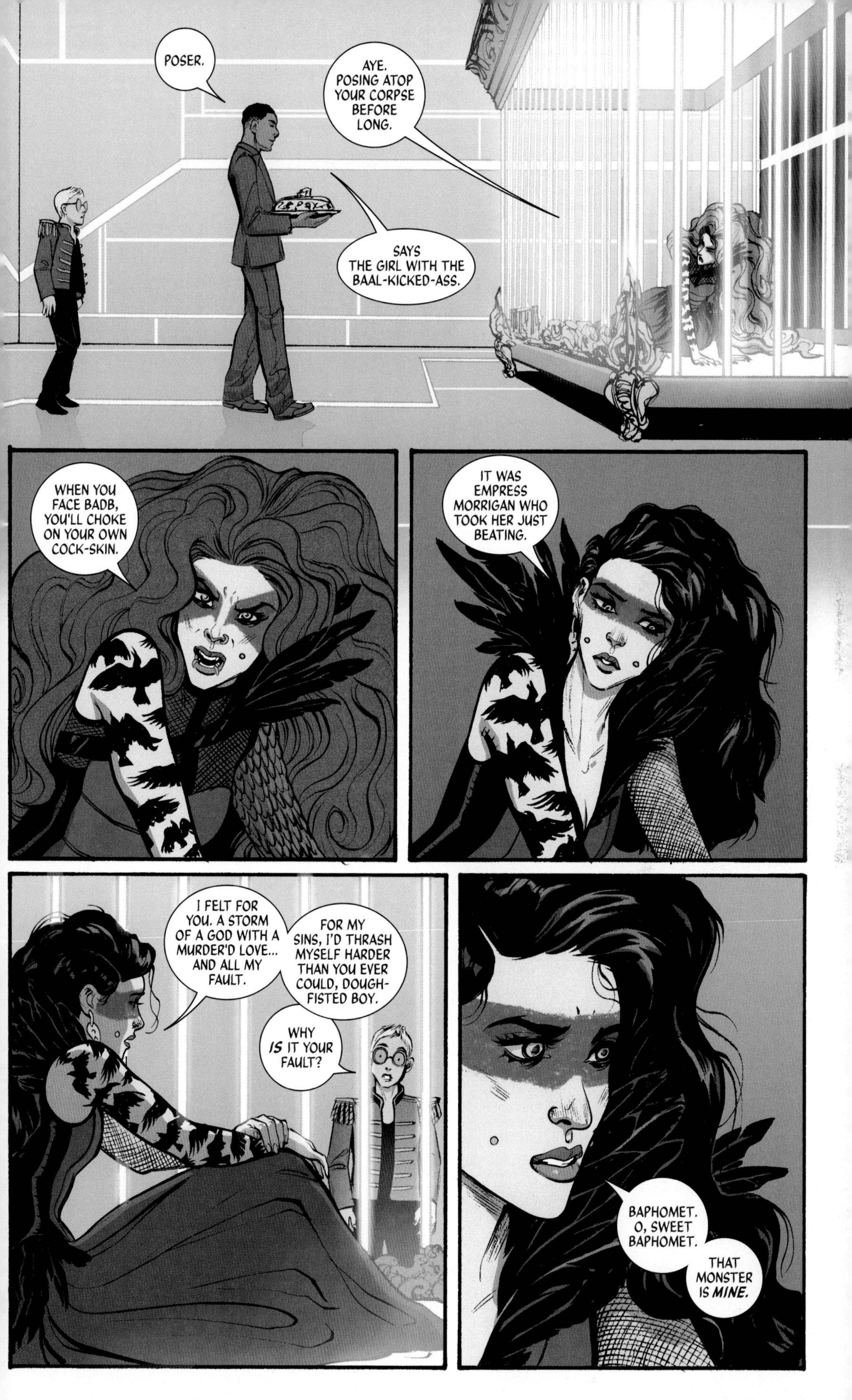
POSER.
AYE. POSING ATOP YOUR CORPSE BEFORE LONG.
SAYS THE GIRL WITH THE BAAL-KICKED-ASS.
WHEN YOU FACE BADB, YOU'LL CHOKE ON YOUR OWN COCK-SKIN.
IT WAS EMPRESS MORRIGAN WHO TOOK HER JUST BEATING.
I FELT FOR YOU. A STORM OF A GOD WITH A MURDER'D LOVE... AND ALL MY FAULT.
FOR MY SINS, I'D THRASH MYSELF HARDER THAN YOU EVER COULD, DOUGH-FISTED BOY.
WHY *IS* IT YOUR FAULT?
BAPHOMET. O, SWEET BAPHOMET.
THAT MONSTER IS ***MINE.***

NONE MORE

2012–2014

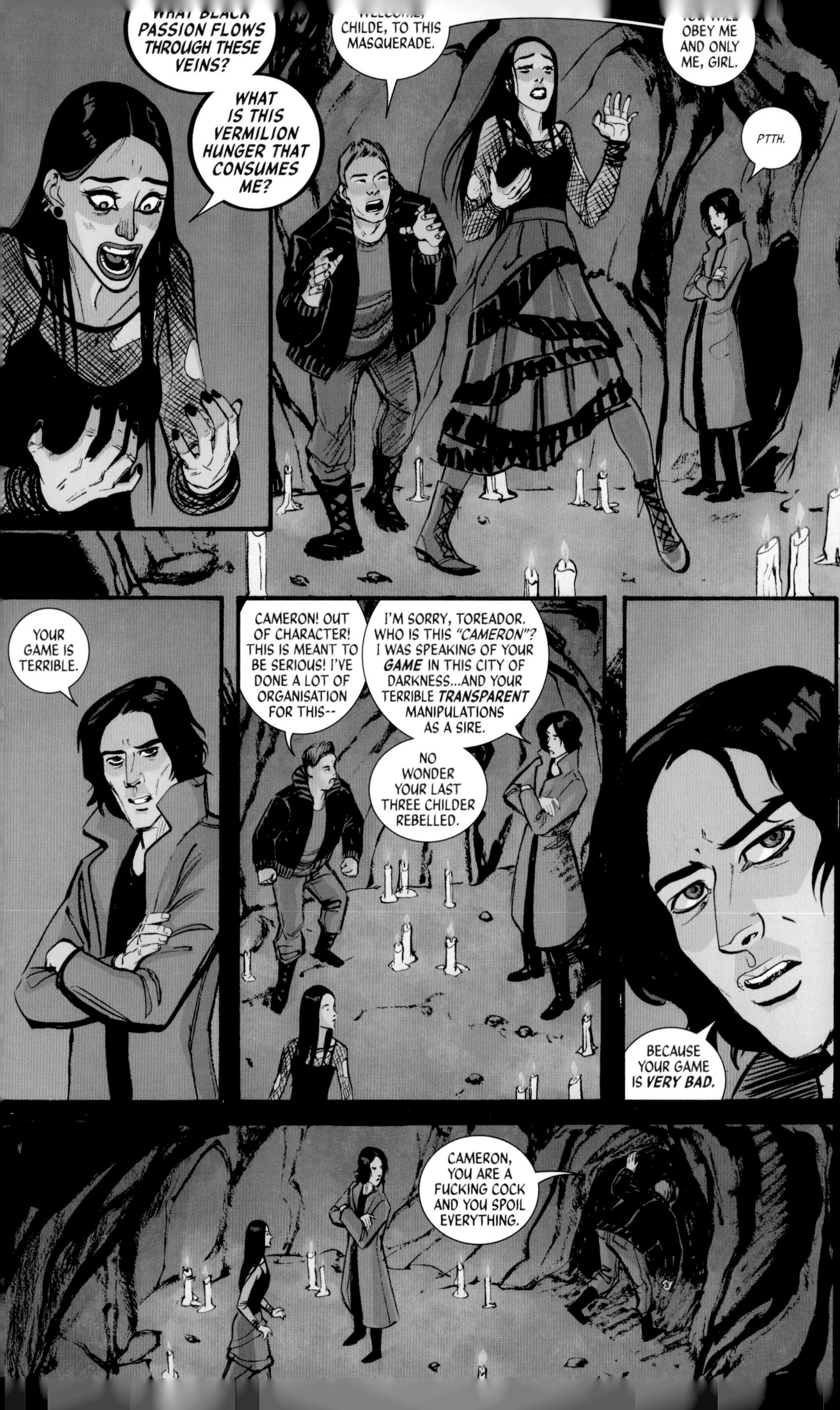
PASSION FLOWS THROUGH THESE VEINS?
WHAT IS THIS VERMILION HUNGER THAT CONSUMES ME?
CHILDE, TO THIS MASQUERADE.
OBEY ME AND ONLY ME, GIRL.
PTTH.
YOUR GAME IS TERRIBLE.
CAMERON! OUT OF CHARACTER! THIS IS MEANT TO BE SERIOUS! I'VE DONE A LOT OF ORGANISATION FOR THIS--
I'M SORRY, TOREADOR. WHO IS THIS "CAMERON"? I WAS SPEAKING OF YOUR GAME IN THIS CITY OF DARKNESS...AND YOUR TERRIBLE TRANSPARENT MANIPULATIONS AS A SIRE.
NO WONDER YOUR LAST THREE CHILDER REBELLED.
BECAUSE YOUR GAME IS VERY BAD.
CAMERON, YOU ARE A FUCKING COCK AND YOU SPOIL EVERYTHING.

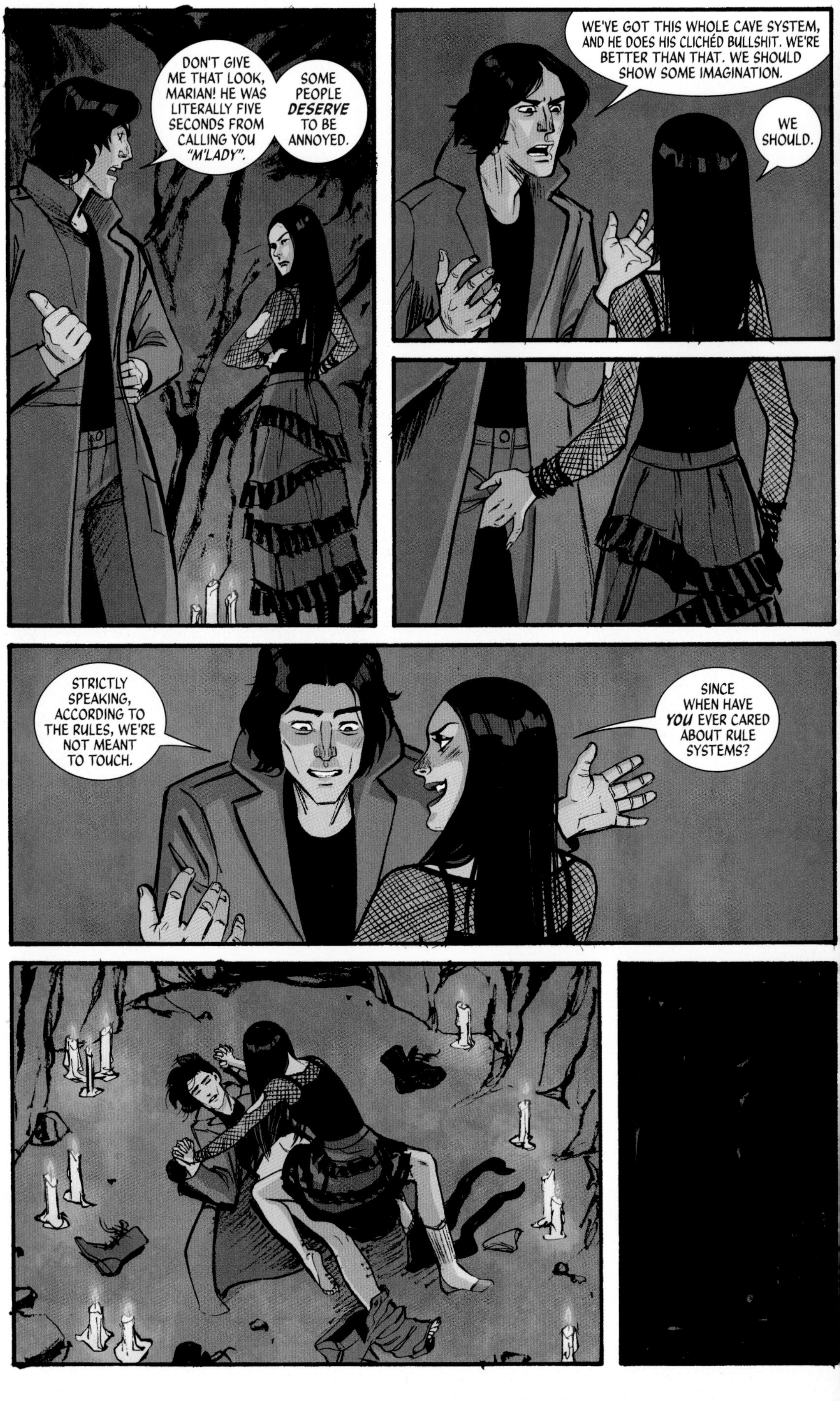
DON'T GIVE ME THAT LOOK, MARIAN! HE WAS LITERALLY FIVE SECONDS FROM CALLING YOU "M'LADY".
SOME PEOPLE DESERVE TO BE ANNOYED.
WE'VE GOT THIS WHOLE CAVE SYSTEM, AND HE DOES HIS CLICHÉD BULLSHIT. WE'RE BETTER THAN THAT. WE SHOULD SHOW SOME IMAGINATION.
WE SHOULD.
STRICTLY SPEAKING, ACCORDING TO THE RULES, WE'RE NOT MEANT TO TOUCH.
SINCE WHEN HAVE YOU EVER CARED ABOUT RULE SYSTEMS?

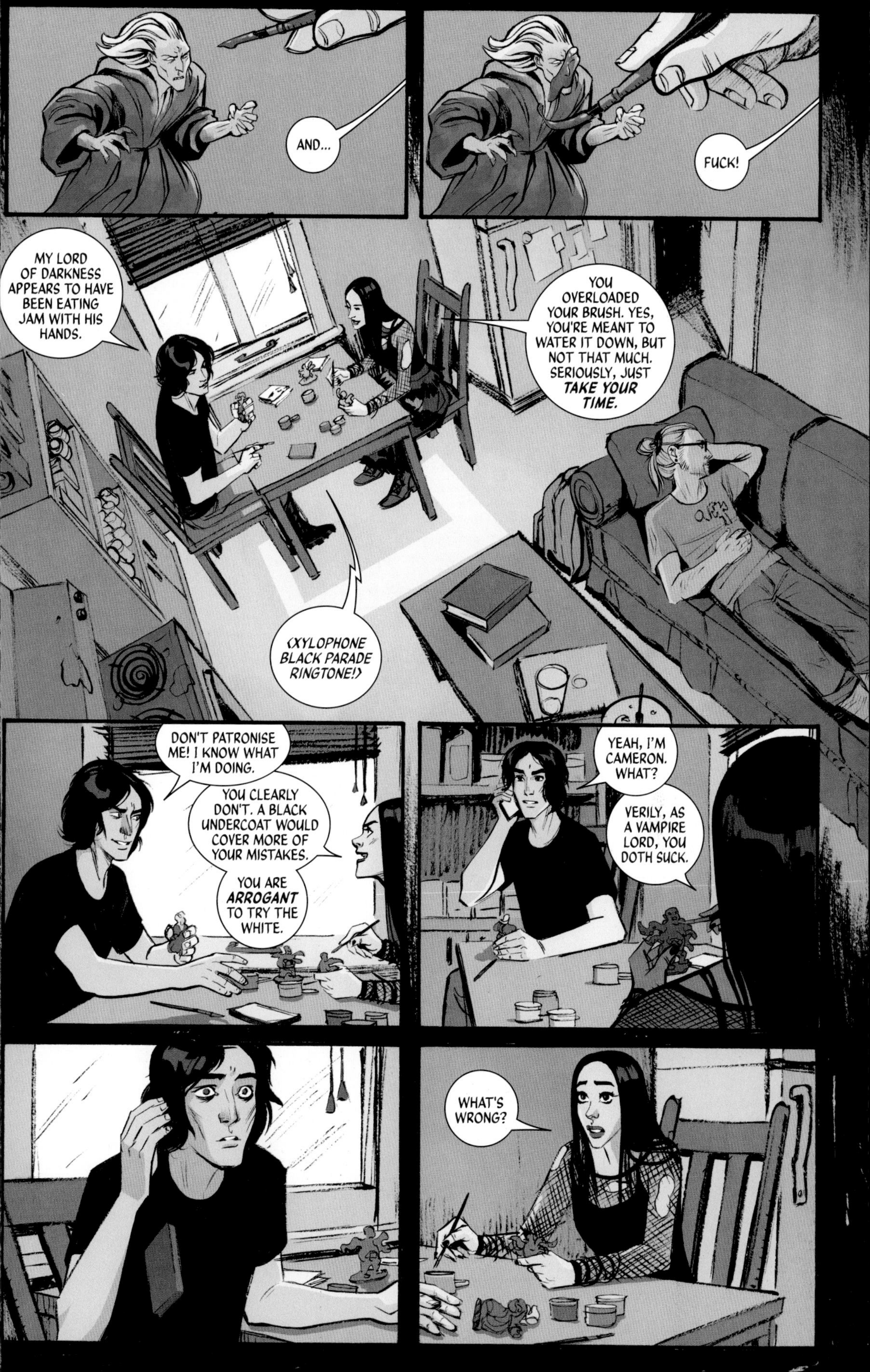
AND...
FUCK!
MY LORD OF DARKNESS APPEARS TO HAVE BEEN EATING JAM WITH HIS HANDS.
YOU OVERLOADED YOUR BRUSH. YES, YOU'RE MEANT TO WATER IT DOWN, BUT NOT THAT MUCH. SERIOUSLY, JUST TAKE YOUR TIME.
<XYLOPHONE BLACK PARADE RINGTONE!>
DON'T PATRONISE ME! I KNOW WHAT I'M DOING.
YOU CLEARLY DON'T. A BLACK UNDERCOAT WOULD COVER MORE OF YOUR MISTAKES.
YOU ARE ARROGANT TO TRY THE WHITE.
YEAH, I'M CAMERON. WHAT?
VERILY, AS A VAMPIRE LORD, YOU DOTH SUCK.
WHAT'S WRONG?

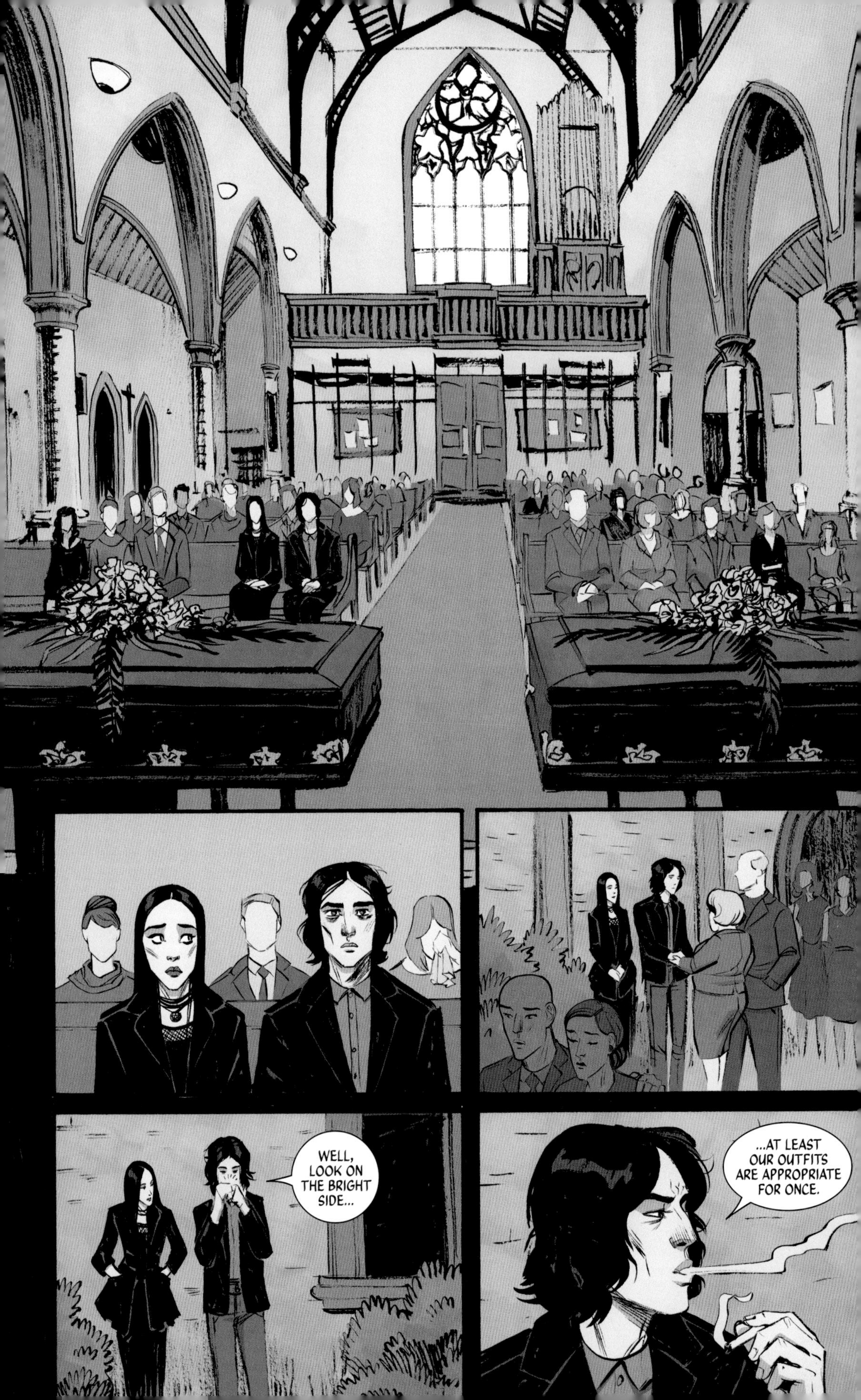
WELL, LOOK ON THE BRIGHT SIDE...
...AT LEAST OUR OUTFITS ARE APPROPRIATE FOR ONCE.

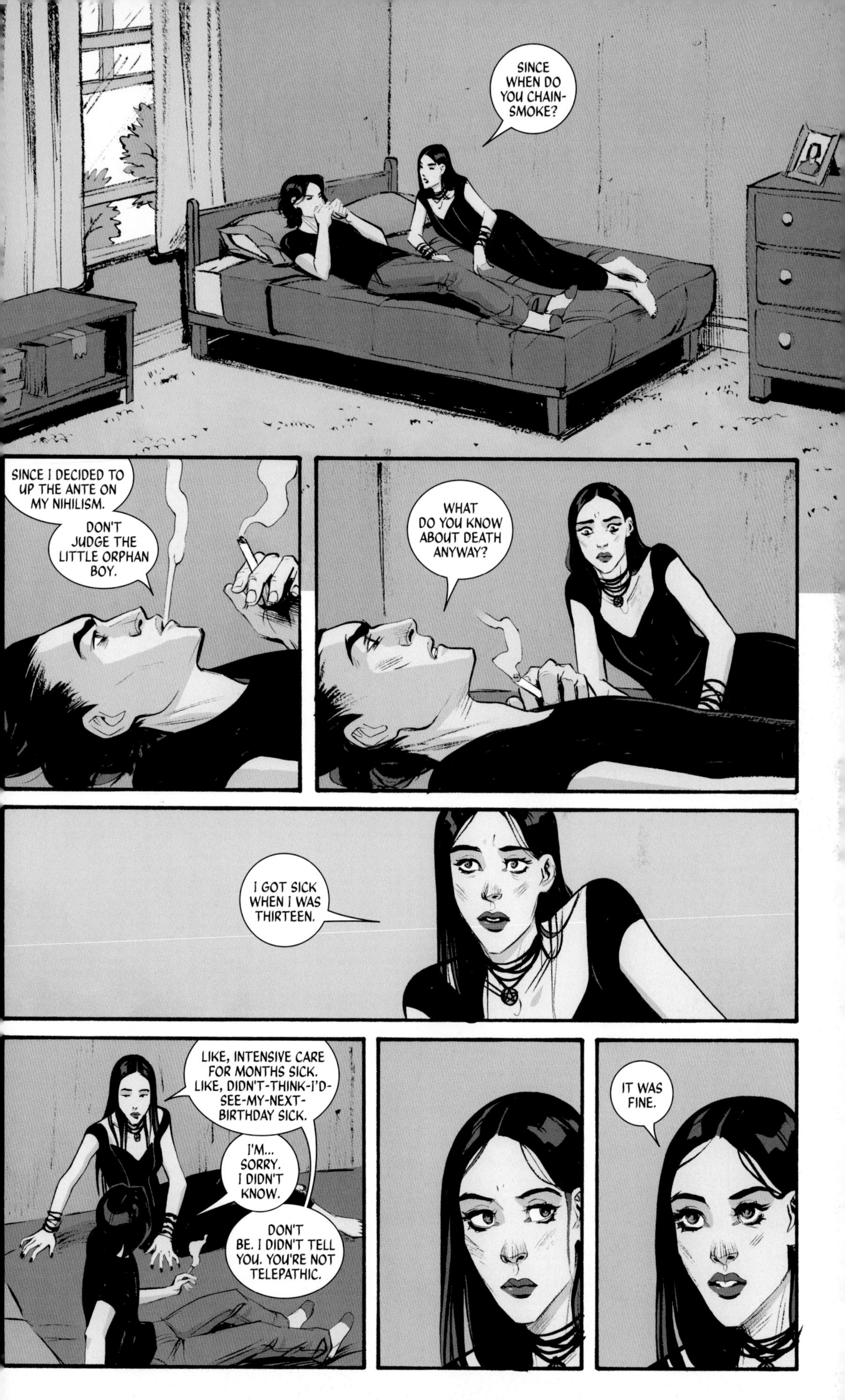
SINCE WHEN DO YOU CHAIN-SMOKE?
SINCE I DECIDED TO UP THE ANTE ON MY NIHILISM.
DON'T JUDGE THE LITTLE ORPHAN BOY.
WHAT DO YOU KNOW ABOUT DEATH ANYWAY?
I GOT SICK WHEN I WAS THIRTEEN.
LIKE, INTENSIVE CARE FOR MONTHS SICK. LIKE, DIDN'T-THINK-I'D-SEE-MY-NEXT-BIRTHDAY SICK.
I'M... SORRY. I DIDN'T KNOW.
DON'T BE. I DIDN'T TELL YOU. YOU'RE NOT TELEPATHIC.
IT WAS FINE.

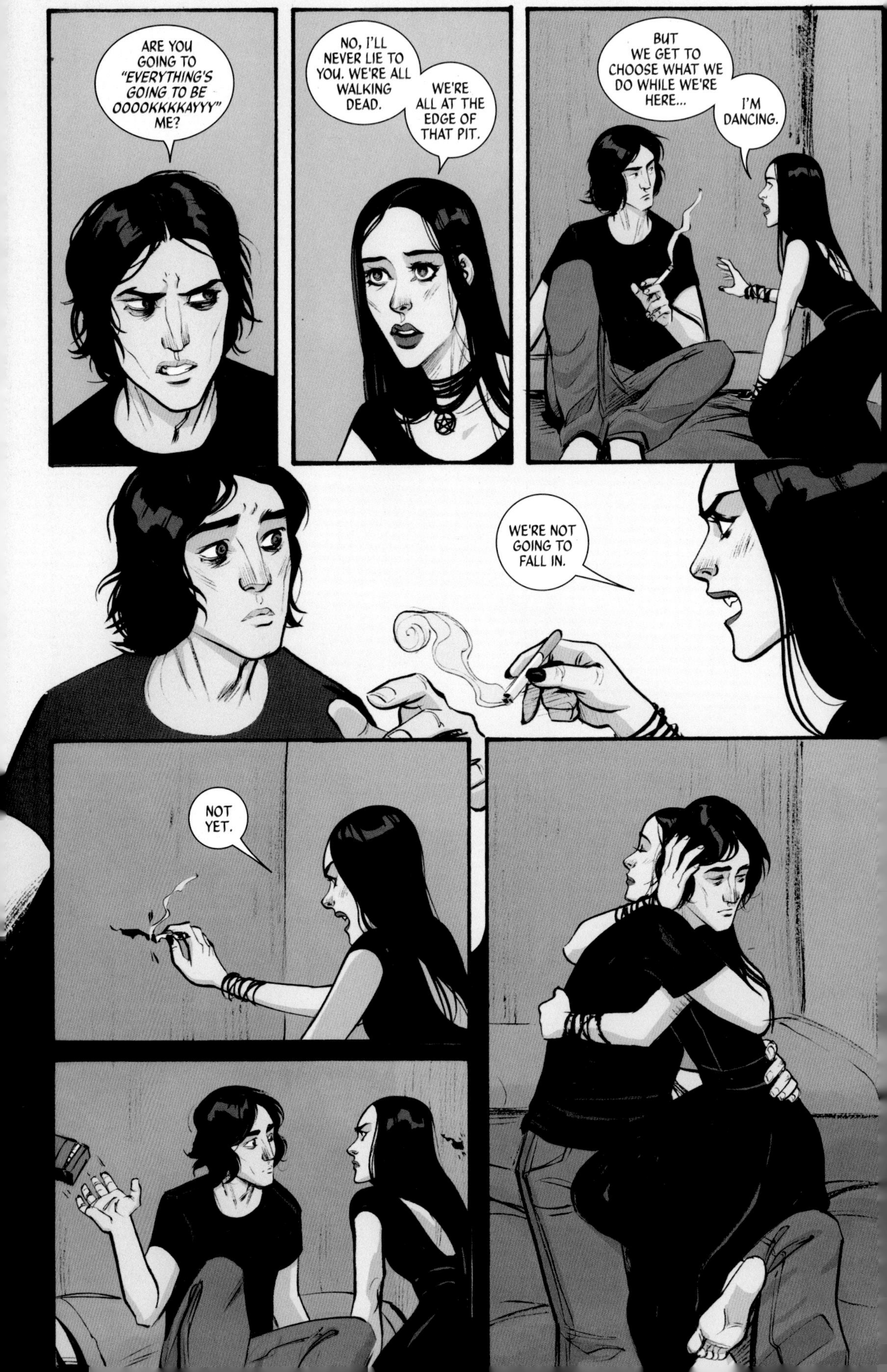
ARE YOU GOING TO "EVERYTHING'S GOING TO BE OOOOKKKKAYYY" ME?
NO, I'LL NEVER LIE TO YOU. WE'RE ALL WALKING DEAD.
WE'RE ALL AT THE EDGE OF THAT PIT.
BUT WE GET TO CHOOSE WHAT WE DO WHILE WE'RE HERE...
I'M DANCING.
WE'RE NOT GOING TO FALL IN.
NOT YET.

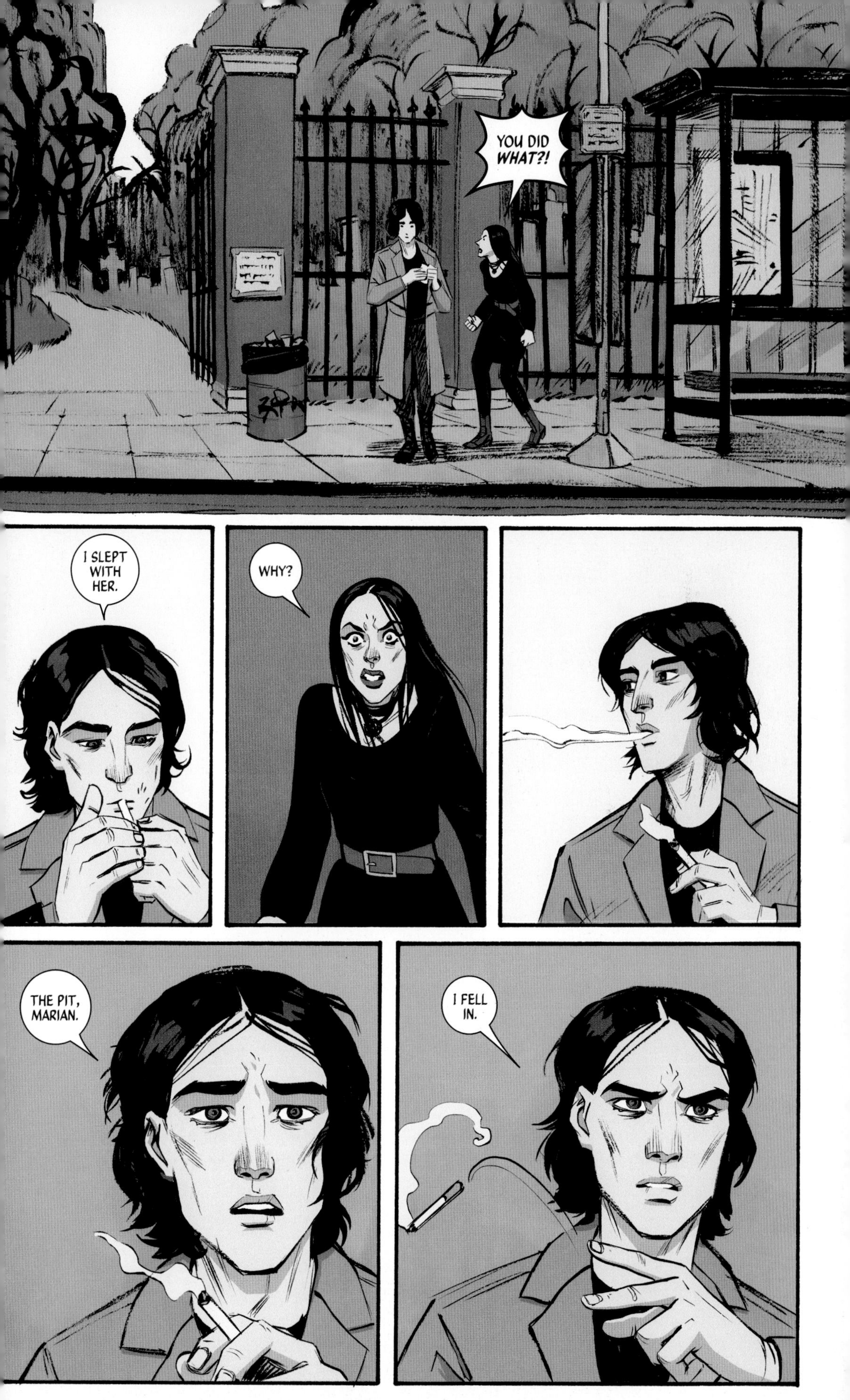
YOU DID WHAT?!
I SLEPT WITH HER.
WHY?
THE PIT, MARIAN.
I FELL IN.

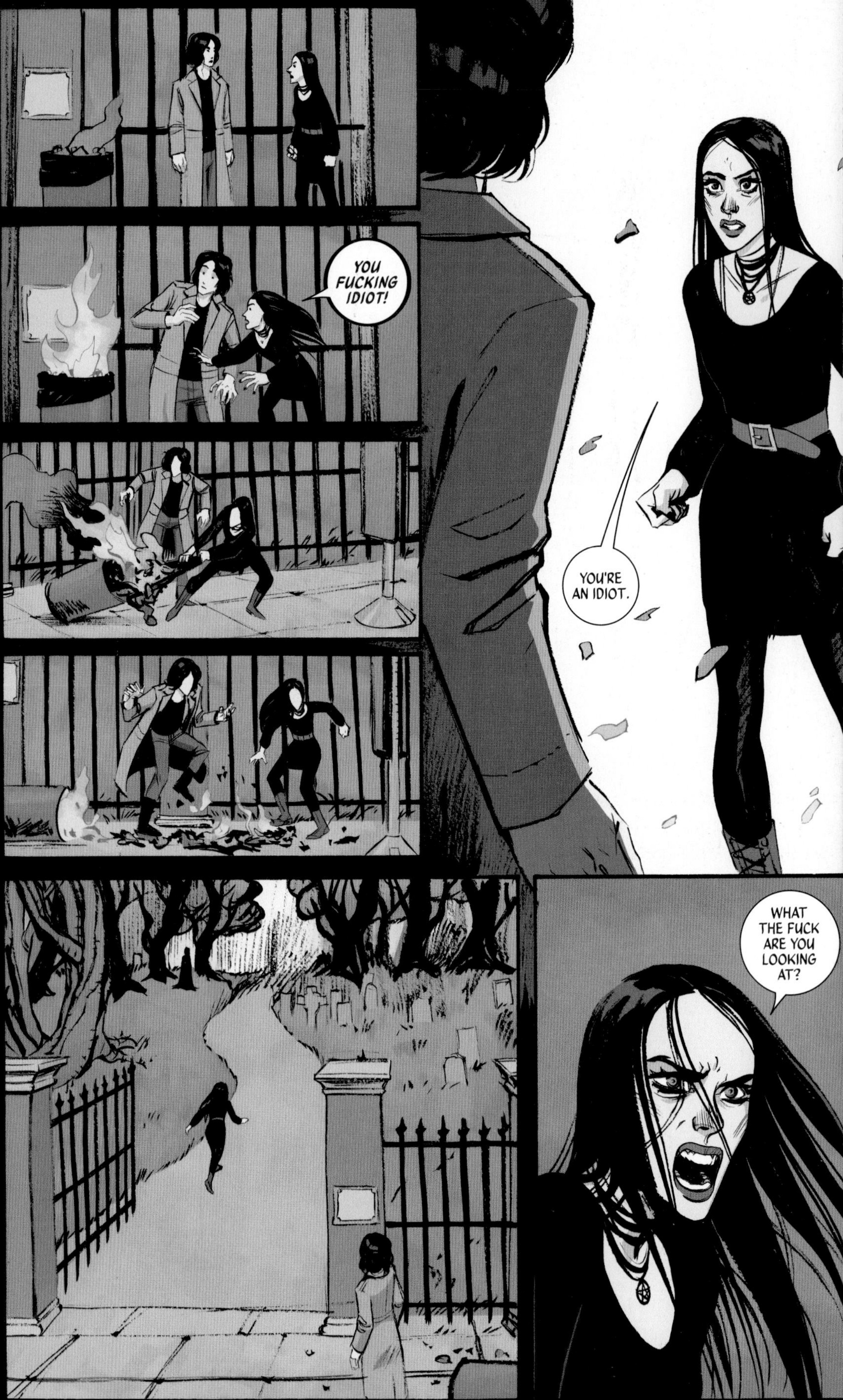
YOU FUCKING IDIOT!
YOU'RE AN IDIOT.
WHAT THE FUCK ARE YOU LOOKING AT?

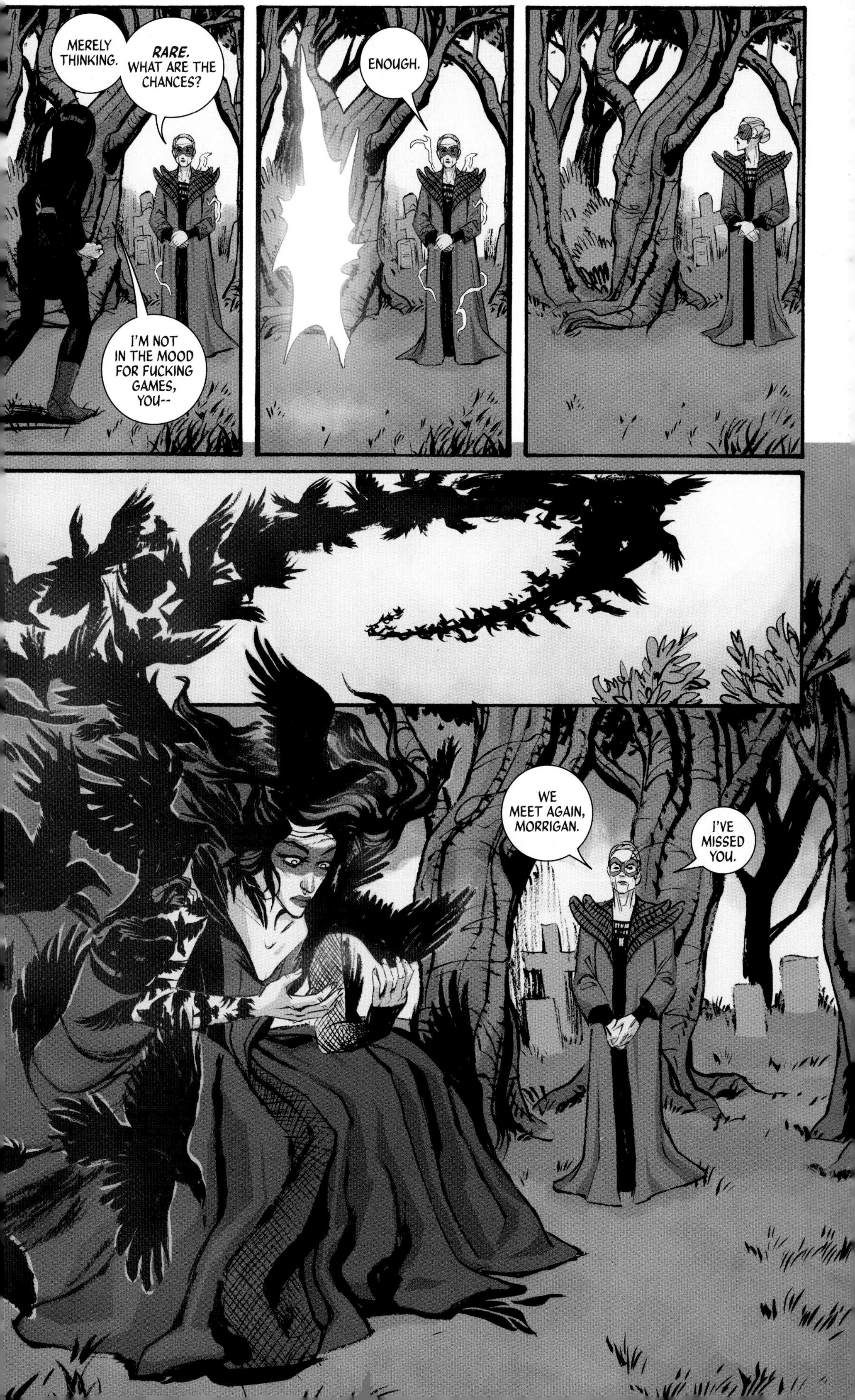

MERELY THINKING.
RARE. WHAT ARE THE CHANCES?
I'M NOT IN THE MOOD FOR FUCKING GAMES, YOU--
ENOUGH.
WE MEET AGAIN, MORRIGAN.
I'VE MISSED YOU.

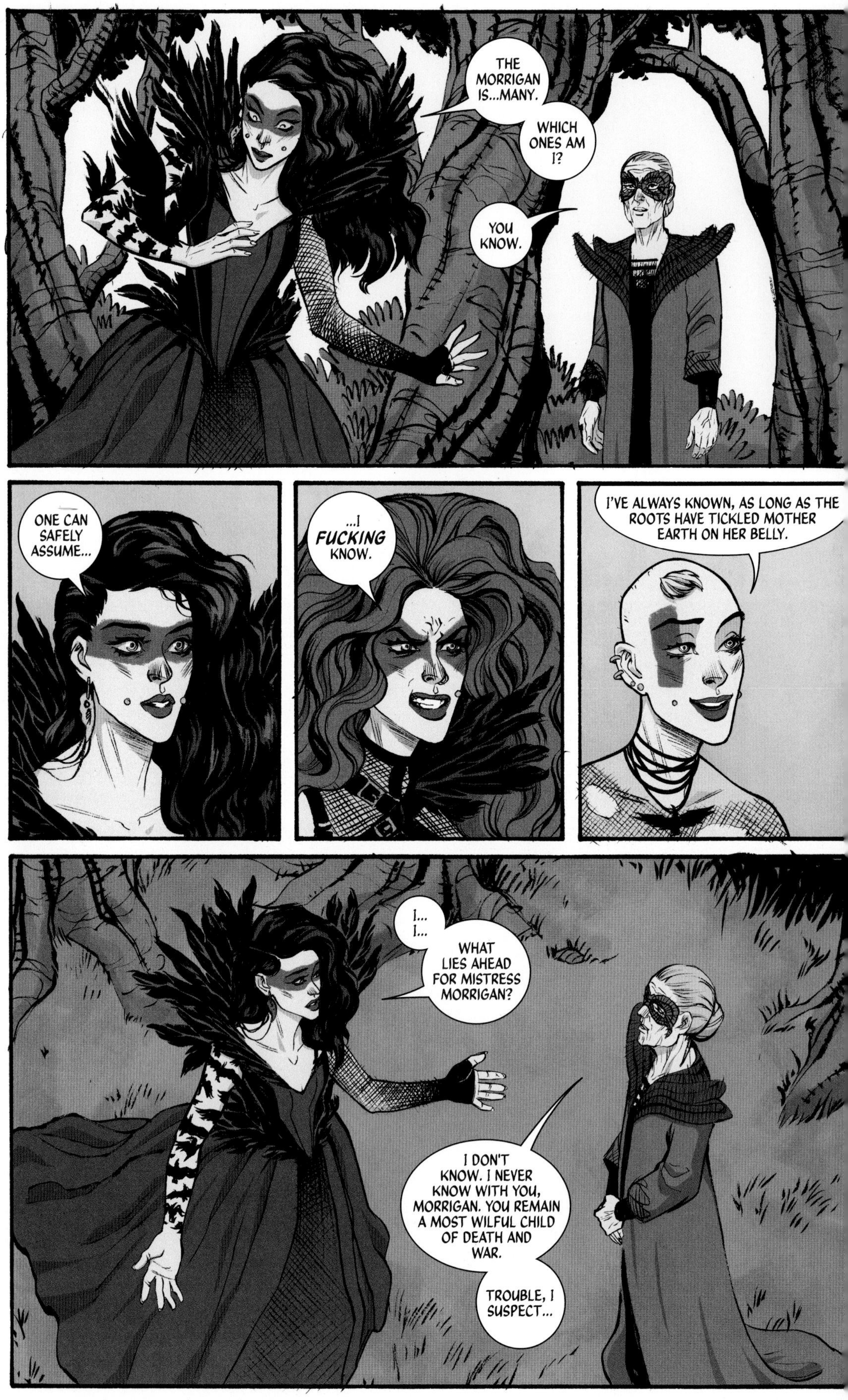
THE MORRIGAN IS...MANY.
WHICH ONES AM I?
YOU KNOW.
ONE CAN SAFELY ASSUME...
...I FUCKING KNOW.
I'VE ALWAYS KNOWN, AS LONG AS THE ROOTS HAVE TICKLED MOTHER EARTH ON HER BELLY.
I... I...
WHAT LIES AHEAD FOR MISTRESS MORRIGAN?
I DON'T KNOW. I NEVER KNOW WITH YOU, MORRIGAN. YOU REMAIN A MOST WILFUL CHILD OF DEATH AND WAR.
TROUBLE, I SUSPECT...

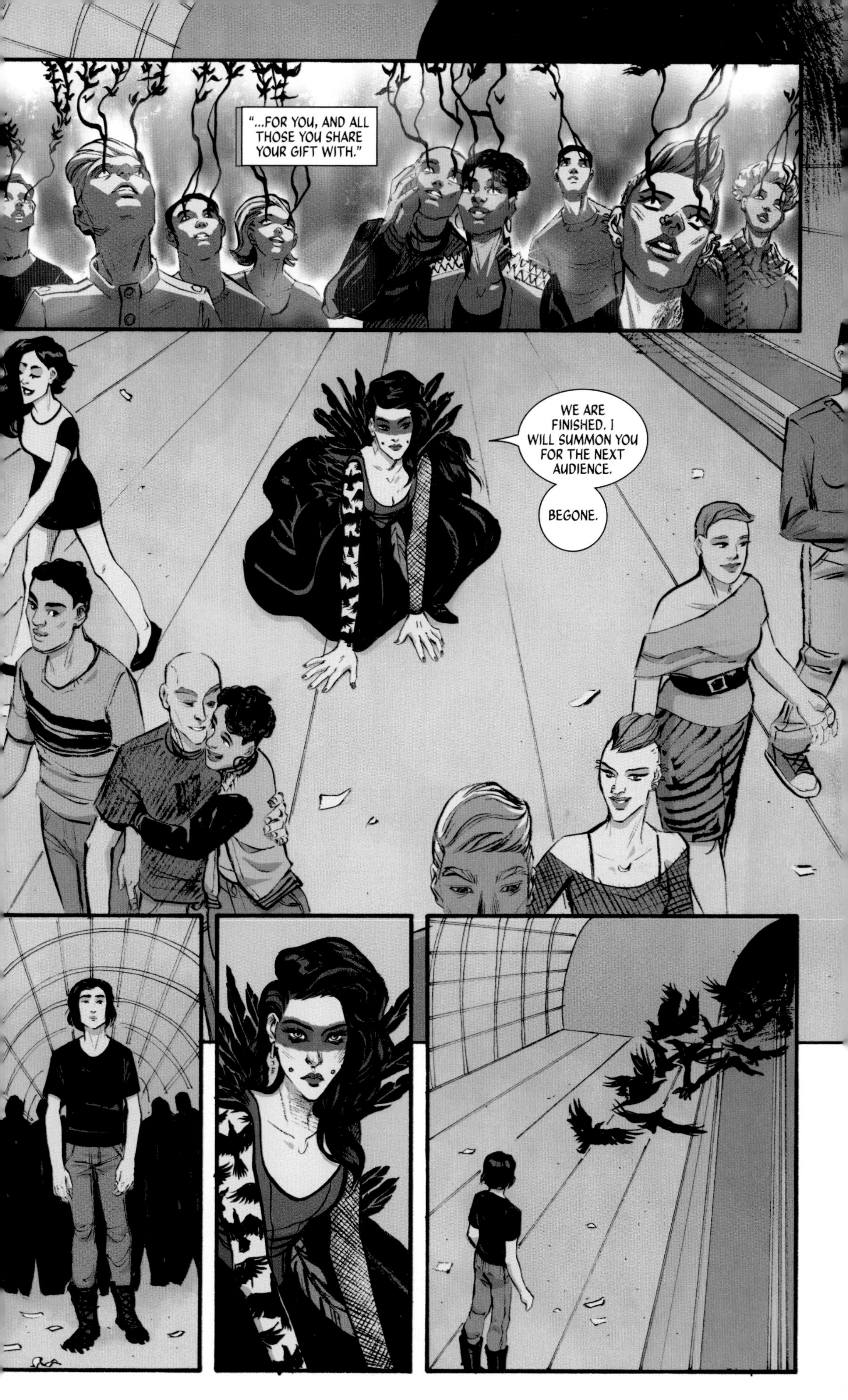
"...FOR YOU, AND ALL THOSE YOU SHARE YOUR GIFT WITH."
WE ARE FINISHED. I WILL SUMMON YOU FOR THE NEXT AUDIENCE.
BEGONE.

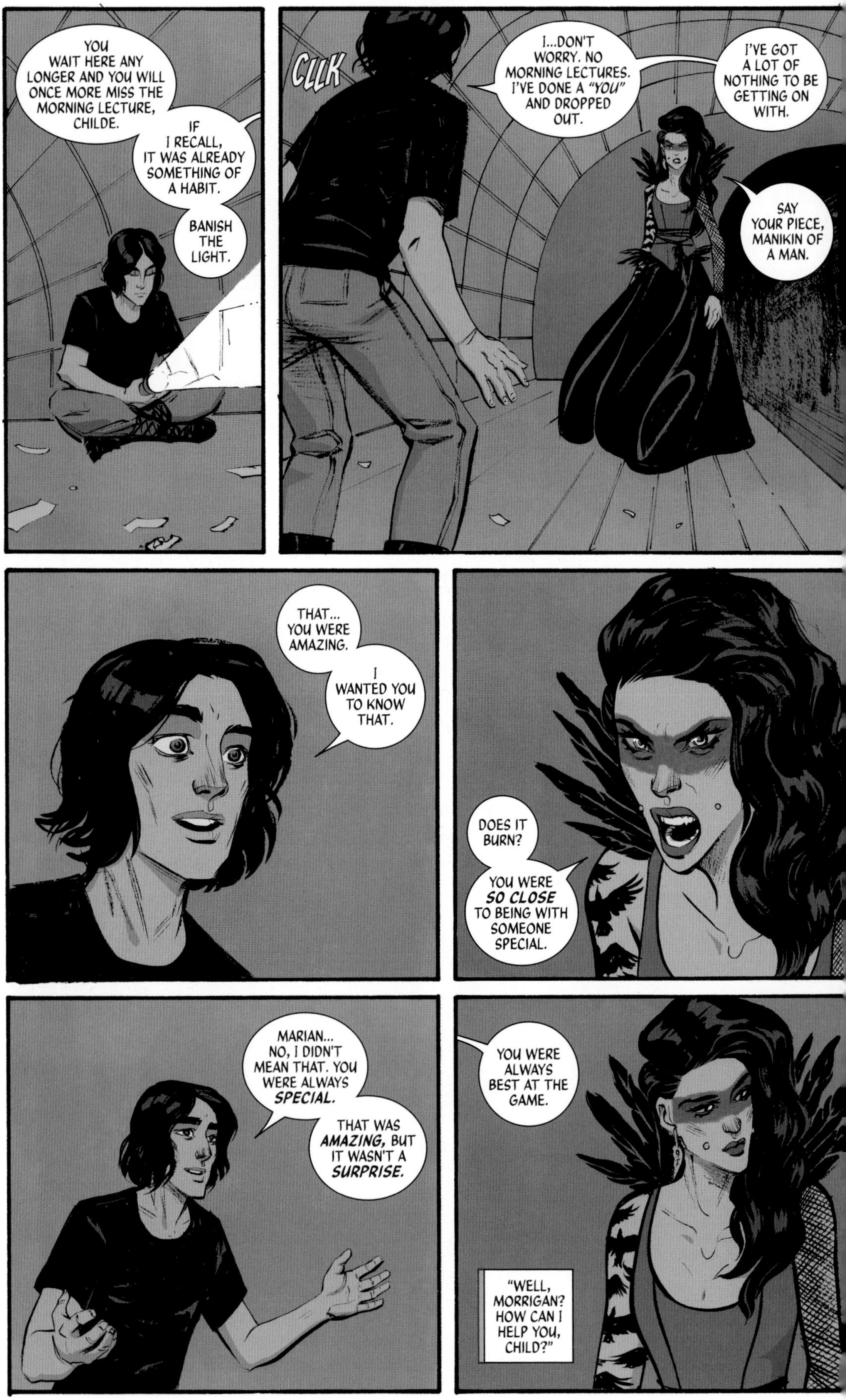
YOU WAIT HERE ANY LONGER AND YOU WILL ONCE MORE MISS THE MORNING LECTURE, CHILDE.
IF I RECALL, IT WAS ALREADY SOMETHING OF A HABIT.
BANISH THE LIGHT.
CLLK
I...DON'T WORRY. NO MORNING LECTURES. I'VE DONE A "YOU" AND DROPPED OUT.
I'VE GOT A LOT OF NOTHING TO BE GETTING ON WITH.
SAY YOUR PIECE, MANIKIN OF A MAN.
THAT... YOU WERE AMAZING.
I WANTED YOU TO KNOW THAT.
DOES IT BURN?
YOU WERE SO CLOSE TO BEING WITH SOMEONE SPECIAL.
MARIAN... NO, I DIDN'T MEAN THAT. YOU WERE ALWAYS SPECIAL.
THAT WAS AMAZING, BUT IT WASN'T A SURPRISE.
YOU WERE ALWAYS BEST AT THE GAME.
"WELL, MORRIGAN? HOW CAN I HELP YOU, CHILD?"

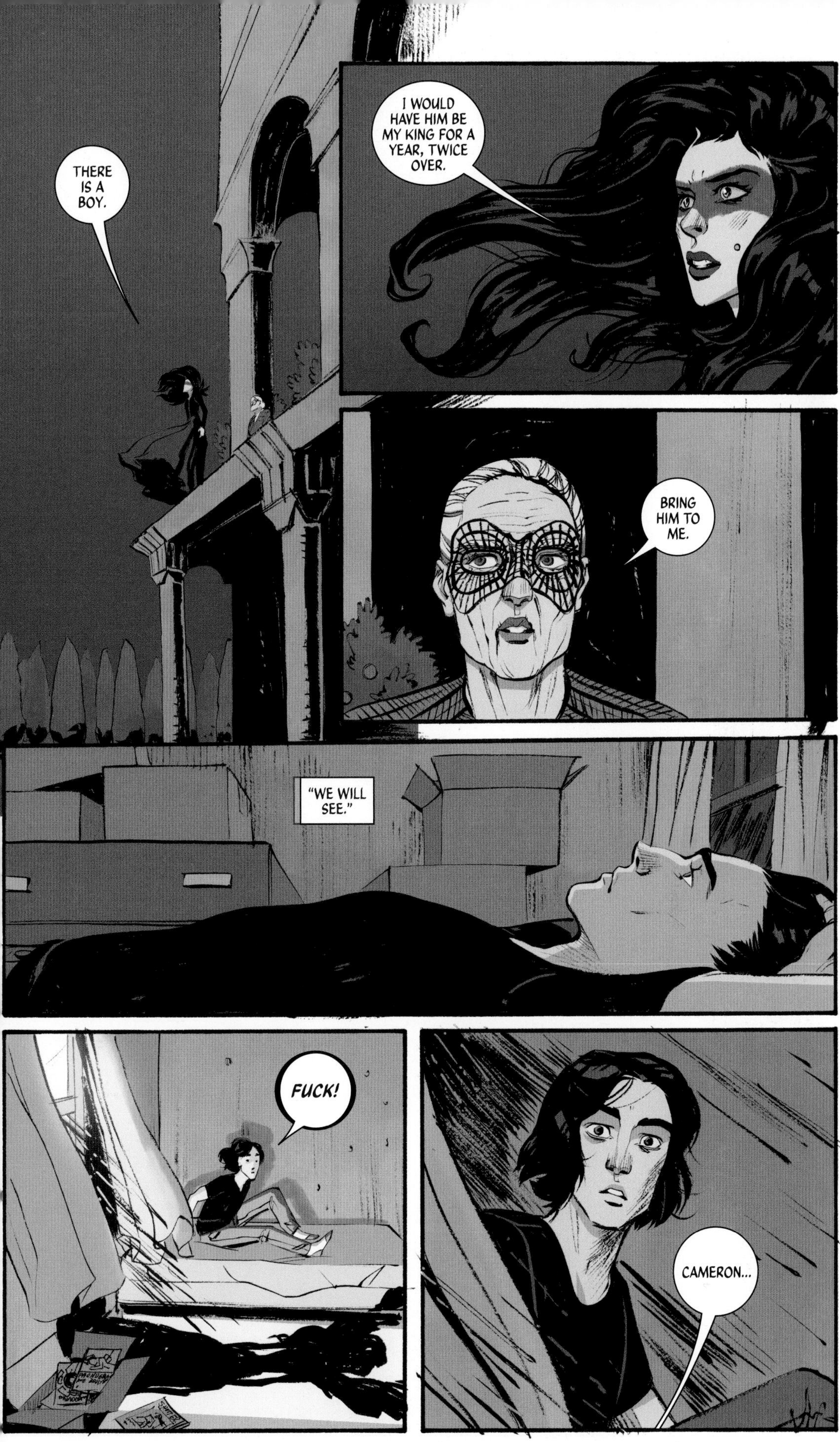
THERE IS A BOY.
I WOULD HAVE HIM BE MY KING FOR A YEAR, TWICE OVER.
BRING HIM TO ME.
"WE WILL SEE."
FUCK!
CAMERON...

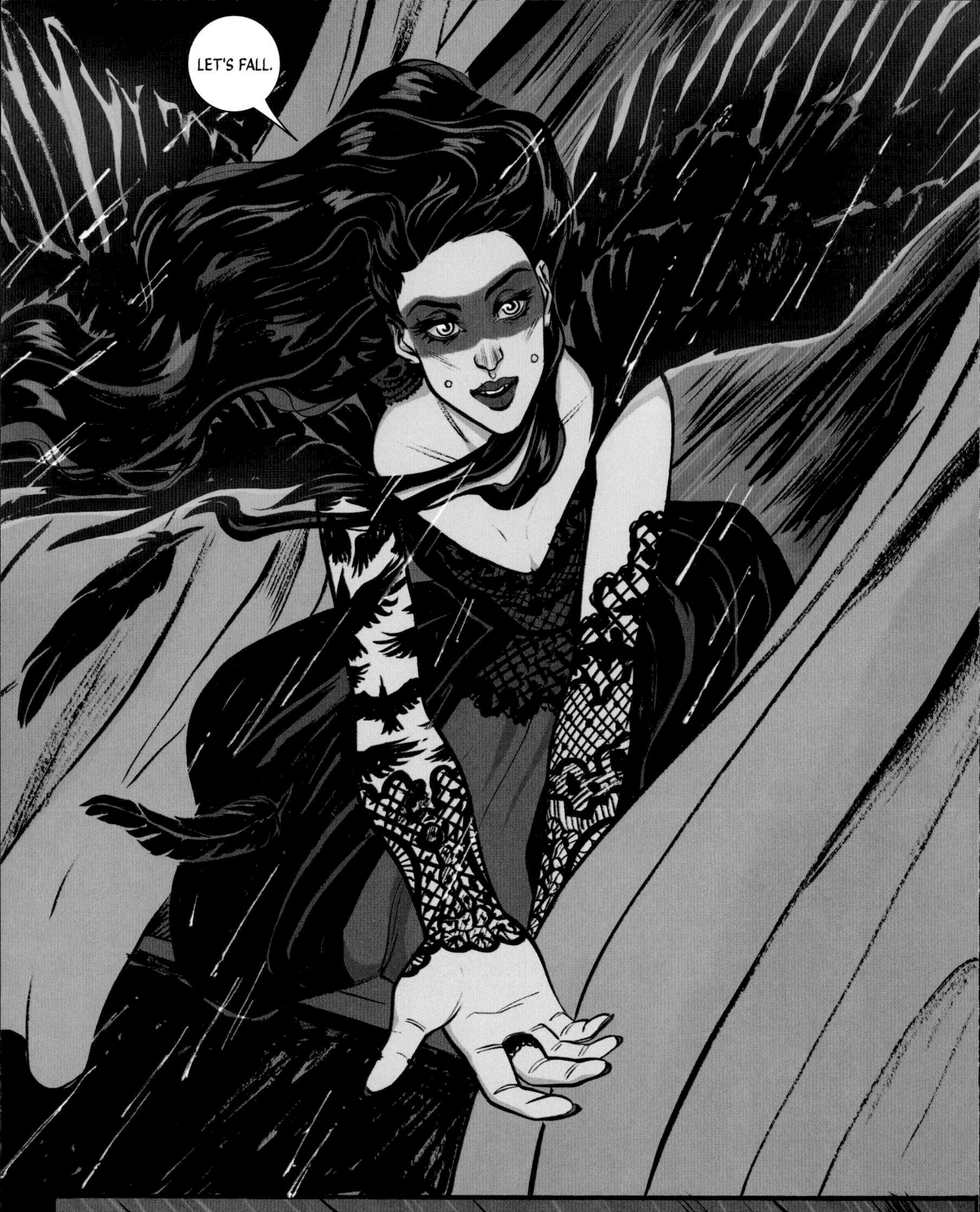
LET'S FALL.

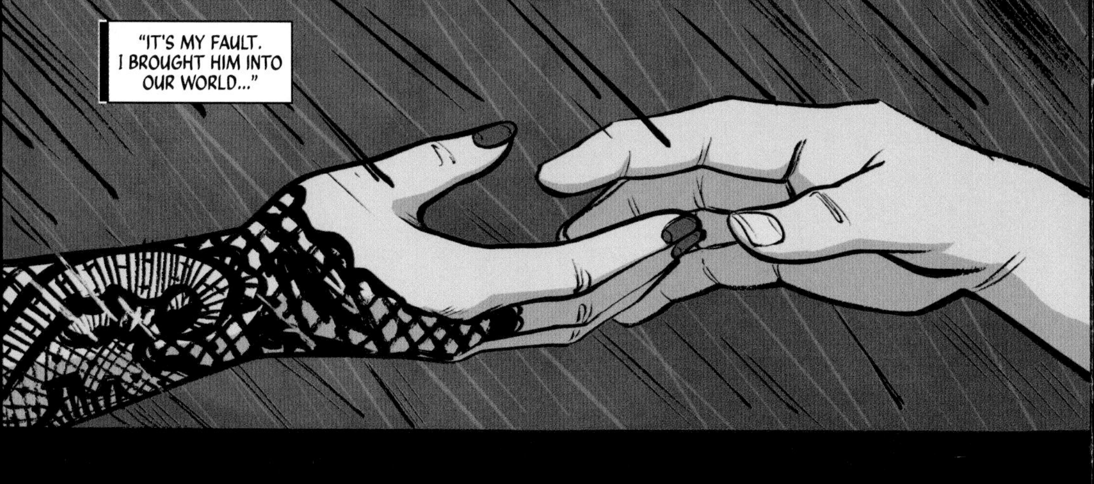
"IT'S MY FAULT. I BROUGHT HIM INTO OUR WORLD..."

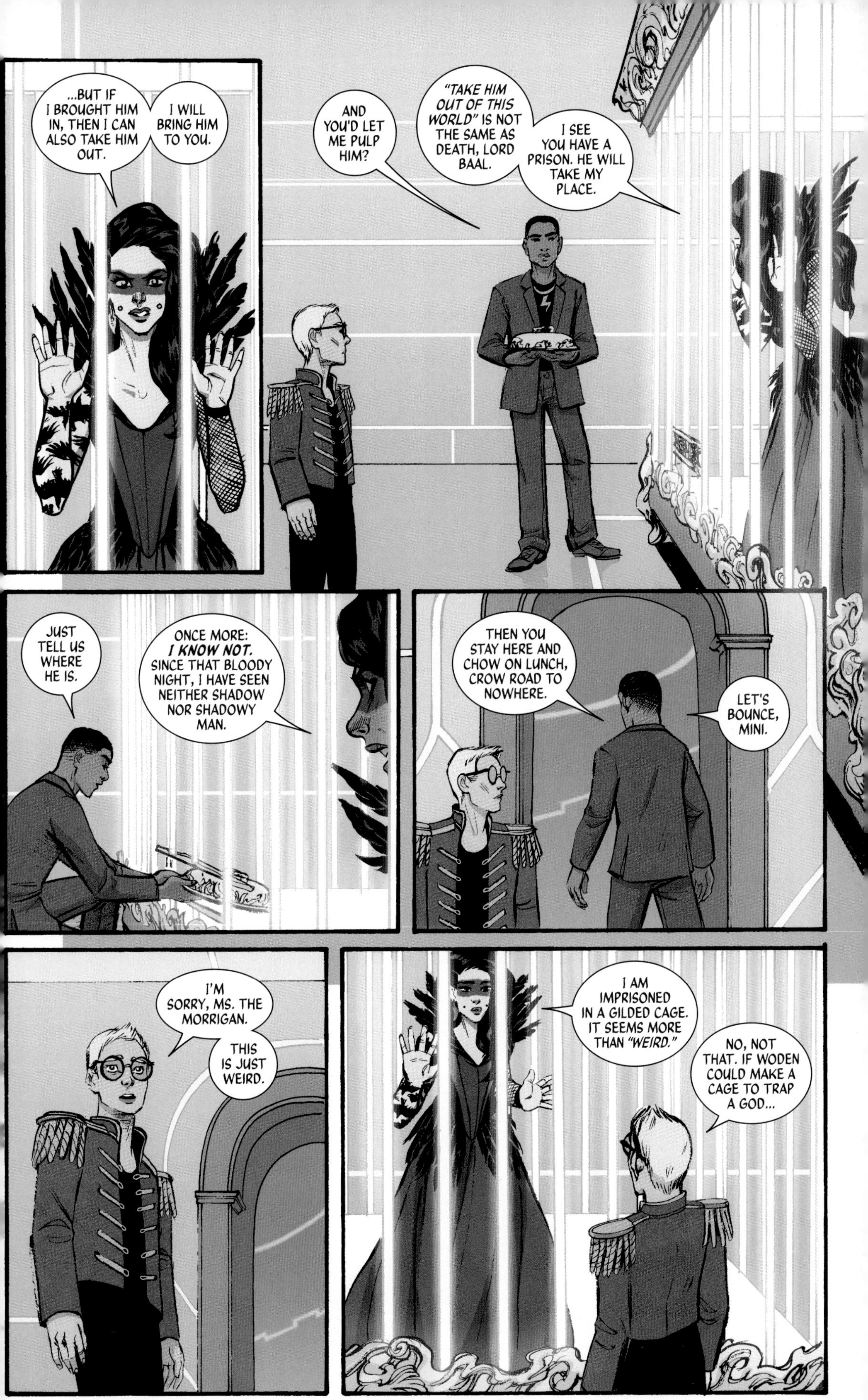

...BUT IF I BROUGHT HIM IN, THEN I CAN ALSO TAKE HIM OUT.
I WILL BRING HIM TO YOU.
AND YOU'D LET ME PULP HIM?
"TAKE HIM OUT OF THIS WORLD" IS NOT THE SAME AS DEATH, LORD BAAL.
I SEE YOU HAVE A PRISON. HE WILL TAKE MY PLACE.
JUST TELL US WHERE HE IS.
ONCE MORE: I KNOW NOT. SINCE THAT BLOODY NIGHT, I HAVE SEEN NEITHER SHADOW NOR SHADOWY MAN.
THEN YOU STAY HERE AND CHOW ON LUNCH, CROW ROAD TO NOWHERE.
LET'S BOUNCE, MINI.
I'M SORRY, MS. THE MORRIGAN.
THIS IS JUST WEIRD.
I AM IMPRISONED IN A GILDED CAGE. IT SEEMS MORE THAN "WEIRD."
NO, NOT THAT. IF WODEN COULD MAKE A CAGE TO TRAP A GOD...

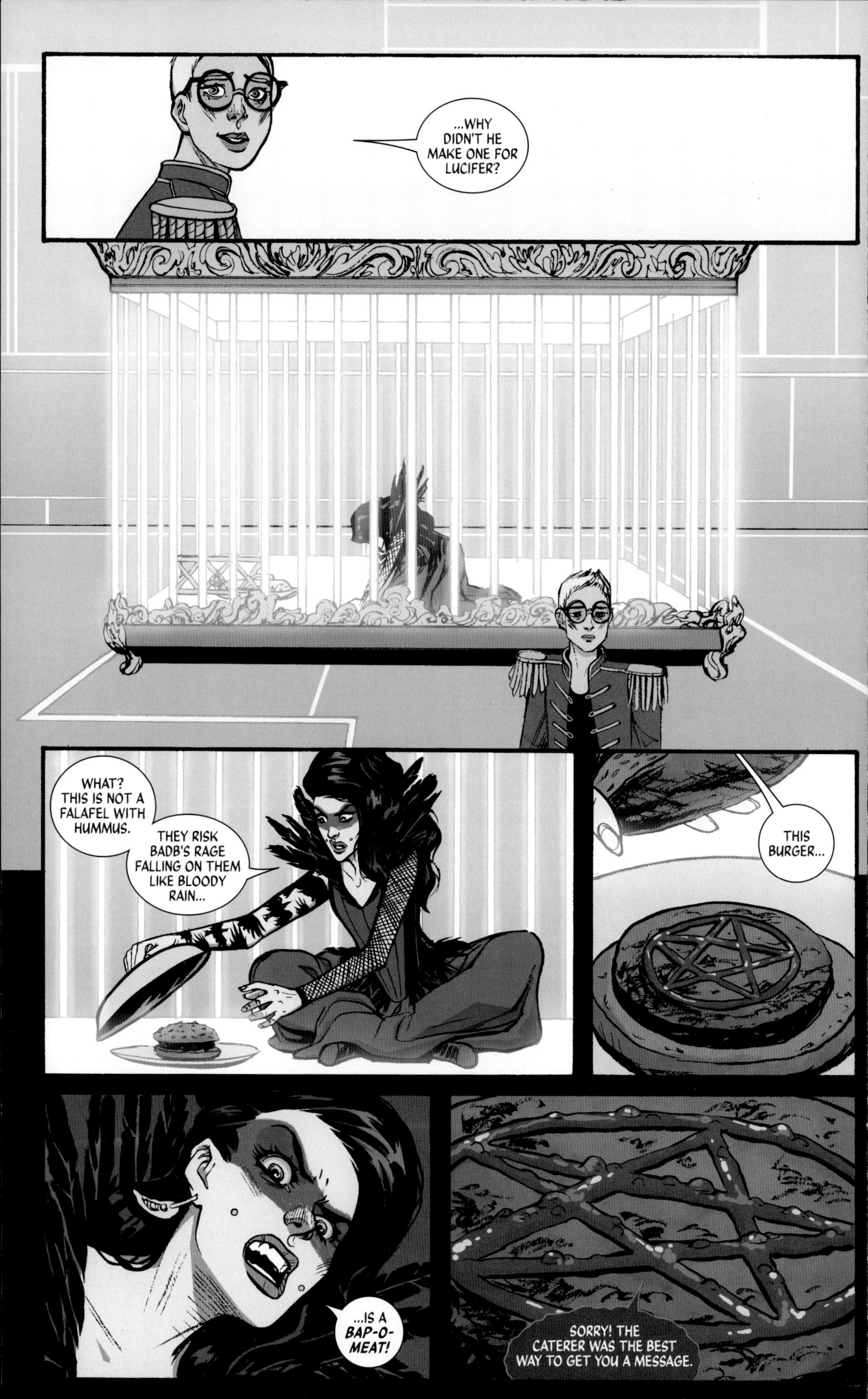
...WHY DIDN'T HE MAKE ONE FOR LUCIFER?
WHAT? THIS IS NOT A FALAFEL WITH HUMMUS.
THEY RISK BADB'S RAGE FALLING ON THEM LIKE BLOODY RAIN...
THIS BURGER...
...IS A *BAP-O-MEAT!*
SORRY! THE CATERER WAS THE BEST WAY TO GET YOU A MESSAGE.

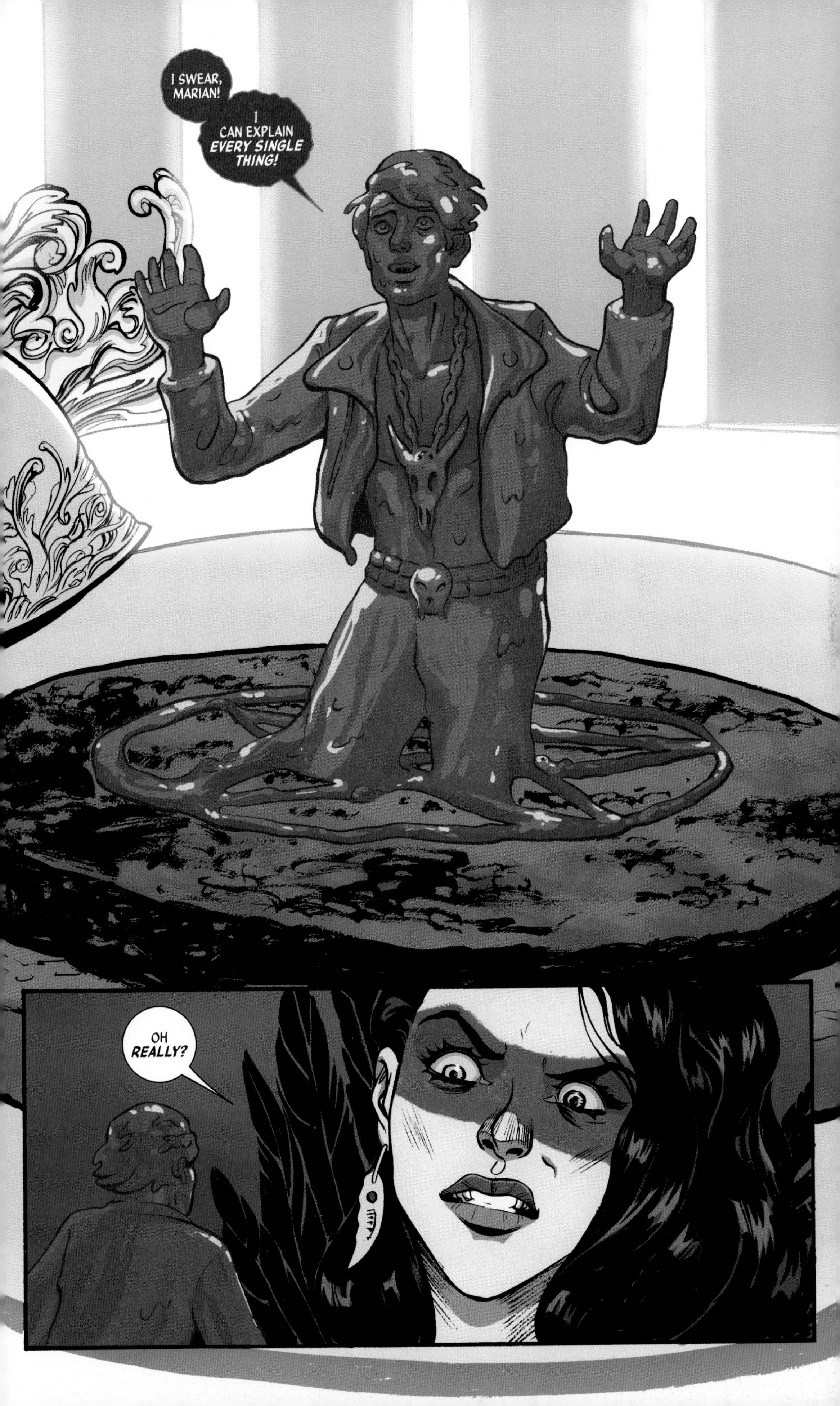
I SWEAR, MARIAN!
I CAN EXPLAIN *EVERY SINGLE THING!*
OH *REALLY?*

NO MORE

9 SEPTEMBER 2014

THE
WICKED
+
DIVINE
THE

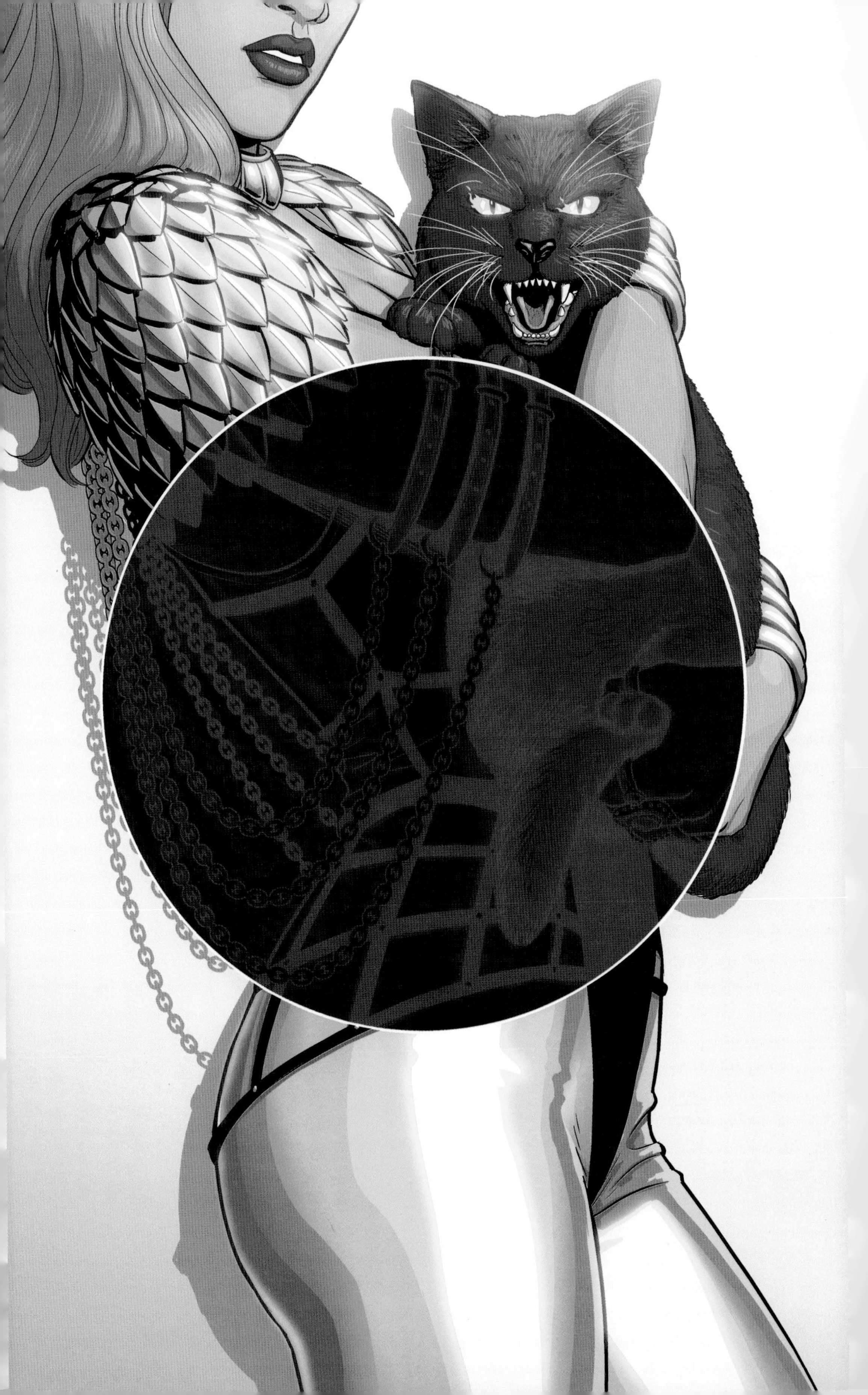

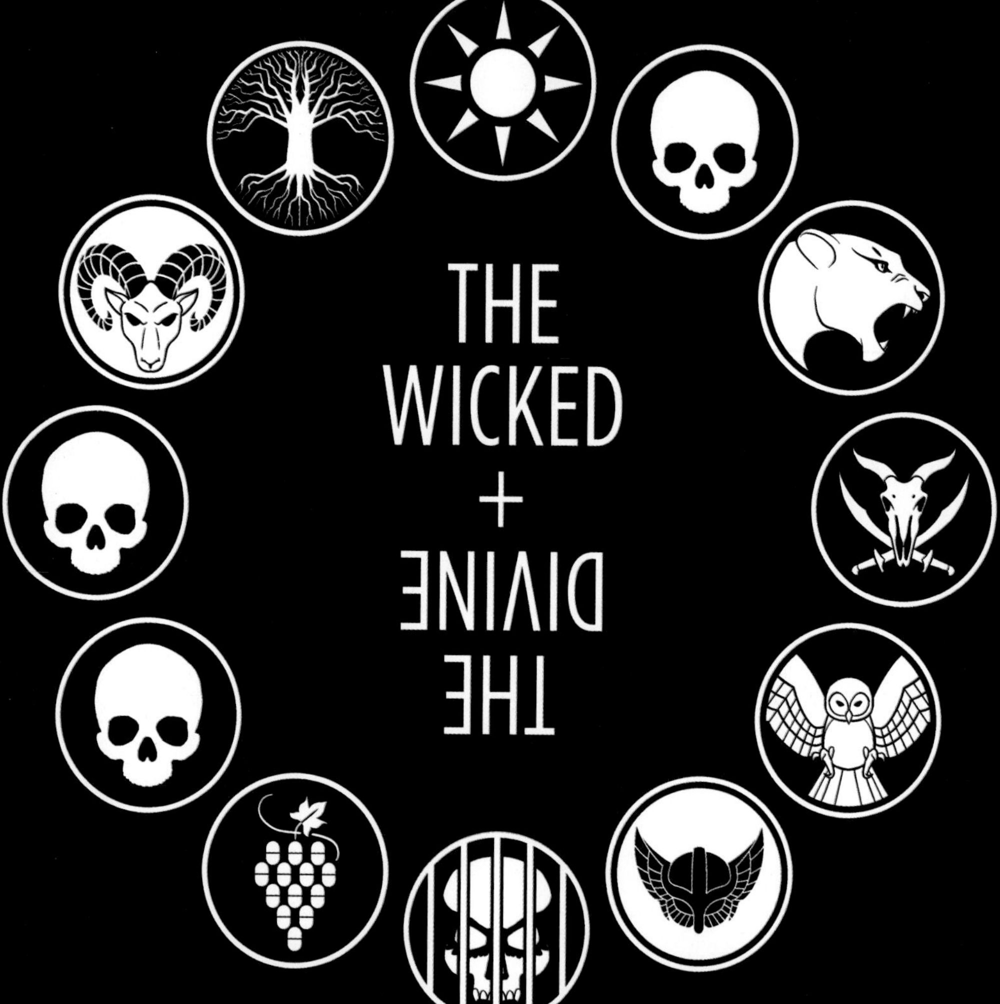
THE
WICKED
+
THE
DIVINE

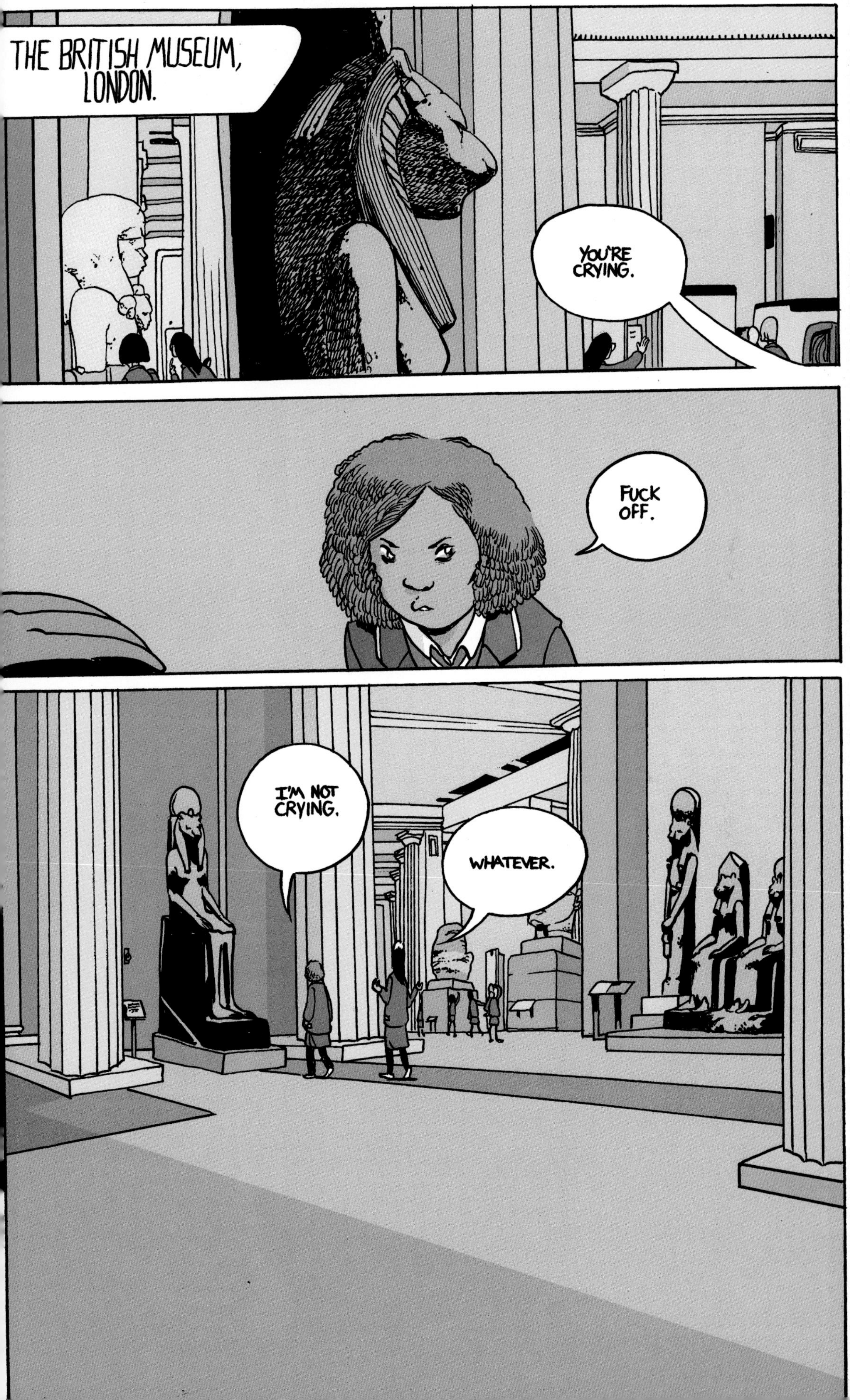
THE BRITISH MUSEUM, LONDON.
YOU'RE CRYING.
FUCK OFF.
I'M NOT CRYING.
WHATEVER.

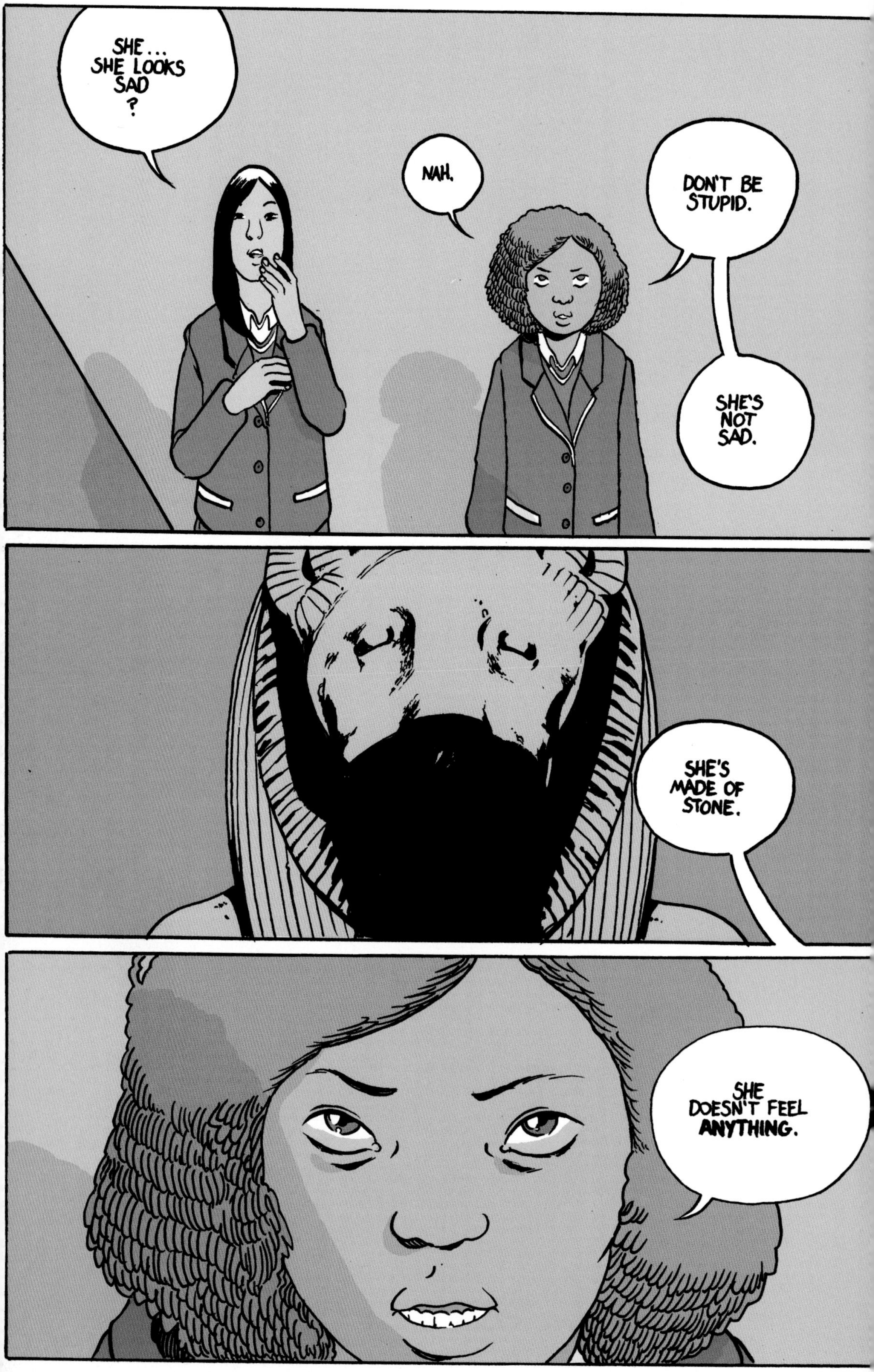
SHE... SHE LOOKS SAD ?
NAH.
DON'T BE STUPID.
SHE'S NOT SAD.
SHE'S MADE OF STONE.
SHE DOESN'T FEEL ANYTHING.

THE LOST CAT

13 JANUARY 2010

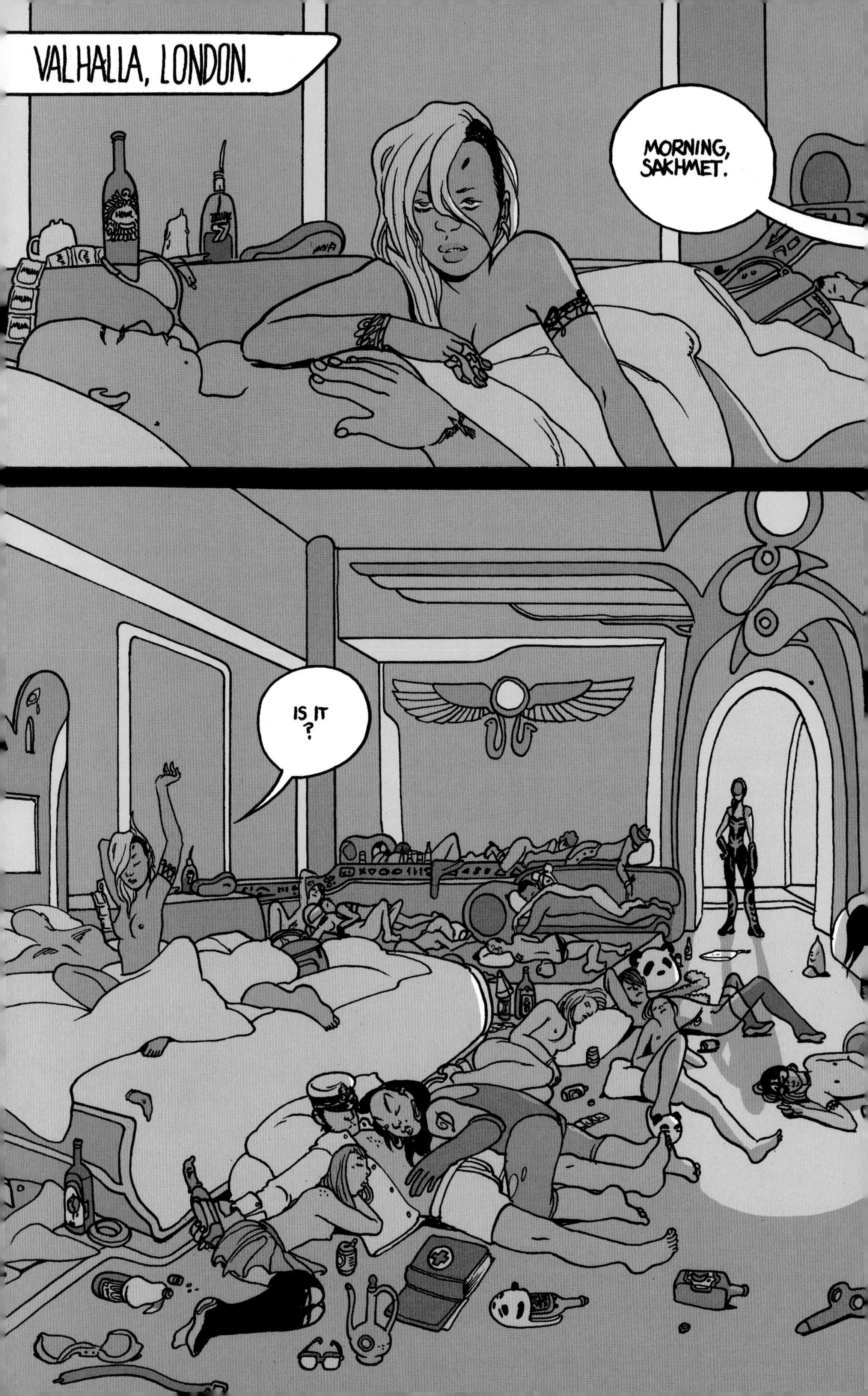
VALHALLA, LONDON.
MORNING, SAKHMET.
IS IT?

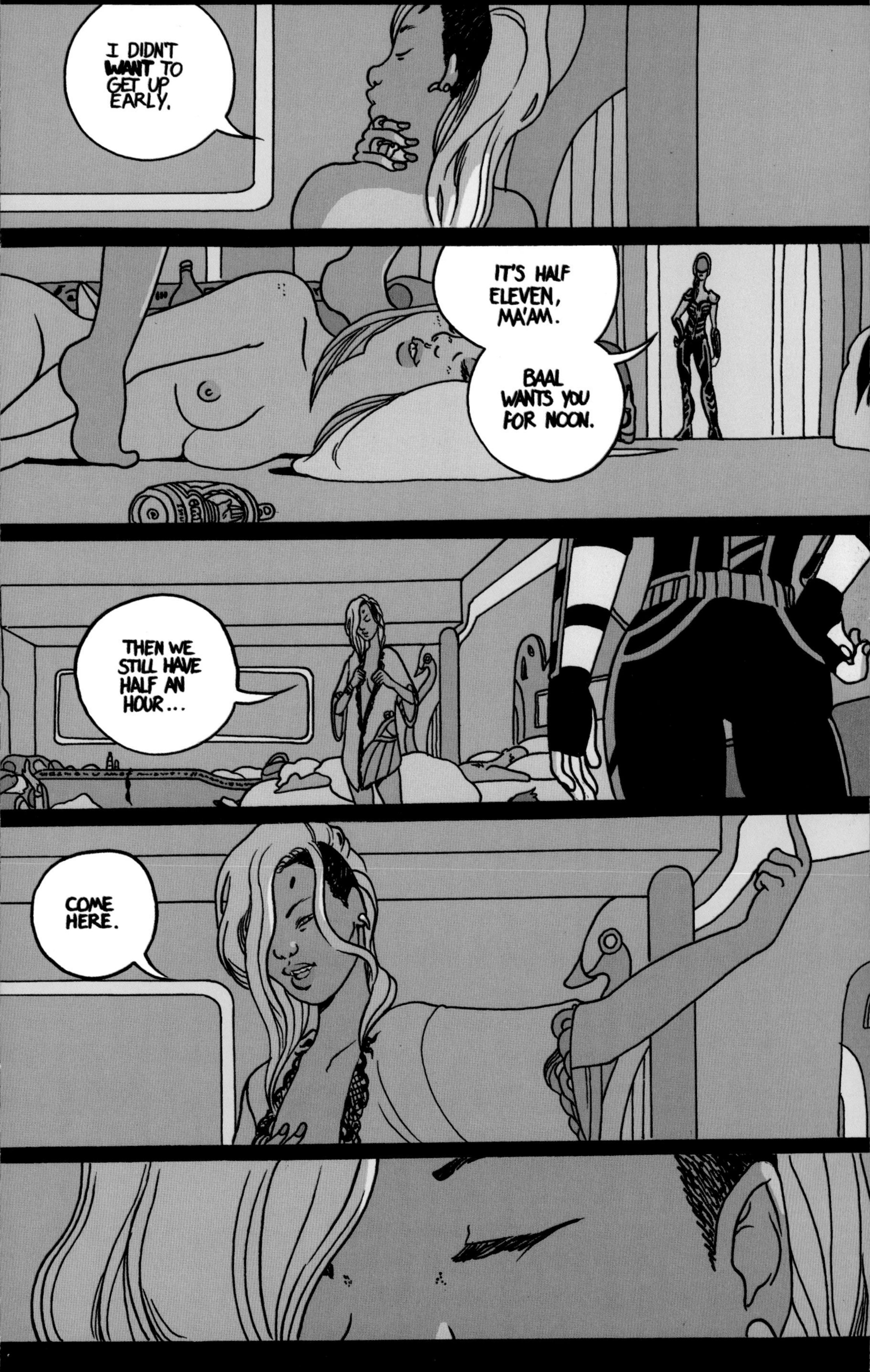
I DIDN'T WANT TO GET UP EARLY.
IT'S HALF ELEVEN, MA'AM.
BAAL WANTS YOU FOR NOON.
THEN WE STILL HAVE HALF AN HOUR...
COME HERE.

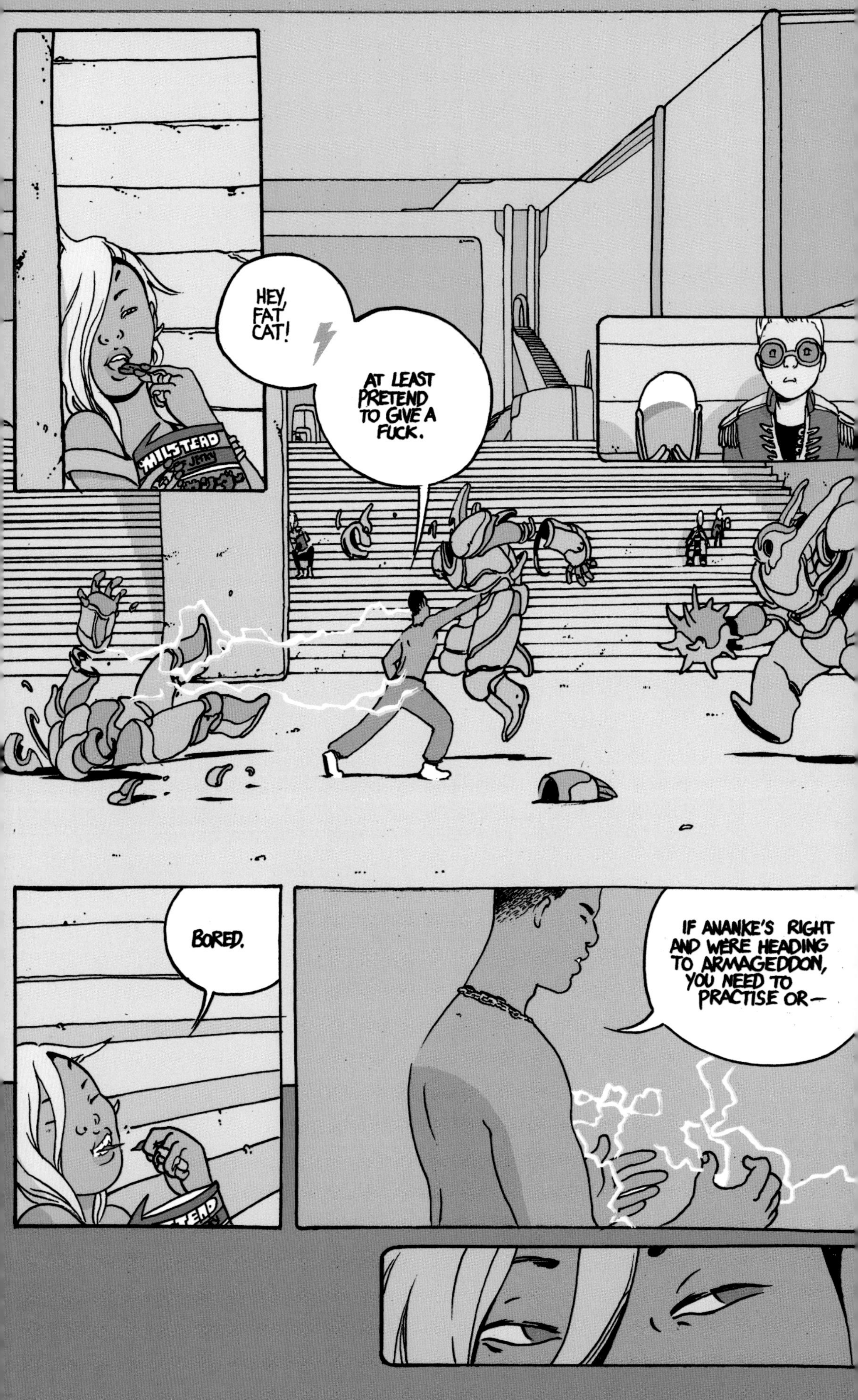
HEY, FAT CAT!
AT LEAST PRETEND TO GIVE A FUCK.
WILSTEAD JERKY
BORED.
IF ANANKE'S RIGHT AND WE'RE HEADING TO ARMAGEDDON, YOU NEED TO PRACTISE OR—

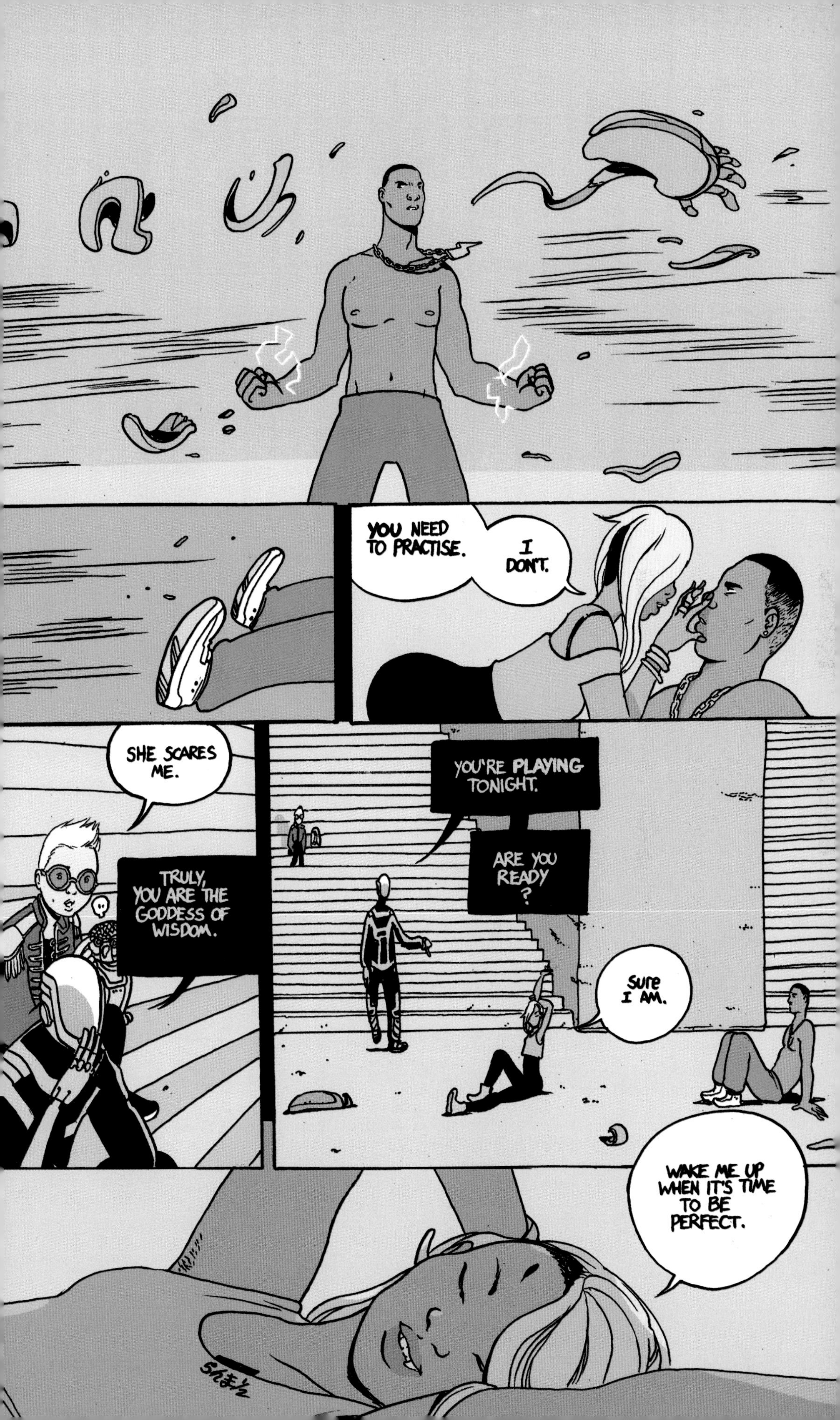
YOU NEED TO PRACTISE.
I DON'T.
SHE SCARES ME.
TRULY, YOU ARE THE GODDESS OF WISDOM.
YOU'RE PLAYING TONIGHT.
ARE YOU READY ?
Sure I AM.
WAKE ME UP WHEN IT'S TIME TO BE PERFECT.

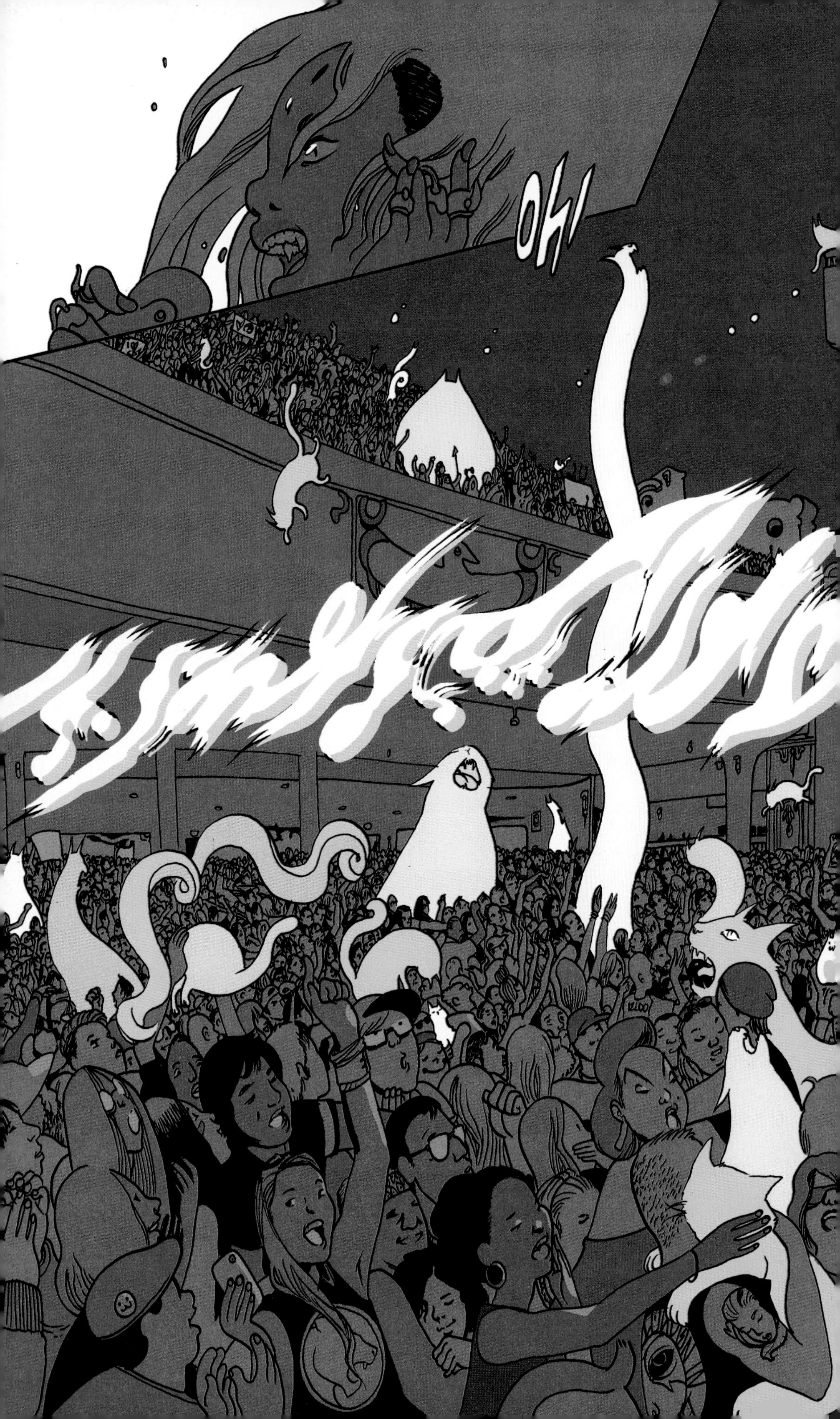
OH!

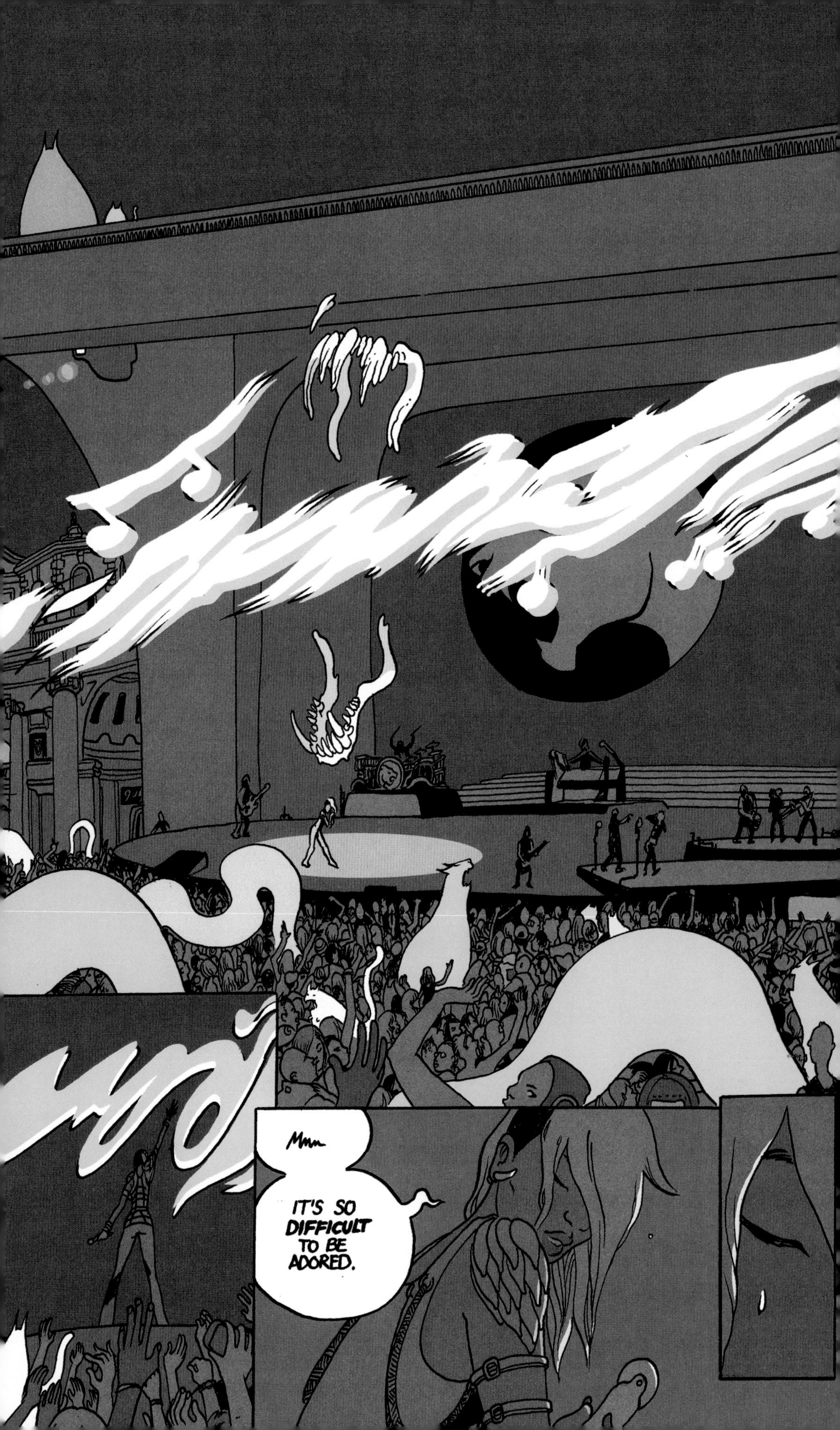
Mmm
IT'S SO **DIFFICULT** TO BE ADORED.

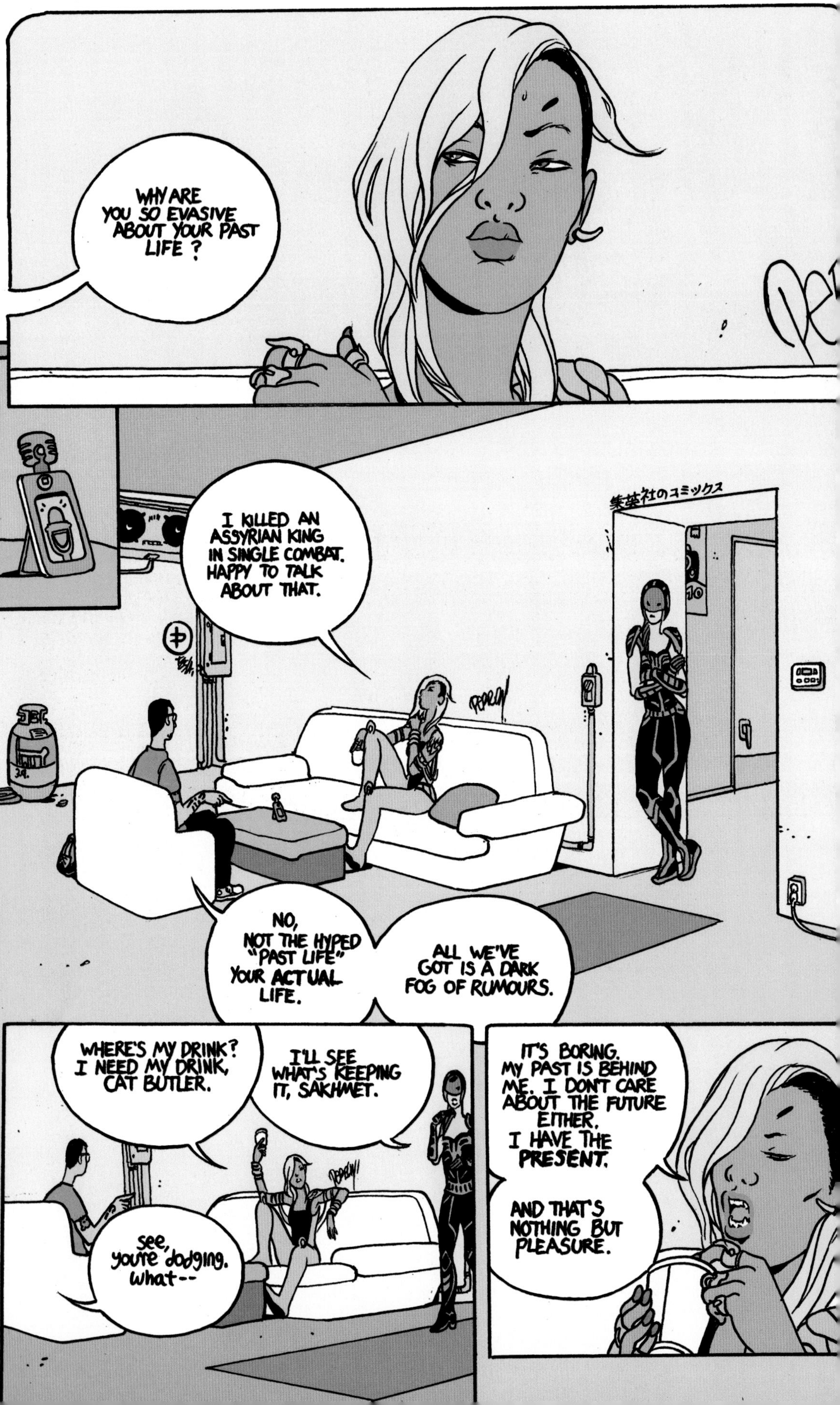
WHY ARE YOU SO EVASIVE ABOUT YOUR PAST LIFE ?
I KILLED AN ASSYRIAN KING IN SINGLE COMBAT. HAPPY TO TALK ABOUT THAT.
集英社のコミックス
NO, NOT THE HYPED "PAST LIFE" YOUR ACTUAL LIFE.
ALL WE'VE GOT IS A DARK FOG OF RUMOURS.
WHERE'S MY DRINK? I NEED MY DRINK, CAT BUTLER.
I'LL SEE WHAT'S KEEPING IT, SAKHMET.
see, you're dodging. what--
IT'S BORING. MY PAST IS BEHIND ME. I DON'T CARE ABOUT THE FUTURE EITHER. I HAVE THE PRESENT.
AND THAT'S NOTHING BUT PLEASURE.

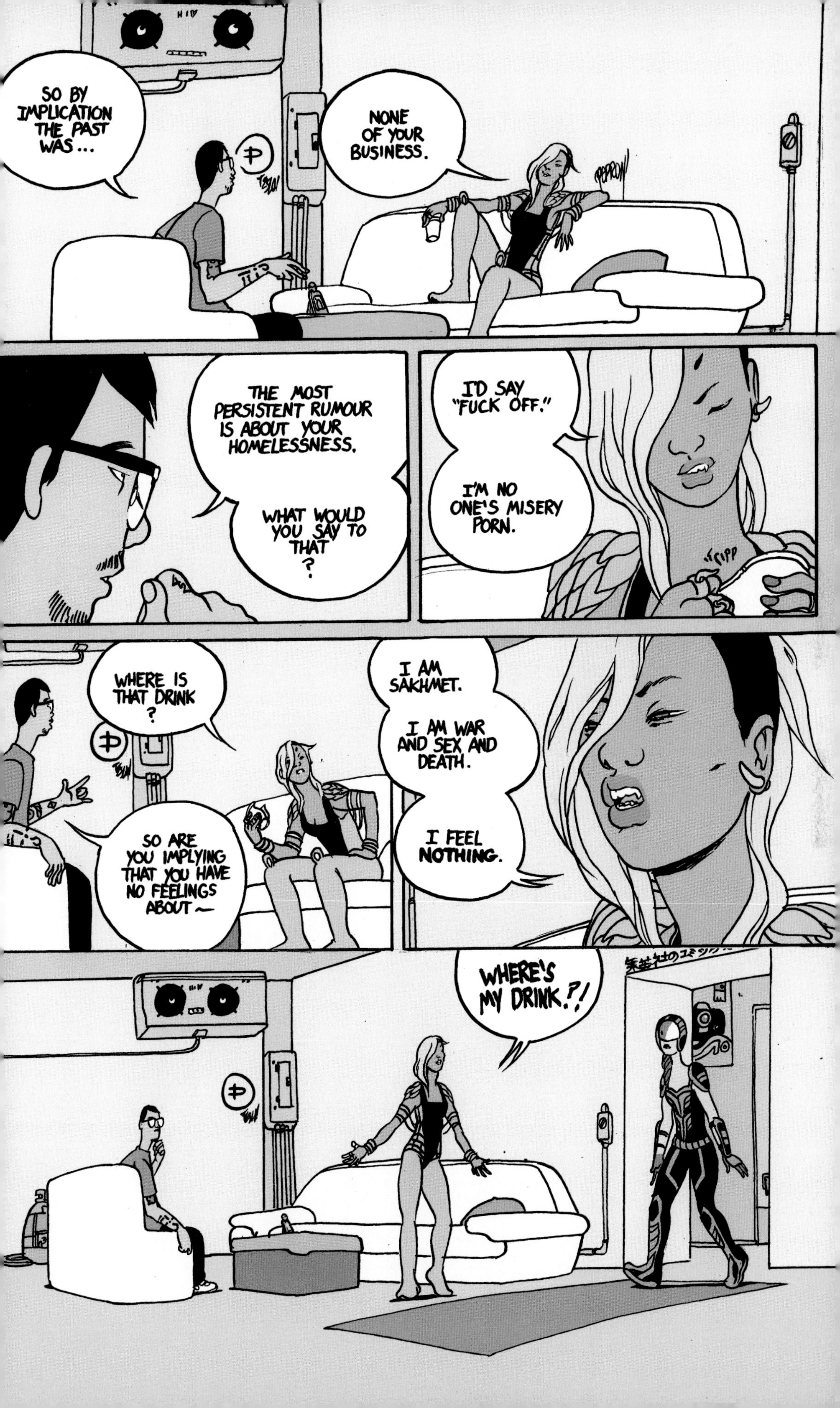
SO BY IMPLICATION THE PAST WAS...
NONE OF YOUR BUSINESS.
THE MOST PERSISTENT RUMOUR IS ABOUT YOUR HOMELESSNESS.
WHAT WOULD YOU SAY TO THAT ?
I'D SAY "FUCK OFF."
I'M NO ONE'S MISERY PORN.
WHERE IS THAT DRINK ?
SO ARE YOU IMPLYING THAT YOU HAVE NO FEELINGS ABOUT~
I AM SAKHMET.
I AM WAR AND SEX AND DEATH.
I FEEL NOTHING.
WHERE'S MY DRINK?!

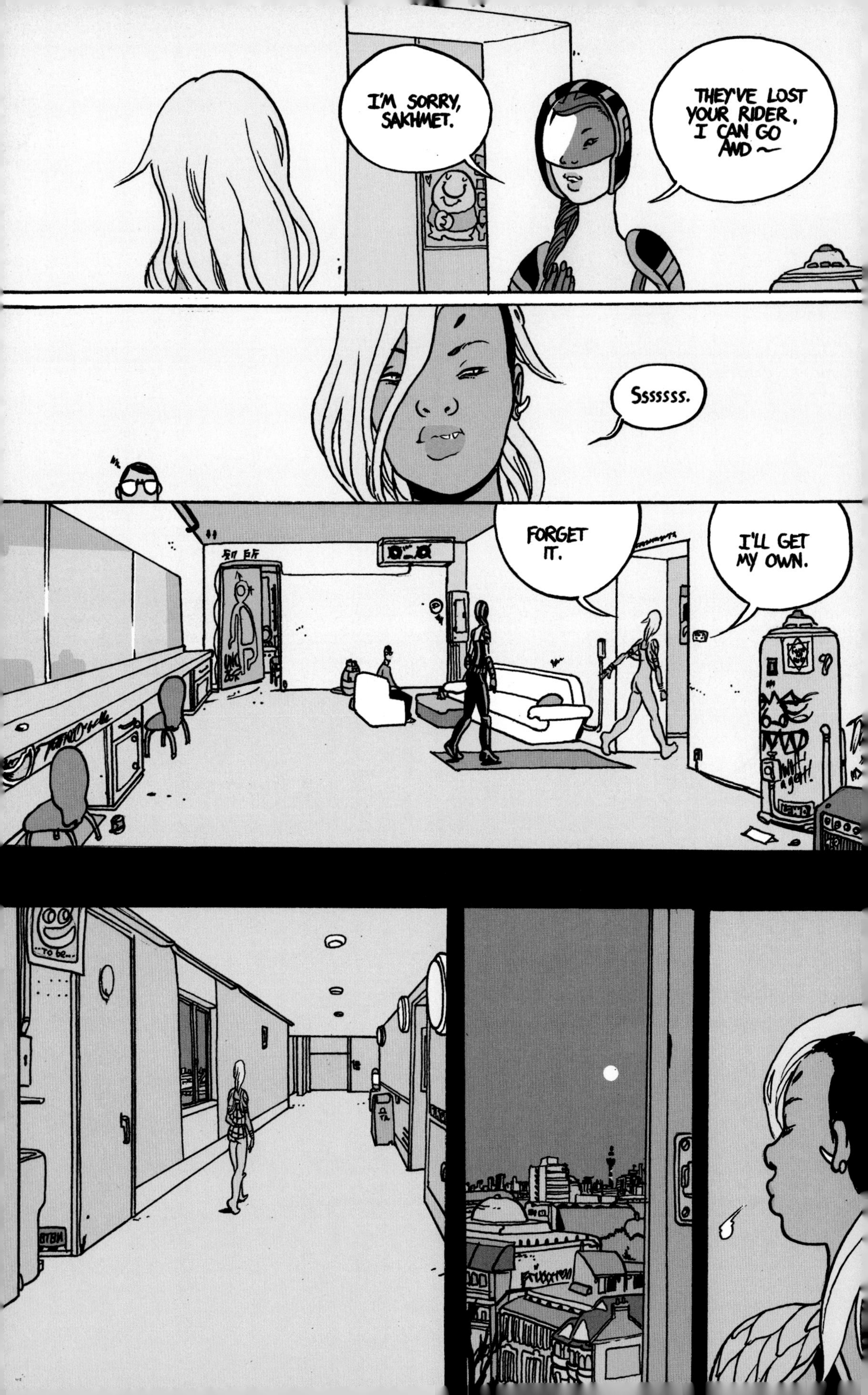
I'M SORRY, SAKHMET.
THEY'VE LOST YOUR RIDER, I CAN GO AND ~
Sssssss.
FORGET IT.
I'LL GET MY OWN.

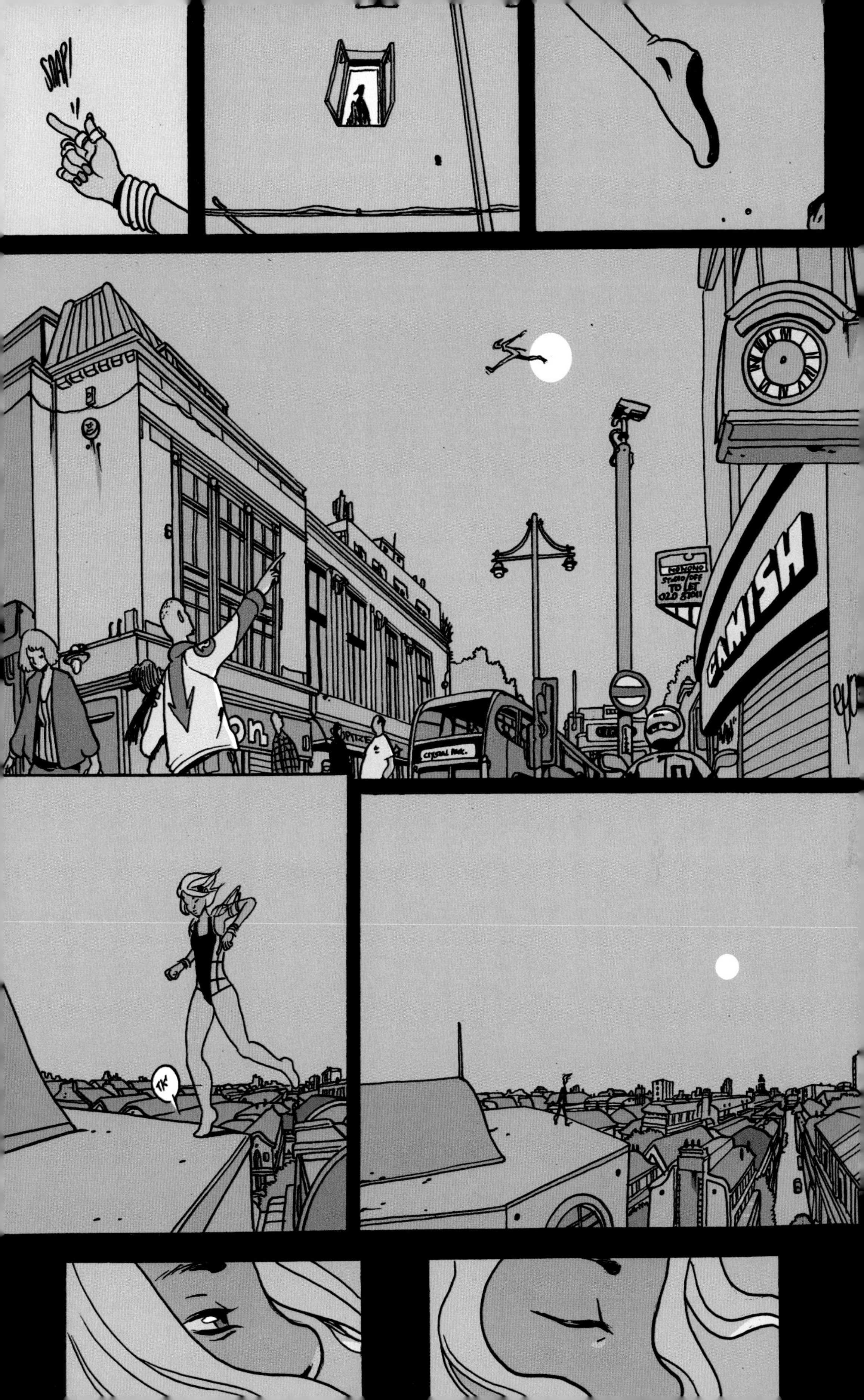
SNAP!
NONONO
STUDIO/OFF
TO LET
CAMISH
TK!

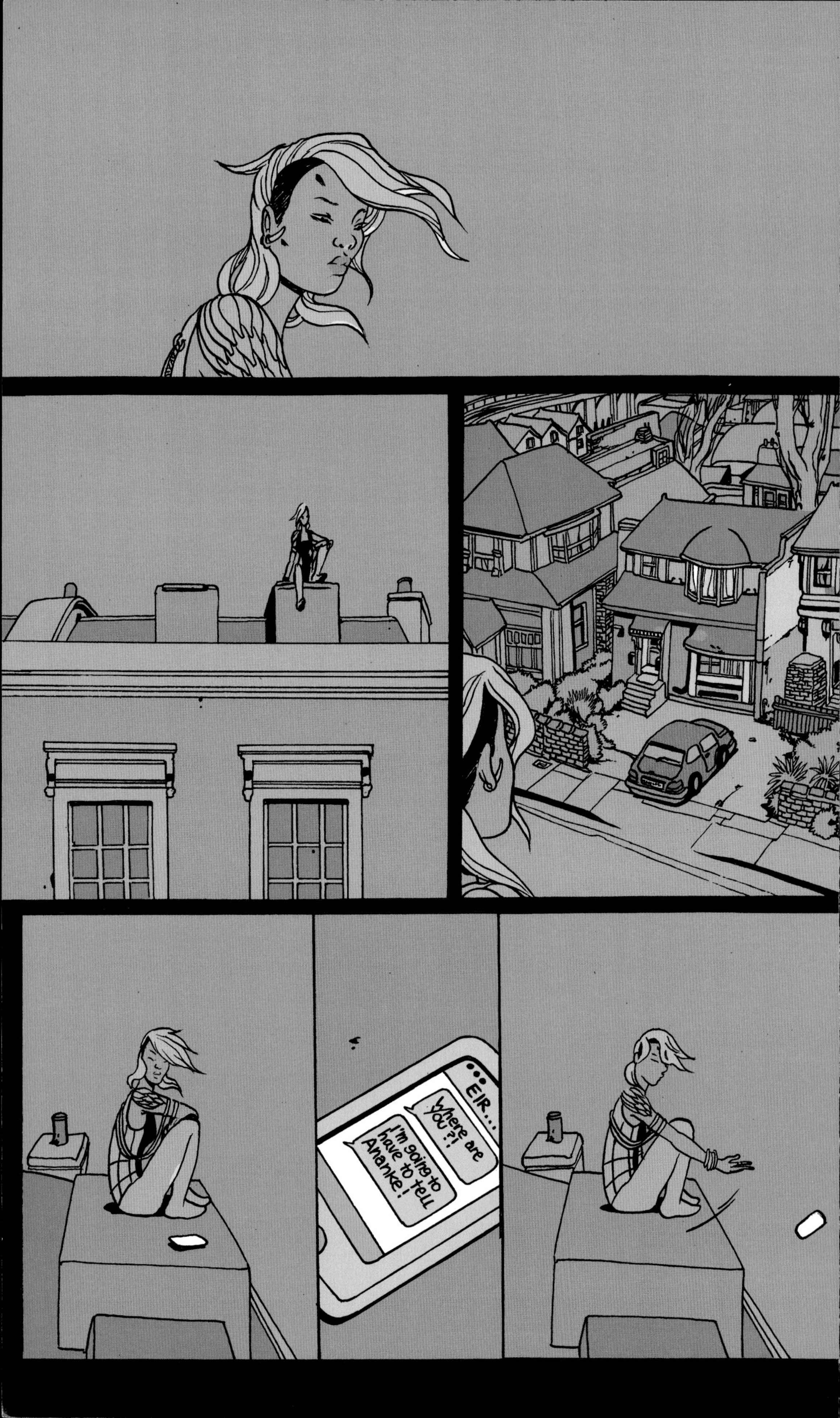
EIR...
Where are you?!
I'm going to have to tell Ananke!

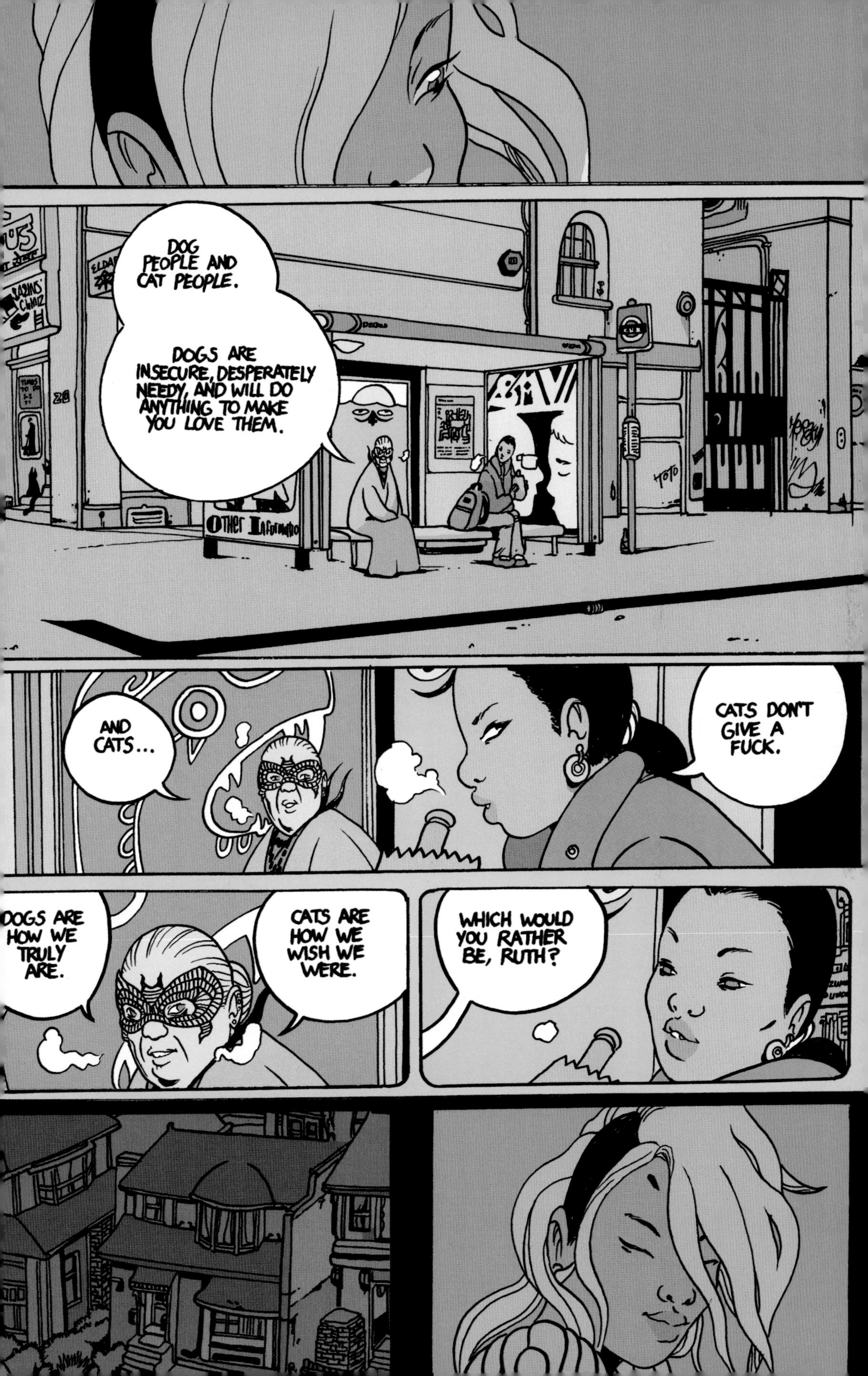

DOG PEOPLE AND CAT PEOPLE.
DOGS ARE INSECURE, DESPERATELY NEEDY, AND WILL DO ANYTHING TO MAKE YOU LOVE THEM.
OTHER INFORMATION
AND CATS...
CATS DON'T GIVE A FUCK.
DOGS ARE HOW WE TRULY ARE.
CATS ARE HOW WE WISH WE WERE.
WHICH WOULD YOU RATHER BE, RUTH?

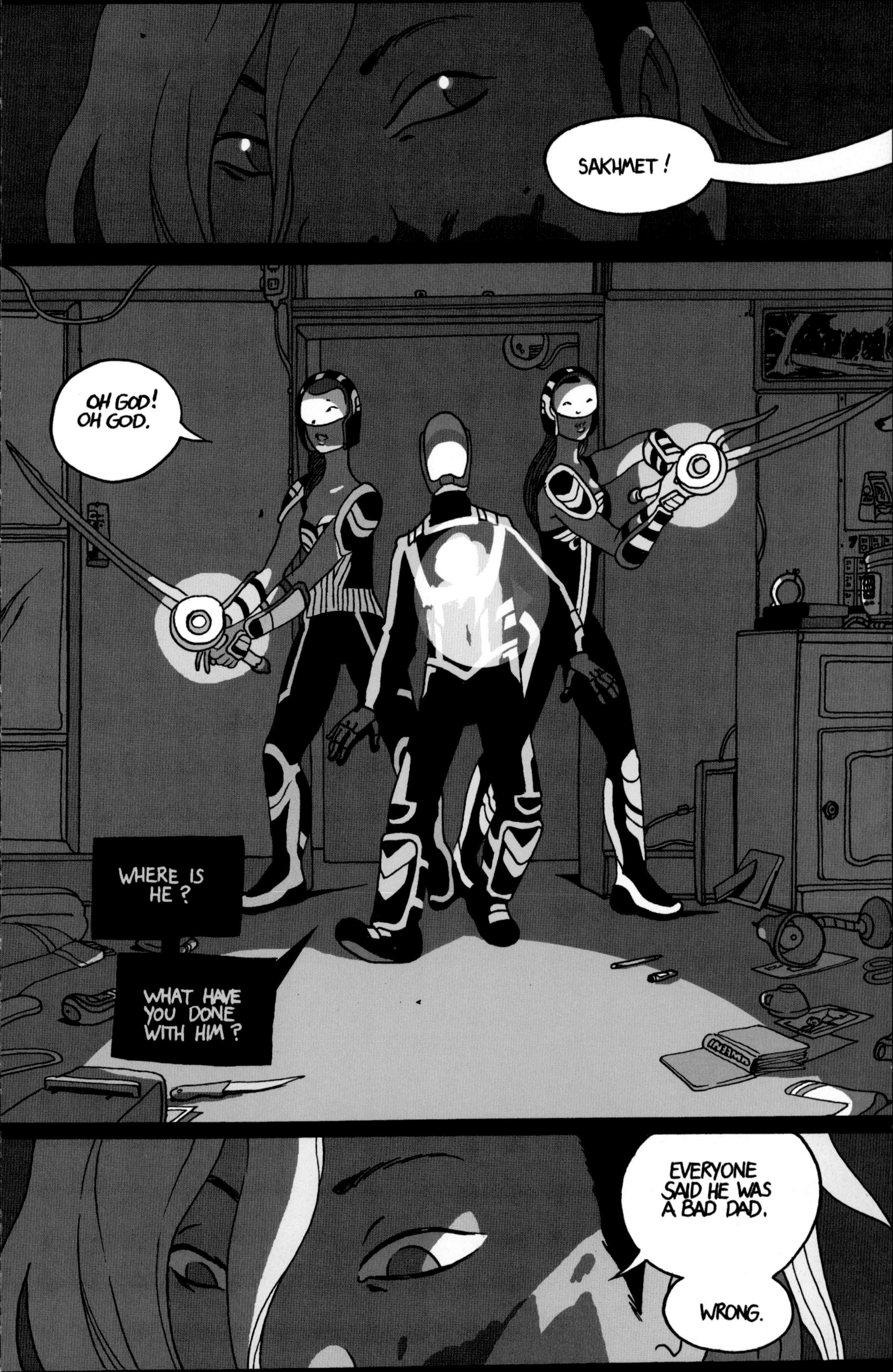
SAKHMET!
OH GOD! OH GOD.
WHERE IS HE?
WHAT HAVE YOU DONE WITH HIM?
EVERYONE SAID HE WAS A BAD DAD.
WRONG.

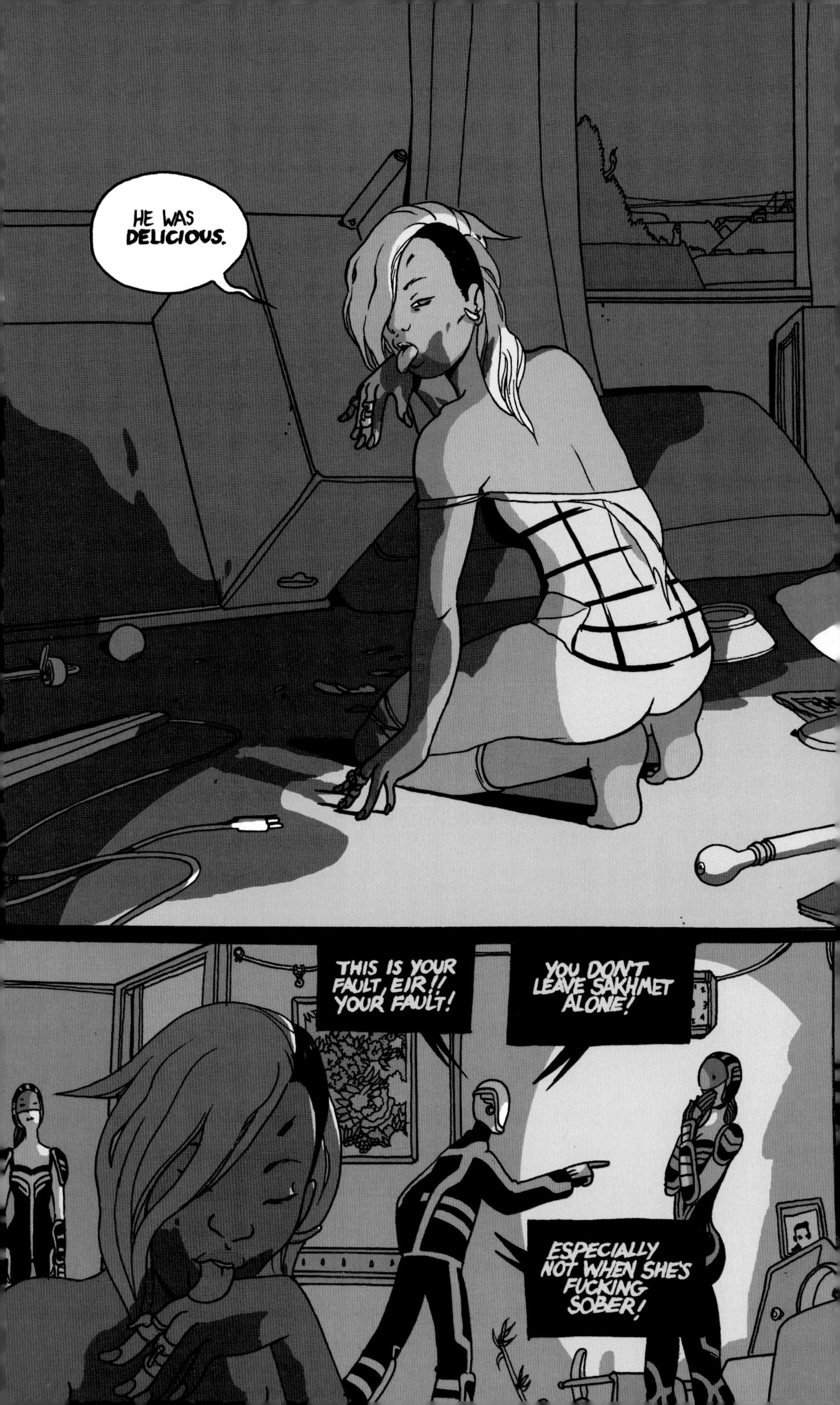
HE WAS DELICIOUS.
THIS IS YOUR FAULT, EIR!! YOUR FAULT!
YOU DON'T LEAVE SAKHMET ALONE!
ESPECIALLY NOT WHEN SHE'S FUCKING SOBER!

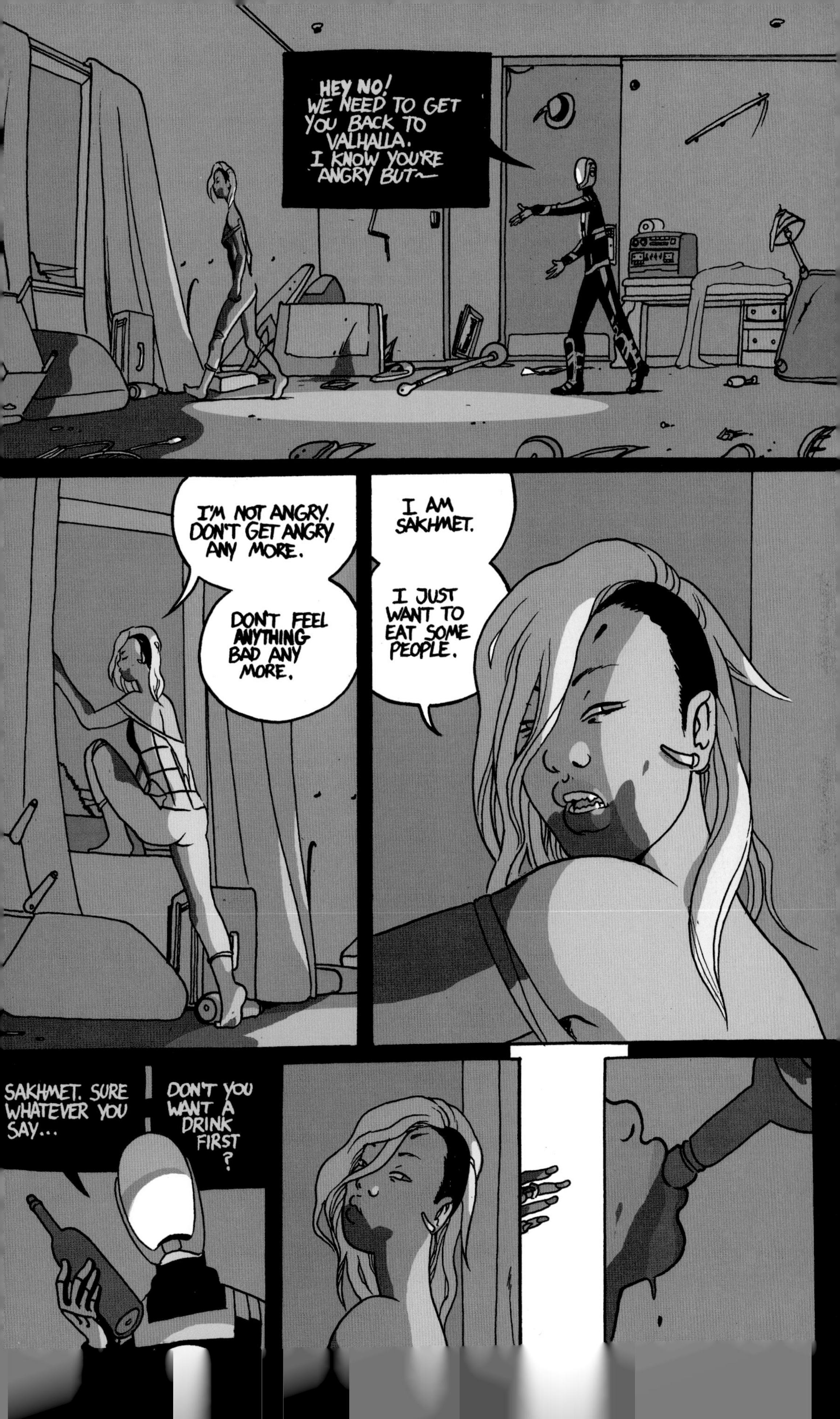
HEY NO! WE NEED TO GET YOU BACK TO VALHALLA. I KNOW YOU'RE ANGRY BUT~
I'M NOT ANGRY. DON'T GET ANGRY ANY MORE.
DON'T FEEL ANYTHING BAD ANY MORE.
I AM SAKHMET.
I JUST WANT TO EAT SOME PEOPLE.
SAKHMET. SURE WHATEVER YOU SAY...
DON'T YOU WANT A DRINK FIRST ?

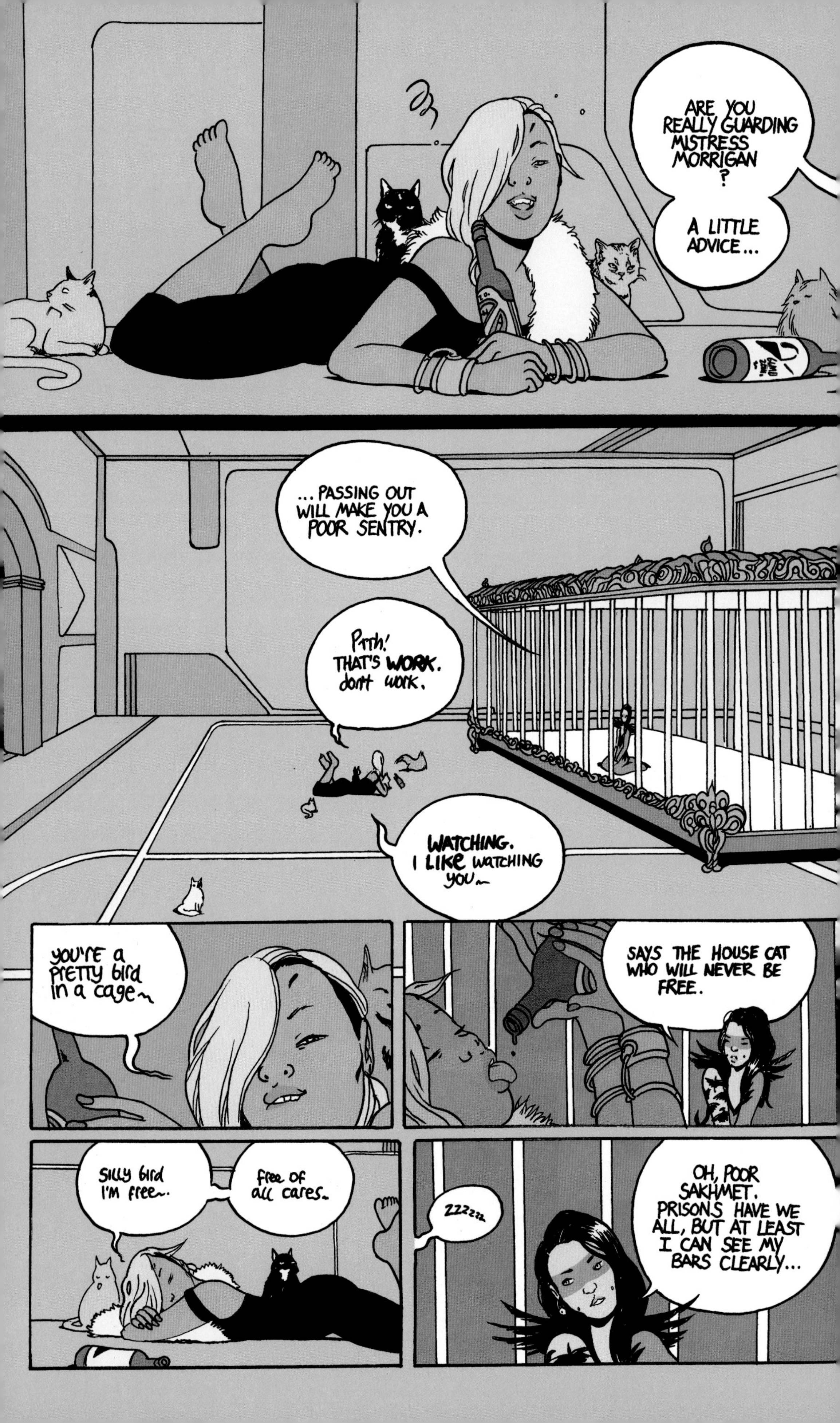
ARE YOU REALLY GUARDING MISTRESS MORRIGAN ?
A LITTLE ADVICE...
... PASSING OUT WILL MAKE YOU A POOR SENTRY.
Prrth! THAT'S WORK. don't work.
WATCHING. I LIKE WATCHING YOU~
you're a pretty bird in a cage~
SAYS THE HOUSE CAT WHO WILL NEVER BE FREE.
silly bird I'm free~.
free of all cares~
zzzzzz
OH, POOR SAKHMET. PRISONS HAVE WE ALL, BUT AT LEAST I CAN SEE MY BARS CLEARLY...

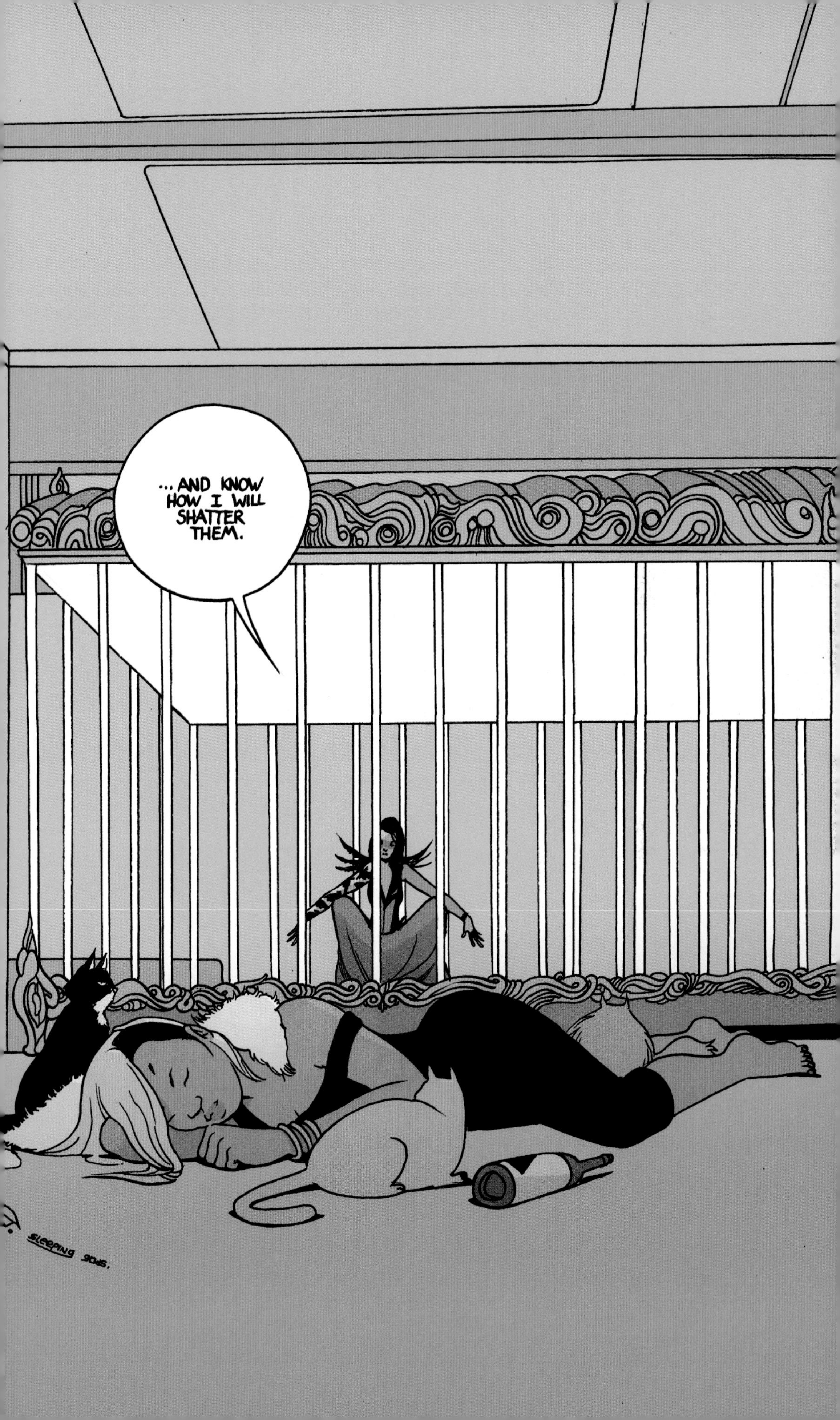
...AND KNOW HOW I WILL SHATTER THEM.
sleeping gods.

THE INEVITABLE CLIFFHANGER

9 SEPTEMBER 2014

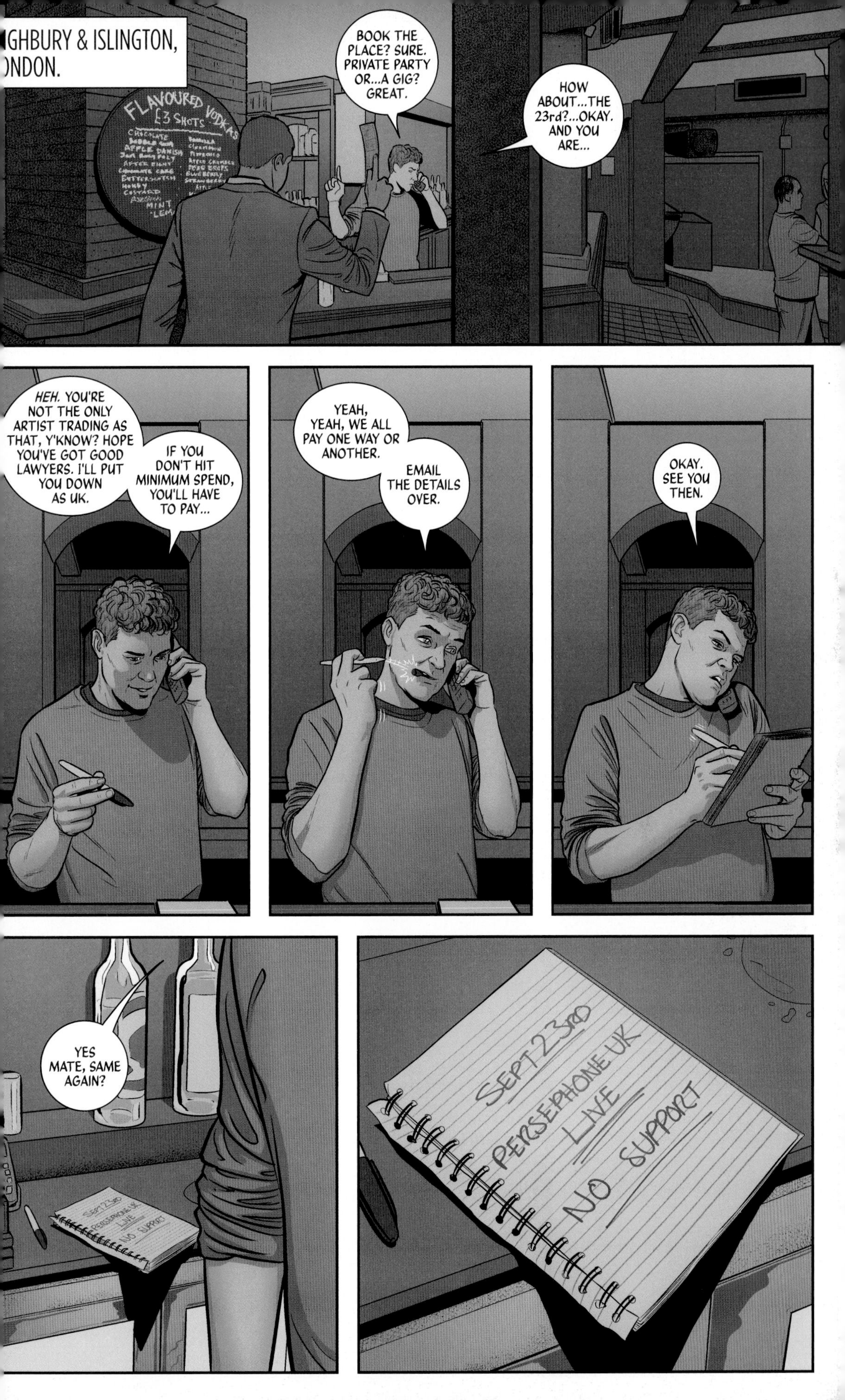
GHBURY & ISLINGTON,
ONDON.
FLAVOURED VODKAS
£3 SHOTS
BOOK THE PLACE? SURE. PRIVATE PARTY OR...A GIG? GREAT.
HOW ABOUT...THE 23rd?...OKAY. AND YOU ARE...
HEH. YOU'RE NOT THE ONLY ARTIST TRADING AS THAT, Y'KNOW? HOPE YOU'VE GOT GOOD LAWYERS. I'LL PUT YOU DOWN AS UK.
IF YOU DON'T HIT MINIMUM SPEND, YOU'LL HAVE TO PAY...
YEAH, YEAH, WE ALL PAY ONE WAY OR ANOTHER.
EMAIL THE DETAILS OVER.
OKAY. SEE YOU THEN.
YES MATE, SAME AGAIN?
SEPT 23RD
PERSEPHONE UK
LIVE
NO SUPPORT

UH-HUH
(SLIGHT RETURN)

9 SEPTEMBER 2014

VIDEOGAMES

As Jamie was away for this arc, we wanted to include an extra page by him in each issue to show that he hadn't just run away and left us. So was born a series of short one-page comics, acting as grace notes or introducing other aspects of the world, tied together by the fact they're all recorded. Hence, *Videogames*. To stress, these are all part of the *WicDiv* canon, which is a phrase we can't write without giggling at ourselves.

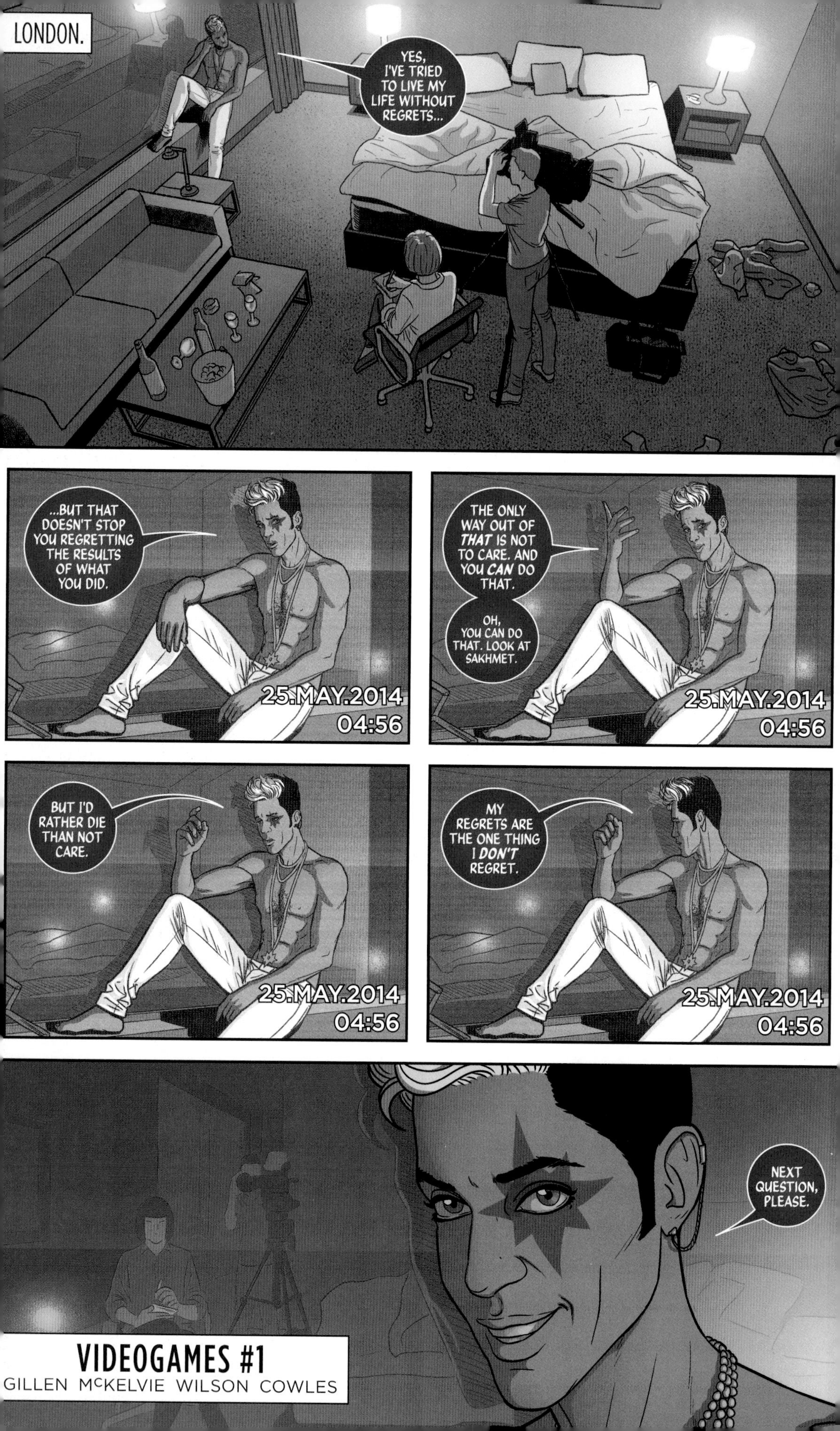
LONDON.
YES, I'VE TRIED TO LIVE MY LIFE WITHOUT REGRETS...
...BUT THAT DOESN'T STOP YOU REGRETTING THE RESULTS OF WHAT YOU DID.
25.MAY.2014 04:56
THE ONLY WAY OUT OF THAT IS NOT TO CARE. AND YOU CAN DO THAT.
OH, YOU CAN DO THAT. LOOK AT SAKHMET.
25.MAY.2014 04:56
BUT I'D RATHER DIE THAN NOT CARE.
25.MAY.2014 04:56
MY REGRETS ARE THE ONE THING I DON'T REGRET.
25.MAY.2014 04:56
NEXT QUESTION, PLEASE.
VIDEOGAMES #1
GILLEN McKELVIE WILSON COWLES

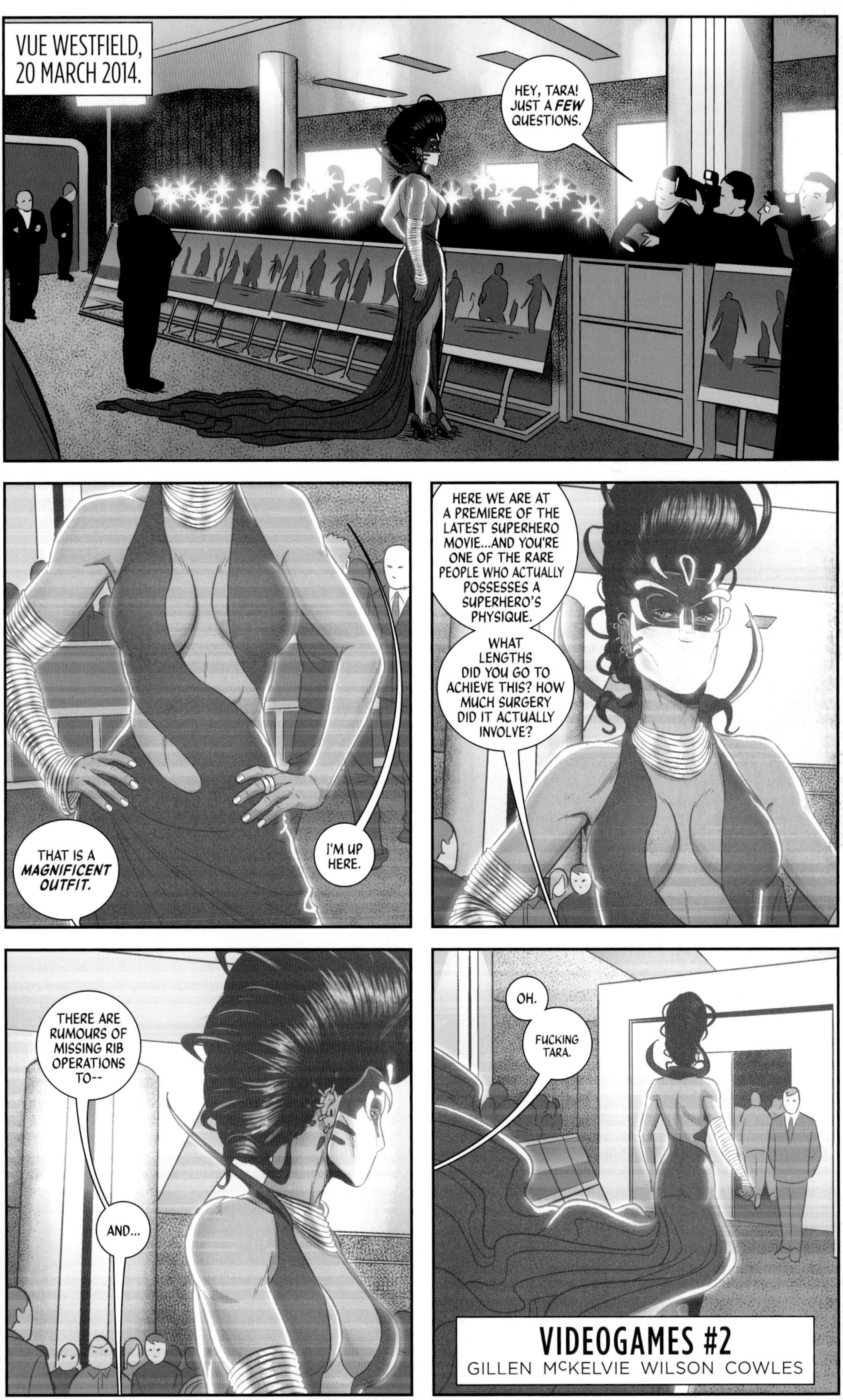

VUE WESTFIELD, 20 MARCH 2014.
HEY, TARA! JUST A *FEW* QUESTIONS.
THAT IS A *MAGNIFICENT OUTFIT.*
I'M UP HERE.
HERE WE ARE AT A PREMIERE OF THE LATEST SUPERHERO MOVIE...AND YOU'RE ONE OF THE RARE PEOPLE WHO ACTUALLY POSSESSES A SUPERHERO'S PHYSIQUE.
WHAT LENGTHS DID YOU GO TO ACHIEVE THIS? HOW MUCH SURGERY DID IT ACTUALLY INVOLVE?
THERE ARE RUMOURS OF MISSING RIB OPERATIONS TO--
AND...
OH.
FUCKING TARA.
VIDEOGAMES #2
GILLEN McKELVIE WILSON COWLES

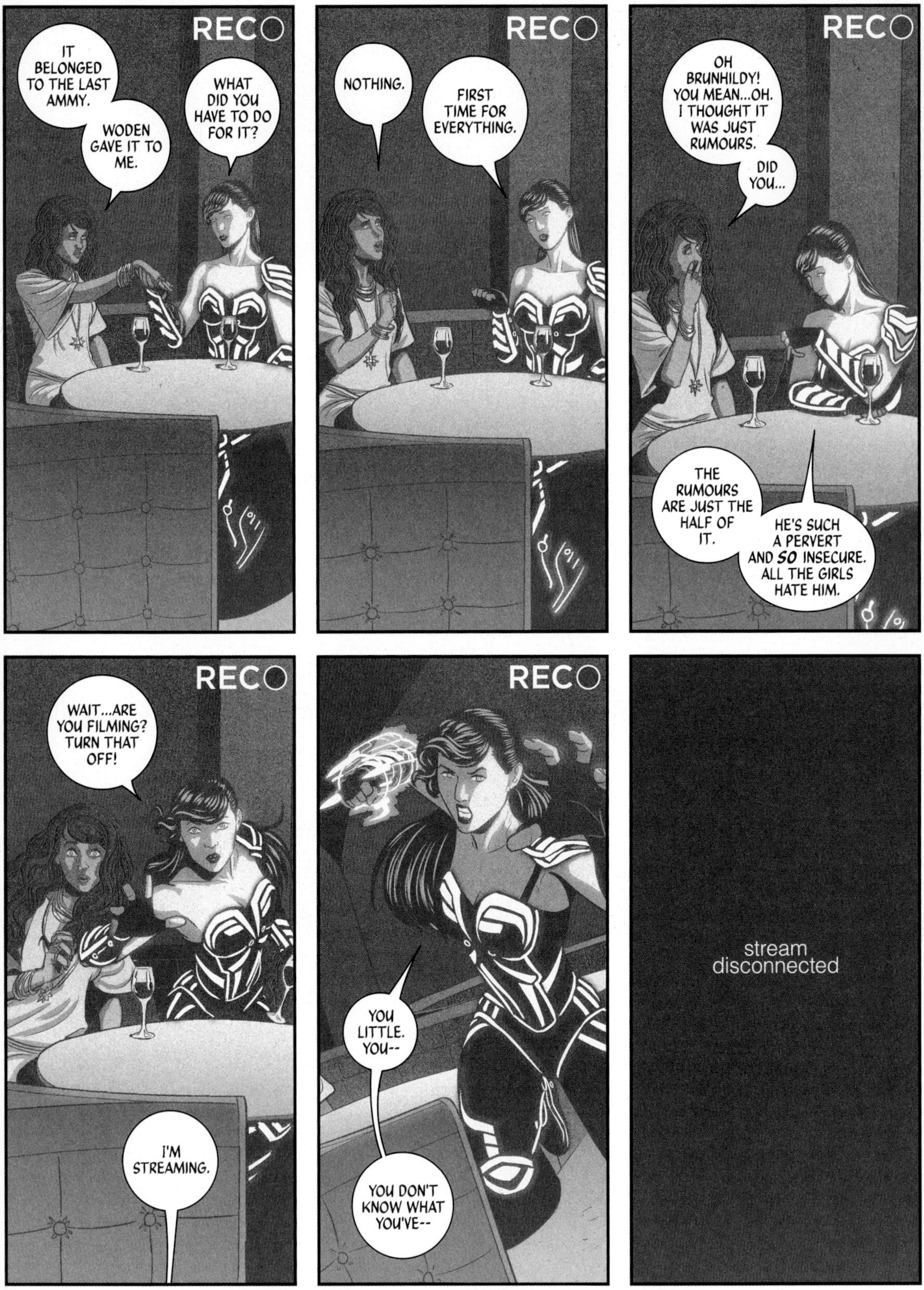
RECO
IT BELONGED TO THE LAST AMMY.
WODEN GAVE IT TO ME.
WHAT DID YOU HAVE TO DO FOR IT?
RECO
NOTHING.
FIRST TIME FOR EVERYTHING.
RECO
OH BRUNHILDY! YOU MEAN...OH. I THOUGHT IT WAS JUST RUMOURS.
DID YOU...
THE RUMOURS ARE JUST THE HALF OF IT.
HE'S SUCH A PERVERT AND SO INSECURE. ALL THE GIRLS HATE HIM.
RECO
WAIT...ARE YOU FILMING? TURN THAT OFF!
I'M STREAMING.
RECO
YOU LITTLE. YOU--
YOU DON'T KNOW WHAT YOU'VE--
stream disconnected

VIDEOGAMES #3

GILLEN McKELVIE WILSON COWLES

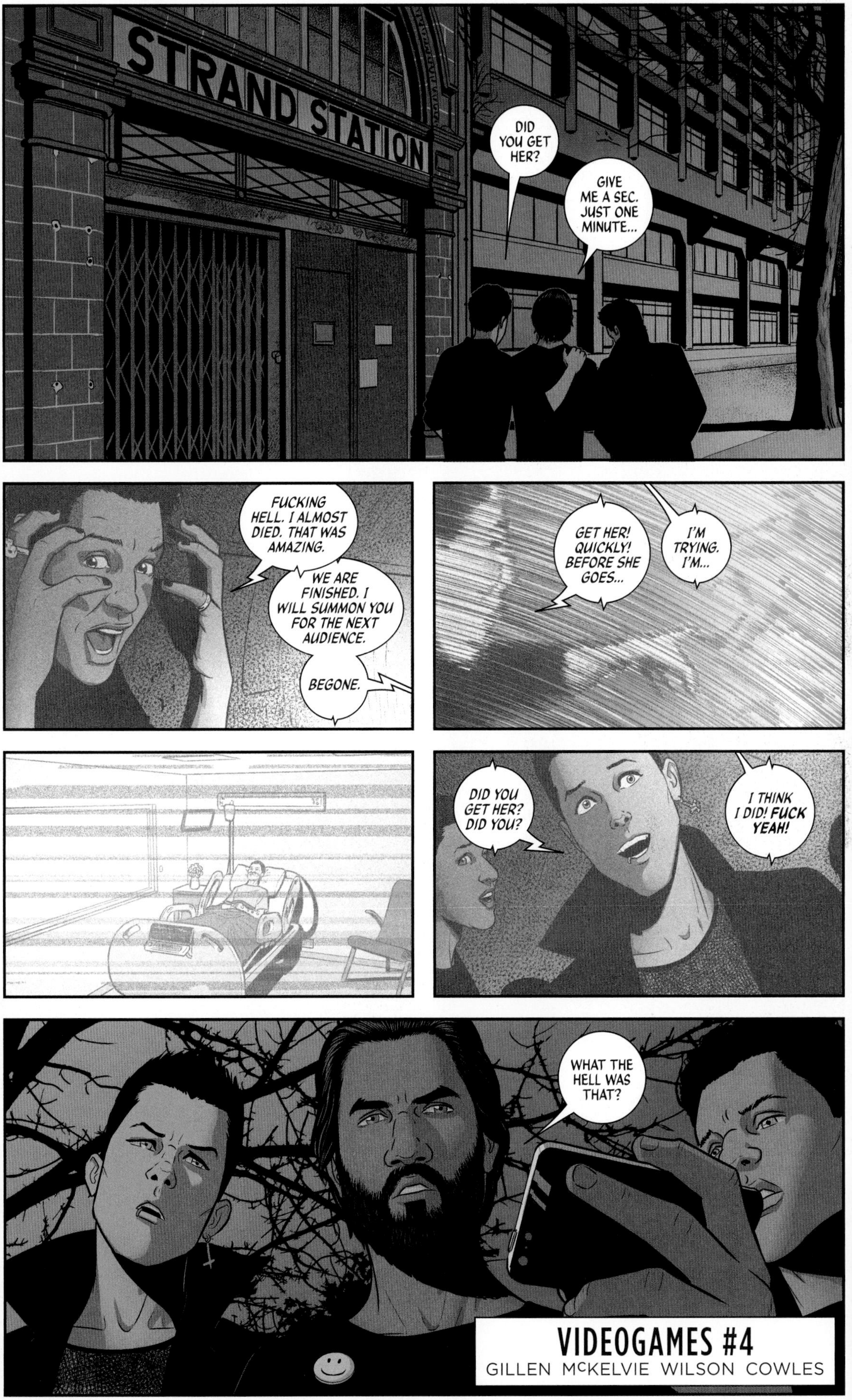
STRAND STATION
DID YOU GET HER?
GIVE ME A SEC. JUST ONE MINUTE...
FUCKING HELL. I ALMOST DIED. THAT WAS AMAZING.
WE ARE FINISHED. I WILL SUMMON YOU FOR THE NEXT AUDIENCE.
BEGONE.
GET HER! QUICKLY! BEFORE SHE GOES...
I'M TRYING. I'M...
DID YOU GET HER? DID YOU?
I THINK I DID! FUCK YEAH!
WHAT THE HELL WAS THAT?
VIDEOGAMES #4
GILLEN McKELVIE WILSON COWLES

VARIANT ART

Our alternate covers were easier to figure out this time: as we
had guest artists on each issue, we decided to let them each
have a cover of their own, to interpret the gods as they saw
fit. As such, Brandon and Stephanie both return to this section
after also having done covers for previous issues. The exception
to this system was issue 14's cover, where we asked Grimes if
she'd like to do one. That seemed like a logical thing to do.

Kate Brown
Issue 12 cover

Tula Lotay
Issue 13 cover

Grimes
Issue 14 cover

Stephanie Hans
Issue 15 cover

Leila del Duca & Mat Lopes
Issue 16 cover

Brandon Graham
Issue 17 cover

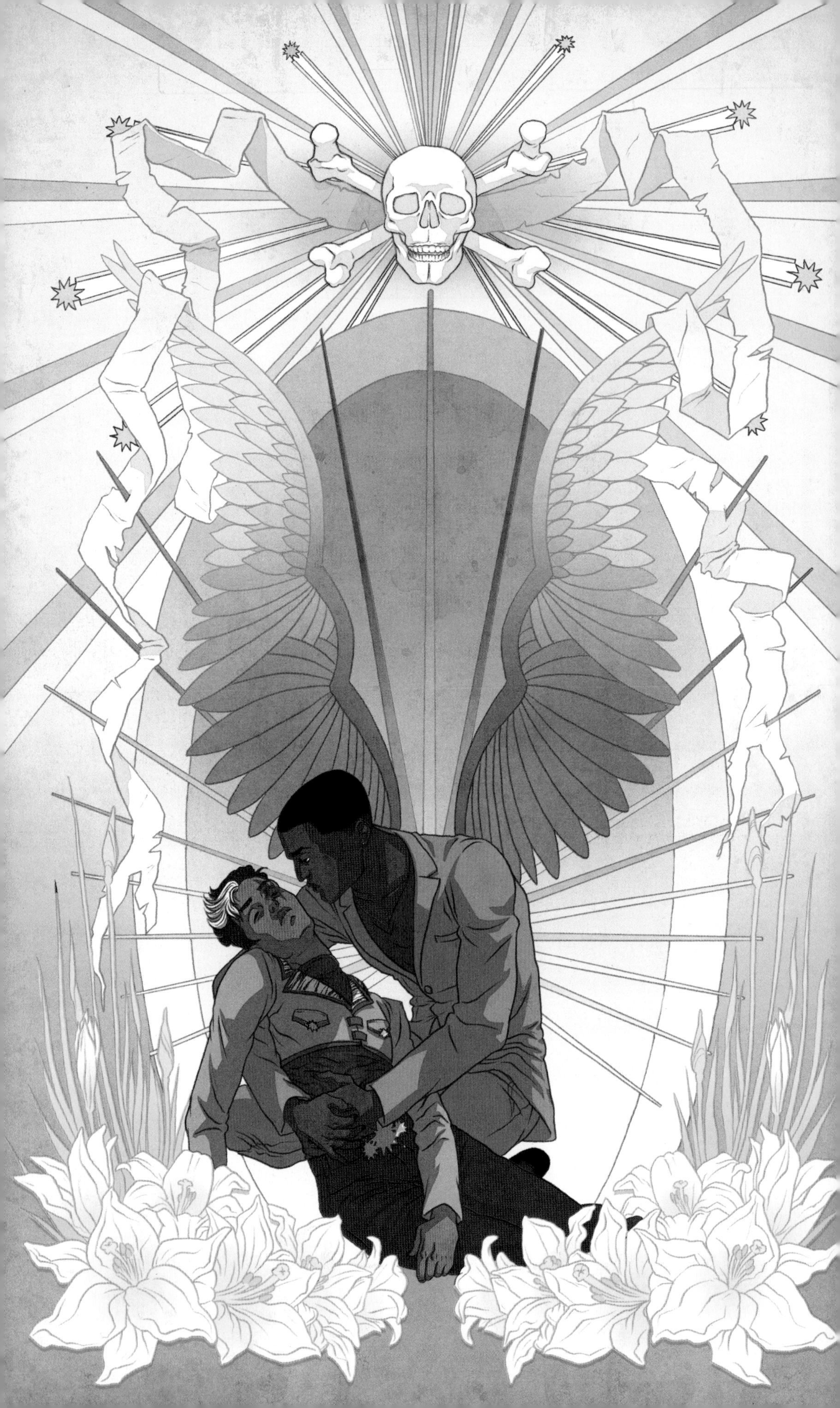

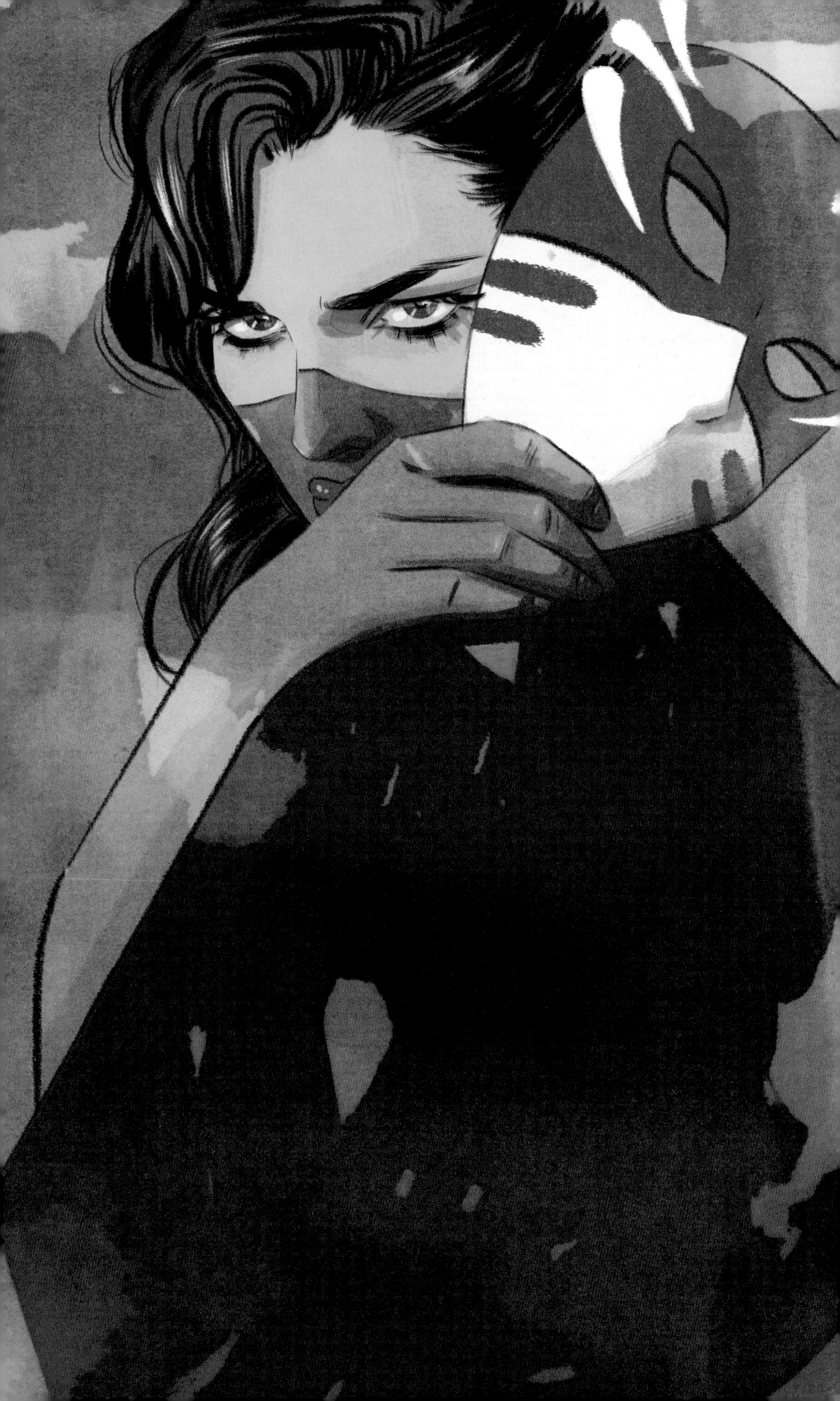

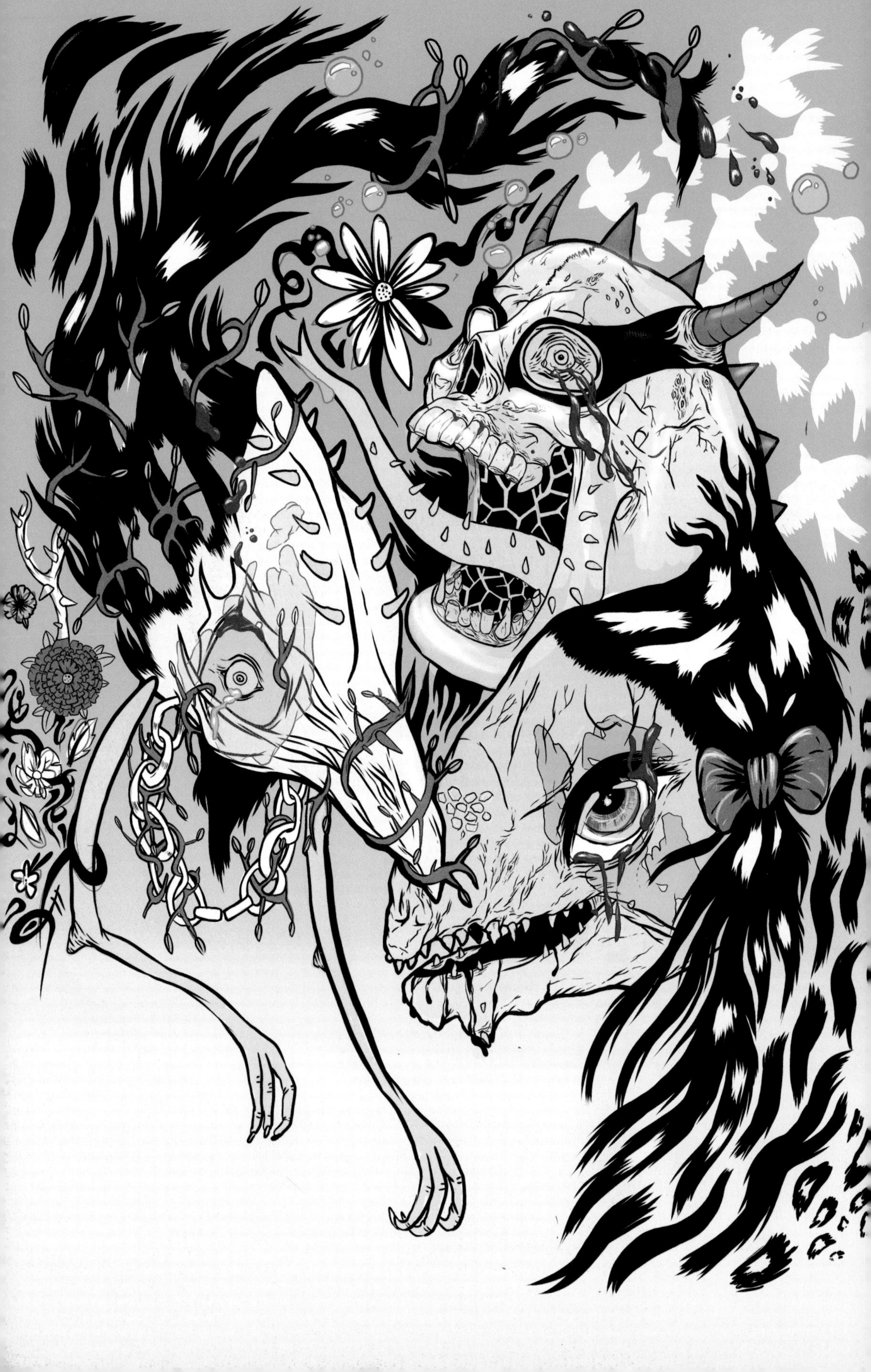

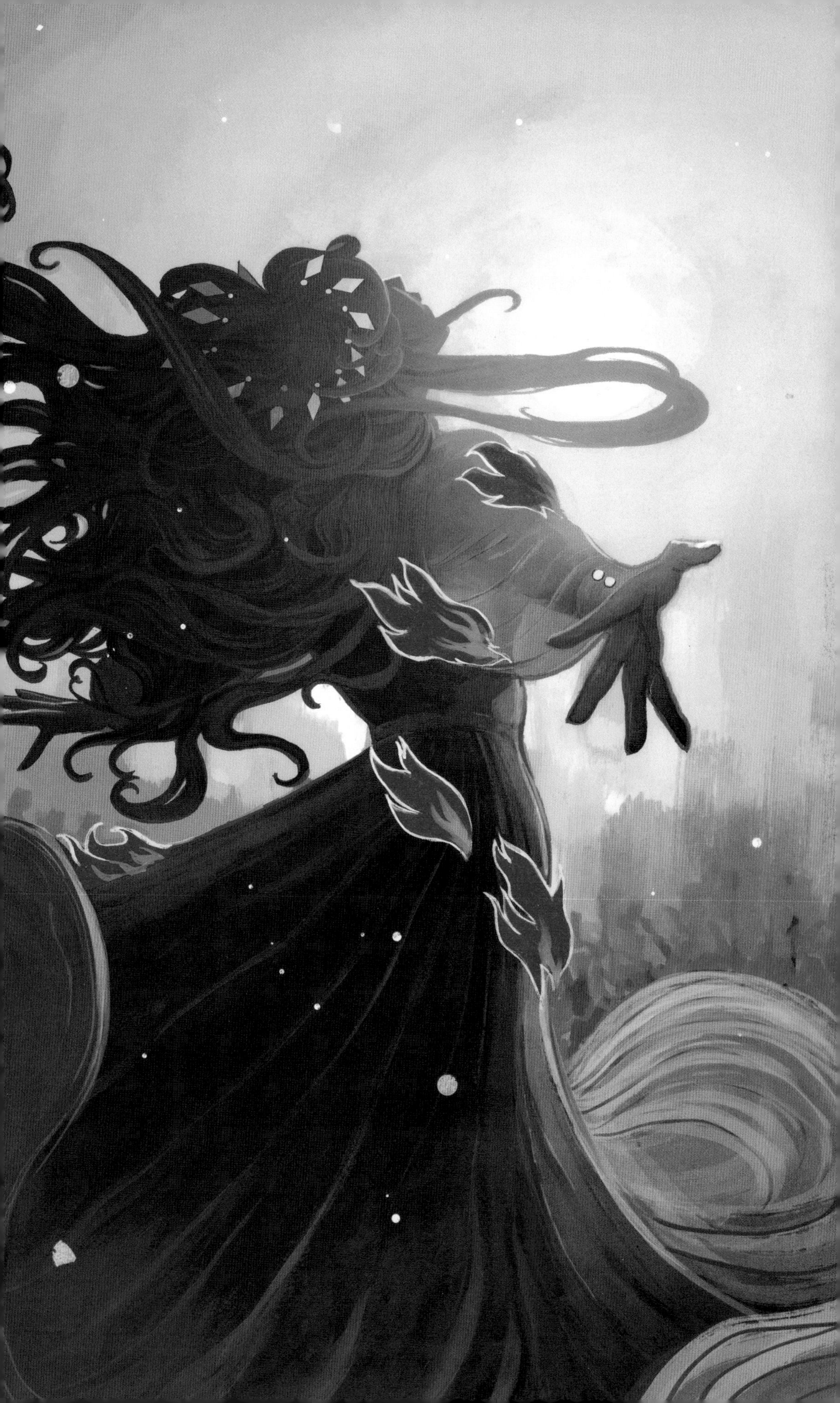

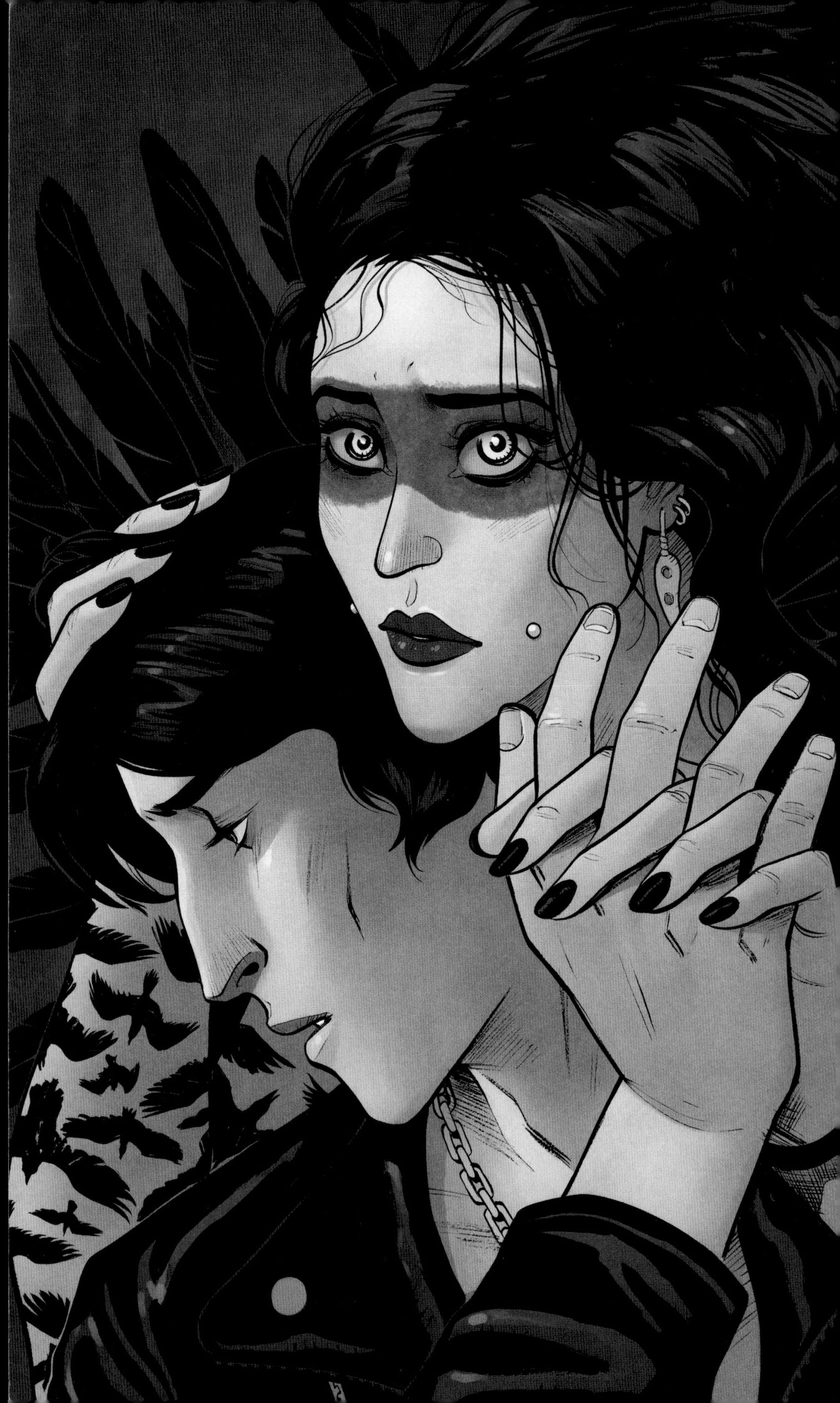

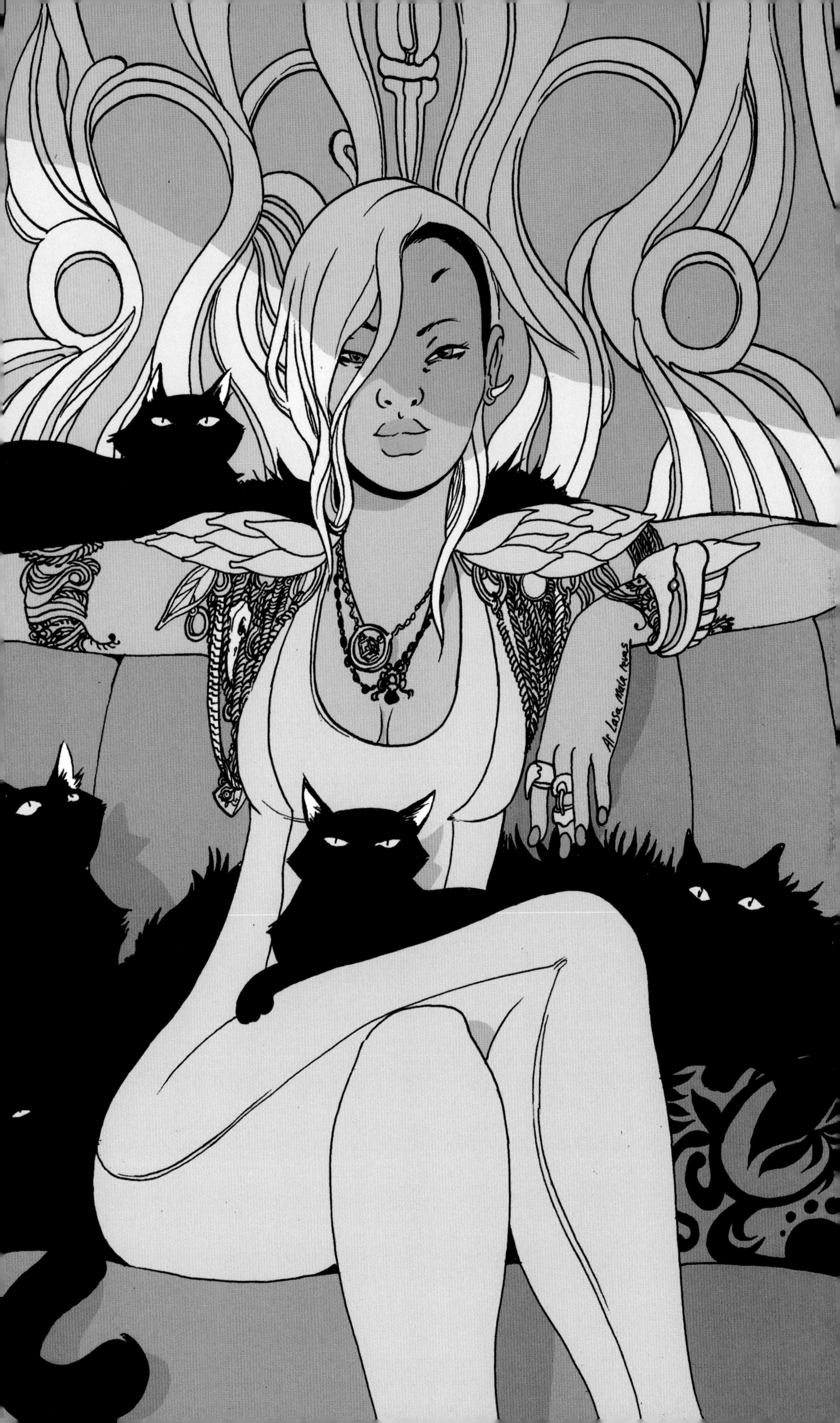

PROCESS

With six radically different issues by six radically different creators, we thought it worthwhile to show how they were done. Also, we have a page of Woden heads we cut out which we thought would be amusing and/or disturbing to show.

Here are some layouts **Kate Brown** puzzled over for the centre spread of issue 12, with a comment from Kate herself:

"I decided, stupidly, to try and shoe-horn Inanna in there somewhere by making his star-icon into a layout. This was quite challenging. Initially, I had it reading down the page as opposed to across as it is in the finals, but this wasn't working so well, and we changed it about a bit until we got something that did. As you can see the bottom-right corner doesn't really change — I often work backwards when doing thumbnails and try to solidify the page-turn first."

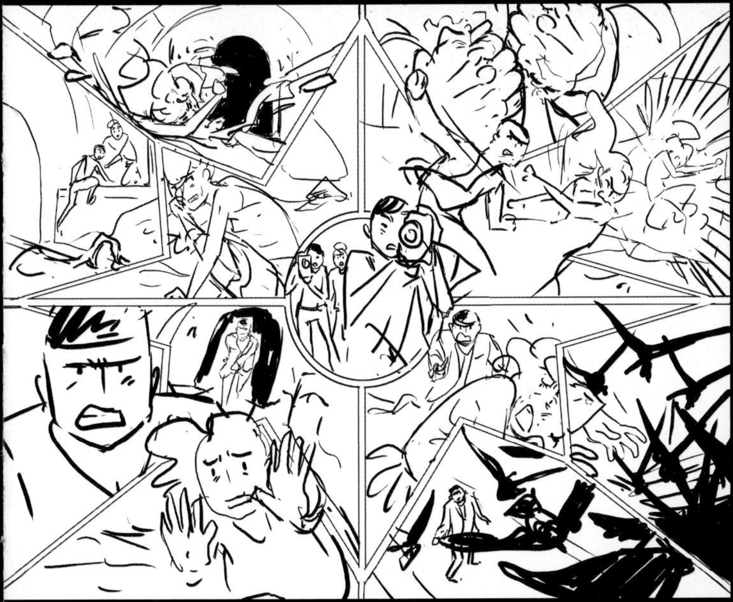

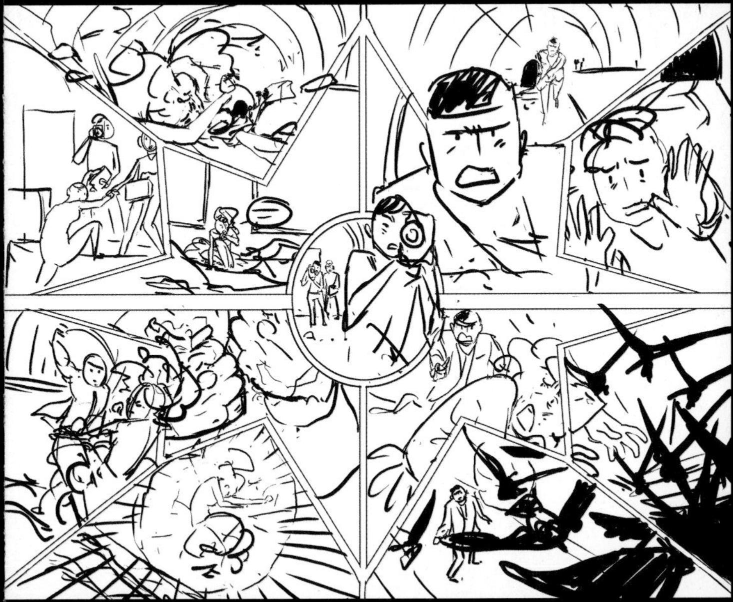

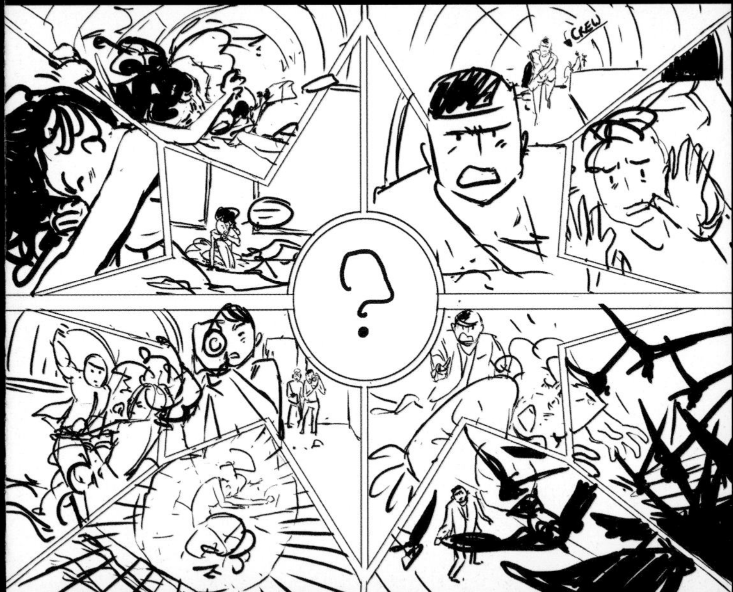
CREW
?

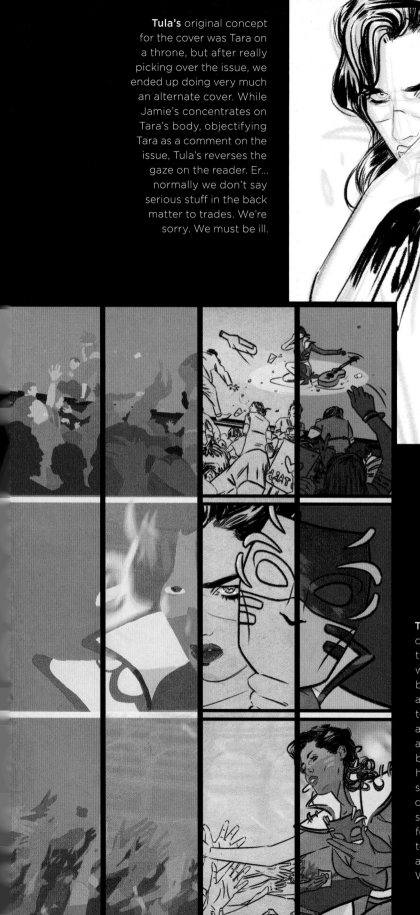

Tula's original concept for the cover was Tara on a throne, but after really picking over the issue, we ended up doing very much an alternate cover. While Jamie's concentrates on Tara's body, objectifying Tara as a comment on the issue, Tula's reverses the gaze on the reader. Er... normally we don't say serious stuff in the back matter to trades. We're sorry. We must be ill.

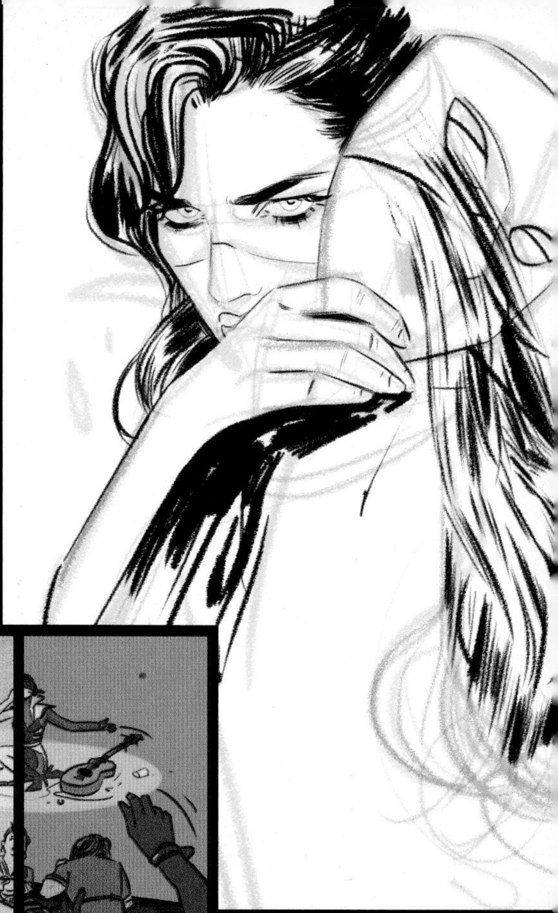

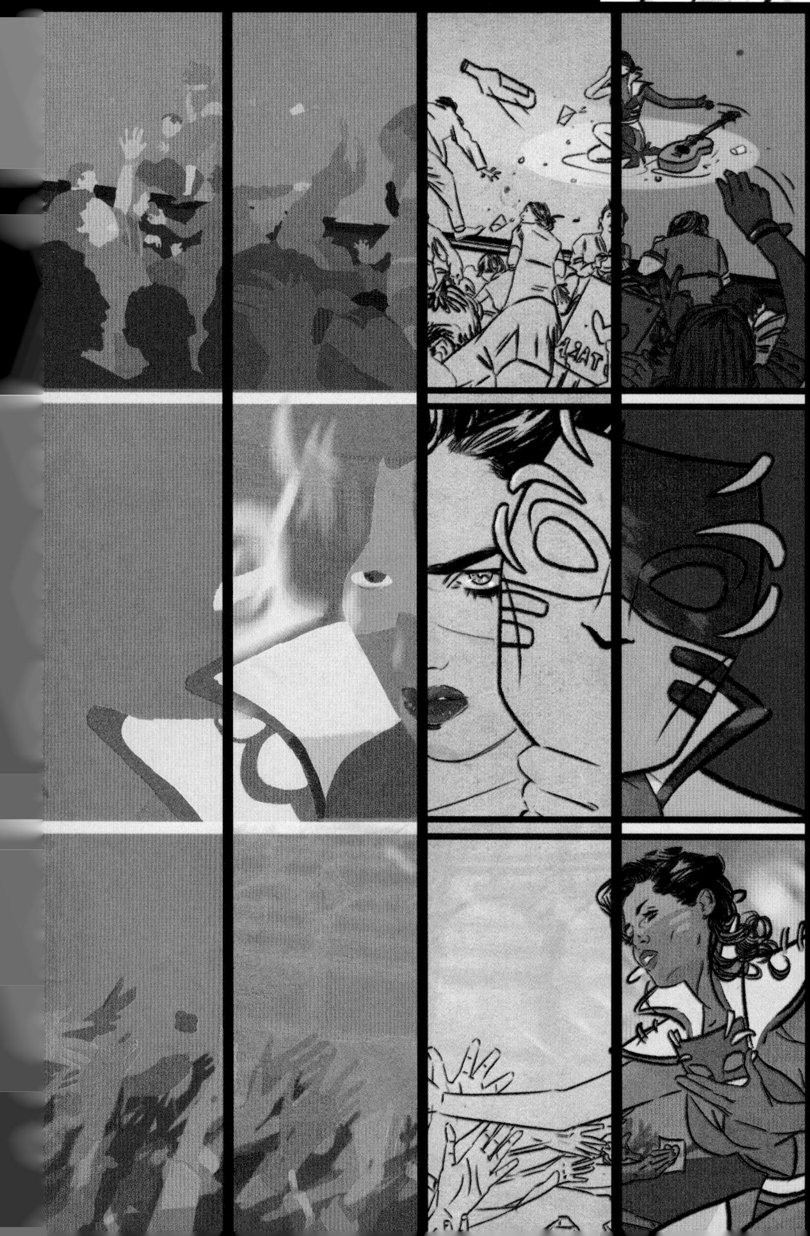

Tula's a non-traditional comics artist, and this was the first time she worked with a flatter. Dee did the basic shapes of colours, allowing Tula to paint on top of them. Tula thought about having someone actually do all her colouring, but we urged her to do it herself. There's something specifically about Tula's choices of colours which seemed appropriate for Tara, and we wanted to use that. Oh no. It's another serious caption. What is wrong with us?

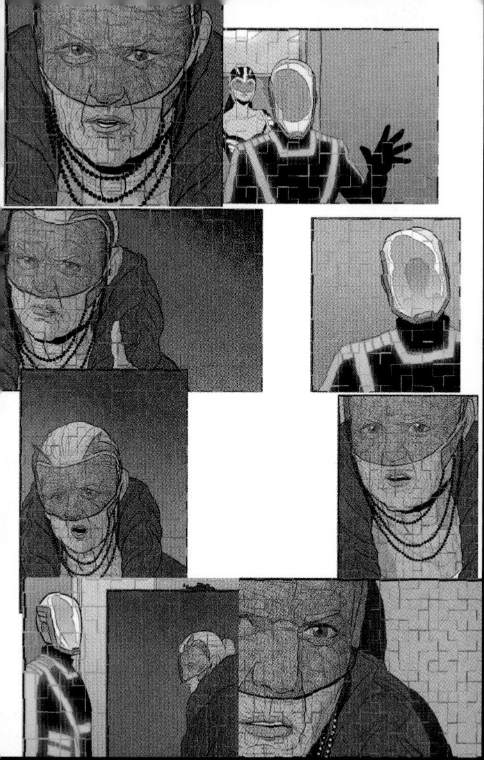

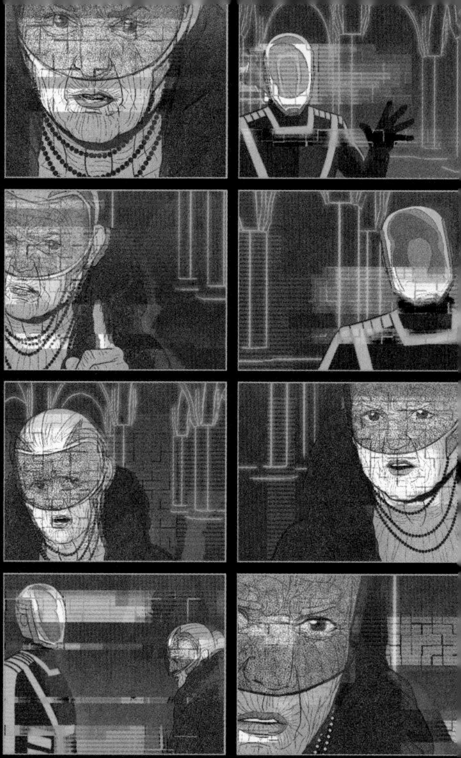

Matt, leaping on the remix aspect of the issue, thought that it may be fun to have a little visual "ghost" of the scene it's sampling from showing through. He started with composite images like so.

Then Matt composited that layer with Jamie re-arranged panels to create the final image If individual artefacts were too distracting, they were tweaked appropriately.

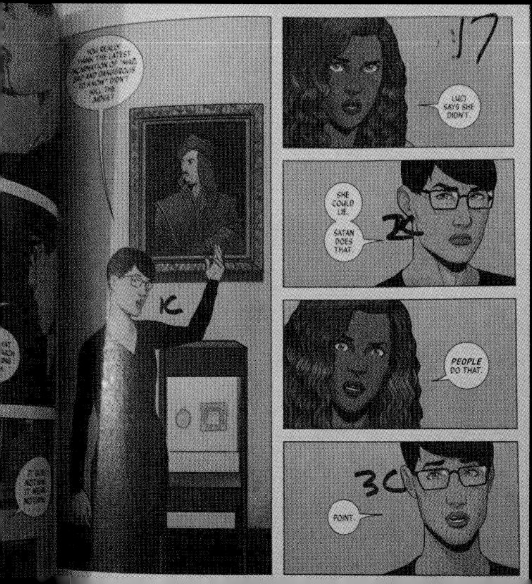

17
LUCI SAYS SHE DIDN'T.
SHE COULD LIE.
SATAN DOES THAT.
PEOPLE DO THAT.
3C
POINT.

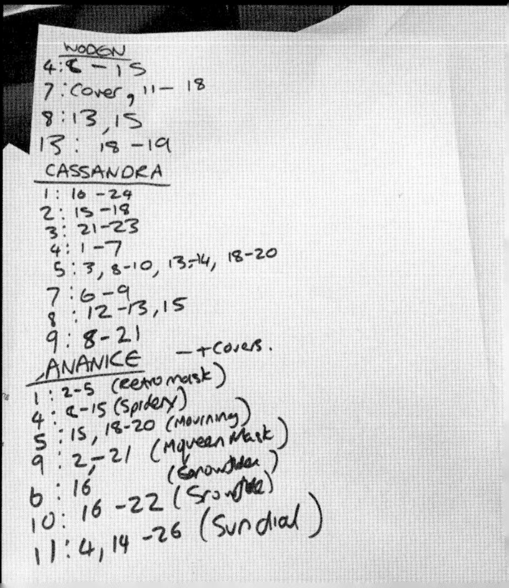

WODEN
4: 6 - 15
7: Cover, 11- 18
8: 13, 15
13: 18 - 19
CASSANDRA
1: 16 - 24
2: 15 - 18
3: 21-23
4: 1 - 7
5: 3, 8-10, 13-14, 18-20
7: 6 - 9
8: 12 - 13, 15
9: 8 - 21
ANANKE — + covers.
1: 2-5 (retro mask)
4: 8-15 (Spidery)
5: 15, 18-20 (Mourning)
9: 2, -21 (Mqueen Mask)
6: 16
10: 16 - 22 (Snowflake)
11: 4, 14 - 26 (Sundial)

f it, Jamie created a palette of Woden's every headshot in the book, which is quite the thing.

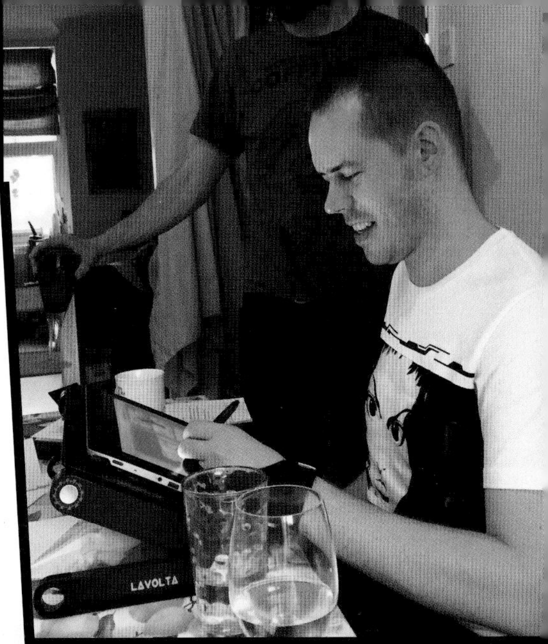
LAVOLTA

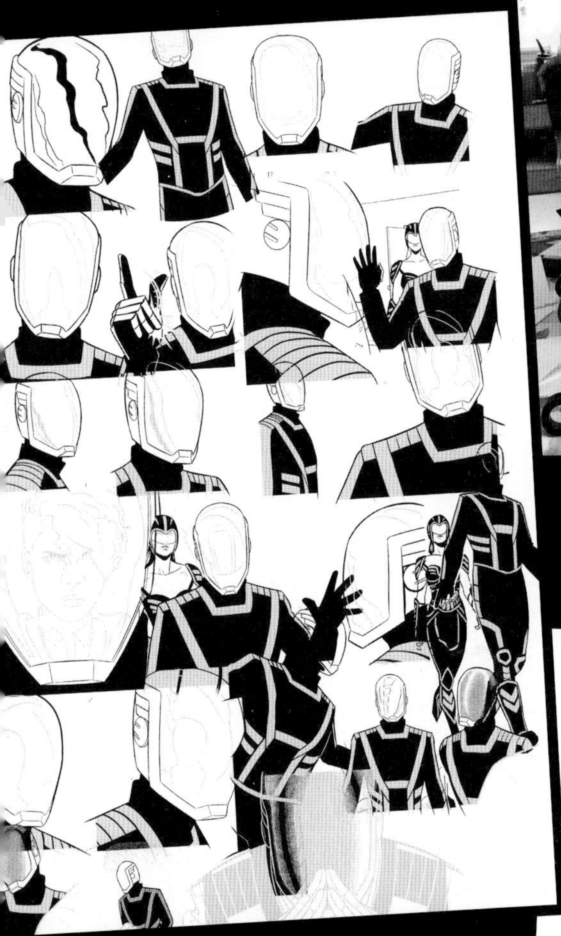

This transcript shows what editor Chrissy managed to note down of Kieron and Jamie's conversation in the height of the Woden reshuffling. You may (hopefully) recognise the "sexy" panels as not

KIERON: We'll have something sexy there. Woden. Woden here. Sexy sexy. Sexy there, sexy Amaterasu, Amaterasu, and sexy image here.

[lots of excitable pointing and instruction]

KIERON: Those two. No wait. That one!

[pause]

KIERON: We haven't got enough sexual enough images!

JAMIE: What if Luci was there, Ami was there, and Cassandra was there?

KIERON: We can't. It forms a column.

KIERON: Wait wait before you move anything! I have to get the rhythm right!

JAMIE: Is it worth squashing those up into a long one?

KIERON: NO.

JAMIE: I mean, you get what's going on?

KIERON: Trust me. I can make this work.

We set up the Dionysus mailing list in issue 7, having no idea what we'd use it for. In the lead in to NYCC, with our plan to sell Dionysus' T-shirts there, we thought it'd be fun to announce it via that. Of course, sending a grotesque commercial mailout felt crass, so we turned it into a continuity insert set just after Dionysus leaves Tara in issue 15.

From: Dionysus <dionyssiankissstory@gmail.com>
Date: Fri, Oct 2, 2015 at 4:11 PM
Subject: A Giggle At the Funeral

FFFFFFFFFFFUUUUUUUKKKKKKYYEHHHHHHHHH!!!

Shit.

No, can't fake it. Sorry, but Brother Dionysus is just got back from seeing Tara.

It's a mess. I'm so... angry?

I didn't exactly do myself proud there. Ended up saying some shit I regret. Only to Woden, but I still regret it. I stay away from Pantheon business. I really do. I've got my work, they've got theirs, and I'm about being there for as many as I can until this is all over. Together, we're immortal. The night's not so dark when we can see by each other's light. You're there for me. I'm there for you.

Wasn't there for Tara though, was I?

Fuck. Fuck. Fuck.

I can't believe it was Baph. I know half of you will hate me for that, but I can't. I still can't.

You ever been let down that bad?

Maybe I've always just been rainforest frog carrying a scorpion on my back. What a surprise! It stabs me.

Standing there, I wanted to fight them all. I'm not a fighter. I'm a lover. I've always stayed away from the Pantheon. The stink of Woden in that place. Hate it. They came to me, and in my church we're all equal. They've been barred since they've locked up the Morrigan. They don't get my communion if they act like that.

None of you know what they did to her to bring her in.

I only came to them at because of Tara. Sorry, girl. Never met you. Can't but help feel it was my fault.

I wanna be your messiah. It's not complex, guys.

I want you to go and call a person you love who you haven't talked to for a while. Call them and tell them that you love them and your life was better for having them in it.

If you don't have anyone like that, just hug yourself, even if you don't love yourself. You should. You're better than you give yourself credit for.

God. Got to get back. No time for this. Coffee is kicking in at least.

So...

LET'S SEE YOUR HANDS IN THE AIR!

<Plug for NYCC T-shirts deleted, as it's kind of irrelevant>

Okay. I'm done. Peace out.

Sleep when you're dead.

Love
Dio.

Having worked with **Stephanie** on *Journey Into Mystery*, Kieron had an idea of Stephanie's process. Like Jamie, he wrote certain sequences in Marvel method, to allow her to interpret things in her own style. The experience taught Kieron that Stephanie was really good at compressing dramatic images into a multi-panel page and remaining powerful — as such a fight sequence which would normally have been much longer was compressed into a few pages, like so.

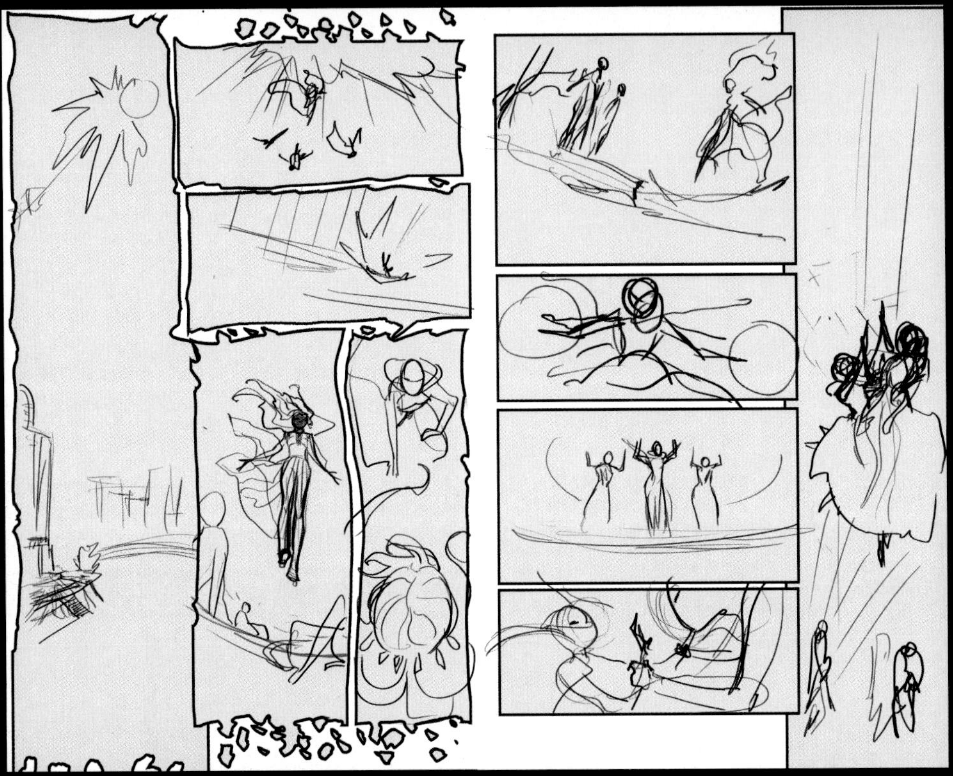

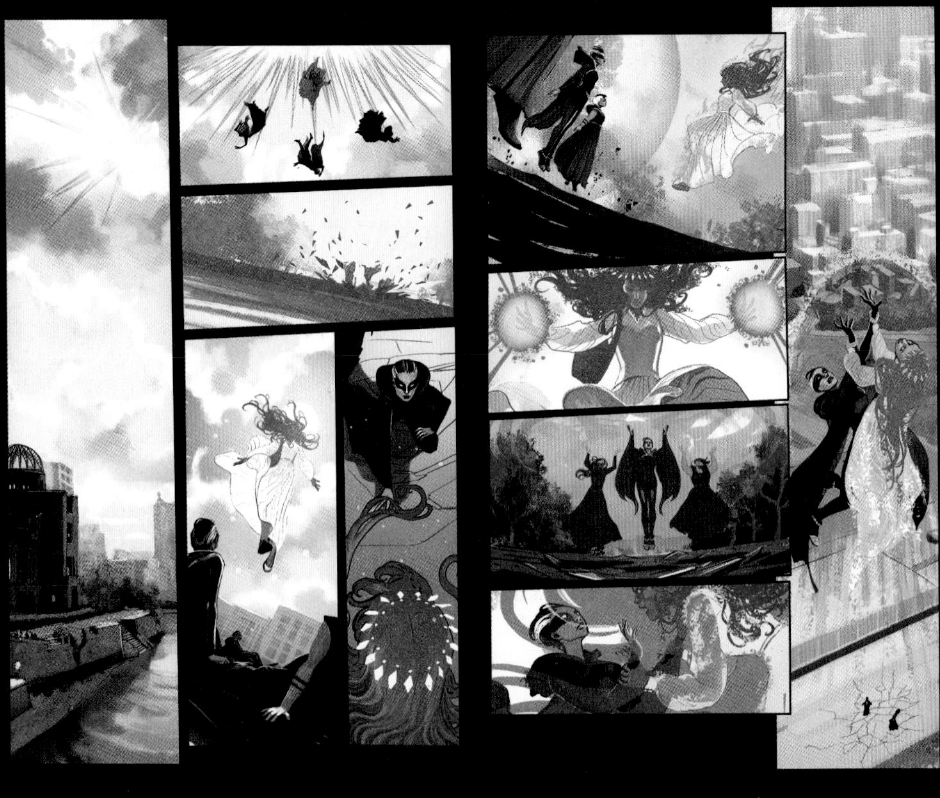

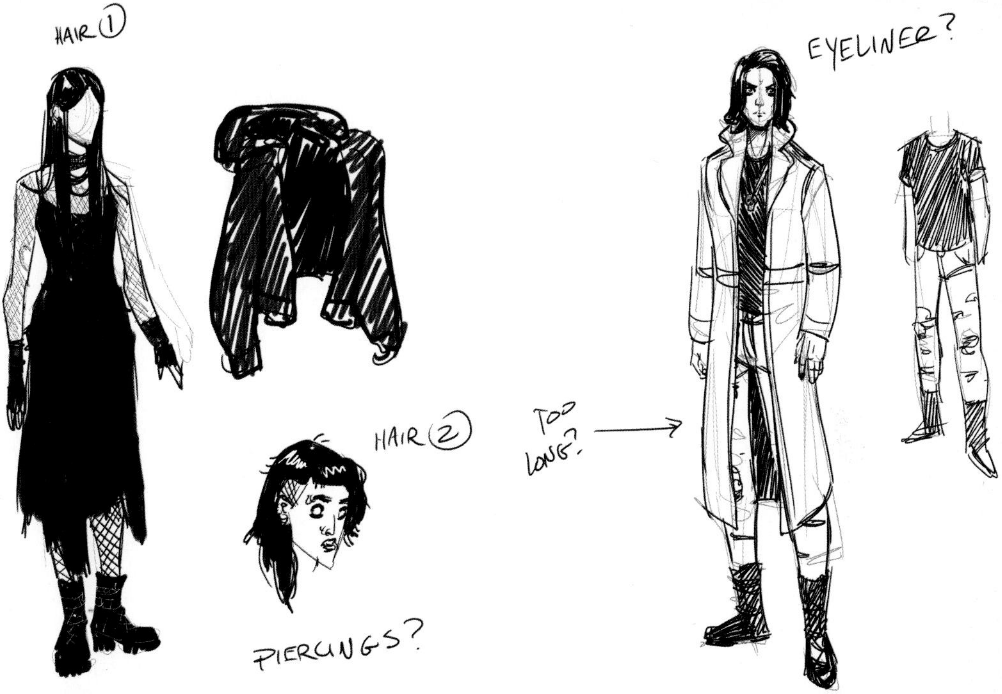
HAIR ①
HAIR ②
PIERCINGS?
TOO LONG?
EYELINER?

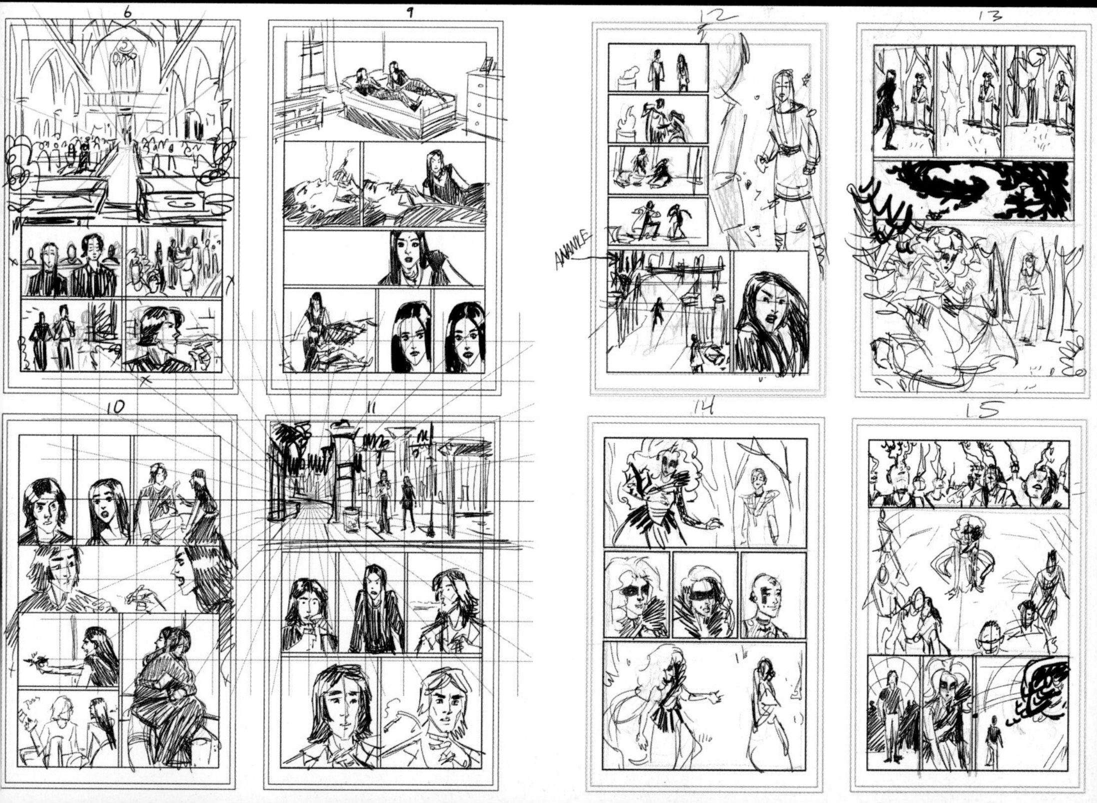
6
9
12
13
10
11
14
15
ANANKE

I'm not crying
Whatever.

She's made of stone.
She doesn't feel anything.

Morning, Sakhmet.
Is it?

Baal
Woden
Minerva.

Maybe a closer shot or
another panel closer in?

At least pretend to give a fuck.
Bored.
If Ananke's right and we're headed to an armageddon, you need to practice and--

You're playing tonight.
Are you ready?

oh
It's so hard to be adored

I'm sorry, Sakhmet--
They've--
Forget it. I'll get my own

How do you feel
about her snapping the window open?

Sakhmet. I know you're angry--
I mean --
I'm not angry--
I am Sakhmet
I just have to
Sakhmet, sure--

Are you really
silly--
Oh, poor

...and know how I will shatter them.

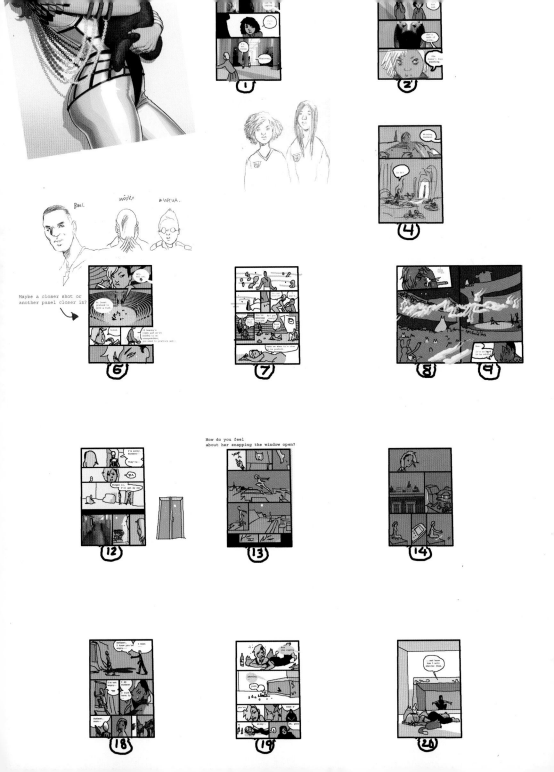

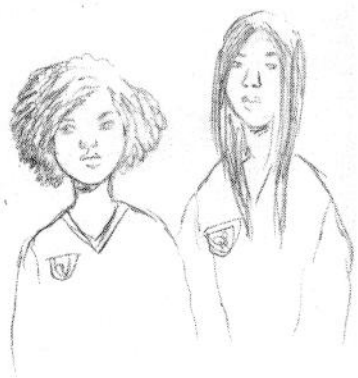

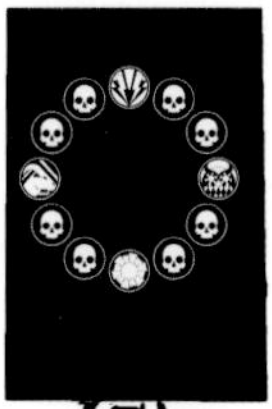

3

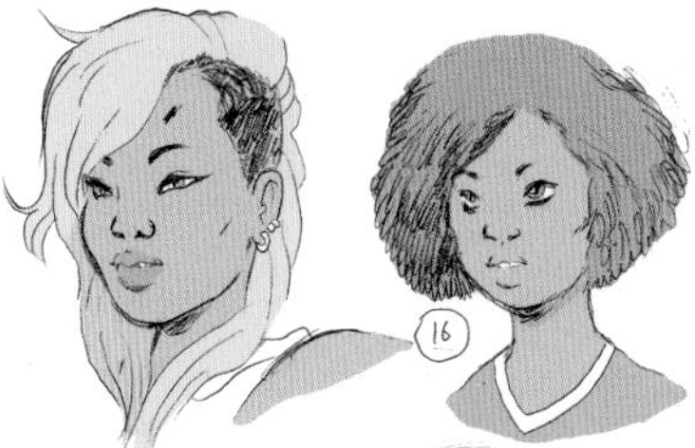
16

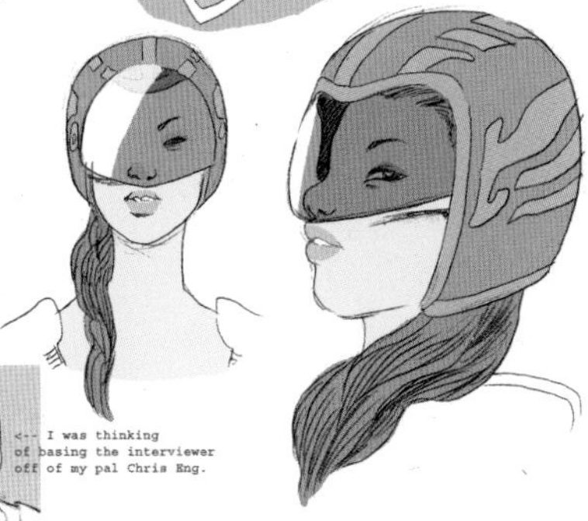

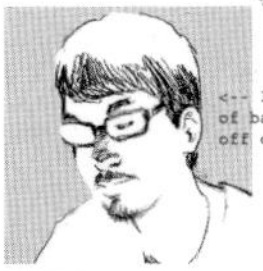

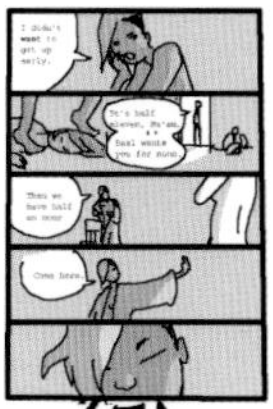
Come here.

5

<-- I was thinking of basing the interviewer off of my pal Chris Eng.

Maybe tiny panels showing her hand and the phone recoreder

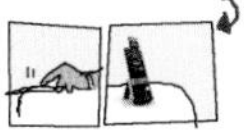

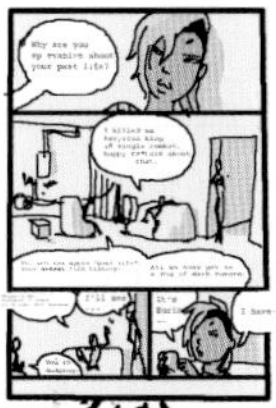
I have--

10

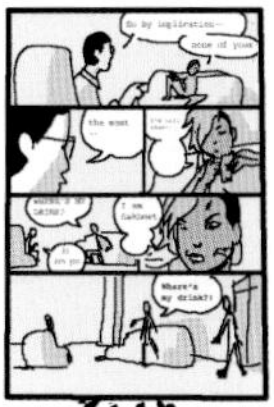
Where's my drink?

11

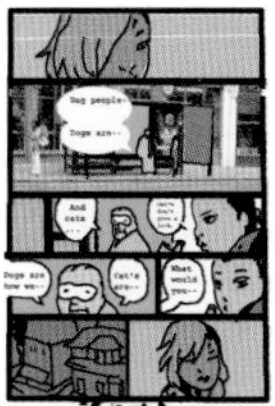

15

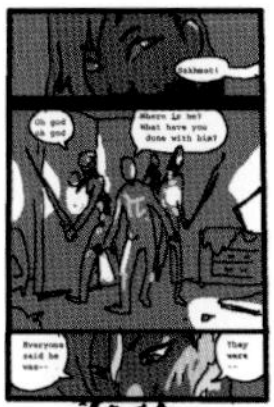
Where is he? What have you done with him?

16

With pages 8 and 9 being a spread-- there isn't a page turn reveil here any more---

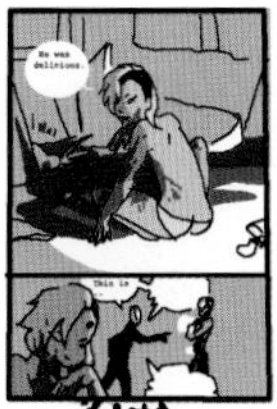
He was delirious.
This is

17

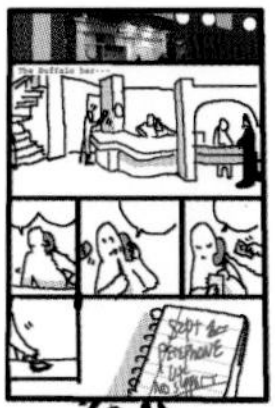
The Buffalo bar--

21

ALSO BY THE CREATORS

THE WICKED + THE DIVINE

VOL. 1: THE FAUST ACT
#1—5 COLLECTED

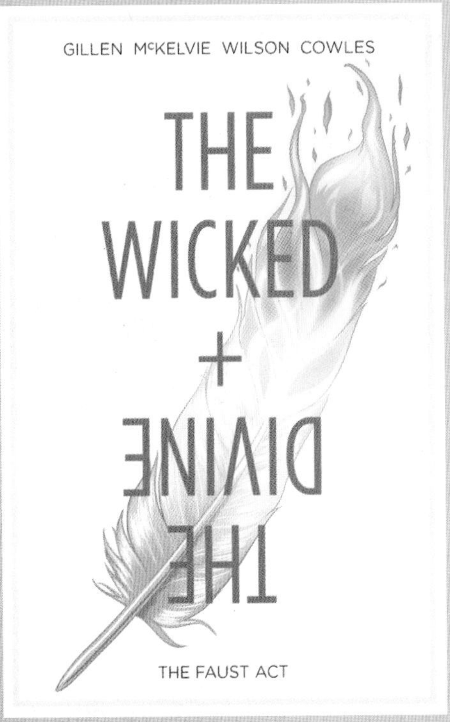

GILLEN McKELVIE WILSON COWLES
THE WICKED + THE DIVINE
THE FAUST ACT

VOL. 2: FANDEMONIUM
#6—11 COLLECTED

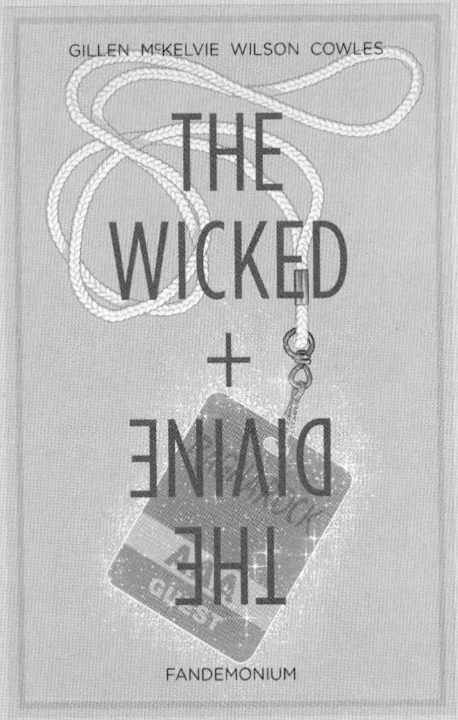

GILLEN McKELVIE WILSON COWLES
THE WICKED + THE DIVINE
FANDEMONIUM

SUBURBAN GLAMOUR

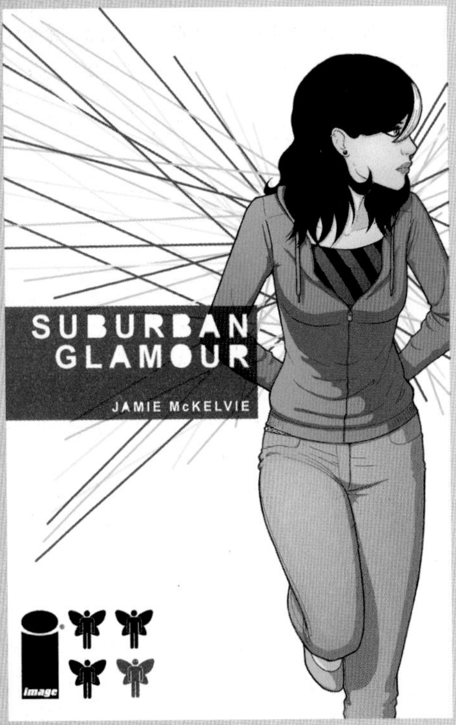

SUBURBAN GLAMOUR
JAMIE McKELVIE
image

THREE

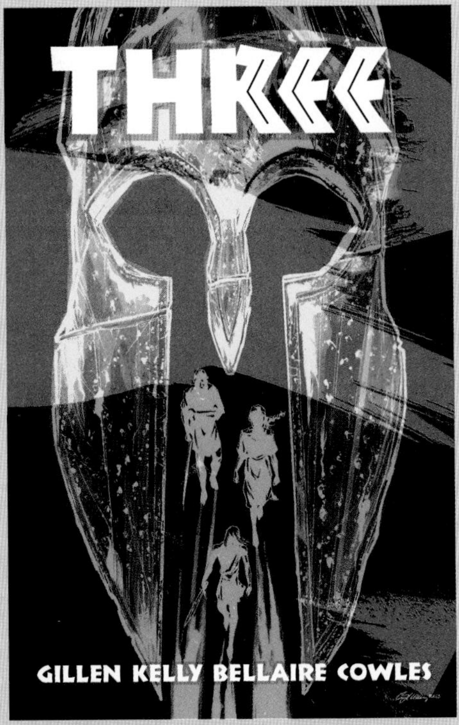

THREE
GILLEN KELLY BELLAIRE COWLES

PHONOGRAM

VOL. 1:
RUE BRITANNIA

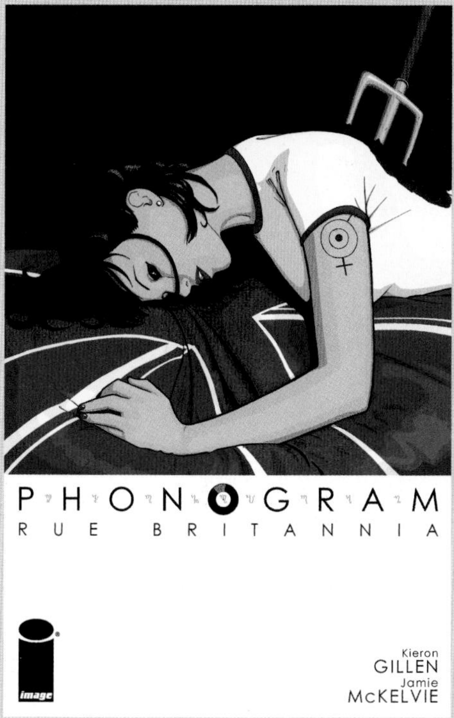

PHONOGRAM
RUE BRITANNIA
image
Kieron
GILLEN
Jamie
McKELVIE

VOL. 2:
THE SINGLES CLUB

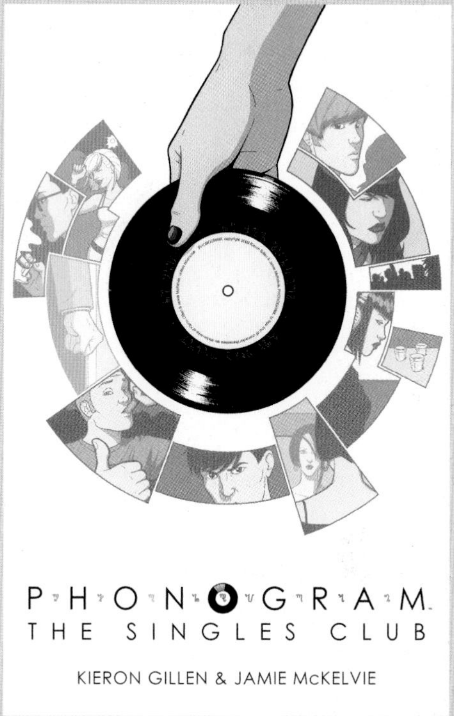

PHONOGRAM
THE SINGLES CLUB
KIERON GILLEN & JAMIE McKELVIE

VOL. 3:
THE IMMATERIAL GIRL

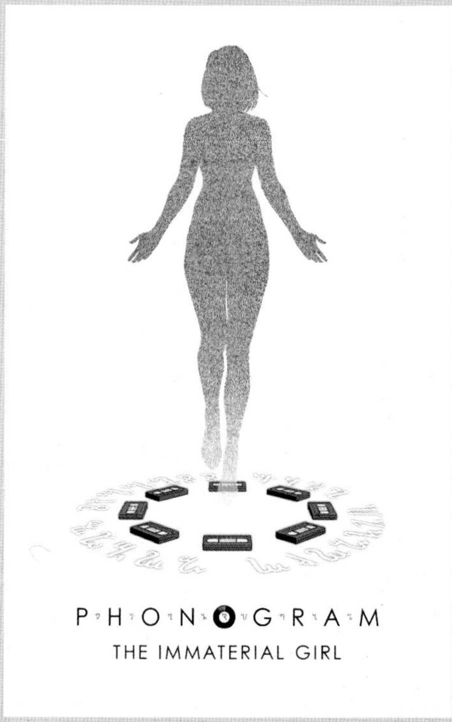

PHONOGRAM
THE IMMATERIAL GIRL

FOR FURTHER INFORMATION ON
THE WICKED + THE DIVINE:

www.wicdiv.com

major news, new issues, merchandise.

#WicDiv

the hashtag on twitter for WicDiv Discussion

WicDiv

the general tag on tumblr for the community.

bit.ly/WicDivPlaylist

the ever-updated Spotify Playlist for the series.

Kieron Gillen is a writer from Britain. His work includes this and work that is not this.

Jamie McKelvie is an artist from Britain. His work also includes this and work that is not this.

Matthew Wilson is a colourist not from Britain. His work includes work with Brian K Vaughan now, so doesn't have to do this any more, so we'd probably better treat him nice in case he leaves us.

Kate Brown is an artist/writer from Britain. Her work includes *The Unicorn And The Woodsman*, *Tamsin & The Deep* and *Fish & Chocolate*. She likes the word "and."

Tula Lotay is another artist from Britain. Her work includes *Supreme: Blue Rose*, *Heartless*, *Bodies* and trying not to die when she organises Thought Bubble in Leeds every year.

Stephanie Hans is an artist from France. Her work includes *Angela: Asgard's Assassin*, *1602: Witch Hunter Angela* and *Angela: Queen of Hel*. Her work does not include Angela Lansbury, who is amazing with no involvement of Stephanie Hans.

Leila del Duca is an artist from the United States of America. Her work includes *Shutter*, *The Pantheon Project* and hitting Kieron when he misspells her name again.

Brandon Graham is an artist/writer standing behind you, watching silently, but if you turn around he'll be gone. You live only by his good graces. Do not anger Brandon Graham. His work includes *King City*, *Multiple Warheads*, *Prophet*, *8house: Arclight*, editing the anthology *Island* and standing behind you, watching silently.